DEMOCRACY AND NATIONAL IDENTITY IN THAILAND

NIAS – Nordic Institute of Asian Studies
Studies in Contemporary Asian History
Series Editor: Robert Cribb, Australian National University

Democracy and National Identity in Thailand

Michael Kelly Connors

NIAS – Nordic Institute of Asian Studies
Studies in Contemporary Asian History 7

First published 2003 by Routledge/Curzon, London & New York

Revised edition published in 2007 by NIAS Press
NIAS – Nordic Institute of Asian Studies
Leifsgade 33, DK-2300 Copenhagen S, Denmark
Tel.: +45 3532 9501 • Fax: +45 3532 9549

Typeset in 10 point Warnock by Donald B. Wagner

Produced by SRM Production Berhad Sdn
Printed and bound in Malaysia

British Library Cataloguing in Publication Data
Connors, Michael Kelly
  Democracy and national identity in Thailand. - Rev. and
  updated ed. - (Studies in contemporary Asian history ; 7)
  1.Nationalism - Thailand 2.Democracy - Thailand 3.Thailand
  - Politics and government - 20th century
  I.Title
  320.9'593

ISBN-10 87-7694-002-0
ISBN-13-978-87-7694-002-7

For my parents

Elizabeth and Michael

and

for Kobchai

Contents

Preface to the paperback edition

I AM GRATEFUL TO GERALD JACKSON AND NIAS Press for proceeding with a paperback edition of *Democracy and National Identity in Thailand*, and to Leena Höskuldsson for providing close copy-editing. For the cover, the distinguished Thai Photographer Ajaan Manit Sriwanichpoom kindly allowed us to use his wonderful picture 'The Future'.

I have taken this opportunity to clear up some obscure prose and to fix a number of mistakes that appeared in the hardback edition, but I have, in the limited space available, and wanting to keep to the original text, only made minor changes in most chapters, including a clearer statement in Chapter 3 regarding my approach to nationalism.

I have also added a glossary and a list of acronyms to facilitate ease of reading. In the hardback edition a decision was made to list only a small proportion of sources used in this book in the Select Bibliography. That decision is carried over here. Full citations, mostly of documentary and Thai language sources, are provided in the endnotes of each chapter.

Chapter 10 contains the most substantive change to the book, with an extended discussion of the Thaksin period of government. Chapter 10 takes the reader through the Thaksin years and then raises the possibility of the emergence of a new movement for political reform. At the time of writing in September 2005 it was clear that a movement against Thaksin would take shape, but its form and politics were as yet unclear, although a heavy dose of monarchism was apparent. By April 2006 there was reason to consider revising Chapter 10. Facing immense pressure for his resignation (following allegations of corruption and abuse of power) and after a meeting with King Bhumiphol, Thaksin announced an election to be held in early April 2006. That election has now passed into history as a farce. Faced with a boycott from the liberally inclined Democrat Party Thaksin's party, Thai Rak Thai, won the kind of victory that Thaksin had long dreamed about, virtually capturing the full house, but at the cost of credibility and a functioning government.

It remains unclear how events will unfold, and any analysis of them will be better served by the passage of time. Although events have now moved beyond those discussed in Chapter 10, I have decided to leave the chapter untouched. I believe that the analysis of political reform offered there remains relevant. As Thai elites continue to contest regime form, taking broadly liberal and authoritarian positions, the best hope for Thailand's majority remains self organization and a non-nationalist politics. In that sense I believe the analysis of democratic ideology and national identity offered in this book will remain relevant for some years to come.

The first edition of *Democracy and National Identity in Thailand* received some generous reviews, some of which also contained useful criticisms of the book's shortcomings. I have attempted to address some of these. In response to Professor Robert Taylor's comments in *Asian Affairs* that Thailand is a good example of relatively successful political socialization, I have added a brief comment in Chapter 2 on what I consider to be the normative politics behind the concept of political socialization and why a critical appraisal of Thai nation-building remains appropriate despite its relatively bloodless character (in contrast to its neighbours).

Anthropologists reviewing this book, including Professor Michael Herzfeld (*Journal of Asian Studies*) and Dr Andrew Walker (*Journal of Contemporary Asia*) welcomed the overview it presents but quite rightly demanded that work be done on how Thai ideology is received, negotiated and even subverted. I can only concur with this suggestion, although I could not do such work in this book. *Democracy and National Identity* was primarily an attempt to map the historical evolution of modern Thai ideology and its intersection with western political thought. I wrote it by accident. I went to Thailand in the mid-1990s expecting to do a much narrower study on 'the people as a figure of fear' in contemporary Thai thought, and found myself without a compass – no general work on traditions of democratic thought in Thailand in the English language. As I studied literature going back to the 1930s that portrayed the Thai people as unfit for democracy I realised I was actually mining Thai democratic thought. All liberal democratic thought seems to be about the unfit nature of common people for the exercise of democracy, and I thus moved to this theme. The project thus became larger, an attempt at providing a sustained overview, covering the second half of the twentieth century, of the formation of Thai national identity and its intersection with democratic ideology. The nature of an overview, such as this book is, is that it misses much that is particular to a period and perhaps it tries to fashion continuities where there may be none; thus I make no claims about this work being a 'final treatment' nor do I claim that the ideology I map is passively accepted by people. More in-depth studies, more periodically focused, more historically driven, and more grounded ethnographic research (and better financed) will no doubt bring into question many of the formulations I have made here either implicitly or directly.

My conclusion that Thailand is a deeply ideological society, with the monarchy at the centre, may not be all that surprising, but the route to this conclusion was at that time largely un-tread. Along the way I was guided by the pioneering work of excellent Thai scholars, whose work the reader will find heavily cited in the notes.

If the research contained herein is gradually superseded, I have immodest hopes that the critical methodological approach used in this book will inform at least some people's understanding of the ideological aspects of democratization. It seems to me that critical studies of democratization would benefit from an analysis of the way that nationalized democratic ideology works to discipline people, rather than to liberate them. That is the point of the book, a point which is largely ignored in most studies of democratization.

I will not repeat here the thanks I owe to the many people who assisted this project, as these appear in the original acknowledgements. But I wish to once again acknowledge my debt to Kobchai. He was always there to help when Thai language sources got tricky or when gloom over the project set in. Despite his deep love for his country and its institutions, and his protestations (and sometimes indifference) about what I was writing, he continued to offer love and support. Without him, this book would not have been written.

Acronyms

ARD	Accelerated Rural Development
CDA	Constitution Drafting Assembly
CDC	Constitution Drafting Committee
CDD	Community Development Department
CFD	Confederation for Democracy
CI	Counter-insurgency
CPD	Campaign for Popular Democracy
CPT	Communist Party of Thailand
CSC	Constitution Scrutinizing Committee
DDC	Democracy Development Committee
ECT	Electoral Commission of Thailand
IPPS	Institute for Public Policy Studies
JPPCC	Joint Public-Private Consultative Committee
KAF	Konrad Ardenauer Foundation
KPI	King Prachatipok's Institute
ISOC	Internal Security Operations Command
LAD	Local Administration Department
LDI	Local Development Institute
NAP	New Aspiration Party
NCC	National Culture Commission
NCCC	National Counter Corruption Commission
NESDB	National Economic and Social Development Board
NGO-CORD	NGO-Coordinating Committee on Rural Development
NIB	National Identity Board
NLA	National Legislative Assembly
NRC	National Reconciliation Commission
NSC	National Security Council
NPKC	National Peace-Keeping Council
PDDC	Project to Develop Democratic Citizens
PDP	Palang Dhamma Party
PRC	Political Reform Committee
SFT	Student Federation of Thailand
SMEs	Small and Medium Enterprises
SSAT	Social Science Association of Thailand
STP	Samakki Tham Party
TRT	Thai Rak Thai Party
UCL	Union of Civil Liberty
USOM	United States Operations Mission

Glossary of terms

barami	prestige/charisma/store of *kammic* merit (Buddhist)
democrasubjection	a neologism designating the way in which people are subjected to imaginary forms of self rule.
ekkalak	identity
hegemony	to rule through a measure of spontaneous consent, the condition under which subordinate populations are integrated into elite projects (Gramsci).
interpellation	hailing, the naming of something within an ideological discourse
jao-poh	godfathers (mafia-like figures)
kanphattana	development
khwampenthai	Thainess
muan-chon	masses
muban	village
nai-amphur	subdistrict officer/sheriff
nathi	duties
phalang phaen din	forces of the land
phonlameuang	citizen
prachakhom	forum/assembly
pracha-rat	people-state (civic state/civil state)
prachasangkhom	civil society
prachatipatai	democracy
ratthathammanun	constitution
sakdina	a Thai form of feudalism centred on control of labour and land
saksri	honour
sithi	rights
tambon	subdistrict
thammarat	good governance
thongthinniyom	localism
thotsaphitrachatham	ten kingly virtues (see note 102, chapter 3)
udomkan	ideals/ideology
watthanatham	culture

Acknowledgements

THE DEBTS INCURRED IN THE WRITING OF THIS work go back a long time. Much of the research for this book was undertaken while I was a recipient of an Australian Postgraduate Award. I was also the beneficiary of a three-month research scholarship based at the Research School of Pacific and Asian Studies at the Australian National University, where I was fortunate to discuss my work with Craig Reynolds and Harold Crouch. Research undertaken in 2001 was supported by a grant from the British Academy. I hope this book is some repayment for the taxes that supported this project.

My studies into Thailand began in 1994 under the guidance of Noel Battye at the University of Melbourne. Writing a fourth-year dissertation on Thai politics, I hit upon the idea that became the basis for this book – democrasubjection. His encouragement of my work, and his scholarly knowledge of Thailand, are remembered fondly. Under the supervision of Phillip Darby and John Dryzek at the University of Melbourne, I commenced doctoral research into Thai democratic discourse. As is the norm in these things, I rabbit-hopped from topic to topic even before my supervisors could bat an eyelid. The broad freedom I was granted by them provided a wonderful space to explore all the nooks and crannies that my rather wandering research led me to. When I did finally get to write up the research, Phillip and John proved to be hardy and critical supervisors, forcing me to address weaknesses and strengthen my line of argument. When I went to Thailand to conduct fieldwork in 1996–7, Prudisan Jumbala from Chulalongkorn University kindly agreed to watch over me (a university requirement). In between tea and aromatic pipe smoke, Ajan Prudisan politely listened as I burdened him with questions and polemic. His apparently happy tolerance was matched by friendly assistance in getting me access to a number of Thai political notables. Finally, Peter A. Jackson acting as co-supervisor read a penultimate draft of the dissertation and offered many valuable comments. Collectively, I thank all of these intellectual mentors for their generous spirit and guidance.

What began as a dissertation became a book, and in the process I have benefited greatly from communication with Bill Callahan and Kevin Hewison. Both offered invaluable advice on possible improvements. I have taken up many of their ideas. Finally, a special thanks must go to my colleague at the University of Leeds, Duncan McCargo. His energy, support and intellectual exuberance played a considerable part in this book seeing the light of day.

It is also appropriate that the influence of Thai scholars on my understanding of Thai democracy and politics be recognized. While the interpretations and judgements of Thai democracy are my own, it would have been a much harder journey without being able to read the work of Nakharin Mektrairat, Kriangsak Chetthaphanuanit, Kasian Tejapira, Sombat Chanthonwong and Chalermkiat Phiu-nuan, and of the highly productive Political Economy Centre at Chulalongkorn University. One can only hope that much of the excellent work in the Thai language will one day find a wider audience through translation.

In the course of researching and writing the book, I was privileged to befriend a great number of people. So many were helpful that I cannot begin to thank them all. In particular, I would like to thank the members of the Graduate Seminars in Left and Social Theory at Chulalongkorn University, and the members of the Kirk University Study Group, in particular Ajaans Ek, Chettha, Chonlathit, Praphat and Bonsung. Librarians at Chulalongkorn University and Thammasat University helped ease the pain of locating material. Colleagues at Thammasat University, where I taught in 1998–9, provided a friendly atmosphere for writing up much of the research. Patamawadee Pochanukul kindly located a number of difficult sources and answered a number of obscure inquiries. Jean-Michael Sands kindly assisted with transliteration of Thai names. Michael Nelson provided several articles cited in this book. He has also been a source of interesting and friendly differences of opinion. A different version of Chapter 7 originally appeared as 'Political Reform and the State in Thailand', *Journal of Contemporary Asia*, 29, 2, 1999. That article was due to the promptings of Ji Ungphakon, and reflects a number of discussions (debates!) I have had with him.

Friends have been a large part of seeing this project through. Lucy Chesser, Theresa Wyborn, Asvin Phorugnam and John Jennings provided endless support and refuge. In particular, Bill Calder and Graham Willett encountered many evenings of discussion on my research, and never once looked bored. It is friendships such as these that make the lonely task of writing bearable. I must offer special thanks to Kobchai, who more than anyone kept me sane and on track throughout most of this project. His love and support sustained me. Finally, I would like to dedicate this book to my parents Elizabeth Connors and Michael Connors.

Despite the efforts of myself and the support of so many, errors of interpretation and fact may remain. It is customary to assume responsibility for these: I do so willingly.

M.K.C.
Leeds, March 2002

1

Introduction

Talking democracy

SOME TIME AGO THE LATE KUKRIT PRAMOJ, ONE-TIME Prime Minister and wit, observed that 'The Swiss do not talk about democracy or politics at all, but they have democracy. The Thais on the other hand talk about democracy and their own politics non-stop, but they haven't got democracy just the same.'[1] Kukrit's aside highlights a fascinating aspect of Thai political discourse: the existence of an endless inquiry into the meaning and status of Thai democracy against a background of Brahman divinity in the Chakri Court, acts of compulsive vote-buying by politicians, and *coups d'état* by military cliques, seemingly 'in accordance' with the 'general will' of the people.

Kukrit was right: democracy is endlessly talked about. From pontificating newspaper columnists to scripted radio instruction on being a good democratic citizen, talk of democracy is ubiquitous. Remarkably, democratic instruction goes on whether an elected or unelected government is in office. Even in remote villages, government officials utter Abraham Lincoln's dictum that democracy is a system of government for the people, by the people and of the people. However, Kukrit's claim that Thailand had 'no democracy' was contrary to the belief held by many intellectuals who worked close to state agencies and envisaged a significant role for these agencies in advancing political development. These intellectuals did not view democracy as a final product, but as part of a statist developmental project from which the state could draw legitimacy.

Now while 'democracy' has been utilized to enhance regime legitimacy in Thailand, it is often considered as having played second fiddle to 'development' and 'security'. In a fascinating account of the use of political language in Thailand, Chai-Anan Samudavanija and Kanok Wongtrangan found that references to 'democracy' in coup announcements between 1932 and 1981 were relatively rare and, when made, were generally negative.[2] Work of this kind tends to downplay the importance of democratic ideology in Thailand. The present book shows how democracy has been integral to the general developmental metaphor that actors in the Thai state use to construct national ideology for hegemonic purposes. Let me now anticipate some of the arguments that follow.

Thai statist ideas on democracy transcend the limited notions of procedural democracy that dominate mainstream Western political science. The latter is a putative science of processes, institutions and empirically observed behaviour that

1

focuses on the competitive circulation of elites through electoral mechanisms. By contrast, democracy in the Thai statist view is conceptualized as an ideal psychological, almost spiritual, condition of the people and their capacity to be self-governing. Notably, when authoritarian governments ruled they extolled a democracy far more idealistic than actually existing democracies. In part, the ideal served as a delaying mechanism, functioning to buffer bureaucratic and military rulers from other claimants seeking access to state power. While the Thai state was fighting the spectre of communism in the 1960s and 1970s, it let loose the unnamed ghost of disciplinary liberalism (in the form of developmental democracy), to haunt the Thai people. Put simply, the people were not yet ready for self-rule.

The implementation of a moral project of rational citizenship by state actors has been a common feature of most regimes, military or civilian. The purported aim has always been to educate the people for responsible citizenship. Thailand's liberal democratic transition has been accompanied by new programmes of civic education by non-state activists, educators and academics. This book is an attempt to make sense of these projects.

Chapter 2 contains a consideration of how democracy and democratization are loaded concepts, dependent on an ideological reading of the 'West' and how these readings have been deployed in understanding Thai politics. Taking up the suggestion of Arturo Escobar to consider 'development' as a discursive formation that aims at the production of 'objective' knowledge to aid strategies of intervention,[3] the book focuses on political development and its relationship to strategies of hegemony and government. This aspect of Thai politics has been largely neglected because much academic literature on Thailand is tied to what Paul Cammack has called the doctrine of political development, a doctrine that neutralizes questions relating to power and domination.[4] This book's organizing theme is that democracy has been deployed as a disciplining practice. In making a case for this position, I indicate how Gramscian and Foucauldian insights on hegemony and governmentality help in the critical exploration of democracy.

This book illuminates the hegemonic and governmental role that 'democracy' has played in Thailand. This is studied first in the deployment of democracy by authoritarian regimes, and second in the context of Thailand's political liberal-ization. My central focus is neither the sociological generalization of the forces that have structured Thailand's democracy through its phases from statist to liberal moments, nor the institutional modalities of each form of democracy. Rather, foregrounded is the articulation of ideological moments of democracy, that is, its place in a discursive struggle over how to signify the political realm by forces in the state.

Chapter 3 considers the period from the overthrow of the absolute monarchy to the mid-1960s. It describes how the broad ideological horizon opened up by the overthrow of the absolute monarchy shifted modes of legitimation in Thailand. Chapters 4 and 5 present extended accounts of statist democracy from the 1960s to the 1990s. I argue that there was a coherent articulation of democracy with the problem of development. These chapters present a close reading of the historical contexts that threw up political development notions of democracy in Thailand. In this period liberal democracy, as a project to be realized, became a *de facto* aspect of national ideology, and functioned in hegemonic practice. Chapter 6 studies the attempt to articulate Thai identity and the monarchy to democracy, an important if not central component of the disposition-creating aspect of Thai democratic discourse.

Chapters 7, 8 and 9 are concerned with making sense of contemporary ideological shifts in Thai politics. Having established the general contours of statist notions of democracy in the preceding chapters, greater focus is given in the last chapters to contestations of democracy and citizenship. The shift is warranted by my desire to highlight the fact that new hegemonic strategies and contestations have come to occupy the discursive spaces opened up by the process of democratization in Thailand. Rather than suggest plans for further entrenchment of the democratic rules of the game—the focus of most writings—I focus on the emergent disciplinary democratic imaginary in Thailand. In doing this, I draw on Kasian Tejapira's contribution to understanding the basic liberal-globalizing/communitarian split in Thai political discourse.[5] In my treatment of these two broad trends I note, like Kasian, that these strategies are linked to alternative conceptions of the state, and that they are likely to direct political debate into the future. However, the very real contestation between them is constrained by a shared political liberalism and a common commitment to the triadic national ideology of 'nation, religion and monarchy'.

More specifically, in Chapter 7 I present an argument for rethinking Thailand's so-called 'People's Constitution' as an attempt at embedding liberal imperatives in the Thai state. I present an extended analysis of the social forces and agendas behind the new constitution. On the basis of the background material presented in that chapter, Chapter 8 studies the position of liberalism in the new democratic imaginary. The principal argument made in that chapter pertains to the ideological shift that recentres liberalism as a present possibility, rather than a latent condition. Chapter 9 considers the position of progressive democratic discourses located in NGOs and in the theorizing of intellectuals, in relation to the hegemonic project of the new liberalism. It considers the manner in which progressive notions of democracy, development and community are being appropriated and inserted into new disciplinary imaginings of the Thai nation.

Chapter 10 provides an overview of the Thaksin challenge to the liberal democratic project and concludes with an argument for the relevance of 'democrasubjection' for understanding processes of democracy and democratization.

The thematic unity of this book is comprised of the critical argument that both liberal and statist moments of democracy in Thailand were/are projects of what may be termed 'democrasubjection': the subjection of people to imaginary forms of self and collective rule. 'Democrasubjection', as an idea, can be applied to any time and place where the terms of democratic political discourse are ideologically directed.

Democrasubjection is a necessary condition of the problem space of democracy where nominal political equality, or its possibility, is subject to practices of power that are exploitative and interest-driven. It involves tying national-peoples to myths of self and nation, as subjects in the process of self-realization and agency. This book is about the hegemonic work that democracy does.

Notes

1 *The Nation*, 18/9/78, p. 2.

2 Chai-Anan Samudavanija and Kanok Wongtrangan, *Phasa thangkanmeaung* [Political Language], Bangkok: Samakhom sangkhomsat haeng prathet thai, 1983, pp. 36, 58–63.

3 Arturo Escobar, *Encountering Development: The Making and Unmaking of the Third World*, Princeton: Princeton University Press, 1995, pp. 5–6.

4 Paul Cammack, *Capitalism and Democracy in the Third World*, London: Leicester University Press, 1997.

5 Kasian Tejapira, 'Globalizers vs Communitarians: Post-May 1992 Debates among Thai Public Intellectuals', paper presented to Annual Meeting of the US Association for Asian Studies, Honolulu, 11–14 April 1996.

2 Making democracy mean something

Contemporary notions of Thai nation and identity are informed by narratives that have been told and sold as authentic stories of the coming into being of the Thai nation, so much so that they have become part of the common-sense way of seeing things for many people. In everyday speech and assumption, Thailand and its people are often taken as natural fact, as if the 'Thai people' and their territory have always existed. Yet no national people, as such, exist independently of imagining them to exist. Even the most ardent exponents, such as Anthony Smith, of the idea that nations have consequential roots in past ethnic formations recognize that, in its modern form, the nation requires conscious 'reinterpretation' and 'rediscovery' of the 'living past' by nationalist intelligentsias.[1] Ethno-symbolists, such as Smith, claim that nationalism and national identity are often symbolically recovered forms of authentic pre-modern ethnic identity, under the conditions of the modern state and citizenship. These conditions mark the transition from *ethnie* to nation. It is this 'recurrence' of identity, in different forms and under different conditions, that is said to account for the power of nationalism – it has roots in the past, in which people have emotional investment, and can be mobilized for contemporary symbolic purposes. This is to say that the ethno-symbolists broadly read history as nationalists do. What this means in the Thai context is that the Thai are as the Thai say. Or are they?

When historical forms of the *ethnie*-cum-nation are paraded as evidence of recurrence, this is usually little more than a reconstruction of the present reaching into the past.[2] In the Thai context, the recovery of the past by nationalist intelligentsias produces a fabled history of great kings and deeds, and assumes that there is a conscious collective actor (the Thai people). This is little more than fiction. When Sulak Sivaraksa, the contemporary doyen of Thai national identity, writes '[t]he Siamese must have realized their own identity before intercourse with the West,'[3] of whom does he speak? When he writes, 'They did not want to share much of their identity with the *khaek* [foreigners]',[4] whom does he mean by 'they' – who, in other words was policing the boundaries of this assumed identity and determining the rights of entry, and why does he accord these guardians collective status as 'all Siamese'? It is doubtful that even 18th- and early 19th-century elites were conscious of their later status (in the annals of official history) as collective actors of the nation. Sulak's are the concerns of the present, and disclose this much about national consciousness – that the 'image of communion' within the nation, requires a historical subject that can speak to the present as if it almost-always existed.[5]

It has now become commonplace in academic studies to note that the attempt to form a national people involves multiple processes of discursive construction that are never quite successful at encompassing their intended targets. Thailand, in that sense, is not particularly unique. From the fiction of a Thai and Buddhist people to the very physical existence of the land, one can uncover a history of construction.

From David Streckfuss we learn how the idea of an all-encompassing 'Thai people' emerged in an encounter with Western anthropological fetishism for race. Faced with late nineteenth-century French attempts to expand their empire by seeking to provide 'protection' to the Lao peoples then under Siamese control, the ruling Chakri dynasty counteracted by mobilizing racial categories. By designating Lao people as 'Thai', the dynasty laid claim to legitimate guardianship over them.[6] We learn, from Kamala Tiyavanich, of a Bangkok elite frustrated by the divergent and localized Buddhist practices of the regional clergy and the subversive threat posed by wandering forest monks. Against this religious chaos, an image of Buddhist order definable by Bangkok-centric practice and scriptural interpretation was successfully projected.[7] From Thongchai Winichakul we learn that Siam itself was conjured in a world of power and cartography, replacing different notions of space and sovereignty with imitations of the territorial nation-state – or what he terms a 'geo-body'.[8] These are just a few of the critical studies that alert us to the nonsense that is the 'national' essence.

If scholarly critique works to undo the essentialism of the nation myth, then the very practices of the 'Thai' people place the idea of a Thai identity in the realm of oppositional politics. In language one will find strategies that privilege locality and dialect over standard Thai. People continue to confound attempts at state control of religion, a key component of Thai identity. In illegal border crossings the fixity of the national border is mocked and daily transgressed. Perhaps most significantly of all, in the many acts of unexamined resistance that sustain difference and dignity in daily life, the elegant invocation by authorities to be 'Thai' is gently reduced to a rhetorical rubble. For those who embrace the sentiment for difference, the phrase 'discursive construction of national identity' is but a euphemism for the untold symbolic and real violence that is done in the name of sameness. Clearly, the politics to create, appropriate or resist Thai identity is a contested and ongoing one. If Benedict Anderson's influential notion of nations as imagined communities focuses on the technologies (print media) that spread language communities and provide the material means for reconceptualizing time and place, it may be said that the fragility and even subversive nature of imagining portends the inability of the territorial state to ever quite succeed in the production of national homogeneity.[9] Still, states and their intellectual allies do try.

The present book explores the modern deployment of democratic discourse and Thai identity, as carriers of sameness, by state and non-state actors. This chapter lays down a general orientation to this problem by first considering the disciplinary power of 'the doctrine of political development' and its paradoxical assumption that a national people have to be created in order to be represented. Second, a conceptual tool for understanding this project of sameness is elaborated. The concern is to explore how democracy and identity are disciplinary technologies utilized for the purposes of hegemony by forces, in and out of the state, for the construction of a 'people-body', an imagined body of people around which the state plans and for whom it purportedly speaks.

Political development and order

Anyone writing on the politics of any country necessarily acquaints themselves with a canon, the stock-in-trade literature which provides commentators with a common language, without which one cannot speak, or at least without which one will not be heard. It is common to assume that such literatures are ivory-towered productions, of little practical relevance, and mostly self important. Let me suggest that this, at least in the case of Thailand, is not the case. Political writings from the position of mainstream political science have had an impact on forms of ideology and practices of government.

Typically, observers of Thai politics absorb the orientation to order found in political development literature (1960s–1970s) and its successor, democratic transition and consolidation literature (1980s–1990s). This literature has importance because the discourse of political development was not merely an academic exercise; it furnished actors in the Thai state with a technical and interpretative tool with which to design policy prescriptions for order, stability and managed change. Further, it provided them with forms of rationality that seemingly dispensed with neo-traditional political rationalities centred on sacred notions of legitimate power.[10] In short, political development became a discursive formation, loosely defined, authorizing state actors to go to work on the material resources of nation building (the people) and aim for their incorporation into modernized institutions.[11] Today, one will still find many adherents of theories of political development in the Thai bureaucracy. Whole generations of graduates are being schooled in a discourse of order that would seem to have passed its heyday in the West. Some books on politics published in 2005 and sold in university bookshops around the country have bibliographies that list nothing published after the 1970s; prime among the entries are the luminaries of 1960s American political science: Easton, Verba, Pye, Huntington (in his first incarnation), and others. These authors are read not as intellectual history, but as holding the key to understanding how Thailand might make the transition to a modern democracy. This adherence is paradoxical; privately many Thais are despairing of ever developing democracy given the seeming resilience, even functionality, of what they perceive as Thai-specific practices of patronage and hierarchy. Yet despite the seeming recalcitrance of Thai politics to 'modernity', academia and the bureaucracy continue to use political development 'theory' to design programmes of democratic reform. Why?

Perhaps the answer lies in the utility that this body of thought has for governors. Political development theory has as its object of concern the problem of order over people when the dawn of modernity breaks over an alleged pre-modern past, and 'things fall apart'. In the name of managing change, state actors deploy an array of institutional, cultural-socializational and leadership strategies. This seeking of order brings into being an ensemble of concepts discursively unified by the object-focus such concepts strategically name and seek to transform. Concepts such as political culture, rationality, socialization, and citizen, emerge around the problem of embedding democracy. These concepts frame the people as an object to be worked upon and reformed. Within this discursive formation a way of speaking emerges that sets the subject, the developer, authorized by this discourse, into a relationship of leadership, guidance and surveillance over the mute-rational object of the 'people'. Yet it is characteristic of political development discourse that it aims to make the object (the people-body) speak the language of modernity, to embody the principles of its teleology in the creation of a speaking subject – the tempered democratic citizen. Within this discourse, then, lies a coherent strategy of citizen construction, the creation of a self-governing subject, which is simultaneously a component of the broader hegemony sought by the state. This book attempts to show different moments of this order, from the period of statist democratic discourse to the liberal-communitarian discourse of more recent times which, notwithstanding the Thaksin era, remains strong.

The development ethos long preceded the sub-discipline of political development and can, for instance, be traced back to imperial trusteeship and colonial administration.[12] However, one distinctive aspect of political development literature is that it engaged with Third World elites as partners in the quest for modernization. It addressed them as policy makers and planners, holders of the key to order and stability, without which the fragile world of post-colonial states would break up or be run over by the 'communist menace'.

More specifically, the import of political development discourse and its application in developing countries derives from its orientation towards capitalist modernization. It provided policy makers and planners with a map on which to strategically mark pathways to development facilitative of a capitalist economy and, eventually, a democracy. Its distinguishing mark was the role of a 'hyper-West', nowhere in existence save as an idealized bundle of aspects, as a reference point for development. This involved the attribution of ideal constructs such as progress, individuality, enterprise and rationality to the West, and taking these attributes as the end point of development. This imagining of the West, or what has been called 'Occidentalism', frames also the assumptions of much of the literature on political development and democratization.[13]

This literature was shaped by the geo-politics of the Cold War era. In her exhaustive study of political development literature, Irene Gendzier notes the utility of behavioural political science to US foreign policy, especially its role in counter-insurgency and in justifying the existence of authoritarian states as buffers against the consequences of mobilization during modernization.[14] Concerning Thailand, Peter Bell suggests a firm relationship between Western conceptions of Thai society and their utilization in counter-insurgency strategies.[15] Bell offers the example of research by prominent academics Herbert Phillips and David Wilson. Phillips and Wilson, writing in the 1960s, expressed a fear that the development of a rationalized bureaucracy in Thailand would pose dangers for regime legitimacy. From their perspective, Thais did not seek self-determination, preferring to be led by a government that had the 'attributes of a strong, wise, but indulgent father'.[16] It was expected that a modernized bureaucracy would not be able to fulfil what Phillips and Wilson described as people's traditional expectations of a paternalistic state. They recommended, therefore, the revitalization of traditional functions of government in which benevolent rule was emphasized and ritualized for the sake of internal security.[17] This work epitomized much of the entrenchment of the social sciences in the work of counter-insurgency. This often involved mapping managed cultural change, while proposing the retention of useful aspects of tradition for purposes of authority and order.[18]

Paul Cammack notes that political development theorists attempted both theoretical elaboration and to develop a doctrine related to 'a transitional program for the installation and consolidation of capitalist regimes in the third world'.[19] This programme, ideologically anti-communist, required a certain telos, or endpoint, to rationalize its recommendations. That telos was order, conceived as state-capacity to manage its internal and external affairs within the parameters of a capitalist economy. Political development, as the synonym of order – expressed in nation building, as projects of national integration, as institution building, as projects of normative socialization – became, in effect, the conscious problematic from which generic themes of nationalism, democracy and identity could be addressed as matters of social engineering and, as goals, advanced towards by rational planning. Such planning required knowledge of the object to be nationalized, democratized and identified: the people. As a discourse, then, political development was imperialist in its ambitions, cannibalizing other discursive formations and turning them into objects of its own rationality: the nation, identity and democracy all became rationalized by the logics of the developmental position; they became things to be planned for. Thus the emotive resources of the state, located in appeals to the 'nation' and the 'people', had a parallel existence as objects for developmental experts to form. This *getting to know and manage the people* brings into focus what may be termed the 'people-problem': that is, what forms of government in the many aspects of modernizing life can be utilized towards the end of people-order? As it happened, this issue of management was often directed towards the peasant and brought into being a literature concerned with personality typologies, achievement strategies and political socialization. By means of some behavioural alchemy, analysts from the social sciences hoped to turn the parochial peasant into a self-conscious modern 'man', one capable of change, empathy and rational choice.[20]

Although many authors within the political development field eschewed notions of ideal modernity and were cautious regarding the extent to which developing countries would ever reach such a state, rarefied versions of the West did aid in mapping trajectories for developing countries. As will be shown in the course of this book, the doctrine of political development provided the modernizing elites of the Thai state, from the 1960s onwards, with a powerful problematic from which to order and act on the 'people-problem' in a way productive for hegemonic ends. It would be wrong to conclude, as does Yogesh Atal, that in Thailand 'scattered-piecemeal research...[makes] it difficult to assess the impact of political science in the functioning of governments'.[21] Indeed, he suggests that non-utilization was likely. A study of the rationalities of government in Thailand provides ample evidence of utilization and constant interaction between political scientists and state actors. Political scientists were habitually eager to spell out their role in providing the intellectual means by which to develop and bring security to Thailand.[22] Furthermore, they were among the leagues of social scientists eager to lecture military personnel and civil servants, as well as sit on numerous committees. By such means did their influence become dispersed through the system.[23] Although political science faculties were, and to some extent remain, schools of public administration designed to feed students into the expanding bureaucracy,[24] in the 1960s the growing theoretical pursuit of politics brought forth the possibility of doctrinally informed governmental practice.[25] However, in estimating the relevance or impact of political science, even Thai academics Sombat Chantornvong and Chulacheeb Chinawanno suggest that the models taught, among them structural-functionalism, political process and political culture, were of little relevance to the Thai context.[26]

The importance of political development studies, as it took root in Thailand, was not necessarily in developing successful and applicable models. Its importance lay in naming a particular approach to the problem of development that focused on the difficulty of entrenching democratic rule, the contingencies of transformation, and the requisite need for management of change centred on the capacity of the state. Cammack's study of Western theorists demonstrates that regardless of the varying positions on political development, there was common agreement on the need for certain transitional mechanisms on the path to liberal democracy, a view shared by political scientists in Thailand and those working on Thailand. This view was reflected in the influential work of Fred Riggs. We now come to what might be regarded as the Western language canon of Thai political science.

Fred Riggs, writing in the 1960s, refashioned notions of a prevailing bureaucracy in Thailand into the theory of bureaucratic polity, and provided the paradigmatic interpretation of modern Thai politics.[27] Riggs shared political development theory's basic premise of societies being evolutionary organisms. This *organismic* metaphor, as David Apter terms it, when applied to developmental processes, 'explains equilibrium maintenance, the capacity of systems to survive under conditions of change by means of internal adaptation and differentiation.'[28] Riggs was part of the intellectual currents justifying transitional mechanisms on the road to modernity. Conceptualizing Thailand through the organismic metaphor, Riggs sought to define the nature of the Thai polity so as to both rationalize and prescribe further action in the interests of system maintenance and adaptation. The basic problem was one of modernization: how to institute modern governmental forms that best served the functional stability of the body politic in moments of transition from tradition to modernity, without triggering instability and radicalism (malintegration).

Riggs posited that the bureaucracy effectively constituted the political field.[29] The bureaucratic polity drew its legitimacy not through appeals to electoral constituencies, as he imagined happened in the West, but through the operation of rival cliques aiming at parcels of state control.[30] The layers of bureaucracy, military and civil, were the polity's constituency: 'the bureaucratic apparatus, instead of serving largely as an administrative function, became also the primary arena of political rivalry.'[31] It was, then, a system of closed inputs lacking the institutional mechanisms of Western democracies. In this absence he located the prime obstacle to further development:

> The great obstacle to further modernization of the Siamese polity lay not in the construction of the bureaucracy, which could surely, if adequately directed, give effective and efficient service…. That flaw, rather, lay in the lack of a guiding force outside the bureaucracy capable of setting its goals and keeping its agents under effective control.[32]

This statement reveals the nodal point organizing much of the doctrinal work on Thai political development: the seeking of extra-bureaucratic players to police the functioning of an emergent liberal state. This problem becomes the story-line of much subsequent literature.

While Riggs disclaimed Thailand as a 'perfect example' of the bureaucratic polity model, others have written as if the bureaucratic polity was a defining feature of Thai politics.[33] Subsequent work within this paradigm sought to determine whether the bureaucratic polity had been transcended by gauging the balance of power between bureaucratic and non-bureaucratic forces.[34]

Characteristically, the central tenets of Riggs' model were enriched by the cultural incantations of various exponents. Theorists deployed a number of related themes to explain the inability of the Thai masses to form a counterweight to the bureaucracy: Thais were said to pursue interests vertically through patron-client mechanisms rather than in horizontal interest groups;[35] Buddhism depoliticized the impoverished masses;[36] Thais were politically apathetic, they lacked discipline and had cultural habits of reverence which installed political deference.[37] In their analysis of the open-period of Thai politics (1973–6), David Morell and Chai-Anan Samudavanija argued that the mass demonstrations, class polarization, political instability and democratic contestation of that era were premature, born of uneven economic and ideological development, a dysfunctional moment restored, albeit brutally, by a military coup.[38] In a later piece, Chai-Anan suggested that Thais were, in the lead-up to the 1976 coup, nostalgic for an earlier era of 'stability and security'.[39] Culture, in this manoeuvre, becomes a handy rationalizing tool. The appeal to culture is of particular importance in the Thai adaptation of political development theory. In this regard many of Thailand's most prominent political scientists attempted to analyse Thai political culture and the means by which it could be reformed to fit the demands of a liberal democracy. Class struggle in this analysis is effaced and replaced by the question of the management of political development and the need to attend to various dysfunctional moments in the body politic.

If political culture was one axis on which political development revolved, the other was the question of institutionalization. Questions of institutionalization, leadership and party formation have thus accompanied developmental enquiries into the 'problem' of the Thai polity.[40] These were the underlying questions accompanying the debate on whether the 'bureaucratic polity' was still a viable model in the 1980s. Noting the failure of the bureaucratic polity model to explain the high levels of extra-bureaucratic political participation in the 1973–76 period, Pisan Suriyamongkol and James Guyot ventured that the 'bureaucratic polity was at bay'.[41] Strengthening their argument was the military's failure to amend the constitution in 1983. The authors asserted that the institutionalization of democratic processes had defined new rules of the political game.[42] Chai-Anan Samudavanija was less hopeful, suggesting that the 'contested terrain had shifted from state dominance to the dynamic formation of alliances among strategic groups of which state power elites are but one element'.[43] Unlike Pisan, Chai-Anan failed to see how this represented a new polity. Characterizing the situation as 'semi-democratic', as 'Thai-style' democracy, Chai-Anan argued that the emerging societal forces had been co-opted into the logic of the bureaucratic polity.[44] This co-option into semi-democratic forms was presented by Chai-Anan as an appropriate instrument of political stability, one in which the bureaucratic and non-bureaucratic forces share power and 'continually engage in bargaining and adjusting their strategies in order to maximize their power'.[45]

More innovatively, Anek Laothamatas described the new polity as a system of *liberal corporatism*. He claimed that the emergence of business in the 1980s, politically expressed through representative associations and their work within the Joint Public-Private Sector Consultative Committee (JPPCC), had made redundant the bureaucratic polity model:

> The political regime at work in Thailand, at least in the realm of economic affairs, is no longer a bureaucratic polity, but not because non-bureaucratic forces have gained power at the expense of bureaucratic forces. Instead, it is because both forces are strong and autonomous, and the decision-making of the regime has ceased to be monopolized by the military-bureaucratic elite.[46]

The transformation had delivered Thailand to a higher developmental stage involving the distribution of power along liberal corporatist lines.[47] Clearly, Anek's model was simply an alternate method of analysing the rise of non-bureaucratic forces: it remained firmly within the political development paradigm. Anek linked his argument of liberal corporatism to a conception of business groups as progressive forces for democratization. For Anek, business groups are important actors in society's struggle to escape state dominance. Unlike theorists who sought institutional arrangements welding together old and new social forces, Anek described a new polity. The idea of liberal corporatism forges a key conceptual link in political development theorizing on Thailand: the liberal corporatist polity was envisaged as the latest instalment delivered by strategic struggle under conditions of modernization.

The most traumatic malintegrative moment since the 'open period' of 1973–76 was the crisis of 1991–92, beginning with a coup against an elected government in February 1991. In those years a coalition of moderate forces united to demand a democratic constitution and the resignation of an unelected prime minister. Speaking of these events, Surin Maisrikrod contended that the bureaucratic polity – composed of the government, the military and the monarchy – remained resilient, due to the failure of non-bureaucratic forces to institutionalize democratic processes to their advantage, particularly in the realm of political party formation.[48] However, within and without the bureaucratic polity, there had been a polarization between conservatives and reformists whose programmes for Thailand differed sharply.[49] Here, Surin argued, lay the basis of the ensuing conflict. On the nature of this contestation he commented that 'Thailand may have entered a new era of political radicalization which pits the old elites against the new'.[50] The new elites were said to favour bureaucratic efficiency and open competition as against the old guard's yearning for the status quo.[51] Surin convincingly argued that a political shift had occurred within the Thai bourgeoisie and middle class, representing a global trend towards diminishing the role of the state and enhancing the capabilities of the private sector.

Much of the work that appeared in the post-1992 period was concerned with elaborating the conditions for liberal democracy and the obstacles that needed to be overcome. Such work was characterized by similar themes: the interaction between structures and agents, the much lauded growth of the middle class, the question of political culture and the role of astute leadership in the transition.[52] What is significant in much of this work is the manner in which the standard categories of political development, democracy and the analytical couplet of 'society and state' are taken as given units of analysis. This flows, of course, from its position within the genre of political development theory. In being part of this general literature, the work also exhibits some typically Orientalist readings of Thailand. Writers in this frame have all sought to make sense of the Thai polity as a problem, as a lack. One of the early statements of this current of thinking was appropriately titled 'The

Problem of Democracy in Thailand.'[53] Much subsequent work on Thai democracy has the simple status of subtitle to this text.[54]

The various systems proposed to understand Thai politics by different authors make sense only in terms of what Thai politics is not: not democratic; not fully endowed with a civil society; only partially corporatist; endowed with vertical complexes of patron–client relationships rather than horizontal cleavages. While marked by the individual styles of its authors and their applications, the doctrine of political development emerges forcefully in this literature. The subthemes of order and control, of dealing with the people-problem, are present in theorists' considerations of institutionalization and political culture. The general categories of modernity, development and rationality, which inhabit this literature, are discursive cloaks hiding the fact that it is real people doing real work: ordering people towards hegemonic ends, under the guidance of the doctrine of political development. In more recent times, the focus of order has shifted from the state, so central to political development theory (in its metaphor of order), towards the significance of a normatively conceived civil society in producing a stable democracy and rooting a liberal ethic. Civil society builders are, like their predecessors, order builders. As will be shown in the later chapters of this book, there is discernible ideological continuity between them.

The significance of political development, from the 1960s onwards, as a framing tool emerged in the contradiction between the theorists' liberal aspirations to establish procedural democracy, and the apparently recalcitrant nature of the countries upon which a liberal regime was to be grafted.[55] However this recalcitrance was expressed – as lack of a political culture supporting democracy, the threat of irrational mass mobilization, the poor level of institutionalization and process – a position of opting for less-than-liberal forms of rule was embraced. Thus authors such as Samuel Huntington argued the need for strengthening state institutions, regardless of their regime form, such that they have the capacity to manage and lead change; as he succinctly put it: 'The primary problem is not liberty but the creation of a legitimate public order.'[56]

Strengthening institutions effectively meant removing them from societal influence.[57] It was expected that a series of manoeuvres would be undertaken by the state to produce stability and order, and slowly incorporate a widening body of competent citizens into the polity. Daniel Lerner, for example, expected that while motivational strategies at the individual level could have results in the short term, the payoff from civic education and socialization would take at least a generation; he thus effectively endorsed non-democratic means of government in the meantime to control the high expectations of the masses.[58] The view here is clear: only by painstaking foresight and clever manipulation of the resources available could state elites hope to succeed in winning order from their populations and be able to move towards democracy. It is this stance that Cammack names the doctrine of political development – a doctrine for a 'transitional programme' towards liberal democracy and capitalism in developing countries, with the state as the prime actor.[59]

Significantly, conscious of the leadership inherent in managed change, Lucien Pye, a leading formulator of the doctrine, and supporter of authoritarian control of information during the transitional period, explained that in mass/elite relations, 'ruling elites of some countries are in a position essentially analogous to that of persons employing psychological warfare across national boundaries.'[60]

Let me make some general observations about Pye's insight. Imbued with this warlike orientation, modernizing elites developed political rationalities to address the 'people-problem'. This was an ethos separate from, and not reducible to, people's sovereignty and legitimacy (democracy). It thus required its own conceptual apparatus, for if the people were conceived as a body of objects to calculate, reform and work on, then the source of the state's legitimate sovereignty does not lie in the people but is vested in the state's knowledge complexes as expressed in programmes of development. Also, the question of legitimacy becomes instrumental, residing in state efficacy and delivery; international legitimacy was bestowed on regimes that could control their populations. There was, in abstract, no need to always have recourse to the fiction of a democratically socially-contracting people. However, given the prominence of the discourse of nationalism in developing states, new states necessarily operated at several levels in terms of political rationality, and the question of a sovereign people was never absent.[61] One might speak of a dual movement here, where the posture of the state towards the people was not simply one of formation of rationalities for reform, but also entailed rhetorically appealing to a sovereign people. Thus there is an irrepressible tension between the rationality of government as a project shaping the conduct of people not yet capable of self-rule, and the universal appeal to represent the sovereign people. In Western political development theory, enmeshed as it was in the theories of procedural democracy and the management of order, the quest to root state sovereignty in a body of citizens was displaced, but not suppressed, by the examination of the 'actual' processes of existing democracies. The behavioural revolution removed questions of legitimacy from the purview of much of political science. However, intellectuals close to the state in 'developing' countries, who were motivated in terms of rationalizing rule to the people, needed to take account of popular sovereignty as an ideological resource. This tension created a permanent movement between broad questions of legitimacy and the lower-level rationalities of specific practices of government. Actors in the Thai state, influenced by the doctrine of political development, had to negotiate the latent contradiction that lay at the heart of the doctrine's proposed subject/object relations: how could mute-rational objects (the people prior to modernity) ever be the sovereign basis on which the state could claim to speak, except *post-facto*, given that the people as sovereign citizens were not yet existent? This contradiction sanctioned the many projects of citizen formation in Thailand. This contradiction is a useful starting point for examining the essentialism that underlies the fiction of democracy. Having defined something of the positions underlying this work, it is now necessary to outline the operative concepts structuring this inquiry.

Hegemony

The Gramscian notion of hegemony is open to various readings: two basic issues concerned Antonio Gramsci's rendering of the concept. In its earliest usage it related to the strategic problem of securing proletarian leadership and dominance.[62] With the failure of the Italian proletariat in the early 20th century to reach any hegemonic position, Gramsci undertook a historical study of the Italian elites and their modes of power assumption. The state in these studies was conceived as a historical process combining political society and civil society, composing what Gramsci termed the integral state. Very generally, his studies noted that the Italian bourgeoisie had failed to hegemonize (to control and lead by a measure of spontaneous consent from those led) the social field of civil society and that it had been incorporated into the ruling strata through a process of passive revolution that did little to bring revolutionary bourgeois values to bear on the Italian social formation. Whatever the specificities of Gramsci's study of Italy, his theoretical rendering of the Italian experience spawned a new conceptual apparatus that was highly productive for thinking about the forms of rule in society, their historical base, and the modes of subjugation of people to dominant principles and interests of a ruling strata.[63]

Gramsci was interested in asking how, in societies of relatively advanced capitalism, a position of hegemony could be attained so that the main integrative element of the social formation was, apparently, the consent of those who were exploited and oppressed within it. Gramsci's notion of hegemony as an answer to this conundrum went beyond simplistic notions of ideology as false consciousness to a concrete study of the historical emergence of blocs and their articulation of domination and consent through state and civil society apparatuses, such that they could maintain some degree of equilibrium in the social formation.[64] Ideology was only one element of the hegemonic achievement, so too were administrative functions, mechanisms of soft coercion as structured in the rule of law, the distribution of economic concessions to strategic groups, and so on. Gramsci's study of hegemony correlated to a dual conception of state. First, he saw the state as an institutional ensemble, or the coercive apparatus for the practice of domination. Second, he posited the notion of the integral state, which entailed the coupling and dynamic interaction of the state as institutional apparatus and the organization of politics and civil society elements.[65] Gramsci was, at times, certain that the institutional ensemble corresponded to moments of force while civil society corresponded to moments of consent. At other times he recognized that political society itself played a part in organizing consent.[66] Gramsci explored the concrete forms of the integral state, most productively through a study of Taylorism, noting the articulations and social controls that emerge from non-state arenas (conceived in the narrow sense).[67] He called for a study of cultural and economic apparatuses and the manner in which they could be articulated to hegemony.

Gramsci may be read as understanding modernizing societies as having shifted from rule primarily by force (domination) to rule primarily by consent, organized through multiple sites within civil society and state. However, his study of the articulation of hegemony was cognizant of the hybrid character of domination and consent, of hegemony's uneven and fragile nature, and of the role of intellectuals in the reproduction and organization of hegemony. Intellectuals, across a range of sectors (for example, education, churches, press, ministries, private foundations) are, in his conception, charged with the task of organizing the long-term viability of class rule through contributing to the strategic maintenance of hegemony in its various moments and by articulating the particular interests of ruling groups to the general interest.[68]

According to Gramsci, hegemonic status for any class (or class fraction) entailed having successfully drawn other classes and groups under its leadership through a series of measures aimed at compromise and ideological identification. However, domination, as the moment exterior to a comprised hegemony, was a necessary counterpoint for those strata excluded from the articulation of a hegemonic apparatus. For Gramsci, then, hegemony was subject to the pressures of political struggle and the dialectic of resistance inherent in class compromise. Domination was always a present possibility should consent break down. As will be seen in this work, the various democracy projects carried out in Thailand are hegemonically motivated, which is to say that while they function as attempts to create order and identification with a political order, their capacity for universal control is strictly limited, and order is also achieved by many other means.

This book focuses on the 'democratic aspect' of a broader hegemonic project. In doing so, it studies the articulation of democratic hegemony at concrete conjunctures. It attempts a broadly Marxist political-historical study without recourse to economic determinism. This frame grants efficacy to the political moment expressed as ongoing strategies of domination and hegemony and their reconstitution, through the varied institutional, ideological and economic matrices that make up an articulated, social formation. In concrete terms, this means presenting an exposition of the differential articulation of democracy with national ideology, and an explanation of those articulations in terms of the political struggles in the evolving Thai capitalist social formation.

In seeking to delimit this study, democracy here is conceived as composing one component of what Bob Jessop terms a hegemonic project, where hegemony is (following Gramsci) understood as the

> interpellation and organization of different class relevant...forces under the 'political, intellectual and moral leadership' of a particular class (or class fraction) or more precisely its political and intellectual and moral spokesmen. The key to the exercise of such leadership is the development of a specific 'hegemonic project' which can resolve the abstract problem of conflicts between particular interests and the general interest.[69]

Hegemony, Jessop argues, can be secured through the mobilization of support behind a concrete, national popular program of action which asserts a general interest in the pursuit of objectives that explicitly or implicitly advance the long term interest of the hegemonic class (fraction) and which also promotes particular economic-corporate interests compatible with this program.[70]

A hegemonic project, then, involves the strategic use of institutional, social, ideological, material and moral resources in the mobilization of a particular view that facilitates the continuing dominance of interests articulating, or articulated in, that project.

Democracy, as a metaphor for the capacity of a political community to be self-governing, is one component in the production of hegemony. It names a political community as one bound by common interest and fate, as if there were not always irreparable differences, interests and a constant flow of power in the maintenance of the myth of common interest. Democracy, then, can be seen as doing the hegemonic work of universalizing particularistic interests. To the extent that democracy proceeds in this manner, one may speak of *democrasubjection*, or the subjection of people to imaginary forms of their own rule (see below). However, while hegemony, as a multiple category of consent-producing practices (by economic, social, psychological and ideological means), is useful as a descriptive generalization, it is too expansive to explore and name specific sites at which the potential for consent is produced.

At what sites does power work to make people feel and act like citizens in a democratic community? For those interested in one aspect of the production of consent, that is, the creation of particular subjectivities as a field in which identity effects are potentially produced, it might be better to recognize the distinctive localized, bureaucratized or privatized forms that power moves through in an effort to shape orientations, as potential elements of a broader hegemony (in articulation). On this aspect, Gramsci noted that in ideal bourgeois societies where the notion of the free autonomous individual was realized, the brutal hand of domination was lifted and in its place was the 'individual [who] can govern himself without his self-government thereby entering into conflict with political society.'[71] To the extent that one wishes to study how such self-government is procured by particular practices of power, and has potential hegemonic effects in that it articulates the individual to a social order, the employment of Michel Foucault's notion of government can be productive.

Government

Foucault's notion of governmentality provides important insights into the processes of democrasubjection. It is argued below that examining the attempted construction of the democratic citizen from the dual perspective of hegemony and governmentality is a productive and critical exercise for understanding the aporia that attaches to 'democracy'. The aporia, or insoluble contradiction, of democracy is marked by the space between the rhetoric of the sovereign people and their non-existence from a development perspective. Democrasubjection seeks to overcome this contradiction by filling the space with hegemonically and governmentally conceived projects that seek to bring 'the people', who will be the subjects of democracy, into being. In this respect the coupling of hegemony and government proposed here follows Barry Smart, who sees in Foucault's notion of government a deepening complexification of hegemony. For Smart,

> it is in the work of Foucault that an analysis of the various complex social techniques and methods fundamental to the achievement of a relationship of direction, guidance, leadership or hegemony is to be found.[72]

Foucault's work, according to Smart, 'revealed the complex multiple processes from which the strategic constitution of forms of hegemony may emerge.'[73] To see how this might be so requires an accounting of Foucault's notion of governmentality and its relation to power.

To be definitional, governmentality involves the operation of certain modes of power, emergent in situated rationalities, capable of shaping conduct, towards the production of order in any specified field. On Foucault's notion of governmental 'rationalities', Colin Gordon has suggested that we understand this as 'a way or system of thinking about the nature of the practice of government (who can govern, what governing is, what or who is governed)' in multiple fields.[74] If these varying governmentalities are to be understood as forms of power, this would suggest something of an identity between government/power.

This is, indeed, Barry Hindess' reading of Foucault, and one broadly followed here. Hindess notes that Foucault attempted to overcome potential misreadings of his work that conflated domination and power. In order to do this Foucault had to strike against prevalent notions of power which posited relations of a linear and asymmetrical type. For Foucault, power was immanent in all social relations as an effort to shape the conduct of things. This is basically the meaning he attributes to government. Given the premise of free subjectivities, inherent in the application of government is the possibility of resistance and an alternative shaping of things that defy any production of order in a field of power. For Foucault, the practice of government is not domination, as Hindess tells it, because it goes to work on a range of free, or potentially free, subjects, who may wrestle with its effects and subvert its outcome. Power operates in a space of subjectivities which are given to choice and reflection, but which are equally bounded by the discursive discipline that holds in that space.[75] The import of this Foucauldian insight is only clear when the notion of governmentality is set against the general approaches to power by political theory.

As Foucault puts it, governmentality, in the context of a state's turn to practices informed by political economy, is defined as the ensemble formed by the institutions, procedures, analyses and reflections, the calculations and acts that allow the exercise of this very specific, albeit complex form of power, which has as its target population, as its principal form of knowledge political economy, and as its essential technical means apparatuses of security.[76]

It will be useful to unpack this quotation. As McNay notes, Foucault conceptualized modern societies as characterized by the 'tri-angular power complex: sovereignty – discipline – government'.[77] While traditionally political theory was preoccupied with the art of sovereign power, resident in the ruler, Foucault noted that it had not been attuned to the actual practice of government. His definition of governmentality, or rationalities of government, is prefaced by noting the rise of practices of government beyond the simple 'maintenance of one's principality' (the question of sovereignty), and how the emergence of government introduced principles of economy, as the management of one's household, into 'the management of the state'.[78] Political theory, lured by the grand narratives of the sovereign individual and the social contract, for example, has, by and large, missed the actual productive practices of government. This Foucauldian displacing of the themes of political philosophy, as Hindess notes, suggested a whole new field of inquiry – the specific rationalities of government that lay under and below the claims of the right to rule and the obvious forms of domination in the practice of discipline. These rationalities were concerned with questions of management of the population and social forms of the organization of that management.[79]

In Foucault's sketched outline, the formation of political economy, as a body of knowledge concerned with the uses of resources for the development of national wealth, entailed a multiple mapping of things and persons. Thus, within modern society, new forms of knowledge/power complexes emerged with their own rationality separate from, but historically always in relation to, questions of sovereign power and discipline.[80] These forms of knowledge, Foucault suggests, have their means of realization in apparatuses of security. Such apparatuses take the form of various techniques which secure specific objectives over the social body in particular fields. As Peter Miller and Nikolas Rose put it:

If political rationalities render reality into the domain of thought, these 'technologies of government' seek to translate thought into the domain of reality, and to establish 'in the world of persons and things' spaces and devices for acting upon those entities of which they dream and scheme.[81]

It was by focusing on emergent rationalities in the many fields to be governed that Foucault could say, pace Nicos Poulantzas, that '[m]ay be what is really important for our modernity...is not so much the etasisation of society as the "governmentalization" of the state'.[82] By suggesting governmentalization of the state Foucault was not denying the existence of the 'state', but attempting to historicize it as a contingent outcome of the play of many rationalities and practices of power that had accumulated inside and outside the institutional apparatuses of the state.

With this account in mind, it is not surprising that while Foucauldian studies of specific forms of governmentalization develop detailed inventories of technologies of productive control, they do not, generally, go on to ask the broader questions of how such forms of control are integrated within the broader capitalist context.[83] However, for some, the notion of governmentality does illuminate how a strategic unity of distinct regimes and centres can take hold in society. Miller and Rose, for example, note that Foucault's understanding of government is an attempt to understand indirect means for 'aligning economic and social and political conduct with socio-political objectives'.[84] Nevertheless, while Foucault's master-works were discrete studies, his lectures on governmentality pointed to the possibility of a thematics of unity of the discrete discursive practices of capitalist modernity. Certainly, this was conceived differently from Gramscian notions of a hegemonic bloc governing downwards from a steering position. That Foucault analyses the rationalities of power in discrete instances means that his work presents a picture of contingent macro-power emerging from different micro-functional practices; and while he might conceive of some systemic form of governmentality over the social whole, this is always a contingent construction irreducible to any essence or point of origin.

Towards the idea of democrasubjection

The concerns of democrasubjection differ from the field understood as political socialization (the acquisition of political values studied by social scientists).[85] Studies of political socialization are often normatively oriented to a given order, seeking to understand maturation or deviance measured against a given, often liberal, value frame. In that sense, political socialization studies, through various techniques, are part and parcel of responding to the people-problem. When applied to third-world societies, the concept of political socialization is deployed in prescriptive terms – *why are people the way they are now, and how shall we remake them?* The use of democrasubjection in this book is restrictive, it does not look at acquisition of ideological traits or reception by intended subjects. This book looks at the interaction of different practices external to the subject, which is to say it focuses on government and hegemony, and leaves the question of impact bracketed. Nevertheless the book proceeds on the premise that democrasubjection is at least partly successful in making people into national-citizens. Clearly, it is a restrictive concept, but it does provide a conceptual clearing space for approaching democracy in a critical manner.

In the movement between projects for reform of political subjects/citizen construction and grandiose claims regarding the sovereignty of the people, complementary strategies of hegemony and governmentality converge in the practice of what may be termed democrasubjection – the subjection of people to imaginary forms of their own rule. Here 'imaginary' is understood as the discursive and ideological effects that produce a way of seeing that might be otherwise, given different conditions. Such ways of seeing imprint on social relations a really existing nature (to think and act like a citizen for example). The generalized experience of this imagined realm, for subjects, is shaped by the discursive limits imposed by apparatuses of security and the broader hegemonic conditions under which subjects live.

Schematically, the deployment of democracy, as a metaphor of the common good, proceeds within two parallel moments. First, there is the moment of broad hegemony conceived as a specific historical formation of cemented leadership by a historical bloc over a social formation, framed by moments of state-building, ideological practices, economic development and conjunctural politics. Within this historical condition democracy may variously be advanced as an ideological state, an institutional form, a project to build. Underlying these possibilities, either alone or in combination, is the organization of a centre that aggrandizes for itself the capacity to speak for the common good. Second, there is the moment of democracy as a political rationality, or specific project of government, aimed at creating practices of self-government. This may be framed as the production of capacity for the practice of citizenship and the promotion of civic virtue through which the particular is transcended, such that individuals act in a manner commensurate with the common good (the particular of the elite universalized). To the extent that a moment of democratic hegemony becomes effective in dispositional terms, by orientating people to particular ways of seeing and acting as citizens of a political community, then we are studying the effects of government situated within the problem space called democracy. To give specificity to this discrete area of governmentality and hegemony, it may be named democrasubjection. As theoretical constructions, neither hegemony nor governmentality are exhaustive of the forms of power operative in society, nor do they work in an enduring balance; rather, as organizing concepts for enquiry, they point to a critical reading of democracy as democrasubjection.

Democrasubjection, or 'people in democratic subjection', refers to the potentially oppressive dimension of democracy, the never-succeeding project of subjecting people to new institutional and ideological forms of power in the construction of democratic subjects. This is more than a play on words: it is an attempt to suggest some productive insights that flow from a recognition of the constructedness of subjecthood. It also draws on Althusser's noting of the ambiguity of the term 'subject':

> In the ordinary use of the term, subject in fact means: (1) a free subjectivity, a centre of initiations, author of and responsible for its own actions; (2) a subjected being who submits to a higher authority, and is therefore stripped of all freedom...the individual *is interpellated as a (free) subject in order that he shall submit freely to the commandments of the Subject, ie, in order that he shall (freely) accept his subjection...There are no subjects except by and for their subjection.*[86]

This derivation of 'democrasubjection' does not signify agreement on Althusser's structuralist reading of the subject, which extinguishes meaning (1). Democrasubjection is understood more as a strategy, within a more general hegemonic project, than an actual state. It may succeed in having some dispositional consequences, in terms of producing 'consent' (as an inculcated propensity to see or do things in particular ways by self-volition).[87] Likewise, the Althusserian model of 'total' ideology is eschewed here, in favour of a more limited sense which points to the production of closure, a placing of limits on ways of seeing, in a discursive formation, and this closure's instrumentality for hegemonic blocs.

Ideologically speaking, then, a citizen, in moments of practice and identification, might be seen as a subjective place of closure inhabited by myths of nationhood and animated by the equivalence of nation and self, produced by such identifying closure. Certainly, across the globe, and no less in Thailand, much effort is expended on producing a political subject able to recognize itself as a modern political citizen, who is held to be an autonomous agent, and capable of consenting to participate in a political community. Althusser's notion of *interpellation* is useful for making some general remarks on this. He maintained that a necessary precondition for the maintenance and reproduction of capitalist society was the extent to which its ideological systems were perpetuated.[88] To examine this, Althusser grappled with how the subject internalized ideology, and he famously concluded that ideology was constitutive of the subject: 'Ideology interpellates individuals as subjects.'[89] By this Althusser meant that ideology, as a representation of the imagined relations of individuals, is a process through which the subject 'negotiates' its relationship to societal forces (material ideological apparatus). The 'negotiation' takes place at the level of subject (mis)recognition of itself when it is interpellated, or hailed, by outside subjects or institutions.[90] When a subject (mis)recognizes that a discourse is addressed to herself/himself, and responds as the addressee, then the subject is thoroughly implicated in ideology. Thus, Althusser claims that actually the negotiation described above (interpellation/(mis)recognition) does not take place because '[t]he existence of ideology and the hailing or interpellation of individuals as subjects are one and the same thing.'[91] The subject only ever was an ideological production.[92]

We have in Althusser the strongest statement on the fictive nature of subjecthood, such that lines of resistance are not intelligible. Here the questions of subject autonomy, of consent and resistance, make no theoretical sense. While the idea of interpellation remains a suggestive way for theorizing the discursive making of subjects, for it points to a permanent process of subject constitution, Althusser denies the agential nature of interpellation and the possibility of resistant readings of subject status because interpellation is presented as a formal rather than real process (since ideology and the subject are the same thing). Inasmuch as one might recognize the limits of 'interpellation' as an account of subject constitution, it can nevertheless function to name a particular elite orientation which seeks to construct particular ways of being by addressing people as citizens.

Furthermore, an underlying assumption of the chapters that follow is that the democratic aspect of both the statist and liberal hegemonic project entails the discursive citation of what Poulantzas calls the 'isolation effect', an effect in which subjects recognize themselves as citizens or individuals rather than class subjects, and which produces forms of politics relevant to this being a 'person' in a nation, separate from class politics and identity.[93] As Poulantzas argued, the isolation effect cannot be read simply as an automatic process derived from the structural isolation of individuals through commodity production and their de-classed relation to the political region as individuals, mediated by 'juridical-political ideology' and legal institutions.[94] Rather, this effect must be organized and constantly articulated as the common-sense operative subjectivity, as a form of subjectivity involving a particular imagining of the political community and one's location in it.

Projects of dominatively defined citizenship function as constant interpellative appeals to the desired subjectivity. This is not to say they are effective or not subvertible, but it is to say that they form a crucial component of the ideological struggle to combat the 'people-problem', or the problem of organizing the people productively. Part of the democratic aspect of hegemonic projects in Thailand, both statist and liberal, is precisely the attempt to make manifest and operative the structural potential of the isolation effect, to make it politically operative and organize the population around concepts of citizenship. That is to say that the isolation effect is consciously organized for as a political project. The more organized ideological strata in the state do seek the organization of a national imaginary and a citizen conducive to self-rule. It is for this reason that there exists a durable tradition of practices of government in the Thai state concerned with developing within the people particular subjective orientations that are held to be the civilized condition of modernity, among which is the production of a democratic temper. It is also why it is possible to meaningfully speak of projects of democrasubjection.

Admittedly, the notion of democrasubjection circumscribes a relatively narrow area of study that focuses on analysing an aspect of the relationship between hegemony and governmentality around representations and practices of democracy. This work seeks to illuminate how democratic discourse and the propagation of forms of citizenship-practice contribute to the practice of hegemony – by constituting a national political imaginary, a political community, at the level of ideology.[95] This does not exhaust the hegemonic apparatus in Thailand. Indeed, rather than attempt the over-ambitious project of determining the total nature of the state in Thailand and its hegemonic apparatus (as a complex unity of historical blocs, national and international, condensed as the integral state) this work will present a discrete analysis of several moments of democracy (statist/liberal/communitarian) as part of a contribution to an understanding of the complex of ideological forces that play a part in articulating the Thai social formation. Such a study is neither exhaustive of an understanding of the political and ideological realms of Thai society, nor is it necessarily the central aspect of the constitution of hegemony of the Thai state. Other studies could legitimately focus on, for example, the coercive nature of much of social life beyond the constitution of the political imaginary, the market and its impact on subject constitution, and the practices of neo-patrimonialism. The mix of powers, repression and localities in Thailand is as complex as anywhere. However, it is beyond the bounds of this work to present an articulation of the complex unity of hegemony and domination in Thailand. As a research project such work, pursued by a community of critical researchers, would need to attend to the many ideological forms that fabricate life, and the many concrete social relationships that are structured into strategic dominance. It would demonstrate the emergence of historic blocs that are capable of, and which are defined by, the direction of societal projects around the problem spaces of the economy (as a project of development and national commitment) and security (as a project of national identity and sovereignty). Clearly, given this wide scope, the study of realized hegemony in Thailand certainly is not the aim of this work. In any case, hegemony should not be understood as a static condition, but rather a condition that is fought for and resisted. If we consider Gramsci's notion of attained hegemony we might wonder if it is even possible. It involves the successful presentation and indeed historical necessity of a group's corporate interests being universalized, and in which a dominant 'party' brings about

> not only a unison of economic and political aims, but also intellectual and moral unity, posing all questions around which the struggle rages not on a corporate but universal plane, and thus creating the hegemony of a fundamental social group over a series of subordinate groups[96]

Another limit of this study is that it does not approach the study of Thai democracy in terms that emphasize resistance and conscious counter-hegemonic strategies that rework the national-popular imaginary. It is taken as given that resistance is a permanent possibility and is an inherent part of the discursive workings of power in identity formation. Regarding Thailand, one can find in Peter Vandergeest's work an attempt to highlight counter-hegemonic strategies in the appropriation of state propagated rights discourse by Thai peasants and farmers.[97] This project of recovery is to be supported. Certainly, in focusing on hegemony and state ideology this book misses much of the dissonance that pervades even official ideology and its reception by the population.[98] Yet the attempt to study the dominative work that democratic discourse does, necessarily means focusing on projects that emanate from those pursuing hegemonic strategies. This is not to say there is no escape. Indeed, in the worker and peasant movements of Thailand one sees acts of resistance and rebellion with the potential to fundamentally transform the existing social formation. But this book focuses on the 'other side': the hegemonic productions of the elites and their project of subjecting people to imaginary forms of their own rule. This is a justifiable focus, given the relatively little attention that has been paid to it. What is more, by uncovering these processes, it becomes possible to take to task the liberal and communitarian refashioning of democracy, which have recently emerged, as part of a new project of people-subjection. The present book aims to illuminate how historical forms of democracy must be understood as practices of power (hegemonic and governmental) in specific sites and for specific purposes. Mainstream studies of democratization are internal to these practices of power, for they largely reproduce its ideological categories. The study of democrasubjection seeks to demystify these practices of power.

Something also needs to be said about the conceptualization of citizenship used here. This is not a sociological study of the emergence of institutionalized relations between states and subjects. Democrasubjection, in its productive aspect of citizen construction, is distinguished from positivist and critical readings of citizenship because, as a conceptual category, it seeks a transcendence of the ambivalent tension between seeing citizenship positively, as in the Marshallian tradition of a bagfull of enabling rights and obligations, and critically, as a strategy of rulers to stave off class conflict.[99] Democrasubjection, being a discursive account of citizenship, sees citizenship as the possibility of a productive enactment of a mythical political community by subject-citizens within the limits set by hegemonic blocs.

If democrasubjection might be a theoretical category – organizing our understanding of the construction of democratic subjection through the discourses of citizenship – it may also be the name properly given to a particular practice of power. I am developing here the idea that it is better to see democrasubjection as a political project, rather than an actual state. This requires a constant engagement with the objects of that project and consequently a continual reformation of the project in response to real-life resistance and obstacles. In making this point I hope to move beyond an ideology-critique of citizenship as serving bourgeois capitalist values, towards an elaboration of the social and political forces that go into its making. Here, then, democrasubjection might best be defined as any articulated project formed at the intersection of the ideological interpellation of individuals into citizen-subject status within the frame of the nation, and the governmental practices that take up the raw material of people for productive reform. Clearly, as the politics of cosmopolitan citizenship take shape, the sphere of this practice of power is extended. What is significant, is that the term directs our attention to the dominative side of citizenship. To this end citizenship is now read as an enabling discursive resource for social control and active internalization of the given normative frame.[100]

In the chapters that follow I will attempt to present a situated reading of projects of democrasubjection. My approach is expository as well as critical. I take an expository stance since what I am saying regarding democracy in Thailand is unorthodox and there is a need to present textual evidence. I interpolate this expository approach, however, with critical comments pertaining to democrasubjection. By using both hegemony and governmentality, a dual critique may be formed. Let me now briefly summarize the argument as it will emerge in the chapters that follow.

In studying the hegemonic aspect of democracy, we are looking at the interpellation of the subject-cum-citizen into the nation, as an identified member of a political community. The extent to which identification occurs is the extent to which it is possible to speak of hegemonic effects. The democratic aspect of hegemony operates at the level of appeals to legitimate sovereignty and the production of relevant metaphors substantiating this claim. Practices of government are linked to the production of dispositional orientations and the very being of the subject-citizen. These practices are orientated to subject-citizen realization and take the form of technological rationalities of management and reform of the subject, although there are attempts to articulate these with questions of sovereignty. By taking on this dual perspective it becomes possible to explore the contradiction surrounding the claiming of legitimacy, on the basis of popular sovereignty, when state and social actors seek the very creation of citizens on whose behalf democracy is supposed to function. This is another way of reintroducing one of the latent contradictions of the political development doctrine: how can a political philosophy of popular sovereignty hold, when there are no citizens to speak of, just objects of reform? Thinking about democracy in this way entails a demystification of popular sovereignty by pointing to its fragile constructedness.

Also, a focus on the governmental level, on the political rationalities that lie behind hegemonic discourses on democracy, helps explore the question of 'consent' raised by Gramsci. These rationalities aim at the construction of consent by proposing means towards the formation of pliable citizens with particular subjective orientations and identifications towards the political. This is why thinking between hegemony and governmentality might also be productive in any enquiry into the workings of a democracy. It is also why the term democrasubjection was coined. This term captures both the global level of projecting a sovereign power as the focus of unity to which people are to be subjected, as well as the making of that subjection through the very practices of becoming a citizen.

Democrasubjection, as a project, is always unfinished. Progressive battles are fought in the name of popular sovereignty and citizenship, which is to say that people are not simply the mute objects of power. In that sense, it is best to think of democrasubjection as a project, rather than as an actual state. While there is a never-ending quest to subjugate, order and exploit in the name of an elite-defined common good, there is also resistance, and subversive reversals that accompany any play of power. The field is never secured. Finally, a qualifier – hegemony and government, in this book, are theoretical categories through which I attempt to do some exploratory work on 'democracy'. These categories narrow the field of investigation, as well as claim too much; alas, this is always the hazard of isolating out from complex social fields several issues for investigation.

Notes

1 Anthony Smith, *Myths and Memories of the Nation*, Oxford: Oxford University Press, 1999, p. 9.

2 My reading of nationalism follows a historical modernist and constructivist perspective. Smith as an ethno-symbolist is right to consider the potency of myth and memory as sources for symbolic nationalist politics, but these are forms of ideological struggle and their potency emerges in context, not by virtue of their authenticity. Smith's ethno-symbolism has taken him close to a modified version of the idea of 'invented tradition', but instead of ideology we have 'sincerity'.

3 Sulak Sivaraksa, 'The Crisis of Siamese Identity' in Craig Reynolds (ed), *National Identity and Its Defenders: Thailand Today*, Chiang Mai: Silkworm, 2002, pp. 33–48, p. 33.

4 *Ibid.*

5 See Anderson, who famously said of the nation, 'It is imagined because the members of even the smallest nation will never know most of their fellow-members, meet them, or even hear of them, yet in the minds of each lives the image of their communion.' Benedict Anderson, *Imagined Communities: Reflections on the Origin and Spread of Nationalism*, (2nd Edition) London: Verso, 1991, p. 6.

6 David Streckfuss, 'The Mixed Colonial Legacy in Siam: Origins of Thai Racialist Thought, 1890–1910', in Laurie Sears (ed.) *Autonomous Histories: Particular Truths, Essays in Honour of John Smail*, Madison: Center for Southeast Asian Studies, University of Wisconsin, 1993, pp. 123–53.

7 Kamala Tiyavanich, *Forest Recollections: Wandering Monks in Twentieth-Century Thailand*, Chiang Mai: Silkworm Books, 1997.

8 Thongchai Winichakul, *Siam Mapped: A History of the Geo-body of a Nation*, Honolulu: University of Hawai'i Press, 1994.

9 Benedict Anderson, *Imagined Communities*, p. 6.

10 On traditional rationalities of power, see Stanley Tambiah, *World Conqueror and World Renouncer: A Study of Buddhism and Polity in Thailand Against a Historical Background*, London: Cambridge University Press, 1976.

11 See Michel Foucault, *The Archaeology of Knowledge*, trans. A.M.Sheridan Smith, London: Routledge & Kegan Paul, 1972.

12 See Phillip Darby, *Three Faces of Imperialism: British and American Approaches to Asia and Africa, 1870–1910*, New Haven: Yale University Press, 1987.

13 James Carrier, 'Introduction', in J. Carrier (ed.) *Occidentalism: Images of the West*, Oxford: Clarendon Press, 1995, pp. 1–32. Carrier suggests a brief definition of Occidentalism as 'stylized images of the West', p. 1.

14 Irene Gendzier, *Managing Political Change: Social Scientists and the Third World*, Boulder: Westview Press, 1985.

15 Peter Bell, 'Western Conceptions of Thai Society: The Politics of American Scholarship', *Journal of Contemporary Asia*, 12, 1, 1982, pp. 61–74.

16 Herbert Phillips and David Wilson, 'Certain Effects of Culture and Social Organization in Internal Security in Thailand', Memorandum Rm. 3786-ARPA (abridged), The Rand Corporation, 1964, *ibid.*, p. 8.

17 *Ibid.*, pp. 7–8.

18 See Eric Wakin, *Anthropology Goes to War. Professional Ethics and Counterinsurgency in Thailand*, Wisconsin: University of Wisconsin, Center for Southeast Asian Studies, Monograph no. 7, 1992.

19 Paul Cammack, *Capitalism and Democracy in the Third World,* London: Leicester University Press, 1997, p. 1.

20 See, for example, David McClelland, 'The Impulse to Modernisation', in M. Weiner (ed.) *Modernisation: The Dynamics of Growth,* New York: Basic Books, 1966; A. Inkles and D. Smith, *Becoming Modern: Individual Change in Six Developing Countries,* Cambridge MA: Harvard University Press, 1974.

21 Yogesh Atal, 'Arrivals and Departures: The Case of Political Science in Asia', in D.Easton, D.J.Gunnell and M.Stein (eds) *Regime and Discipline: Democracy and the Development of Political Science,* Ann Arbor: University of Michigan Press, 1995, pp. 249–68, p. 264.

22 See, for example, Khana ratthasat mahawithayalai ramkhamhaeng, *Sarup phonkan kanprachum thangwichakan ratthasat kap kanphathana prathet 8 thanwakhom 2525* [Conclusions from an Academic Meeting, Political Science and Development of the Country], Bangkok: Khana ratthasat mahawithayalai ramkhamhaeng, 1982.

23 Precha Hongrailert, interview with the author, Bangkok, 24 March 1997.

24 See Sombat Chantornvong, 'Political Science in Thailand: A Brief History of the Discipline' (in English), in Phonsak Phongpaeo (ed.) *Thitthang khong ratthasat thai]Directions in Thai Political Science],* Bangkok: Samakhom nisit kao jula-longkon mahawithayalai, 1985, pp. 189–201, pp. 190–4.

25 Sombat Chantornvong, 'Major Trends in Teaching', in *ibid.,* pp. 201–17, p. 210.

26 Sombat Chantornvong and Chulacheeb Chinawanno, 'Problems of the Profession', in *ibid.,* pp. 226–8, p. 227.

27 Fred Riggs, *Thailand: The Modernization of a Bureaucratic Polity,* Honolulu: East-West Centre Press, 1966. For a Marxist critique of modernization theory in general and Riggs in particular, see Kevin Hewison, *Thailand Politics and Power,* Manila: Journal of Contemporary Asia Publishers, 1989, pp. 3–13.

28 David Apter, *Rethinking Development: Modernization, Dependency and Postmodern Politics,* Newbury Park CA: Sage, 1987, p. 20.

29 Riggs, *Thailand,* p. 96.

30 *Ibid.,* p. 364.

31 *Ibid.,* p. 148.

32 *Ibid.,* p. 131.

33 *Ibid.,* p. 396.

34 Neher and Bidya note the prevalence of the bureaucratic polity model among Thai political scientists. See Clark Neher and Bidya Bowornwathana, 'Thai and Western Studies of Politics in Thailand', *Asian Thought and Society,* 11, 31, 1986, pp. 16–27, p. 16.

35 For an example of this type of analysis see Clark Neher, *Politics and Culture in Thailand,* Ann Arbor: Center for Political Studies Institute for Social Research, University of Michigan, 1987. Also see Norman Jacobs, *Modernization without Development: Thailand as an Asian Case Study,* New York: Praeger Publishers, 1971. Jacobs uses the Weberian notion of patrimonial authority to explore Thai political culture.

36 Somboon Suksamran, *Buddhism and Political Legitimacy,* Bangkok: Chulalongkorn University Research Report Series, no. 2, 1993.

37 Thinapan Nakata, 'Political Culture: Problems of Development of Democracy', in Somsakdi Xuto (ed.) *Government and Politics of Thailand,* London: Oxford University Press, 1987, pp. 168–95.

38 David Morell and Chai-Anan Samudavanija, *Political Conflict in Thailand, Reform, Reaction, Revolution*, Cambridge: Oelgeschlager, Gunn and Hain, 1981, p. 311.

39 Chai-Anan Samudavanija, 'Thailand, A Stable Semi-democracy', in L. Diamond, J.Linz and S.M.Lipset (eds) *Democracy in Developing Countries*, London: Lynne Rienner Publishers, 1990, pp. 271–312, p. 281.

40 See William Siffin, *The Thai Bureaucracy: Institutional Change and Development*, Westport: Greenwood Press, 1966; Suchit Bunbongkarn, 'Political Institutions and Processes', in Somsakdi Xuto (ed.) *Government and Politics of Thailand*, London: Oxford University Press, 1987, pp. 41–74; Kramol Thongthammachart, *Toward a Political Party Theory in Thai Perspective*, Singapore: Southeast Asian Studies Centre Occasional Paper, 1982, no. 68.

41 Pisan Suriyamongkol and James Guyot, *Bureaucratic Polity at Bay*, Bangkok: Graduate School of Public Administration, National Institute of Development Administration, 1985, p. 37.

42 *Ibid.*, p. 60.

43 Chai-Anan Samudavanija, 'State Identity Creation, State Building and Civil Society 1939–1989', in C. Reynolds (ed.) *National Identity and its Defenders, Thailand: 1939–1989*, Clayton: Centre for Southeast Asian Studies, Monash University, 1991, p. 75.

44 Chai-Anan Samudavanija, 'Thailand, A Stable Semi-democracy', pp. 297–302.

45 *Ibid.*, p. 310.

46 Anek Laothamatas, *Business Associations and the New Political Economy of Thailand: From Bureaucratic Polity to Liberal Corporatism*, Singapore: West View Press, 1992, p. 161.

47 *Ibid.*, pp. 168–9. See especially p. 171: 'the participation of business in the policy making process and its exertion of influence over the bureaucracy may be considered as a progressive stage in the political development of a society with a strong tradition of operating in a bureaucratic polity'. See pp. 154–5.

48 Surin Maisrikrod, *Thailand's Two General Elections in 1992: Democracy Sustained*, Singapore: Research and Discussion Notes Paper no. 75, Institute of Southeast Asian Studies, 1992, pp. 4–5.

49 Surin Maisrikrod, 'Emerging Patterns of Leadership in Thailand', *Contemporary Southeast Asia*, 15, 1, 1993, pp. 80–96. See especially pp. 89–93.

50 *Ibid.*, p. 84.

51 *Ibid.*, p. 86.

52 For examples, Surachart Bamrungsuk, 'New Strengths – Old Weaknesses: Thailand's Civil-Military Relations into the 2000s', paper presented to Interdepartmental conference, Faculty of Political Science, Chulalongkorn University and Department of Politics and Public Administration, University of Hong Kong, Hong Kong, 17–18 May 1996. On pacted transition see Park Eunhong, 'A Study on Democratization: Comparative Analysis of the Periods between from [*sic*] 1973–1976 and from 1992 to the Present', paper presented at 'Asia in the Next Century Forum', Centre of Asian Studies, Chiang Mai University and Korea Institute of Southeast Asian Studies Program, 5 February 1996.

53 Thinapan Nakata, 'The Problem of Democracy in Thailand: A Study of Political Culture and Socialization of College Students', Ph.D. dissertation, Vanderbilt University, 1972. Also see Thinapan Nakata, 'Political Culture: Problems of Development of Democracy', in Somsakdi Xuto (ed.) *Government and Politics of Thailand*, London: Oxford University Press, 1987, pp. 168–95.

54 See for example Kamol Somvichian, 'The Thai Political Culture and Political Development in Modern Thai Politics', in Clark Neher (ed.) *Modern Thai Politics: From Village to Nation*, Cambridge MA: Schenkman, 1979, pp. 153–69; Kramol Thongthammachat, *Kanmeuang lae prachathipatai khong thai* (Thai Politics and Democracy), Bangkok: Ho.jo.kho. bankit trading, 1976. This text introduces the notion of democracy as a way of life and thus as a matter of cultural norms (pp. 258–9); Amon Raksasat, *Anakhot chart thai* [The Future of Thailand], Bangkok: Rongphim kromyuthasuksa thahanpok, 1976. This book suggests building democracy with regard for Thai culture and argues for expanding the role of the monarchy. The most sophisticated approach is found in Chai-Anan Samudavanija, *Panha kanphathana thang kanmeuang* [Problems of Political Development], Bangkok: Samnakphim julalongkon mahawithayalai, 1993.

55 Paul Cammack, *Capitalism and Democracy in the Third World*, London: Leicester University Press, 1997, p. 123.

56 Samuel Huntington, *Political Order in Changing Societies*, New Haven: Yale University Press, 1968, p. 7.

57 *Ibid.*, pp. 20–4.

58 Daniel Lerner, 'Toward a Communication Theory of Modernization', in L. Pye (ed.) *Communications and Political Development*, Princeton: Princeton University Press, 1963, pp. 327–50.

59 Cammack, *Capitalism and Democracy*, p. 123.

60 See Lucien Pye, 'Communication Policies in Development Programs', in L. Pye (ed.) *Communications and Political Development*, pp. 229–33, p. 232.

61 As Preston suggests, post-colonial elites in 'developing' countries were strongly influenced by the doctrine of nationalism as a resource for modernization. See P.W.Preston, *Discourses of Development: State, Markets and Polity in the Analysis of Complex Change*, Aldershot: Avebury, 1994, pp. 4–7.

62 Christine Buci-Glucksmann, *Gramsci and the State*, London: Lawrence and Wishart, 1980, pp. 47, 111–36.

63 It would be quite useful to draw many parallels between modern Thailand and Gramsci's Italy, given the nature of the bourgeoisie in Thailand. Indeed, John Girling has produced a very suggestive piece in this direction, drawing on the notion of passive revolution and hegemony. See John Girling, 'Thailand in Gramscian Perspective', *Pacific Affairs*, 57, 3, 1984, pp. 385–403.

64 Buci-Glucksmann, *Gramsci and the State*, p. 38.

65 Antonio Gramsci, *Selections from the Prison Notebooks*, London: Lawrence and Wishart, 1971, pp. 262–3.

66 For the myriad meanings that might be read into hegemony see Perry Anderson, 'The Antinomies of Antonio Gramsci', *New Left Review*, 100, 1976/7, pp. 5–78.

67 Gramsci, *Selections from the Prison Notebooks*, pp. 279–80, 301–10. Gramsci's comments on rationality and Taylorism hint at some kind of 'apparatus', but it is ideologically conceived as an effect of capitalism and the factory, it is not 'rationally' driven by the power/knowledge paradigm as Foucault would have it. See pp. 270–278.

68 *Ibid.*, pp. 5–25.

69 Bob Jessop, *State Theory: Putting Capitalist States in Their Place*, London: Polity Press, 1990, pp. 207–8.

70 *Ibid.*, p. 208.

71 Gramsci, *Selections from the Prison Notebooks*, p. 268.

72 Barry Smart, 'The Politics of Truth and the Problem of Hegemony', in D. Hoy (ed.) *Foucault: A Critical Reader*, Oxford: Blackwell, 1986, pp. 157–73, p. 160.

73 *Ibid.*

74 Colin Gordon, 'Governmental Rationality: An Introduction', in G. Burchell, C. Gordon and P. Miller (eds) *The Foucault Effect: Studies in Governmentality*, Chicago: University of Chicago Press, 1991, pp. 1–52, p. 3.

75 See Barry Hindess, *Discourses of Power: From Hobbes to Foucault*, Oxford: Blackwell, 1996, pp. 97–113.

76 Michel Foucault, 'Governmentality', in Burchell et al. *The Foucault Effect*, pp. 87–104, p. 101.

77 Lois McNay, *Foucault: a Critical Introduction*, London: Polity Press, 1994, p. 117.

78 Michel Foucault, 'Governmentality', p. 92.

79 Barry Hindess, 'Politics and Governmentality', *Economy and Society*, 26, 2, 1997, pp. 257–72, p. 259.

80 Michel Foucault, 'Governmentality', p. 101.

81 Peter Miller and Nikolas Rose, 'Governing Economic Life', in M. Gane and T. Johnson (eds) *Foucault's New Domains*, London: Routledge, 1993, pp. 75–138, p. 82.

82 Michel Foucault, 'Governmentality', p. 103.

83 For a critique of this nature see Boris Frankel, 'Confronting Neo-Liberal Regimes: The Post-Marxist Embrace of Populism and Realpolitik', *New Left Review*, 226, 1997, pp. 57–92.

84 Miller and Rose, 'Governing Economic Life', p. 76.

85 I am responding here to Robert H. Taylor's argument that what I am really describing is 'political socialization'. See his review of the hardback edition of this book in *Asian Affairs* 34, 3, 2003, pp. 346-347. In a very kind review, Taylor argues that what I see as hegemonic processes are really quite successful processes of national integration without the level of bloodshed seen elsewhere. While I accept this point, with qualifications, accepting the relative lack of bloodshed (in contrast to Burma or Indonesia) does not mean there is no need for a critical study of ideology in Thailand.

86 As should be clear from this, my notion of 'democrasubjection' derives from Louis Althusser, *Lenin and Philosophy and other Essays*, 2nd edn, London: New Left Books, 1977, p. 182. Foucault also points to this duality in the notion of subject. See Michel Foucault, 'Afterword: The Subject and Power', in H. Dreyfuss and P. Rabinow, *Michel Foucault: Beyond Structuralism and Hermeneutics*, Chicago: The University of Chicago Press, 1983, pp. 208–26, p. 212.

87 For an extended discussion on the subject/subjected dichotomy see Etienne Balibar, 'Citizen Subject', in E. Cadava, P. Connor and J. Nancy (eds) *Who Comes After the Subject?*, London: Routledge, 1991, pp. 33–57.

88 Althusser, *Lenin and Philosophy*, pp. 127–8.

89 *Ibid.*, p. 160.

90 By misrecognition Althusser meant to point out how the subject sees itself as the source of meaning when in fact it is simply an effect of meanings around which it is brought into being by interpellation.

91 *Ibid.*, p. 163.

92 Whatever the fate of the Althusserian project, this aspect of Althusser's attempt to bridge the ideological and the material remains a potent one around which contemporary theorists move. See Stuart Hall, 'Introduction: Who Needs Identity?', in Stuart Hall and Paul du Gay (eds) *Questions of Cultural Identity*, London: Sage, 1996, pp. 1–17.

93 Nicos Poulantzas, *Political Power and Social Classes*, London: New Left Books, 1973, pp. 130–4.

94 *Ibid.*, p. 133.

95 See Barry Hindess, 'Citizenship in the Modern West', in B. Turner (ed.) *Citizenship and Social Theory*, London: Sage, 1993, pp. 18–35. I am following, here, certain ideas in the post-Marxist camp. As Hindess notes, the notion of citizenship relates to the idea of a political community as having a common civilizational ethos to which a citizen should aspire. This stands against the idea that citizenship is a real category, which determines the functioning of democracies. Against what Hindess calls 'realization work' (citizenship as an assumed realized state of rights and obligations) and the critique of citizenship as an ideological mystification, Hindess suggests that citizenship can be a way of thinking about the political which can result in unforeseen consequences (pp. 31–2). In essence, Hindess hints at a discursive conception of citizenship. See also Chantal Mouffe, 'Preface: Democratic Theory Today', in C.Mouffe (ed.) *Dimensions of Radical Democracy: Pluralism, Citizenship and Community*, London: Verso, 1992. Mouffe also hints at a de-essentializing of the idea of an existing political community (as if it really exists in a commonality of interests) and proposes that modern political communities be seen as a 'discursive surface of inscription' on which competing interpretations construct and act (p. 14).

96 See Gramsci, *Selections from the Prison Notebooks*, pp. 181–2. For Gramsci, hegemony is never conceived as having been secured but, as Boggs puts it, '[h]egemony is part of a dynamic, always-shifting complex of relations, not the legitimating core of a static and all encompassing totalitarian rule'. See Carl Boggs, *The Two Revolutions: Antonio Gramsci and the Dilemmas of Western Marxism*, Boston MA: Southend Press, 1994, p. 163.

97 See Peter Vandergeest, 'Siam Into Thailand: Constituting Progress, Resistance and Citizenship', Ph.D. dissertation, Cornell University, 1990; also Peter Vandergeest, 'Constructing Thailand: Regulation, Everyday Resistance and Citizenship', *Journal for the Comparative Study of Society and History*, 35, 1, 1993, pp. 133–58.

98 I have in mind here that my focus could reproduce the dominant ideology thesis which has been persuasively critiqued by N. Abercrombie, S. Hill and B. Turner, *The Dominant Ideology Thesis*, London: Allen and Unwin, 1980. Regarding the question of the diversity of democratic attitudes, such that it would be mistaken to imagine passive reception of ideology, see John Dryzek, *Democracy in Capitalist Times: Ideals, Limits and Struggles*, Oxford: Oxford University Press, 1996.

99 For the former position see T. Marshall, *Class, Citizenship and Social Development*, Chicago: University of Chicago Press, 1977. For a suggestive outline of the latter position see Michael Mann, 'Ruling Class Strategies and Citizenship', in M. Blumer and A. Rees, *Citizenship Today: The Contemporary Relevance of T.H. Marshall*, London: Cambridge University Press, 1996, pp. 125–44.

100 Indeed, Bryan Turner has hinted at this, but in a positive fashion, seeing citizenship as a kind of secular solidarity in modern societies. See Bryan Turner, 'Contemporary Problems in the Theory of Citizenship', in B. Turner (ed.) *Citizenship and Social Theory*, London: Sage, 1993, pp. 1–18.

3

Before the doctrine

From constitutional democracy to Thai-style democracy

Our realm is vast and the population is great. The eyes and ears of our king, and the eyes and ears of the government officials cannot reach out to all the people . . . Thus there arose the need to change the form of our government to that of the civilized countries. The way to do this is to make the joys and sorrows of the people known to the eyes and ears of the administrators . . . Those who rule must fulfill the needs of the people . . . This is the rule of democracy where the people are the master. For this reason the people have their representatives who are their spokesmen.[1]

(Phahon Phonphayuhasena, Prime Minister of Siam, 1933–38)

PRIDI PHANOMYONG, ONE OF THE LEADERS OF THE 1932 revolution which overthrew the absolute monarchy in Thailand, was moved several decades later to consider the failure of the People's Party to establish democracy in Thailand. He offered a sketchy explanation focusing on the role of egoism, the degeneration into divisiveness (characteristic of even the French revolution, he noted), and the continued survival of old-regime elements in the post-1932 order, particularly in the bureaucracy. Pridi also repeated a story that is often told at seminars on democracy even to this day, that when officials talked about the importance of the new constitution (*ratthathammanun*) villagers thought it was the child of an important person.[2] The story may be read in several ways. Clearly, it highlights the different world-views of the new rulers and the population. It also points to the fact that while the state may have been characterized by administrative integrity of sorts, and possessed internationally recognized sovereignty, its proclaimed citizens remained distant and undisciplined in terms of the new democratic ideology that the government, and future governments, propagated. Despite the administrative reforms of King Chulalongkorn that brought about a centralized state apparatus, the state was far from able to reach down to the lowest levels and shape the conduct of people. Distant villages, constant movement, and a hardy rejection of the encroaching state made it difficult for the state to turn its rhetoric even into a semblance of reality. Meeting occasionally for ceremonial, financial and legal purposes, state officials and villagers may be envisaged as having a long and uneasy stand-off, right into the present. Penetration of the 'vast land' and 'great people' has been a central aim of state officials. Part of this penetration involved the elaboration of democratic ideology as a way of bringing subjects into relations with the state. A stated ambition of the modernizers from the 1930s to the late 1950s was to break down the population's perceived reverence and fear of authority so that they might become self-governing. In a number of attempts at subject reform and citizen construction, projects of democrasubjection were unevenly put into practice, well before the arrival of the doctrine of political development in the 1960s. This chapter is an account of the context in which these new projects emerged and the conditions under which they were transformed.

Capitalism, the nation and the possibility of citizenship

In the mid-to-late nineteenth century the monarchy emerged as the organizing centre for the rise of a modern state system in Thailand. By a process of adaptation and control over other social forces, it was able to inaugurate a hegemonic project of state modernization. In doing this, new ways of seeing emerged. Although Thailand escaped formal colonization, the military, industrial and social progress of the West greatly influenced the elite.[3] Their actual engagement with the West and their selective application of Western-derived ideology (nationalism, constitutionalism) and technology (state apparatuses, armies) ensured that elites were caught in the discursive frame of Orientalism. They saw the society over which they ruled as somehow delinquent and inferior, and in need of form and rationality (seen as attributes of the West).[4] As Carol Breckenridge and Peter Van Der Veer note, Orientalism was not merely a way of thinking, but 'a way of conceptualizing the landscape of the colonial world that makes it susceptible to certain kinds of management.[5] In bringing under heel the disparate populations that made up the kingdom, elites increasingly embraced a civilizing posture towards their subjects. A form of internalized Orientalism may be said to have informed the practice of 'developing' states and their intelligentsia.[6]

Additionally, Occidentialism, or an imagined West of rational order and progress, animated this Orientalism, providing it with goals and indices of progress and new political rationalities. These basic points have some application in the Thai context, particularly because Siamese elites experienced an epistemic rupture such that the tasks of modernity could only be referenced to Western conditions. As active participants in this Orientalist frame, and providing it with its necessarily hybrid disposition *vis-à-vis* the peculiarities of Siam, the elite emerged as a historical class of state modernizers.

With the overthrow of the absolute monarchy in 1932, 'democracy' emerged as a troubled component of national ideology. The broader social and economic basis for a discourse of citizenship and democracy had been developing for generations. King Chulalongkorn (1868–1910) had built the administrative structure of the nation-state in the late nineteenth century in response to the threat of imperialism, and as a measure to entrench monarchical rule against noble feudalistic tendencies.[7] John Girling describes the form this state building took as a 'colonial-style, centralized, functionally differentiated bureaucratic state'.[8] Additionally, all the outlying regions that form modern-day Thailand were brought under control.[9]

The bureaucratic centralization and modernization of the state were accompanied by the gradual abolition of the *sakdina* system. Seksan Prasertkul has described this system as being composed of the *phrai* (indentured peasant) system of corvee labour and a ranking system of the population.[10] In effect, the *sakdina* system was a specifically unique form of pre-capitalist mode of production, sharing some similarities with European feudalism.[11] Structurally, the *sakdina* system was under threat from the commercialization of agricultural production, and the newly 'liberalized' trade regime resulting from the British-imposed Bowring Treaty of 1855. Integrating itself into this economic regime as regulator and private beneficiary, the monarchy pursued the dual task of forming a centralized, territorially fixed administrative structure and of providing the conditions for a capitalist economy. These developments necessarily impacted on the class structure and gave rise to new national imaginings.

First, the Chakri state succeeded in replacing the subjugation of *phrai* (serfs) to local masters with a new juridical status as subjects of the state. The gradual abolition of *phrai* status (1905) and slavery (early 1900s), which created a universal class of nominally free subjects, reflected the shift to free labour for commercialized agriculture and a shift from corvee to monetary tax as the basis for state revenue. This ushered in a new period of governor/subject relations. As Peter Vandergeest notes, the new nation builders 'attempted to individuate people so that they could be regulated by the institution of citizenship'.[12] Also, by moving against regional monarchies and tributary states, and winning the subjection of the regions to Bangkok, the monarchy was able to implement financial, judicial and military functions of a modern state.[13]

For Thongchai Winichakul, a significant ideological accompaniment to these developments was a shift in the cosmological representation of space in Siam, which was modelled on the Buddhist 'three worlds' account of various levels of existence from celestial to bestial. He argues that a 'modern' understanding of 'borders' was absent, until the Siamese elite found themselves confronted with Western cartography and demands to clearly delineate the boundaries of rule.[14] Emerging out of this encounter with imperialism and the grave imperative to respond, was the 'geo-body' of Siam, a new spatial imagination of territorial and bordered sovereignty. This was a central condition for nurturing national identity.[15] Thongchai's insight builds on the critical account of nations as 'imagined communities' developed by Benedict Anderson.[16] For Thongchai, national space was constructed by the mediation of maps and visual representations, such that it could be discursively deployed to provide 'a component of the life of a nation'.[17] The 'geo-body', then, is not simply to be understood as a physically bounded space, but a space in which to discursively act. The emergence of the nation-state in Siam was also the birth of its geo-body as a representational space around which other discourses could coagulate, particularly those related to sustaining notions of an organic community.[18] Although Thongchai is prone to flights of determinism, granting agency to discourse, and viewing human actors as mere instruments of discourse, his notion of the 'geo-body' is a profoundly critical one, aware of the constructed nature of nationhood, even its seeming physicality.[19]

As new administrative structures spread across the newly bordered Siam, integration was sought even at the most local of levels. On the workings of the new administrative regime, Siffin notes that a figure close to the powerful Prince Damrong Rachanuphap younger half-brother of King Chulalongkorn, visited British-controlled Burma and returned with various ideas relating to administrative measures for the integration of local areas into national administration. In the 1890s the Interior Ministry, under Damrong's leadership, expanded. Censuses were carried out to map the population.[20] Of particular significance were the Local Government Acts designed to integrate local 'village leaders' into state administration as conveyers of policy and, increasingly, as registrars of the local population, performing various licensing and policing needs.[21] Speaking in 1892 on the rationale of local-level administrative reforms which would empower village-level leaders, Damrong explained:

> I want to make them all equal citizens. If we can have such a base for our administration we will naturally be able to mobilize the people, to investigate crimes, and in general to direct the people more easily than in the past.[22]

Finding expression in this short statement are emergent forms of governmental rationality relating to guidance and surveillance through citizenship. Such rationalities would be the basis for attempts to cast the newly created subjects into various productive moulds.

The advance of territorial sovereignty, administrative integrity and penetration into the local areas, required a remaking of processes of state legitimization. While King Chulalongkorn's achievement was the transformation of the dynasty into a territorially bounded monarchy and the development of a modern state apparatus, the significant contribution of King Vajiravudh's regime (1910–25) was in providing the ideological weaponry (the triadic Nation, Religion, Monarchy) required to gather the various network of peoples, that Chulalongkorn had caged, into a sense of nationhood.[23] In propagating this triadic ideology, Vajiravudh shrewdly drew on existing Thai and Western formulations of identity, adding 'nation' to the identity markers of religion and monarchy. The triad came to be the three pillars of the 'civic religion', a related set of symbols and patterns which fill up the meaning of life, connecting it to some sacred entity and destiny.[24] As Benedict Anderson notes, Vajiravudh's administration began to systematically utilize school education, propaganda and the writing of history for the purpose of producing 'endless affirmations of the identity of the dynasty and the nation'.[25] The potential of this ideology, in modified form, was most fully utilized in the decades following the revolution of 1932, as the state embarked on a project of creating a national identity, using drama, music, literature and textbooks.[26]

Nationalism, as a universal language incorporating chosen subjects in a given territory, provided the discursive basis for the development of ideological citizenship; it provided a model of the individual delinked from the hierarchical structure of the *nai* (master) and *phrai* relationship, and made possible the constitution of a juridical subject of law. This challenged the dual traditional rationalities of the monarchy premised on Brahmanical conceptions of divine kingship and Buddhist conceptions of sovereign power legitimated by the monarch's protection and embodiment of the Thai version of the *Thammasat*, the Buddhist legal and cosmological code.[27]

Ideologically, these developments were well under way during Chulalongkorn's reign. Mid-nineteenth century textbooks inculcated among elites the notion of citizen duty to the secular state.[28] Likewise, as the revenue base of the state moved towards taxing the population, taxpayers were increasingly seen as part of a newly emergent secularized state.[29] Notions of bourgeois individualism were also propagated which stressed reason, individual capacity and choice beyond fatalistic conceptions of karma.[30] Most importantly, the idea of developing a citizen's morality and knowledge was related to the development of the nation itself.[31] During the next two reigns, the idea of the Thai nation was further developed around a mythic history of the Thai race.

David Streckfuss has pointed to the importance of the colonial encounter for understanding the discourse of 'Thainess' – the essence of 'who we are'.[32] Streckfuss notes that in struggling to define who would be Thai, when faced with French protectionist claims over Lao people, 'the Thai ruling elite creatively adapted the logic of race in delegitimizing French claims and in formulating a sense of "Thainess"'.[33] While Siam had erstwhile been a multiethnic entity, the attempt to contain imperialist encroachment and maintain sovereignty generated new elite-designated identities over the peoples contained in Siam's emerging borders. Speaking to a royal commissioner, Chulalongkorn suggested caution in the designation of identity:

> [Y]ou must remember that if you are speaking with a westerner on the one hand and Lao on the other, you must maintain that the westerner is 'them' and the Lao is Thai. If, however, you are speaking with a Lao on the one hand and a Thai on the other, you must maintain that the Lao is 'them' and the Thai is 'us'.[34]

Racial categorization brought into being, to follow Thongchai's 'geo-body' neologism, the 'people-body' – the Thai. The conscious slide between 'us' and 'them' would be a constant internal tension of Thai identity, for this was nothing other than the imposition of a centralized identity over a disparate population, some of whom were, according to circumstance, sometimes inside and sometimes outside the designated identity. The word 'Thai' was a call to unity, a recognition that people were not sufficiently Thai and had to be made so. Thainess became a discursive field upon which the people-body would be formed, and a myth of origins was essential to its functioning.

In standard history and classroom teachings, the ethno-base of the nation is uniformly presented as based on a southern migration from China by the many T'ai-speaking people. Yet these diverse peoples become subsumed under a central Thai identity constructed in Bangkok. This historical origin became the discursive basis on which central Thai chauvinism worked to marginalize other ethnic groups.[35] The year 1939 marked the pinnacle of this project when Prime Minister Phibun Songkram changed the name of Siam to Thailand, as part of his strategy to reclaim parts of Laos. E. Bruce Reynolds explains the relevance of this move:

> Ostensibly Thailand represented a more accurate translation of the Thai term 'Muang Thai', but it was well understood that the change reflected an aspiration to bring all neighboring peoples ethnically related to the Thai under Bangkok's rule. In the expansive view of Phibun's chief ideologue, Luang Wichitwatakan, these included not only the Lao, the Shans, and the T'ai peoples in southwestern China, but the Cambodians as well.[36]

In 1927 Prince Damrong, the 'father' of royalist versions of history in Thailand, drawing on ideas that had been developing within aristocratic circles, presented what would become the definitive statement of the characteristics of the Thai people.[37] Damrong explained Thai dominance in Siam, going back 700 years, on the basis of their possession of certain characteristics that he defined as 'Love of National Independence, Toleration, and Power of Assimilation'.[38] As Damrong presented it, through love of national independence the Thais had successfully fended off threats to the nation; because of toleration for different beliefs and customs other races did not hate the Thais; and through clever assimilation of different cultures the Thai people gained the benefit of other civilizations.[39] These 'miraculous' characteristics of the imagined Thais, expressive of their 'Thainess', are still often repeated.

One of the consequences of the rise of national discourse within the bowels of the monarchical state, and its continuance under the emergent post-1932 authoritarian state, was the disciplinary use of nationalism to stave off any challenges to power that might come from the growing non-royalist fractions of the capitalist class, as well as potential political dissidence. This class had been in formation over the previous century and largely had Chinese origins.[40] In 1911, in response to the growing republicanism within China and among Chinese immigrants in Siam, Vajiravudh passed the Nationality Act, which simultaneously acted to exclude and include different sections of the Chinese population.[41] This inclusion and exclusion, and the use of various measures to stamp out the speaking of foreign languages, set the scene for a long history of state efforts to marginalize the Chinese, both workers and capitalists. Seksan has suggested the underlying logic behind these moves:

> [B]y dividing the Chinese into natives and aliens, the Thai state was able to weaken the capitalist class politically and re-establish its political dominance in

the relationship with the local bourgeoisie, it was a situation in which capitalism was allowed to grow but not the political influence of the capitalist class.[42]

This was the basis on which the Thai variant of bureaucratic state capitalism was able to develop, forcing the predominantly Sino-Thai capitalist class into relations of dependence with actors in the state.

Constitutions, politics and the new state

A pervasive interpretation of the revolution that overthrew the absolute monarchy in 1932 is made by Riggs, who noted that '[t]he revolution confirmed but did not create a more basic transformation in the structure of the Thai government, which had already taken place.'[43] Given that significant changes in the state had already occurred in the 1890s, Riggs considered the events of 1932 as merely the 'substitution of one oligarchic elite by another.'[44] Certainly the governments that immediately followed the revolution of 1932 were marked by compromise and struggle between competing fractions of the elite centred in the military, bureaucracy and the palace. These struggles have led to an interpretation of post-1932 politics as a politics of 'faction constitutionalism', which David Wilson famously described as 'the drafting of a new constitution to match and protect each major shift in factional dominance.'[45] At one level this is a fair description, given the frequency of coups d'état and constitutional revision in Thailand. However, recognizing the instrumental uses to which constitutions were put does not mean that 'democracy' was irrelevant to the post-revolutionary order. This interpretation of constitutionalism also downplays the significant changes ushered in by the revolution.

On overthrowing the absolute monarchy in June 1932, the revolutionary People's Party built on earlier discourses of national citizenship to formulate a new conception of an individual's relationship to the state. The revolution's intellectual leader Pridi Phanomyong, a French-educated lawyer, was well versed in Western constitutional and utopian radical thought, and this is reflected in a crucial text, the *Announcement of the People's Party*, issued during the revolution. The *Announcement* criticized the monarchical state as dishonest, corrupt and indifferent to the people's sufferings. Furthermore: 'The king's government held people as slaves...animals, and did not consider them as human beings. Thus, instead of helping them, it continued to plant rice on the back of the people.'[46] The *Announcement* further attacked the arbitrary and nepotistic rot of the monarchical state.[47] It also marked a forceful reconceptualization of the relations between the state and the people:

> People! Let it be known that our country belongs to the people and not to the king as was deceived. Our forefathers had rescued the freedom of the country from the hands of the enemy. The royalty only took advantage and gathered millions for themselves.[48]

In this same declaration the six principles of the People's Party were outlined, the main features of which were to maintain sovereignty of the nation, to provide employment and education, to formulate a national economic plan and for all to have equal rights, freedom and liberty.[49]

While abstractly embracing the people as the sovereign basis of government, Pridi also exhibited the 'civilizing' tendencies of the elite. In his 1933 economic reform plan that promised 'equality of opportunity' and government employment for all, Pridi revealed the modernizing disposition that the revolutionaries held in their assumed role of guardians of the people.[50] This role entailed a modification of the principle of liberty. Speaking of the economic wellbeing of the people as a prior principle to complete liberty, Pridi notes: 'Complete personal liberty is not possible under any social system, such liberty is always limited by the good of society.'[51] In Pridi's view the people needed to be led in their economic development up a higher civilizational scale.[52] As Pridi put it:

> We may compare our Siamese people to children. The government will have to urge them forward by means of authority applied directly or indirectly to get them to co-operate in any kind of economic endeavour.[53]

It was around these interrelated ideas of the nation, economic development and modernization that state democratic discourse emerged. Democracy was seen as just one more component in the package of modernity towards which the new elite aspired, and would in turn involve the formulation of projects for its realization.

Another significant change involved the more effective use of the state apparatuses, separated from monarchical caprice and extravagance, which put in place the long-term conditions for effective practices of specific governmentalities around located problems. Importantly too, administrative power was spread more evenly and away from the dictates of 'born rulers'. 'Commoners' assumed positions of power next to aristocratic hangovers. In line with this trend, the 'permanent' constitution, promulgated in December 1932, proclaimed that titles of birth no longer inhered privilege and laid down the basic rights of people (Article 12).[54] In the post-revolutionary period, the formal political arena expanded to embrace a form of 'parliament without parties', with those pushing for the establishment of political parties seen as harbouring malign counter-revolutionary intent. However, the revolutionary grouping known as the People's Party continued to function. The revolutionaries also put in place a ten-year plan towards full representative democracy. For ten years parliament would be composed of two categories of MPs: first, those elected from local-level elections who would then go on to elect members for a national parliament; and second, those selected by the revolutionary regime. After ten years the second category of MPs would be abolished. This plan stalled with the rise of the military faction within the People's Party; in 1940 the constitution was amended to extend the role of appointed MPs for a further twenty years, thus ensuring the stability of the government.

Another indication of significant change after 1932 was the shift towards economic intervention in order to mobilize national capitalism.[55] Regarding the former, it is possible, Kevin Hewison argues, to look beyond the intriguing struggles in the decades following the revolution and discern the emergence of 'haphazard, state-led industrialization' and, more generally, the role of the state as 'policy maker, financier and model investor' of capitalism.[56] This was a decisive break with the almost laissez-faire attitude of the absolute monarchy and its use of state apparatuses for private gain. Within the general parameters of this new state, different elite fractions struggled. Once secured, power networks of allied capitalists, military elites and bureaucrats were in a position to benefit economically, and through such patterns of alliance, state actors became rentiers.[57]

The fact that the revolution had stopped far short of purging the palace element meant that a latent royalist threat remained. This threat manifested itself in the rebellion led by Prince Boworadet in October 1933, which indicated the sheer reticence of aristocratic elements to submit to the revolution. The regime was forced into strategies of mild 'terror' and political parties were banned. The Protection of the Constitution Act (1933) curtailed free speech.[58] By the late 1930s the struggle for control of the state had led to various measures that sat uncomfortably with the democratic rhetoric of the regime. The rise of the military faction in the People's Party, led by Phibun Songkhram, was indicative of this. The emergence of the military in the state was rooted in post-revolutionary circumstances, in the concrete political struggles of the day and the emerging structural power of military leadership *vis-à-vis* other elite groups. This trend was attenuated after the onset of World War II.

However, it would be wrong to see the post-revolutionary bureaucratic and military state as simply the inheritor of the centralized apparatus of the modernizing absolute monarchy; rather, it sought to bend this apparatus towards wider degrees of elite involvement, and to further develop modern rationality for governance in nationalistic and democratic terms.

In the late 1930s the intial democratic intent of the regime was overshadowed by xenophobic nationalism. This was expressed in a number of anti-Chinese measures, and was coupled with the promotion of civilized Thainess through the issuing of what were called state preferences (*ratthaniyom*). These state preferences were the first extensive project, apart from developments in education, of subject reform aimed at producing a modern citizen. They prescribed standards of behaviour for the people, including: the use of modern dress, eating and bathing codes; loyalty to the nation; respecting the king, flag and anthem (which described Thailand as a democratic state); instructions to cooperate in building the nation; and a preference calling on Thais to carry out their civic duties including promoting a common identity as Thai.[59] Importantly, along this line of civilizational thinking, the new state elites issued a Cultural Maintenance Act which proclaimed 'It is the duty of the Thai people to practice national customs and promote prosperity of Thailand by conserving and revising existing customs.'[60] It defined culture as 'qualities which indicate and promote social prosperity, orderliness, national unity and development and morality of the people'.[61]

This fascinating period in Thai history, when the state issued decrees in excess of their possible policing, was not simply a Phibun initiative but corresponded with broader elite civilizational projects.[62] Indeed, Yoshifumi Tamada notes that Phibun's cultural policies were supported by the People's Party including Pridi, as they were in formulation well before Phibun's turn to autocratic leadership. Significantly, justification for the preferences was made in terms of 'public opinion'. According to Phibun, state preferences were

> similar to the proper type of etiquette to be observed by all civilized people. In this term is included 'public power' which is derived from public opinion. Public opinion brings public power...and this enables either reformation, or the suppression of a minority of people who are too stubborn to be reformed.[63]

The civilizing work of the regime was justified also in terms of democracy:

> This is the government of the people, by the people for the people. Therefore it is quite natural that this government will attempt to do anything according to...public opinion, regarding public opinion as the guideline for public administration.[64]

Yoshifumi Tamada notes that Phibun's populist nationalism was more egalitarian in rhetoric than the nationalism of Vajiravudh. His invocation of democracy also indicated that the fusion of people and the nation-to-be, through the rhetorical device of democracy, was a significant element of the new Thai nationalism, even though Phibun was discredited for his wartime alliance with the Japanese and expelled from office in late 1944.

After the war a reconciliatory alliance emerged between the liberal faction of the People's Party and royalists. A constitution was issued providing for a bicameral parliament, with the upper house appointed by the lower house. Provision for the organization of political parties was made. The military sat in the shadows. It seemed possible once more that a liberal constitutional regime might emerge. Civilian sections of the bureaucracy and the old liberal guard of the People's Party were favouring such a system, as were royalists who now saw a constitutional system as the only defence against dictatorship.

This potential basis for elite forms of democracy gave way, however, once more to military might in the late 1940s. Splits within the civilian regime, economic deterioration and resentment within the military of civilian interference in their affairs paved the way for another military takeover of power. In this context, the return of royal exiles after the war is significant. A number of these began to organize a royalist element in the parliament led by Khuang Apaiwong, along with support from Kukrit and Seni Pramoj.[65] This faction allied with the military in seeing the pro-Pridi government over-thrown in 1947, subsequent to accusations that Pridi had been involved in the murder of the young King Mahidol in 1946. This royal resurgence provided some basis too for the project of recentring the monarchy in national ideology.

It is a mistake to imagine that the monarchy disappeared as an ideological force until its rehabilitation in the late 1950s. Since 1932 the institution of the monarchy remained in use as an aspect of political legitimacy and as a focus for aristrocrats to maintain and advance their position. Struggles continued even after the abdication of King Prachatipok in 1935. Conservatives continued to seek an extension of the constitutional role of the monarchy through to the late 1940s.[66] Even during the height of the ultra-nationalism of the Phibun regime the monarchy still counted. Phibun, in a 1940 address opening the Democracy Monument, noted the importance of the monarchy as an inviolable institution so that it could 'be a factor letting all people unite harmoniously as one'.[67] He went on, however, to say that if the king failed in his duties it could lead to the collapse of the nation and lead even to hatred of the king himself.[68]

Although the late 1940s signalled the dominance of the military in determining who held power, parliamentary forms of government, along with elections, were basically retained until the late 1950s despite brief suspensions. Nevertheless, the 1950s was characterized by a series of coups, corruption and parliamentary impotence. Political parties, as cliques of bureaucratic capitalists and royalists, as well as reforming middle-class elements, provided the day-to-day drama of politics, as did the manoeuvring within bureaucracy for control. Electoral corruption was also common.[69] The coup of 1958 led by Sarit, however, seemingly no different than the seven (five successful) coups that had followed the 1932 revolution, sought to provide a new ideological basis to state stability and to shift the contest of political power decisively outside parliament and its constitutional trappings. Importantly, given the geo-politics of the period, Sarit was also bolstered by US military support and aid. He was thus able to deploy material and ideological resources to effectively address the question of regime identity in a statist direction.

In the preceding period, democracy had been used both as part of the national ideology and as a rhetorical defence for the pursuit of interest among elite fractions. The constant coups and Cabinet shifts reflected the inability of any enduring power bloc to emerge. This changed with Sarit's success in aligning with US security interests, and by winning over sections of the royalists. A hegemonic bloc, in which the military took the leading role, emerged. It is important to note here that the overthrow of the absolute monarchy ushered in a period of permanent contestation between the monarchists and the People's Party. At the same time, as a new political order emerged centred on the state and bureaucracy, political power became something of a football, maddeningly sought after, occasionally groped, even productively directed at times, but always elusive. Within this contest for political power a complex of economic and political fractions emerged that denied the state a constant basis for directing broad hegemonic projects that could win enduring support. Despite this, even if elites could not agree on the terms of political contest (as the litany of coups and constitutions suggests), attempts were made to propagate abstract notions of democracy to the people as part of the production of national identity.

Democracy and citizenship in the post-revolutionary period

In the following section a closer look at post-revolutionary democratic discourse up to the Sarit regime is presented. This is not merely a matter of antiquarian interest; a number of elements of modern-day ideology were distilled in this period, as were embryonic projects of democrasubjection.

The political tension between the People's Party and the palace was naturally reflected in official discourse. In this context, just what to call the new regime was by no means clear: a tension between the appellations 'limited monarchy', 'democracy' and 'constitutional system' was evident. In a 1933 Department of the Interior announcement regarding the election of District Representatives (who would then go on to elect half of the first House of Representatives in Thailand) it was explained that in the new form of 'democratic government', called 'limited monarchical power' (rachathipataiamnatjamkat), the highest power 'comes from' the people.[70] The people's sovereignty was, however, to be exercised by the king, who issued laws with the suggestion and acceptance of parliament. The people were called on to help the king who had 'gracefully conferred the constitution'.[71] In an announcement in October 1933 on the election of the House of Representatives, voters were cautioned about the need to elect good representatives because 'Siam at this moment is your responsibility'.[72] As Sombat Chanthonwong's study of the political discourse of the time shows, the meanings of most political terms which had emerged in the previous generation to name new political phenomena were very fluid and contextual, [73] reflecting the difficulty of linguistically capturing the compromise that had been effected in the 1932 constitution. From its initial denunciation of the parasitic monarchy, the People's Party had retreated significantly, initially allowing the palace to retain significant control. The constitution therefore substituted the revolutionary rhetoric of the People's Party with royal piety. The preamble states that the king graciously granted the constitution after considering the people's request. A condition of the grant was the preparatory work undertaken during 150 years of just rule by the Chakri dynasty. It had educated, through the expansion of the civil service, the people such that they were now in a position to have some say in government.[74]

In terms of understanding the evolution of democratic discourse and ideology as forms of power to make particular dispositions, the constitution and those that followed were an important part of legitimating the regimes and of providing a centre-point for the evolution of rights and duties of the new Thai citizen, even if only at a rhetorical level. The 'temporary' constitution issued after the revolution in June 1932 contained no provisions on rights and duties. The four articles dealing with rights and duties in the 'permanent constitution' issued in December, covered equality before the law, freedom of religion and belief 'when it is not antagonistic to the duties of a citizen or when it does not contravene the peace and order or the good morals of the people' (Article 13). People were also given the right, within the bounds to be defined by law, of free movement, residence, property, speech, education, assembly and the right to establish associations (Article 14). As for duties, these were relatively straightforward: respect the law, protect the country, and assist the government by paying taxes and by other means (Article 15).

In a significant development, the Department of the Interior began a campaign to spread knowledge about the constitution, issuing instructions to publicize its existence.[75] Officials were to present the constitution as sacred (*saksit*) by having it delivered on a *paan* (the utensil used for passing objects to monks).[76] Stressing the importance of the people's knowledge of the constitution to political stability, the head of the Department of the Interior noted, 'we do not have complete order in our politics because our people lack considered reason [*khwamphijaranahetphon*]'.[77] There followed a declaration that the people of the nation are all stakeholders, members of a company, who must help the king administer the land.[78] Facing the uncertainty of an untried political democracy, it was commonplace for officials to have concerns about the people's capacity to be good citizens; complaints about the 'disease' of freedom which threatened traditional morality were common.[79]

The concern behind building up people's knowledge was related to the project of the modernizing state. The elite viewed their own 'people' and society as inadequate and in need of development. Rights and duties were components of a modern state that entailed rational use and productive service to the nation. Not only that, the rights contained in the constitution hinted at the basic infrastructure of capitalist freedoms, rights to property and free movement. Concerns with national development, national unity and the quality of its subject citizens required that state officials address themselves to 'the people-problem'. One response to this problem was the publishing of citizens' manuals.

Citizens' manuals

The continuing struggle for an adequate symbolic rendering of the new regime's legitimacy, despite the uncertain outcome of the revolution, is the context in which one should consider the issuing of the *Manual for Citizens* by the Department of the Interior in 1936. This publication aimed at providing people with an understanding of the new regime and its claim to political legitimacy.

A brief exposition of two versions of the manual follows. One was issued in 1936 at a time when the royalist threat remained, although diminished. The second, a revised manual, issued in 1948, appeared when the royalist influence was again being felt both in public discourse and in political circles. Thousands were distributed to the provinces for the edification of officials and literate local notables. As official publications, they present the state orthodoxy of the time.

In the first manual, Siam is said to no longer be an absolute monarchy but a system of democracy, which is described as a 'government of the citizens and by the citizens [*phonlameuang*]'.[80] Drawing on, but reworking, the familial metaphor of the nation propagated by Vajiravudh, the nation is described as 'one big family'.[81] Readers are told that the security of the nation is in the minds of each person. In a revised edition, published a year later, a rationale for the manual is given:

> In every country that has government in accordance with constitutional democracy the people have a duty to study and know their rights and duties…so as to be able to act as a good citizens.[82]

The manual, the reader is informed, was therefore published to assist citizens to be 'persons who love the nation, religion, king and constitution'.[83]

In matters of the above, the 1936 and 1948 editions are very similar. However, a significant shift in tone appears in a parallel discussion on the difference between the idea of a country (*prathet*), a sovereign territory ruled by a state, and a nation (*chat*), a grouping of people of common origins.[84] In the first manual the origin of the state (*rattha*) is described as being based on the need for a sovereign power when people gather together. In such gatherings it is the duty of a country to protect the rights and freedoms of the people and to improve the welfare and status of the people.[85] In the 1948 manual readers are now informed, under the same heading of 'Country', that there must be 'governed and governors' and that the governors must have the capacity to compel the governed to follow dictates which correspond to both tradition and law.[86] To control a nation of thousands of families, there is a need for power that is 'sacred', which can protect those with little power from those who would harm the people. Such power is sovereign, and with it a government can look after the people's livelihood (*dulae thuksuk*).[87]

In both manuals, the status of a citizen is contrasted with that of a slave. While a slave's life was in the hands of the master, a citizen has full rights (*sitthi*) and duties (*nathi*). Slavery, the reader is informed, went against the inherent love of freedom, and was thus unnatural.[88] Rights are defined as having access to political and legal equality and freedom. However, rights are limited so as not to infringe on other people's rights.[89] Freedom is to be constrained by law, for freedom means being 'able to do anything without infringing the law of the land'.[90] Rights include having freedom of movement and expression, to take up any occupation or legal residence, or to set up an association.[91] These are all part and parcel of a generalized liberal presentation of democracy as a system safeguarding individuals.

In terms of a citizen's duties, the 1948 manual reflects the growing administrative control sought by the bureaucracy over the population. In addition to the duties outlined in the 1936 manual (patriotism and defending the country, the payment of taxes, voting, respecting the law, and seeking an education and working),[92] citizens were now expected to report deaths, births and marriages, report building activities and participate in various duties that tied the citizen to the state; citizenship thus became a matter of self-reportage to the distant state.[93]

The discussions on democracy and sovereignty are quite similar in both manuals. While sovereignty is seen as coming from the people, the people are to use their sovereign power indirectly, voting to elect representatives who will control the three branches of government, which, in liberal fashion, are to be kept separate so as to act as a check on each other.[94] While democracy is described as the best form of government in the 1936 manual, a cautious note is struck, because 'it can be disastrous when the people do not know how to use their rights.'[95] Therefore the manual called for the training of citizens.[96]

Evident in both texts is a particular concern to emphasize that democracy does not mean equality in economic terms, but only in political and legal terms; after all, '[i]n every milieu there must be "big people" (phuyai) and "little people" (phunoi), commanders and commanded.'[97]

The manuals are useful in capturing the popular presentation of democracy by the state to the people – a formal presentation of quite liberal forms of democracy. As yet, the highlighting of the monarchy and Buddhism (central to contemporary discourse) as the basis for democracy is not present, neither is there any extended representation that seeks a moral constitution of the citizen in terms of 'Thainess'. However, in noting the absence of capable citizens the embryonic theme of citizen 'know-how' is clearly present. In short, these early manuals contain 'thin' ideological notions of citizenship, a series of citizen depictions as a form of oratory appeal. As members of the nation-state, citizens had a duty to participate, through voting, in the administration of the country; this was what was meant by democracy. The thick elaboration of contemporary democratic discourse where citizenship is deeply entwined with mythologized history and culture had not yet been formed. Democrasubjection, as the dual movement of hegemony and government, remained, as yet, an undeveloped project at this early stage.

The texts discussed are official representations of the new form of political legitimacy. Outside of official circles, intellectuals also took part in naming the new system, defining its elements and its connections with the Thai past and the modern future. Separate Thai-language studies of these intellectual currents by Nakharin Mektraiarat and Kriangsak Chetphathanuan suggest a period of significant articulation of conservative and liberal renderings of democracy. These studies present a detailed picture of monarchical entrenchment into the discourse of democracy. Royalism was initially submerged and struggled for space under the post-revolutionary fervour of the period, but gradually emerged into the mainstream in the post-war period, becoming officially promoted under Sarit. A significant theme in both studies is the permanent state of debate surrounding democracy among elites.[98]

The broad significance of both studies is to highlight the attempt by traditionalists to re-legitimize the monarchy by rethinking and propagating select aspects of traditional Thai kingship. Such re-legitimization included appeals to the notions of the 'father king' (pho khun) as upholding Buddhism in the Sukhothai period (thammaracha) – seen as the dominant principle of kingship before its supposed corruption into divine kingship (*thewada*) under the Brahmanical influence of Khmer thought in the Ayutthaya period. Furthermore, the traditionalists, moving in the direction of elective kingship, suggested that the king governed with the people's consent as long as he ruled according to Buddhist precepts (*aneknikonsomosansamuti*). These ideas had re-emerged during the reign of Chulalongkorn, and would be used by the royalists in the aftermath of the revolution to argue that the ancient form of Siamese government was already democratic.[99] Nakharin demonstrates how this idea of kingship was drawn on by Sarit to eschew the formal election of political leadership; instead Sarit rooted political legitimacy in notions of patriarchal rule and the ability of high-level civil servants and experts to understand the will of the people, and therefore rule with their consent.[100]

An oft-cited article by Prince Dhani Nivat usefully summarizes the ideas of the traditionalist school regarding the monarchy.[101] It is argued that the Buddhist kingship rested on the king as guardian of the *Thammasat*, and on rule in accordance with the ten kingly virtues (*thotsaphitrachatham*).[102] As to the continuance of Brahman practice in the palace, Dhani suggested this was merely ritual and did not imply that the king was god-like.[103]

When Sarit came to power in the late 1950s, in line with the ideological recovery of the monarchy pushed for by royalists he rehabilitated the monarchy, but dumped their apparent liberal aspirations. Few protested.[104] Sarit's assumed purpose in doing this was to use the monarchy as part of a strategy to provide the regime with traditional legitimacy. As described by Thak Chaloemtiarana, Sarit promoted the idea that democratic rule did not require elections, and principally involved government in the people's interest. Questions of institutional form were relegated to matters of historical and cultural specificity. The focus was on order and development.[105] We might see the Saritian formulation on democracy as a passing attempt to end elite conflict, buckle down on the growth of working-class and intellectual dissidence in the 1950s, and also to initiate an ideological catharsis, a purging of the Western liberalism that had informed constitutional governance in the post-1932 era (excluding the war years). In terms of the resurgence of monarchical mythology, this may have been partly motivated by Sarit's own attempt to chew fat from the substantial bone of that institution's charisma (*barami*), by projecting himself in the image of a grand fatherly figure (*pho khun*). However, as Thak notes, it would be wrong to see this as merely a retrogressive ideological step, for in harnessing royalist themes and rearticulating democracy in authoritarian terms, Sarit was seeking a more stable path to modernization.[106]

In the late 1950s and early 1960s, then, notions of Thai-style democracy (*prachathipatai baep thai*) emerged as a basic component of Thai military and bureaucratic ideology.[107] Under Sarit a deliberate shift away from a 'Western' ideology of democratic government occurred, making redundant the use of the citizens' manuals. Sarit's international spokesperson, Thanet Khoman, explained:

> [T]he fundamental cause of our political instability in the past lies in the sudden transplantation of alien institutions on to our soil without careful preparation,

and if we look at our national history, we can very well see that this country works better and prospers under an authority, not a tyrannical authority, but a unifying authority.[108]

It was with this thinking in mind that Sarit's government, having overthrown an elected government in 1958, announced:

> The Revolutionary Council wishes to make the country a democracy...[which]... would be appropriate to the special characteristics and realities of the Thai. It will build a democracy, a Thai way of democracy.[109]

In line with this thinking, parliament was abolished and an appointed assembly came into being. Despite Sarit's death in 1963, his successors continued to describe the regime as working within the confines of Thai-style democracy. The book *Thai-style Democracy and Ideas about the Constitution*, containing radio broadcast transcripts, may be considered representative of this stream of thought.[110]

While pre-Sarit manuals had described democracy in terms familiar to the structure of Western democracies, these broadcasts reflect the transformation of political thinking associated with the Saritian regime. The broadcasts were essentially an attempt to cohere the legacy of Sarit.[111] In the opening broadcast listeners are informed of the need for the new constitution, then being drafted, to be appropriate to Thailand: 'The constitution that we need must be a democratic one and one that is appropriate to the condition of the Thai people.' The broadcaster goes on to attack intellectuals who think democracy must have English or American characteristics.[112] Attacking an emphasis on the institutional forms of democracy, it is argued that 'Thailand at this moment does not have elections and no permanent constitution, but we are a democracy.'[113] This claim is justified by arguing that a system that maintains the people's interests and responds to their needs and which is able to 'gather and use the people's opinions' is the true essence of 'government of the people, by the people and for the people.'[114] Depending on the circumstances, it is said, there are many forms that can fit this essential meaning of democracy. [115] Drawing on royalist discourse, significant claims are made for the Thai past that includes identifying the king's abidance by the ten virtues as an implicit social contract to serve the people.[116] Readers are also informed that King Prachatipok (1923–35) had always intended to grant a constitution, but the premature actions of the People's Party overtook him.[117] However, the text goes on to bemoan that this promising start to democracy was wasted for two reasons. First, Pridi's 'ultra-left' economic plans generated great conflict. Second, because some leaders of the People's Party had been educated in Western Europe they tried to use a Western constitution which did not match Thai realities.[118]

Interestingly, the common argument that the difficulty of establishing democracy in Thailand lies in low levels of education is rejected. Thais are seen as having great democratic potential because 'their generosity and love of freedom coupled with Buddhist training in disposition [*obrombom nisai nai praphutsatsana*]...becomes a sure basis for democracy.'[119]

Furthermore, the broadcasts note that the Revolutionary Council proclaimed as one of its tasks building a Thai-style democracy, an important element of which would be the reform of relationship between parliament and the Cabinet, following Charles de Gaulle's reforms in France.[120] Strangely, then, this exposition of Thai-style democracy identifies a continuity with Gaullist practice; that is, a Western referent underlies and justifies the 'unique' nature of Thai democracy. In later broadcasts Thai-style democracy is seen as part of a legitimate international trend in underdeveloped countries which reject excessive parliamentary democracy and place restrictions on political parties. The rationale for strong executive rule and limits on freedoms and rights in countries with fragile social and economic roots proceeds:

> if we allow unlimited political struggle it will become a struggle without order and discipline [*mai mi rabiapwinai*], and when anarchy [*anathipatai*] emerges it will present dictators with an opportunity to seize power.[121]

Thus, for the sake of political stability, the parliamentary system is disavowed, although with qualifications:

> it is not yet possible to use parliamentary democracy or Western European democracy. In the future, once the country has developed and has economic and social stability, it is possible that parliamentary democracy be used; the evolution of world democracy has been thus.[122]

Conclusion

The propagation of Thai-style democracy was an attempt to end perennial questions of political legitimacy by tapping into traditional rationalities of rule, but which left open the road to the development of a democratic people, once economic questions had been addressed and a middle class had come into being.

By suppressing the institutional elements of 'Western' democracy and then salvaging Thainess as a resource for a distinctive form of democracy facilitative of political stability and economic growth, Sarit's regime was in a position to bring to centre-stage the discourse of development as its source of legitimacy. Economic development and its prerequisites were elevated as regime requirements and outcomes.

Sarit's suppression of elements of liberal democracy had its ideological antecedents not simply in royalist myth but also in the notion of 'public opinion' deployed by Phibun. As Thailand shifted to a new consolidated state form – emergent in its relationship with the US – which brought security to the state and a degree of market openness to the economy, the tensions of Thai-style democracy as a basis for government were soon to be felt. Within a few short years the regime would begin embracing political developmental notions of democracy and fusing them with elements of Thai-style democracy. The shift back to the requirement for rational citizens, not dependent subjects of benevolent regimes that Thai-style democracy implied, would be gradual and contradictory, but it formed the only basis on which the modern state of Thailand was able to discursively interact with and mobilize its subjects as active participants.

Looking at the aftermath of 1932, the political struggles over state-form had led to some ambivalence in the kinds of project emanating from the centre; civilizational, constitutional and traditionalist rationalities competed or complemented each other. Yet no clear and enduring project of democrasubjection had emerged. There had yet to be a coincidence of hegemonic perspectives on nation and citizenship with particular rationalities of citizenship construction. Certainly, both governmental and hegemonic aspects of democracy were in formation, but nothing approaching a stable hegemonic project had crystallized. This is the significance, ideologically, of the Sarit era. With that regime's embracing of traditionalism, within the fold of modernity, crucial aspects of a future project of democrasubjection were put in place, most significantly, the place of culture in the democratic identity of a people: a theme that would later dovetail with the idea of civic culture propagated in political development circles.

To anticipate the next chapter, when state actors began to elaborate a more extensive programme of developmental democracy in the 1960s, greater heed was given to programmes of reform which took the people's cultural position not as in need of transcendence, but rather in need of assimilation into the ways of the modern. This assimilation would be sensitive to the assumed place of the traditional in matters of authority, congruent with the idea of civic culture. Phibun's projects of an idealized modern subject were effectively superseded. In their place more extensive projects of subject reform and citizen construction emerged, which began first with *getting to know the people* and using this knowledge as a basis to go forward. The great cultural leap, by edict, envisaged by Phibun, was replaced with the elaboration of technologies of reform centred on the family, communities, beliefs, production, and so on. From change by edict to the hard work of reforming technology, governmentality had arrived, articulated with the question of producing a sovereign people and democracy.

Saritian Thai-style democracy with its inherent paternalism, and legitimized by a particular reading of history, was challenged by forms of governmentality around development projects and community participation. Thainess, in these projects, would remain an indelible part of the subjection of citizens, but through an integration with the political development doctrine it would be rationalized, categorized, disenchanted, and would become a resource for management towards a Thai modernity. Thus the very Thainess of democracy would become part of the rationalized way of seeing culture and tradition as useful in matters of government. In the reclamation/construction of a posited past, lay a modern project for the construction of citizens. Saritian democracy, then, should not be seen as some atavistic, short-lived throwback; rather it laid the basis for modern projects of cultured democracy, fusing traditionalism with the doctrine of political development.

Notes

1 Cited in Eiji Murashima, 'Democracy and the Development of Political Parties in Thailand, 1932–1945', in Eiji Murashima, Nakharin Mektrairat and Somkiat Wanthana, *The Making of Modern Thai Political Parties*, Tokyo: Institute of Developing Economies, Joint Research Program Series no. 86, 1991, pp. 1–54, p. 8.

2 Pridi Phanomyong, *Ruam khokhian khong pridi phanomyong*, [Collected Writings of Pridi Phanomyong] Bangkok: Samnaknganphim mahawithayalai thammasat, 1982, pp. 357–61.

3 Anrotjak Sattayanurak, *Kanplianplaeng lokthat khong chonchan phunam thai tangtae ratchakan thi 4 thung phutthasakarat 1932* [The Changing World View of the Thai Elite From Rama 4 to 1932], Bangkok: Samnakngan phim julalongkon mahawithayalai, 1997; Nakharin Mektrairat, *Kanpatiwat siam 1932* [The Siamese Revolution of 1932], Bangkok: Samnakphim amarinwichakan, 1997.

4 Edward Said, *Orientalism*, New York: Pantheon Books, 1978.

5 Carol Breckenridge and Peter Van Der Veer, 'Orientalism and the Postcolonial Predicament', in C.Breckenridge and P.Van Der Veer (eds) *Orientalism and the Postcolonial Predicament*, Philadelphia: University of Pennsylvania Press, 1993, p. 6.

6 *Ibid.*, p. 11.

7 See the discussion in Pasuk Phongpaichit and Chris Baker, *Thailand: Economy and Politics*, Oxford: Oxford University Press, 1996, pp. 216–39.

8 John Girling, *Thailand: Society and Politics*, Ithaca NY and London: Cornell University Press, 1981, p. 46. For details see William Siffin, *The Thai Bureaucracy: Institutional Change and Development*, Honolulu: East-West Center Press, 1966, pp. 64–90.

9 Charles Keyes, *Thailand: Buddhist Kingdom as Modern Nation-State*, Bangkok: Editions Duang Kamol, 1989, pp. 54–6.

10 Seksan Prasertkul, 'The Transformation of the Thai State and Economic Change 1855–1945', Ph.D. dissertation, Cornell University, 1989, pp. 1–14.

11 There is a long debate on the nature of the pre-capitalist mode of production in Thailand that I will not enter into here. For the benefit of readers unfamiliar with Thai history, I reproduce two explanations of the *sakdina* system. First, Charles Keyes' glossary definition of *sakdi na*:

> literally 'rank (as indicated by) paddy fields'. During Ayutthayan times and the first half of the Bangkok era, every person in the realm was accorded a status associated with a specific acreage of rice land; the greater the acreage, the higher a person's position in a social hierarchy headed by the monarch. This hierarchy constituted the *sakdi na* system.
>
> (Charles Keyes, *Thailand: Buddhist Kingdom as Modern Nation-State*, Bangkok: Editions Duang Kamol, 1989, p. 225)

Pasuk and Baker propose a definition focused on resource control:

Every resident below the king was theoretically awarded a ranking measured in units of *sakdina* ... The term *sakdina* can be translated as 'power over fields' and, as a result, these rankings have been sometimes confused with feudal land grants. However, there was no land attached to these ranks. An alternative translation is close to the concept of 'resource entitlement'; this gives a clearer indication of the nature of the grant, with the key resource being labour power ... The *sakdina* ranks were an idealization of the king's role as allocator of the key scarce resource of labour power.

(Pasuk Phongpaichit and Chris Baker, *Thailand: Economy and Politics*, Oxford: Oxford University Press, 1996, p. 11)

12 Peter Vandergeest, 'Constructing Thailand: Regulation, Everyday Resistance, and Citizenship', *Journal for the Comparative Study of Society and History*, 35, 1, 1993, pp. 133–58, p. 133.

13 Chaiyan Rajchagool, *The Rise and Fall of the Thai Absolute Monarchy: Foundation of the Modern Thai State from Feudalism to Peripheral Capitalism*, Bangkok: White Lotus, 1994, p. 121.

14 See Thongchai Winichakul, *Siam Mapped: A History of the Geo-body of a Nation*, Honolulu: University of Hawai'i Press, 1994, ch. 2.

15 *Ibid.*, pp. 1–19.

16 Benedict Anderson, *Imagined Communities: Reflections on the Origin and Spread of Nationalism*, London: Verso, 1983.

17 Thongchai, *Siam Mapped*, p. 17.

18 *Ibid.*, pp. 132–5.

19 On Thongchai's discourse determinism consider the following statement: 'The Thai monarchs were merely the instrument of the new discourse and Thainess was nothing but a construct of humble origin.' Thongchai, *ibid.*, p. 12.

20 See Siffin, *The Thai Bureaucracy*, p. 72.

21 See Chai-Anan Samudavanija, *Village, Bureaucracy and Development*, Bangkok: The Public Affairs Group, the Public Affairs Foundation, Friedrich Ebert Stiftung, 1985, p. 3.

22 Cited in Tej Bunnag, *The Provincial Administration of Siam 1892–1915: The Ministry of the Interior Under Prince Damrong Rajanubhab*, Kuala Lumpur: Oxford University Press, 1977, p. 109.

23 Eiji Murashima, The Origin of Modern Official State Ideology in Thailand', *Journal of Southeast Asian Studies*, XIX, 1, 1989, pp. 80–96. For an extended discussion on King Vajiravudh see Walter Vella, *Chaiyo! King Vajiravudh and the Development of Thai Nationalism*, Honolulu: The University Press of Hawaii, 1978.

24 Frank Reynolds, 'Civic Religion and National Community in Thailand', *Journal of Asian Studies*, 36, 2, 1977, pp. 267–82, p. 274.

25 Anderson, *Imagined Communities*, p. 95.

26 Scott Barme, *Luang Wichit Wathakan and the Creation of a Thai Identity*, Singapore: Institute of Southeast Asian Studies, 1993, p. 9. Also see Craig J. Reynolds, 'The Plot of Thai History: Theory and Practice', in Gehan Wijeyewardene and E.C. Chapman (eds) *Patterns* and *Illusions: Thai History and Thought,* Canberra: Richard Davis Fund, Department of Anthropology, Australian National University, 1993, pp. 313–32.

27 See David Engel, *Law and Kingship in Thailand During the Reign of King Chulalongkorn,* Ann Arbor: Center for South and Southern Asian Studies, University of Michigan, 1975, pp. 1–5.

28 Atthajak Sattayanurak, 'Kankoet naeokhit nathi phonlameuang nai rat thai samai mai' [The Birth of the Idea of Citizen Duty in the Modern Thai State], *Ratthasatsan* [Political Science Journal], 14, 3, 1990, pp. 204–27, p. 205.

29 *Ibid.,* p. 214.

30 *Ibid.,* pp. 209–10.

31 *Ibid.,* pp. 218–20.

32 David Streckfuss, 'The Mixed Colonial Legacy in Siam: Origins of Thai Racialist Thought, 1890–1910', in Laurie Sears (ed.) *Autonomous Histories, Particular Truths: Essays in Honour of John Smail,* Madison: Center for Southeast Asian Studies, University of Wisconsin, 1993, pp. 123–53, p. 125.

33 *Ibid.,* p. 126.

34 Cited in *ibid.,* p. 134.

35 Pasuk and Baker, *Thailand: Economy and Politics,* p. 233. For a discussion of contemporary usage of this mythology in the Thai classroom see Niels Mulder, *Thai Images: The Culture of the Public World,* Chiang Mai: Silkworm Books, 1997, pp. 44–52.

36 E.Bruce Reynolds, 'Thai Irredentism and Japan's Greater East Asian Co-prosperity Sphere', paper presented to American Association of Asian Studies Annual Meeting, 22–25 March 2001: online at http://www.uoregon.edu/~iwata/_private/GEACS/new_page_25.htm, retrieved 13/2/2002.

37 Craig Reynolds, 'Introduction: National Identity and Its Defenders', in C. Reynolds (ed.) *National Identity and Its Defenders: Thailand, 1939–1989,* Chiang Mai: Silkworm Books, 1993, pp. 1–39, p. 13.

38 This is Damrong's own translation. See Damrong Rachanuphap, 'Khunatham khong chonchatthai' [The qualities of the Thai race], in Khanakammakan ekkalak khong chat samnakgnan sermsang ekkalak khong chat samnakgnan lekhathikan naiyokratthamontri, *Udomkan khong chat* [National Ideology], 1983, pp. 5–8, p. 7.

39 *Ibid.,* pp. 7–8.

40 Seksan 'The Transformation of the Thai State and Economic Change 1855 1945', pp. 308–23.

41 See Vella, *Chaiyo!* pp. 186–96.

42 *Ibid.,* p. 323. The classic work on the Chinese in Thailand remains William Skinner, *Chinese Society in Thailand: An Analytical History,* Ithaca NY: Cornell University Press, 1957.

43 Fred Riggs, *Thailand: The Modernization of a Bureaucratic Polity,* Honolulu: East-West Center Press, 1966, p. 196.

44 *Ibid.,* p. 112

45 David A. Wilson, *Politics in Thailand,* Ithaca NY: Cornell University Press, 1962, p. 262.

46 The People's Party, 'Announcement of the People's Party (24 June 1932)', in Thak Chaloemtiarana (ed.) *Thai Politics: Extracts and Documents 1932–1957,* Bangkok: Social Science Association of Thailand, 1978, pp. 4–7, p. 4.

47 *Ibid.*, p. 5.

48 *Ibid.*, pp. 5–6.

49 *Ibid.*, pp. 6–7.

50 Pridi Phanomyong, 'National Economic Policy of Luang Pradit Manutham', in Thak (ed.) *Thai Politics*, pp. 110–61.

51 *Ibid.*, p. 148.

52 See, for example, 'Minutes of a Meeting of a Committee to Consider a National Economic Policy at Paruskawan Palace', in Thak (ed.) *Thai Politics*, pp. 161–85, p. 168. Pridi comments to a committee considering his economic plan:

> What we ought to do is not to compare our state of advance to that of people less fortunate than ourselves but rather to that of the people of a civilized nation in order to see how far we still lag behind. And then we ought to make every effort to equal them.

53 *Ibid.*, p. 167.

54 *Ratthathammanun haeng ratchaanajaksiam 2475* [Constitution of the Kingdom of Siam, 1932].

55 Kevin Hewison, *Power and Politics in Thailand*, Manila: Journal of Contemporary Asia Publishers, 1989, p. 34.

56 Kevin Hewison, *Bankers and Bureaucrats: Capital and the Role of the State in Thailand*, New Haven: Yale University Southeast Asian Monographs no. 34, 1989, p. 57.

57 On this see Sungsidh Piriyarangsan, *Thai Bureaucratic Capitalism 1932–1960*, Bangkok: Chulalongkorn University Social Research Institute, 1982.

58 It would take fourteen years and four general elections before political parties were legalized. See Eiji Murashima, 'Democracy and the Development of Political Parties in Thailand, 1932–1945', in Murashima *et. al.*, *The Making of Modern Thai Political Parties*, pp. 1–54.

59 All the state preferences are available in translation in Thak, *Thai Politics*, pp. 244–57.

60 'National Cultural Maintenance Act BE 2483', in Thak, *Thai Politics*, pp. 255–6, p. 256

61 *Ibid.*, p. 256.

62 See Yoshifumi Tamada, 'Political Implications of Phibun's Cultural Policy 1938–1941', Final Report Submitted to the National Research Council of Thailand, February 1994, pp. 1–7.

63 *Ibid.*, p. 21.

64 *Ibid.*

65 Pasuk and Baker, *Thailand: Economy and Politics*, p. 267.

66 See Kobkhua Suwannathat-Pian, 'Thailand's Constitutional Monarchy: A Study of Concepts and Meanings of the Constitutions 1932–1957', paper presented at International Association of Historians of Asia, Chulalongkorn University, Bangkok, 20–24 May 1996, p. 7.

67 'Raignan kan sang anusaowari prachathipatai' [Report on the construction of the democracy monument], *Thesaphiban*, 1940, pp. 442–6, p. 448; 'Khamklao khong pho. no. naiyokratthamontri nai kanboet anusaowari prachathipatai' [Speech of the Prime Minister on the opening of the democracy monument], *Thesaphiban*, 1940, pp. 447–51. The actual

volume number and issue of *Thesaphiban* appear inconsistently on a number of volumes for several years after the revolution, and so for this earlier period citations are by year and page number. Pagination in the volume (normally comprised of twelve issues) is consecutive.

68 *Ibid.*, p. 448.

69 On this period see Girling, *Thailand: Society and Politics*, pp. 108–11.

70 Kong khosana krom mahatthai samnao [Department of the Interior, Propaganda Office], 'Thalaengkan khong kong khosana kanleuak tang phuthaen tambon' [Announcement of the Propaganda Office: The Election of Tambon Representatives], *Thesaphiban*, 1933, pp. 486–9, p. 486.

71 *Ibid.* Similar statements may be found in Luang Norakitborihan, 'Kotmai leuaktang' [Election Law], *Thesaphiban*, 1936, pp. 7–36, p. 13.

72 Kong khosana [Propaganda Office], 'Kanleuaktang phuthean ratsadon' [Election of Members of Parliament], *Thesaphiban*, 1933, pp. 490–9, p. 494. This article provides the text of what may have been the first democracy manual instructing citizens of Siam on selecting responsible, honest and non-materialistic representatives (pp. 495–6).

73 Sombat Chanthonwong, *Phasa thangkanmeuang phathana khong naeo athibai kanmeuang lae sap kanmeuang nai kankhian praphet sarakhadi thang kanmeuang khong thai pho. tho. 2475–2525* [Political language: the development of political explanation and vocabulary in thai political feature writings, 1932–82], Bangkok: Sathabanthai khadisuksa, 1990, pp. 40–54.

74 *Ratthammanun haeng ratchaanajak siam 2475* [Constitution of the Kingdom of Siam, preamble 1932].

75 Krommahatthai [Department of the Interior], 'Reuang raignan kanpoei phrae withikanpokkhong tam ratthathammanun' [Report on methods to disseminate the method of constitutional government], *Thesaphiban*, 1934, pp. 995–6.

76 Banthit Janrotjanakit, 'Kanmeuang wathathanatham reuang kansang khwammai prachathipatai' [Cultural Politics: Constructing the Meaning of Democracy], p. 102, M.A. dissertation, Thammasat University, 1998. Banthit's dissertation includes a useful discussion of the early citizen manuals.

77 Phrayasunthonphiphit, 'Ratthathammanun' [Constitution], *Thesaphiban*, 1936, pp. 1243–68, p. 1254.

78 *Ibid.*, pp. 1247–50.

79 Phrayasunthonphiphit, 'Siam-Prachathipatai' [Siam-democracy], *Thesaphiban*, 1937, pp. 407–14, p. 407.

80 Samnakgnan khosana [Propaganda Office], *Khumu phonlameuang* [Citizens' manual], 1936, p. kor kai.

81 *Ibid.*, p. 4.

82 Samnakngan khosanakan [Propaganda Office], *Khumu phonlameuang* [Citizens' manual], 1937, p. kho. khai.

83 *Ibid.*, p. kho. khwai.

84 Country: *prathet*; nation: *chat*.

85 Samnakngan khosanakan [Propaganda Office], *Khumu phonlameuang* [Citizens' manual], 1936, pp. 12–13.

86 Samnakngan khosanakan [Propaganda Office], *Khumu phonlameuang* [Citizens' manual], 1948, pp. 10–11.

87 *Ibid.*, p. 11.

88 While the first manual makes no mention of King Chulalongkorn's role in the abolition of slavery, notice of this is made in the 1948 version. See p. 18.

89 Samnakngan khosanakan [Propaganda Office], *Khumu phonlameuang* [Citizens' manual], 1936, p. 21.

90 *Ibid.*, p. 26.

91 *Ibid.*, pp. 26–9. In the 1948 version one finds the following definition: 'A right is the power to do anything...that the law guarantees' (p. 22).

92 Samnakngan khosanakan [Propaganda Office], *Khumu phonlameuang* [Citizens' manual], 1936, pp. 152–4.

93 Samnakngan khosanakan [Propaganda Office], *Khumu phonlameuang* [Citizens' manual], 1948. See the later chapters covering the many duties.

94 Samnakngan khosanakan [Propaganda Office], *Khumu phonlameuang* [Citizens' manual], 1936, pp. 43–9.

95 *Ibid.*, p. 154.

96 *Ibid.*, pp. 156–7.

97 *Ibid.* A similar sentiment is found in the 1948 version, p. 235.

98 Kriangsak's study identifies four significant streams of elite democratic discourse that evolved within identifiable groups in the post-revolutionary period: old conservatives, new conservatives, the Soi Rachakhru grouping and the Sarit grouping. See Kriangsak Chetphathanuan, 'Naeo khwamkhit prachathipatai paebthai' [The idea of Thai-style democracy], M.A. dissertation, Thammasat University, 1993. Nakharin suggests, in his study, that two significant schools of thought can be identified which provide the discursive resources for political contest: the traditional school and the Western school. See Nakharin Mektrairat, 'Watthakam kanmeuang wa duay prachathipatai khong thai' [Thai Political Discourse on Thai Democracy], in Nakharin Mektrairat, *Khwamkhit khwamru lae amnatkanmeuang nai kanpatiwat siam 2475* [Thoughts, knowledge and political power in the Siamese Revolution 1932], Bangkok: Sathaban siam suksa samakhom sangkhomsat haeng prathet thai, 1990, pp. 45–85, pp. 45–7.

99 See Nakharin Mektrairat, 'Watthakam kanmeuang wa duay prachathipatai khong thai' [Thai political discourse on Thai democracy], pp. 47–55.

100 *Ibid.*, pp. 53–5.

101 Dhani Nivat, Prince, 'The Old Siamese Concept of the Monarchy', in *Selected Articles from the Siamese Society Journal, 1929–53*, Bangkok: Siam Society, 1954, pp. 160–75.

102 Dhani, *ibid.*, pp. 162–4. The ten virtues are listed by Dhani as almsgiving, morality, liberality, rectitude, gentleness, self-restraint, non-anger, non-violence, forbearance and non-obstruction. Additionally, a king would be righteous if he were to follow the four lines of conduct, which were: to have knowledge of food organization, knowledge of men, to know the ways of winning people's hearts, and to have a way with gentle words.

103 *Ibid.*, p. 171. Readers could usefully consult both Christine Gray, 'Hegemonic Images: Language and Silence in the Royal Thai Polity', *Man* (n.s.) 26, 1991, pp. 43–65; and Christine

Gray, Thailand: the Soteriological State in the 1970s', Ph.D. dissertation, University of Chicago, 1986. These present brilliantly insightful readings of the present dynasty.

104 For one example see the biting criticisms of Kukrit Pramoj by Withakon Chiangkul, *Suksa botbat lae khwamkhit momratchawong kukrit pramot* [A study of the role and thought of Momratchawong Kukrit Pramoj], Bangkok: Samnaknganphim mingmit, 1995. Withakon tends to view Kukrit as a conservative, glossing over his underlying liberal values.

105 Thak Chaloemtiarana, 'The Sarit Regime 1957–1963: The Formative Years of Thai Politics', unpublished Ph.D. dissertation, Cornell University, 1974, pp. 206–19.

106 *Ibid.,* p. 219.

107 Chanwut Watcharaphuk, 'Wiwatthana kanlaksana prachathipatai baep thai' [Evolving characteristics of Thai-style democracy], in Kongbannathikan warasan sethasatkanmeuang, *Bonsenthan prachathipatai thai 2475–2525* [Towards democracy 1932–1982], Bangkok: Sathaban wijai sangkhom julalonkon mahawithayalai, 1983, p. 31.

108 Thak Chaloemtiarana, 'The Sarit Regime 1957–1963', pp. 206–7.

109 Cited in *ibid.,* p. 208.

110 *Prachathipatai baep thai lae khokhit kap ratthammanun* [Thai-style democracy and ideas on the constitution], Bangkok: Samnakphim chokchaitewet, 1965.

111 Thak suggests that Sarit was not a 'thinker' and had not really codified his political thought. This was done by those close to him. See Thak 'The Sarit Regime 1957–1963', pp. 204–5.

112 'Raignan taifa bangkok nai rapsapda' [Weekly report, under the skies of Bangkok], in *Prachathipatai baep thai lae khokhit kap ratthammanun* [Thai-style democracy and ideas on the constitution], Bangkok: Amnakphim chokchaitewet, 1965, pp 1–10, p. 7.

113 'Prachathipatai kheu arai? [What is democracy?]', in *ibid.,* pp. 27–33, p. 29.

114 *Ibid.,* p. 30.

115 *Ibid.,* p. 32.

116 'Wiwathanakan prachathipatai khong thai' [The evolution of Thai ddemocracy], in *ibid.,* pp. 45–53, pp. 45–6.

117 *Ibid.,* p. 48.

118 *Ibid.,* p. 49.

119 'Wiwithanakan prachathipatai khong thai (to)' [The Evolution of Thai Democracy, Continued], in *ibid.,* pp. 55–67, pp. 59–60.

120 *Ibid.,* p. 66.

121 *Ibid.,* pp. 185–6.

122 *Ibid.,* pp. 186–7.

4   Developmental democracy

Villages, insurgency and security

IN HIS MEMOIRS, THE FORMER PERMANENT SECRETARY OF the Interior Ministry, Dr Winyu Angkhanarak, tells of his time as Provincial Governor of Udon Thani in 1969–70:

> [T]he Vietnam war was getting very violent, and in Udon Thani alone we had about 6,000 American airforce, green beret and other military personnel, and about 200 American families. The Governor had eight different American advisors. Red head kids were everywhere, the American dollar at the Udon Thani market was almost like Thai money.[1]

If Americans were increasingly common 'upcountry', so too were so-called 'development monks'. After the inauguration of the first Sangha Act in 1902, governing the organization of the Buddhist clergy, Bangkok authorities systematically sought the withdrawal of monks from community life, and conformity to palace-sanctioned forms of Buddhist monastic life. While previously monks had, according to Kamala, been an organic part of local communities, preaching through the medium of drama, storytelling and dialect, the authorities now sought conformity to authorized texts. Furthermore, there were efforts to ensure a proper respectful distance between the clergy and villagers. Some monks continued to resist this standardization with little success. Then, in the 1960s, the state turned directly to Buddhist monks in an effort to link people to the state. The coming battle with communist insurgency prompted authorities to think instrumentally about deploying monks to villages to propagate not just the Buddhist Dhamma, but also loyalty to the king and nation. Furthermore, harking back to the practices of an earlier time, monks were to take part in community activities (now termed development activities) and dirty their hands in the name of building trust.[2] By targeting the 'poor' northeastern and tribal peoples, the prime objective of the mobilization of the monks was to further national integration. As Somdet Phra Wannarat explained, justifying the sangha's involvement with government programmes,

> through the strengthening of people's attachment to Dhamma, the people will be loyal to the nation, the king, and the government; by adhering to Buddhism the people will better understand each other, thereby promoting national integration.[3]

In 1964 monks were despatched from Bangkok, mostly, to travel from village to village under the Dhammatuta Programme, which aimed at combating communism by revitalizing state-sanctioned Buddhism, winning people's loyalty to the government, nation and king, and promoting national integration and development. Arriving in villages, these ambassadors of Dhamma would lecture the people on health, good citizenship and the benevolent works of the king. In some senses the programme was the beginning of new sustained attempts at ideological penetration of local populations. If monks and Americans formed two prongs of this attack, the third undoubtedly came from officials located in the Interior Ministry, and most particularly the Local Administration Department.

From the mid-1960s a new technological understanding of democracy, blending the themes of Thai-style democracy with the political development doctrine, emerged in the Local Administration Department (LAD). While this synthesis would not displace the use of classical rhetoric—statements about sovereignty and the people's will—it provided a rationality of development linked to localized democratic practice and guidance over the people. Such ideology emerged in the context of new and reactive projects of nation building and extensions of the administrative and ideological aspects of the state, under a new authoritative power bloc dominated by the military/bureaucratic alliance.

With the authoritarian state consolidated by Sarit in the late 1950s, Thailand entered a new phase of economic policy, entailing a degree of liberalization and the growth of import-substitution strategies. This economic development was matched by a deepened alliance with the United States. The Thai elites, conscious of the increasing regional and global geopolitical insecurity of the Cold War context, matched with concerns of possible communist insurgency internally, opened the country to massive US intervention. Vast amounts of technical and strategic aid for use in reactive projects of national integration and, later, counter-insurgency, flooded in.[4] With such resources and imperatives, the geo-body of Thailand was opened up for a new incursion by the pioneers of order, extending to unconquered rural peripheries.[5]

While economic technocrats enjoyed relative autonomy from military interference and pursued a capitalist economic agenda aided by the World Bank,[6] the military and civilian bureaucracy steered the administrative and ideological wings of the state, implementing programmes of rural development, aided by the USA's imperialist political arm, the United States Operations Mission (USOM).[7]

Battling on the fronts of security and rural development in the 1960s and early 1970s, the state was also challenged in urban areas by a series of actors seeking an expanded political arena. Such actors included those supporting a return to constitutional rule, and new urban middle-class and intellectual elements seeking a more democratic settlement.[8] There were three basic political struggles between the early 1960s and mid-1970s. First, there was the intra-elite struggle, which was principally a contest for constitutional forms of rule over arbitrary rule, and therefore may be seen as a form of elite Thai liberalism. Second, another strand, more deeply liberal and idealistic, which gained strength in the late 1960s and boiled over into the 1970s, was the struggle for some form of constitutional and representative democracy. Third, there was the challenge embodied by the Communist Party of Thailand (CPT).

While the pre-1960s struggle for an enduring constitutional settlement had largely been lost, by the late 1960s the political consequences of economic growth were beginning to make themselves felt. University students, primarily the children of the rich and middle-class Sino-Thai, were becoming politically assertive and disgruntled with the stifling political atmosphere under military guardianship.[9] A combination of economic growth and new political confidence led to demands for political liberalization by the new social forces that growth had spawned, and a rejection of the Saritian formula imposed between 1958 and 1968. While this formula was partially lifted in the period 1969–71, when Prime Minister Thanom Kittikachorn experimented with a new constitution allowing for executive dominance by the bureaucracy and military in a parliamentary frame, it was reimposed after a coup led by forces in the government itself. It was claimed, by one of the coup group, that 'the current world situation and the increasing threat to the nation's security required prompt action, which is not possible through due process of law under the present constitution.'[10]

Nevertheless, the political assertiveness of the middle classes in the following years, coupled with economic troubles in the early 1970s which led to anger against Japanese economic dominance, saw new demands for an opening-up of the political system. This time the demands took on the dimensions of a mass movement, and in October 1973, following a bloody massacre of student protesters demanding a return to constitutional rule, regime-leaders Thanom and Prapat went into exile, reputedly pressured by King Bhumiphol. Bhumiphol also took a role in shaping the composition of the appointed interim government and the indirectly elected constitutional assembly that was charged with writing a new constitution. This liberal opening soon intersected with the rise of mass struggle among workers and peasants, and communist insurgency in the rural areas.[11]

With the promulgation of a new constitution in 1974 and elections in January 1975, a coalition of conservative and liberal parties – representative of business and military interests – dominated the government led by Kukrit Pramoj. This coalition was ousted in elections in April 1976 and a similar coalition came to power. The governments of this period were wracked with internal conflict, torn between a reforming impulse and conservative entrenchment. Simultaneously, the governments also had to contend with a rising tide of struggle and popular demands from an increasingly radical student–intellectual–worker alliance. Liberal elite forces reached their pinnacle of influence in the open period of politics of 1973–76, but only under the shadow of an increasingly aggressive and brutal right-wing backlash.[12] Precisely because of the polarization in these years, the period is often seen as a lost opportunity; the elite pact of 'first round' democratization is seen as being undermined by a number of factors, including the mobilization of the masses internally, and the 'communist' victories in Cambodia, Vietnam and Laos. These developments led to a conservative reaction among sections of Thai establishment, including the palace, and the mobilization of mass right-wing organizations to terrorize the popular movement. Ultimately, such forces crushed the pro-democracy movement in the bloody events of 6 October 1976, at Thammasat University, when armed thugs, with the backing of the police and paramilitary elements, shot, battered, mutilated and hanged unarmed students. Using the events at Thammasat as a pretext, a coalition of military, bureaucratic, palace and capitalist forces backed a military coup, once again halting the emergence of progressive forces, as they had done in the late fifties.[13]

The victory of state-security forces against the incipient liberalism of factions of the elite and the democratic aspirations of the popular movement made the CPT the only contender for state power. When the CPT launched its Maoist-inspired armed struggle in 1965, after years of clandestine existence, there was little expectation that at its height in the mid-1970s it would control or be influential in villages with a total population of 3.9 million people.[14] Significantly, one of its strongholds was in the ethnically Laotian northeast – a place that has continually thrown up resistance to central authority, and in which a residual secessionist threat remained.

At the same time the CPT made advances in the north of Thailand. Most alarming for the Thai establishment was the CPT's 'L-plan' which aimed to cut off the northeastern provinces from central authority, making them effectively a neighbouring state of Laos.[15] The territorial advances of the CPT from the 1960s onwards provided an impetus for further and extensive social science research relevant to security. Numerous studies of the hill tribes were proposed, as they were seen as the most vulnerable to communist propaganda.[16] As the uprising grew the regime refused to acknowledge it as a Thai insurgency, imagining instead Chinese inspiration. General Saiyud Kerdphon, a key architect of Thai counter-insurgency, speaking in 1968 on the origins of the uprising, explained that '[i]t does not spring up from internal political processes'.[17] Furthermore, before communist intervention, rural life in the 1950s was in

> an enviable state of rustic harmony.... A docile and politically apathetic peasantry was the backbone of Thailand's agricultural economy. Society was governed by the strong cultural traditions of master-client relations and the tolerant Buddhist ethic which ascribes social status to one's karma.[18]

Good guidance and help would lead the stray back to the righteous path: 'We believe our villagers are essentially loyal and that they are capable, with proper support and motivation, of organizing themselves against communist terror and subversion.'[19]

While the CPT's size is debatable, it was said to have somewhere between 10,000 and 15,000 troops. Its ranks further swelled after thousands of students and intellectuals entered the forests following the 6 October massacre in 1976.[20] Failure to win decisive military victories against the CPT meant that proposals for a politically oriented offensive gradually began to take hold. While there had always been a mix of psychological, political, developmental and military elements to counter-insurgency, until the late 1970s suppression had dominated military thinking.[21] It was in this context of first attempting to integrate local elements into the state, and second of contending with hostile social forces, that Thai statist democratic discourse developed in the 1960s and 1970s. It is to this that we now turn.

Developmental democracy

The period under discussion saw an ideological shift towards what may be called 'developmental democracy'. This involved the gradual immersion of thinking about democracy in terms of how to relate 'Thai characteristics' to democratic rule, and plans towards developing the population such that it was fit for democracy. This project was framed by the doctrine of political development, a doctrine which was deployed in order that state forces could incorporate sections of the population into the state's symbolic codes and its administrative structures. The new democracy was encased in a pastoral-type rationality that sought to lead people towards forms of self-discipline and practice conducive to statist-led developmental democracy.

In the 1960s, the circle of democratic induction conducted by the Ministry of the Interior was restricted to village leaders and local notables. This initial focus on the local level reflected the centrality of village and rural leaders in the state's administrative surveillance and control of the people.[22] Through various agencies, intellectual and administrative, the state put into play discursive regimes aiming to inculcate in selected subjects a particular national democratic ideology. Democrasubjection as a strategic project of state actors to incorporate village leaders and notables, and by extension 'the nation of villages', into its ideological hegemony, was based on a complex discursive practice linking instrumental notions of community development, participation and administrative democracy with the promotion of ethical excellence. Emergent at first, these aspects grew in clarity as the state hegemonic project raced against the communist challenge in the rural areas and the liberal capitalist challenge in Bangkok.

There is certainly a contradiction in the existence of this project and the more general function of the state. While capitalist development was aided and abetted by the economic and administrative arms of the state, and threw up massive disparities in wealth and opportunity, statist democratic discourse rhetorically attacked the pursuit of self-interest and capitalist aggrandizement, promoting a national ideology of the common good. The claimed universal role of the state as guardian of its subjects and definer of the 'good' was secured by its national development work that pitted it, at least rhetorically, against the unbridled profit-lust of capital. In that sense, democracy education was about promoting the state as the articulator of the general will, allowing for the continuance of state dominance over particularistic capitalist actors.

The local administration department and statist democratic discourse

A major imperative in the formation of the new statist democratic discourse was the ongoing effort to compose moral claims for state-defined democracy which would be supportive of the intricate and growing web of state apparatuses and the promotion of development. State-centred discourses postulated a central role for the agencies of the state in propagating and developing democracy. A central task confronting ideologists entailed matching ideological claims about Thai democracy as a developmental democracy and linking this to the existing governmental apparatus that reached across the nation. This was achieved by presenting the state as the universal embodiment of the Thai nation, charged with developing its people materially, spiritually and politically. Such expansive claims were aided also by the deployment of Buddhism and the monarchy.

The security strategy of the 1960s entailed, principally, the intersection of security and administration. This meant pursuing the consolidation of clear administrative hierarchies of the centralized state, coupled with aggressive counter-insurgency programmes at the local level that reached into what Phillip Hirsch has called 'bounded villages'.[23] If the geo-body was the semiotic reference for the articulation of national ideology, it was at the local level that the people could be touched by ideology through concrete projects of community development and democratic propagation. At the local level the state pursued various projects to encourage citizen loyalty to the nation. There, the hegemonic project of inculcating national ideology could meet governmental projects to transform the people into citizens. The aim was clearly to embrace the furthermost village within the integument of the state, and thereby promote the state's administrative and security rationality. Furthermore, promoting preparatory capitalist development work in the village involved making rural culture more facilitative of commerce. The opening of the village also entailed the provision of basic infrastructure such as roads, health, schools and irrigation: the material markers of progress.

Part of this thrust into the village involved a bureaucratic self-critique of its domineering and arrogant relations with the people. This critique, in part, was an attempt to entrench a new rational approach to people management. As part of the bureaucracy's attempt to be more effective an '*Approach Programme*' (*Khrongkan khao thung prachachon*) was launched in 1963 which aimed at making government officials more sensitive in their work with villagers.[24] One senior Interior Ministry official lamented the poor state of relations between the people and officials, characterizing them as feudalistic in attitude. Thus, the programme's major objective was promoting good public relations, 'in order for the people to trust them [the officials]...with the result that the people will have faith in a liberal democratic system'.[25] Officials, apart from studying local language and ways, were beseeched not to be moody, not to speak too much, and to suppress corruption.[26]

The claimed outcome of the project would be a feeling of brotherhood and an end to communist infiltration in the village.[27] Armed with these insights, an army of external officials toured local areas, surveying, quantifying and reporting on conditions – all in the name of better public relations with the people.

As governors, LAD officials saw themselves as harbingers of civilization and rationality. Certainly, that is how King Bhumiphol Adulyadej, who promoted the entry of state agents into village communities, saw it. Speaking of functioning, self-governing communities in distant areas, he noted that 'the only thing they lack is a district officer or an official, and they will be a democracy'. Without such state representatives, the king feared, they could become communists.[28] In the late 1960s, Bhumiphol made it clear that a true Thai-style democracy was one in which people understood the word 'enough', or 'appropriate', and in which people thought comprehensively (of all interests) such that the homeland was secure and the people were considerate to each other, and one where problems were addressed with cool-headedness.[29] Presumably, this is what the state agents would bring to local communities.

Before discussing LAD's democracy propagation efforts, comment must be made about the related department, the Community Development Department (CDD). Emerging first in CDD was the notion of local development focused on village leaders, which was seen as the basis on which villages could develop self-reliance and self-governance. The CDD was established out of a bureau in the Interior Ministry in 1962.[30] It aimed at facilitating rural development on the basis of 'aided self-help'. Among the CDD's stated objectives was the fostering of meaningful local government, sanitation, and an increase in family incomes.[31] In order to achieve such goals, a new bureaucratic regime was established with professional community workers – the bringers of development.[32] The priority given to their leadership of villagers, despite the rhetoric of participation, is nowhere more clear than in the following statement:

> Before the Community Development Department begins developing a community, people of the community have their own traditional ways of working and living. It is therefore desirable for the department to stimulate and encourage the people to desire change.
>
> It is advisable to bear in mind that so long as the people are still contented with what they have or what they are, development is unlikely to be started...lack of interest brings about lack of cooperation which hinders all kinds of development programs.[33]

Along with LAD, CDD was also to promote local democracy, although its focus was somewhat different. Interestingly, when officials from LAD reported to the Cabinet in 1971 on the progress of democracy in the villages, the Education Minister was extremely confused and sought clarification on the difference between democracy and community development projects.[34] His confusion sums up the overlapping measures used to bring the village and local level into the nation.

Background to LAD

The Local Administration Department (LAD) became central to the administrative structure of the Thai state.[35] From the 1960s onwards, it began to acquire substantial organizational power and extend its reach into the villages by virtue of a growing network of officials and elected village heads.

In the reforms of the late nineteenth century, local village chiefs (*phuyaiban*) were effectively tied to the central state. Until recently, once elected to their position they were able to keep it for life.[36] Importantly, the right to occupy these positions was subject to the approval of the centrally appointed district officer (*nai amphur*), and in some instances the provincial governor (*phuwarathchakan jangwat*). They are given a nominal income and are responsible for overseeing issues of law and order, registration and other tasks as delegated. Their own role is, theoretically, supervised by lower-level officials from LAD, but as Pasuk Phongpaichit and Sungsidh Piriyarangsan note, many, in more recent times, have used the position to further their own wealth and thus, more recently, some have reversed their subordinate position to lower-level state officials.[37] Village chiefs take part in non-juristic village committees in which state officials exert considerable influence. Local health officials and teachers also sit in these councils and committees, making them the abode of the village elite. Standing above the village is the subdistrict council (*supha tambol*), a commune form of local government established in 1956 to promote participation in local affairs.[38] *Tambol*s are composed of ten to twenty villages, with village heads sitting on the council along with government officials. Having been subject to varying regulatory changes since their inception, the key issue concerning *tambol* councils is the extent to which they have developed to become functioning bodies for local government. The councils have had a mixed history, falling into disrepair in the early 1960s, with few actually functioning; then interest in them as 'schools of democracy' led to revival in the mid-to-late 1960s. More recently there have been efforts to make them actual bodies of deliberation and governance.[39] Above the local government units lies the bureaucratic empire of the Local Administration Department. LAD has district-, provincial- and national-level offices charged with carrying out state policy. At district and provincial level, state appointees are charged with executive power, but the line of command flows to the central office. There has been considerable pressure for decentralization of state administration in Thailand, coming from local-level businesses and some political parties. The gradual emergence of juristic local government in Thailand is a complex story of bureaucratic resistance and compromised legislative reform.[40] The salient point to be made here is that LAD would justify its hold on administrative power by reference to the lack of democratic readiness of the population and the need, first, for people to learn democracy at the local level through committees and councils under its supervision.

A general statement on its objectives in 1977 suggests LAD's general position within the Thai state:

> The Department of Local Administration is an administrative unit under the Interior Ministry which is part of the central bureaucratic apparatus. It is invested with a role of coordinating and taking the administrative, government and political policy of the state to the people through provincial administrative units.... Apart from this, the Department of Local Administration must promote and support local administrative units to have administrative capacity and be able to distribute public services to the people efficiently and to the satisfaction of the people. *The Department of Local Administration has the objective of social progress and development towards the good life [kin di yu di] and security of life, including the property of the people.*[41]

LAD's broadly defined responsibilities included promoting the wellbeing of local areas and the efficiency of their administrative units, social development, registration of populations, preserving law and order, public safety, aid relief and occupational development. In its initial years it was not delegated any major task related to national democratic development, but the late 1970s saw both political development and the development of a democratic political ideology becoming areas of major responsibility.[42]

While the functions attributed to LAD are subject to change they have, over the years, reflected both a constancy and adaptability. By the early 1980s its breadth of legally sanctioned responsibilities had considerably expanded to include maintaining law and order, internal security, promoting local education and social development, employment promotion, ensuring the wellbeing of the people, developing ideology and the political processes of democratic government, and promoting provincial-level administration and bureaucratic efficiency. All of this was to be pursued with the general objective of remedying the suffering of the people and nourishing their well-being.[43] These specific functions were to be carried out by locally stationed government officials and local leaders, accountable to the centre.[44]

With few offices in its early years (budget, research, public relations, registration), LAD has grown to be functionally differentiated. Its relation to the propagation of democracy is also complex. On the whole, its Election Office was charged with disseminating democratic education as elections drew near. But other divisions within LAD also played a role, particularly the Administration College and the Research and Planning Office.[45]

In the early 1960s, some 7,500 public servants were employed to carry out LAD's assigned functions. They were assisted in their administrative duties by the presence of just over 40,000 village chiefs.[46] By 1972, ten years after its formation, the department employed 10,800 staff. It had also managed to further extend its hold over villages by gradually increasing the number of officially sanctioned village chiefs and subdistrict chiefs and by creating the additional category of 'assistant village chief', so that in 1972 there were some 95,000 semi-official agents of LAD in the villages.[47] By 1978, LAD had some 175,000 villagers in its camp.[48] By 1992 it had close to 21,000 civil servants working throughout the nation. At village level, LAD reports having 64,174 village chiefs and 166,974 village chief assistants.[49] The reports testify to a growing encompassment of the population as various village strata were incorporated into the administrative state either through part-time official duties or as volunteers in mass organizations.

LAD was also central, along with the military, in the building of state-sponsored mass organizations of local defence and development which tied selected villagers into the security state. This focus on local administration and its supportive work in community development and in village self-defence provided its officials with an opportunity to tie administrative practice to the rhetoric of democracy and security in a unique way. Most telling about the ambitions of LAD is the fact that in 1994 it listed 9,850,736 members of mass organizations under its direction – the vast majority (over 8 million) being members of the Self-Defence and Development units.[50] These organizations had grown from local bureaucratic initiative in the 1960s to become national organizations mobilizing millions of members in villages and towns. Each region developed its own form of paramilitary village defence and development teams, but in the late 1970s these were re-organized and villages which housed these forces were known as Self-Defence and Development Villages. The centralization of the forces marked their perceived importance in the fight against communism and for the development of statist democracy.[51] The growth of mass organizations around village and border security created new mechanisms for the distribution of statist democracy, and many of the groups formed were also targeted as sites for propagation.[52] In this respect LAD's principal ideological function was to encase administrative, development and security procedures in the village with ideological meaning – to make its work the work of national will.

LAD democracy

The birth of modern statist ideology on democracy can be located in the counter-insurgency programmes of the 1960s. The ideas and principles articulated in that period within the discourse community of LAD (political scientists, public administrators, government officials, and counter-insurgency specialists within US aid agencies) became the building blocks on which a more articulated intellectual apparatus of democracy was constructed. LAD, as one of the state organizations most bound to local areas, assumed an increasingly important strategic role in counter-insurgency, and in extending the reach of the Thai state. In the 1950s, the American government had funded the Psychological Indoctrination Programme, focusing primarily on anti-communist propaganda – mobile teams would arrive in villages on foot, by elephant or helicopter and 'indoctrinate'.[53] In the 1960s, American advisers worked on developing LAD's capacity in both anti-communist activities and democracy propagation, offering technical and financial aid for a number of projects.

By initiating a series of development projects, among them a democratic programme, the government hoped to derail any communist threat. In a revealing memo on the setting-up of a democracy project, one United States Operations Mission (USOM) official reports on a meeting between himself and top LAD officials regarding democracy. He comments:

> After much discussion...it was agreed that if we teach democracy at this time to the public it might boomerang (because the country is not now a democracy). Therefore it was felt that a training program should be developed for Local Self Government in the Northeast where the present ARD [Accelerated Rural Development Program] is. It was felt that the public must experience this Local Self Government before they may be prepared for further democracy.[54]

Towards the end of 1964 a USOM official wrote an article for the LAD journal *Thesaphiban* about the need for Thailand to begin basic democratic development. He noted that although Pakistan was poor, it was still able to maintain democracy in the villages, while in Thailand there was no mechanism for hearing people's needs in national development.[55]

Since the coup in 1958 a Constitutional Assembly had been formed. Its proceedings were slow and, in response, the press, students and veteran politicians had been pushing for the restoration of constitutional rule. Deputy Prime Minister and Interior Minister General Praphat Charusathian, in a speech on the 'Constitution and the election of MPs', argued that democracy was difficult to develop in Thailand. His essential point was that the 'issue of having democracy rests on the teaching of the people to be democratic first'.[56] The first level of teaching was to begin with state officials, who would then pass on their understanding to the people.[57] Praphat summed up much of the conventional thinking of the time: democracy had to be developed at local level and guided by enlightened officials. Interestingly, Praphat defended, as democratic, the constitution-drafting process his government had initiated on the basis that the framers were a select group of elders, suggesting seniority provided for greater rational input.[58] The argument was clearly derived from Saritian rationality on the nature of democracy.

In 1965, some several years after the development incursion into the villages by the CDD, the Project to Develop Democratic Citizens (PDDC) was launched.[59] Initially, the programme was of an experimental nature and involved the teaching of subdistrict councils in self-management.[60] The project touched briefly on the meaning of democracy, but emphasized more administrative features of the democratic process at a local level. The 'democratic' features of the project were essentially the delegation of minor administrative and public works duties, training in efficient meeting practices, and the training of village heads to promote the democratic system to villagers.

In a meeting of community development workers, the deputy governor of Udon, in explaining the project, noted: 'It is now admitted that because of centralism the cooperation of the people was overlooked and Thailand is [as a result] an underdeveloped country.'[61] Critiquing past practices in which subdistrict officers were in charge of local developmental decisions in the subdistrict council, the governor explained that this 'was not in accordance with the actual needs of the people. Now the local *kamnan* [subdistrict head chosen from the village heads] becomes the chairman through his position.'[62] The meeting was also informed that the new democratic emphasis was to be seen in representative terms. One CDD worker speaking on project planning in the reformed subdistrict council (that would emerge from the PDDC) commented that '[i]n principle it is done by the people and for the people. In practice it is done by the people through their member representatives.'[63]

In official circles the project was presented as an outcome of a study tour to Malaya and the observation of civic action programmes there. In a memo sent by the Interior Ministry to the Cabinet, the Malayan government's use of civic education in which government policy would be conveyed to local leaders was reported.[64] The memo suggested that a civic course similarly be developed in Thailand to convey the 'correct principle of government', which was summarized as: 'Government in a democratic system is government in which the people are sovereign in governing themselves.'[65] Such sovereignty was then defined as having two elements. First, the people have the right to determine policy and supervise national and local administration. Second, the people must carry out their life according to the principles of democracy, which was defined as 'the people have the right to express their opinion and propose their needs.'[66]

Furthermore, the project was to be pursued by encouraging people's participation in developmental activities and in accordance with the principles of community development which held that 'the local people must be the owners of their local work'. But such ownership required certain qualifications: people must have 'knowledge, understanding and realize the value of the democratic form of government.'[67]

The PDDC must be seen in the wider context of the counter-insurgency (CI) programmes and the Accelerated Rural Development (ARD) project which targeted 'vulnerable' villages and attempted quick infrastructural development as a way to counteract the CPT.[68] As the PDDC expanded, priority was given to villages targeted for the ARD project. Inciting the expansion of the project was research jointly conducted by USOM and Thai officials. In one research report Toshio Yatsushiro found that there was a lack of contact between villagers and state officials. One subdistrict doctor complained that he had not seen state officials for two years.[69] Perhaps more alarming for state officials was a study on contacts between villagers and officials. In a study of sixteen villages in the northeast it was found that in a space of four to five weeks, two villages experienced no encounter with officials, six villages encountered one visit, three villages only two to three visits and five villages had four contacts or more.[70] The report also noted the presence of negative attitudes to officials, but qualified this disturbing aspect by noting that northeastern villagers seemed to remain 'passive, obedient and easily governed'.[71]

Various reports of USOM and Thai government departments pointed to the need for rural development as a CI strategy, and the PDDC project was conceived within this larger context.[72] The project also reflected the approach of community development and the contradictory aims of community self-reliance *and* fostering closer relations with the state.[73] In one department manual the PDDC, the ARD and the Approach Programme were seen as complementary; the aim was to make the people express unity with the government and to counteract communist infiltration.[74]

USOM's heavy involvement in providing initial training and technical assistance in the PDDC was complemented by its eager involvement in the establishment of a college for the education of lower-level LAD officials. By 1970 some 60,000 Thai government officials had undergone some training related to USOM assistance.[75] While many activities were technically oriented, there were nonetheless components related to teaching government, administration, behavioural sciences, and social and economic development.[76] What this meant, in ideological terms, was the entry of academic Western political development ideas into governmental practice and academia, giving a more technological edge to the modernizing ethos of the Thai elites.

One particular reflection of this was the growing interest in studying political culture. Beginning in 1967, the first of a series of studies with implications for government was undertaken. These studies sought to determine the level of democratic tendencies among target groups. Sujit Bunbongkan, for example, found that students tended to have an active participant interest in politics.[77] Similarly designed studies sought to determine the democratic orientation of various occupational groupings. In 1972, a team of researchers at Chulalongkorn University's Faculty of Political Science undertook a far-ranging study of political culture among 'ordinary people', teachers and monks in four regions of Thailand. The interpretive findings of the project became a standard way of describing the problems with Thai political culture among LAD officials. Significantly it found that the Thai family fails to facilitate democratic development as it socializes a child into submission. Second, the research pointed to the economic structure as a block to democratic development, pointing to a modernization perspective on the requisites for democracy.[78] In summarizing over a decade of research, it was argued that the majority of Thais had 'a political culture that is both democratic and authoritarian'.[79] While individuals may state a preference for democratic forms of government, this meant little in practice for there was widespread antagonism to opposed viewpoints, and also a lack of rational consideration. Thai political culture, particularly among ordinary people, was not yet modern. The people continued to rely on superstition and fate in explaining events. These attitudes were transmitted in the family. However, as for Buddhism, its promotion of reason, tranquillity, consensus and forgiveness is seen as being a positive force for democracy.[80] Here we see a cartography of the Thai people being constructed. Weaknesses in the moral fibre are detected, the lack of reason and failure to tolerate others makes for a grim view. However, this perceived state is merely the naming of a project on which modernizers had to go to work.

Towards the late 1960s, more interest was shown in developing democratic institutions and the development of a discrete democratic discourse emerged in LAD. In part this was a response to the expected opening of the political structure once the new constitution was promulgated in 1968. LAD had earlier been commissioned to draft the Political Parties Act, to prepare for the anticipated election under the new constitution.[81] Thus articles on political party development became more frequent in the department's internal journal.[82] Also, a series of articles emerged on the need for sustained democratic education and political institutionalization. One significant article, espousing the need to consciously create democratic citizens, drew on the West German postwar reconstruction experience and its programmes of education towards democratic citizenship. The same article noted that in the West people became responsible citizens by learning about democracy at school. Socialization, as the key to democratic citizenship, was being rooted in an idealized view of the West.[83] In line with this thinking, a series of articles appeared linking the theme of democratic learning through practice to political development. Significant in this development was one lecture by Hiran Sittikowit, then an LAD official at the subdistrict level, who spoke in political developmental terms. Commenting that the weakness in the political development process was an obstacle to other development dimensions, he proceeded to seek the root of such weakness and propose a solution.[84] The author claimed that the PDDC was ineffective because, as yet, the people were not aware of the shift from the absolute monarchy to democracy. This comment fed into the theme that had been developing in academic discourse on the nature of Thai political culture.[85] It was suggested that despite efforts to teach democracy, the basic problem remained a lack of support from secondary institutions such as political parties and interest groups and associations.[86] The solution for democracy education, then, entailed going beyond the prescriptive education found in the PDDC and moving towards a whole political development perspective.[87]

This article anticipated many of the themes that would develop in post-1960s projects for democracy. In a further instalment, Hiran developed the theme of educating for democracy by drawing on the role of practice in democratic pedagogy, citing along the way J.S. Mill.[88] Drawing on observational psychology, Hiran argued that a child's disposition came from parental behaviour. Commenting on child-rearing practices in Thailand, he noted the atmosphere of fear that pervaded a child's psychological life and suggested this led to the suffocation of a child's natural curiosity.[89] Thus a more innovative rearing approach was suggested, which involved encouraging the child to be creative and curious, teaching the child to speak confidently and exchange ideas, and to have responsibility.[90] Such themes were developed in later democracy manuals. Hiran's piece was not so novel, but drew on much of the academic discourse found in university journals.[91]

Perhaps most indicative of the prevalence of political development thinking is a book, *Ideas on Thai Political Development,* allegedly written by General Praphat Charusathien, Minister of the Interior (1957–73).[92]

Ideas is composed of a collection of articles addressing aspects of political development including national ideology (*udomkan khong chat*). It also presents an outline of a political development plan. Praphat argued for the integration of traditional national ideology with the new ideology of the civilized world—'democracy'.[93] He suggested numerous measures for the promotion of national ideology, including the design of slogans, the use of mass media, and education of all social sectors.[94] To facilitate political development, a series of measures were called for, including the development of interest groups in Thailand.[95] Also deemed necessary was the development of leadership in the middle class.[96] In terms of developing the masses (*muanchon*) it was, Praphat believed, necessary for a gradual approach to be taken, and the focus should be on 'the ability and the qualification to govern oneself'. This qualification would be met when the masses understood, among other things, that everyone had a duty to preserve the nation, and a responsibility to look after themselves so as not to become a burden for the nation. As for the development of political institutions, it was argued that political parties should be developed from a mass basis, and allow members control over policy.[97]

Finally, Praphat proposed a two-stage development of democracy, focusing first on developing self-government at the local level, with the democratic-minded bureaucracy acting as guardians (*philiang*), educating people in democratic ways.[98] This stage was named 'preliminary democracy' (*prachathipatai beuangton*).[99] In the second stage, if preliminary democracy succeeded, the 'guardians' should withdraw and let the people be independent, and a parliamentary system in which the people's representatives control the administration would come into being.[100]

Praphat's book reflected the political thinking of many statist thinkers in the academy on the need to address the problem of democracy in Thailand by institutional and socializational means directed to psychologically rooting democracy before extending it as a national system. It is not difficult to recognize these positions as condensed notes from Western political development theory. Notably, the insistence on a properly functioning democracy that reflects the will of a self-governing citizenry serves as an alibi for the enlightened state to continue to guide this process. Democracy as order would not disturb the course of economic development, but would assist it.

Increasingly, education for good citizenship became imperative as the state faced unprecedented challenges with the rise of radicalism in the open period. Indeed, in the democratic opening of 1973–76 the Thai ruling class faced a challenge so profound that the period's official history remains an issue of contention.[101] This period was marked by intense social and ideological struggle.

While the state had banned unions in the late 1950s, by the late 1960s workers were becoming active and, in 1972, some attempt was made to incorporate the underground union movement through legislative sanction, a process that ended in the passing of the Labour Relations Act in 1975. When the military regime fell in 1973, an avalanche of strikes and acts of working-class solidarity followed. Unionization and strike rates rose at an unprecedented rate.[102] In addition, almost daily student protests filled the streets.[103] A radical reading public was in formation, pushing the publication of left-wing and progressive political analyses.[104] Radical and business-led political parties formed and won seats in parliament.[105] Reformist monks joined protests and began to criticize not just the hierarchical structure of religious organizations, but of society itself, while right-wing monks incited violence.[106] Farmers and peasants began to organize, pushing for land reform and state measures to alleviate the encroaching commercial economy.[107] While rebellion and a taste for democracy were in the air, so was the sound of guns and war, as the CPT continued to make small strategic advances.[108] The parliamentary regime that was imposed after the protests of 1973 failed to contain these movements with its spoonfuls of reform, leading to the security apparatuses' use of selected assassinations, mass mobilization and, ultimately, the coup of 1976 that placed Thanin Kraivixien in power.[109] Thus the material landscape behind democracy education was one of severe social division and brute violence.

Manual democracy

In this section, three manuals are examined. They were issued successively in support of the Project for the Development of Democratic Citizens. The manuals were used throughout the provinces of Thailand by state officials who sought to 'educate' village leaders and members of local committees about democracy. An exposition of these texts shows how, over time, a more extensive definition of democracy was elaborated.

The *Project for Democratic Citizens* book is a discussion of the PDDC programme and its success up to 1967.[110] It begins, in what will become a characteristic of democracy manuals, with a didactic understanding of democracy. The dictionary, the reader is told, defines democracy as system of government in which the people are sovereign, which is then explained as meaning that the highest political power comes from the people and that the people are the owners of political power.[111] The second dimension of democracy is a system of government in which the people govern themselves. This is immediately given a representative inflection, for 'government of oneself' is defined as the election of a representative whose role is to help determine policy and to supervise the government.[112]

The authors, aware of the impending elections once the new constitution was promulgated in 1968, suggested that democratic education be developed differentially: for urban groups the use of mass media and a focus on rights and duties was suggested, while for the rural populations it was felt a focus on the subdistrict council, and therefore the village elites, would be appropriate.[113] While the subdistrict council was not yet a juristic entity, being closest to the people it could animate the idea of 'by the people, for and of the people', by giving the people some degree of delegated responsibility as well as some funding.[114] As a key element in creating an alliance between the people and the bureaucracy, the PDDC was seen as nurturing a local village political elite that could cooperate with the development and security incursions of the state.[115] This early document has a narrow focus, principally relating democracy to the local level. Present in the document is the emerging political development ethos, not yet explicit nor forcefully put and not yet technicized, but emergent as a frame awaiting a new common jargon.

The next two documents examined, *The Subdistrict Committee Manual* (hereafter *Manual 1*), and the *Subdistrict Committee Manual According to the Project to Develop Democratic Citizens* (*Manual 2*), expand the notion of democracy, relating it more firmly to national ideology and to the problem of 'Thainess' (*khwampenthai*).

Manual 1 was in use in the early 1970s.[116] *Manual 2*, issued before the crackdown in 1976, follows the expanding role of the subdistrict council resulting from the release of funds for its operations by the Kukrit government.[117] Although both documents were issued under different circumstances, there is a similarity in their discussions of democracy, reflecting a continuity of the bureaucracy's relationship with people, regardless of regime form.

Noting that the prime purpose of a restructuring of the subdistrict council was to develop in citizens an understanding of democracy, *Manual 1* stresses that people needed to be given the opportunity to practise democracy at a local level, which would be scrutinized by the central bureaueracy.[118] As a manual directed to members of the subdistrict council, readers are informed that it will be their task to convey an understanding of the value of democracy to others.[119] Notably, *Manual 2* argues that in England, the 'model of democracy', local government, was the basis on which democracy was established. Drawing from the authoritative experience of England it is stated:

> Developing the citizens of Thailand to have knowledge and understanding, and to realize the value of government in a democracy, it is necessary for the people to have the opportunity to practise and have a familiarity of government at the local level first.[120]

There are few differences between the two manuals in their substantive discussion of democracy, so I will discuss them simultaneously, drawing mostly from *Manual 1*.

The royalist interpretation of democratic development is inserted into the manuals, though in a very limited form when compared to later manuals (see next chapter).[121] The manuals claim that little democratic progress occurred after 1932, and while 1932 was a revolution in theory, there was no corresponding 'revolution of the minds of the people' (*patiwat thangjitjai*).[122] A lack of democratic understanding among the people is thus cited as the cause of frequent changes of government.[123] Both manuals note a popular confusion relating to the word 'democracy':

> The ambiguity [of the meaning of democracy] comes from an understanding of the meaning of some actions that are not democratic. For example, take some children, their parents often prohibit them from doing as they please so they will say 'my parents are not democratic'...and even in society when the government doesn't listen to the opinion of the people, people will say the government is not democratic. Such understandings might be true, but they are unclear; there is still the question of what is democracy?[124]

In a move that is replicated in almost all manuals that follow, the meaning of democracy is illustrated in the following manner:

> Democracy (*prachathipatai*) = people (*pracha*) + sovereignty (*athipitai*)....
> Accordingly, democracy may be translated as the highest power belongs to the people.[125]

Similarly, the words of Abraham Lincoln are reported as the most popular meaning: 'government of the people, by the people and for the people'.[126] What then follows is a simplistic distillation of liberal understandings of democracy.

Democracy, the manuals continue, is a system that emerged from the coming of people into society and is based on a number of attitudes and beliefs. First, rather than seeing the people as stupid (*khonngo*), administrators must believe in the goodness of the people and their possession of reason. If leaders are not optimistic then they will 'concentrate power in their own hands' in contravention of the principles of democracy.[127] Second, rather than the state, government and civil servants being the masters (*nai*) of the people, as in the time of absolute monarchy, 'these three bodies are instruments for the wellbeing of the people'.[128] Third, a belief in the rights and freedoms of the private person are seen as necessary. Rights and freedoms, it is stated, are promoted as long as they do not go against the common interest.[129] In both manuals an extended discussion of rights and duties follows. Rights are placed in two categories: civil rights (rights to free movement, property, physical safety; cultural and religious rights) and political rights (freedom of expression, right to peaceful assembly, right to form political parties).[130] Fourth, a belief in the right to change an unsatisfactory government is said to be necessary, and although no method is specified, there 'needs to be a system to allow for change of government'.[131]

Following this liberal presentation, both manuals address the issue of democratic conventions, which are seen as flowing from the above beliefs. It is noted that the 'rules of the game of democracy' are one gauge of 'democracyness' (*khwampenprachathipatai*).[132] The conventions proposed are drawn from existing

Western democracies: free elections, freedom of expression with reason, the rule of law, majority vote with minority protection.[133] Finally, these democratic conventions are to be laid down in a constitution, which 'is very important because it is the highest law which expresses various principles very clearly and prevents the subversion and arbitrary use of power'.[134]

Reflecting the growing scholarship on the nature of Thai political culture, social values and norms, there follows a negative assessment of the Thai potential for democratic rule. Once positively valued during the Sarit era, certain 'Thai' characteristics are now seen as hindrances to democracy. Present too is self-critique by the government agency regarding its relationship with the people. A significant theme in these manuals is to try and break down the notion of paternal government as a permanent state of affairs. The discussion on these points is almost identical in both manuals; citations are mostly from *Manual 1*.[135] It is noted that some people argue that democracy faltered because the governors do not want to bestow full democracy to the people. Partially conceding this point, a defence is raised:

> Because democracy is a system of government that gives wide freedoms and rights to the people, if the people do not know how to use their rights and freedoms in the prescribed limits it will result in trouble or losses to other individuals...democracy is a two-edged sword, it might be very beneficial to people who know how to use the sword and it might be punishment for those who do not know how to use it.[136]

This lack of understanding is traced back to the 1932 origins of democracy in Thailand: '1932 was a revolution in theory only, with there being no revolution of the mind'.[137] In what will become a familiar analogy in later manuals, the acquisition of self-government is compared to the acquisition of omniability:

> At first the child falls, chaps its lips and struggles to walk. Over time the child can walk, but occasionally it falls, but it is better to let it fall than to always assist, otherwise the child would never learn to walk.[138]

Regarding socio-economic obstacles to democracy, the dominance of agriculture is seen as a sign of poor economic development, which results in a popular preoccupation with subsistence, leaving little time for matters of the state:

> The people must use most of their time anxious with the burden of livelihood. Provided that the majority of people remain anxious of their livelihood, it will be difficult for political consciousness...to arise.[139]

Centre-staging a key proposition in political development thought, it is argued that rural conditions of life do not create a middle class with a reasonable economic status that 'supports and promotes the growth of democracy'. In order that this class can arise, the government must support poor farmers. With such structural support and an improvement in their status it is expected that the farmers will 'begin to take an interest and participate in governing themselves in accordance with the democratic system'.[140]

Another solution to the problem of Thai democracy lies in people knowing their rights and duties so that they are in a position to control the government.[141] Furthermore, the people must be brave and express their opinions, which will help the government in determining policy.[142] However, duties must be understood, as well. Educating people for democracy is important, because 'people who have little education are easily persuaded to go the wrong way...which is a major problem Thailand currently faces'.[143]

However, there are certain Thai dispositions that militate against the free expression of opinion. First, the respect for the elderly and seniority means that Thais 'uphold individuals over principles'. Such respect leads to a lack of initiative and ambition in struggling for rights according to democracy.[144] The Thai are also said to be too rigid with their various customs and traditions. Furthermore, they have 'a simple way of life' (*chiwit khwambenyu yang ngai*), which is unwelcoming of change.[145]

The long history of political rule in Thailand is presented as a major obstacle to the development of the democratic citizen. Taking on board the general royalist reading of Thai kingship and its subversion under the influence of Brahman notions of kingship, it is stated that the legacy of kingship lives on in the minds of the people. Since the Sukkothai period, it is argued, Thailand was ruled by absolute monarchy of two types. The first was the *thammaracha* (the righteous Buddhist king) who ruled according to the ten kingly virtues. In such a system the kingship was a form of paternal rule over the children. However, once the capital shifted to Ayutthaya the Thais fell under the influence of the Indianized Khmer and incorporated their understanding of the king as divine. Consequently this 'divided the governors and the governed from each other'. The simple result of this was that the 'governing classes developed privileges and the people became subjected to government'.[146]

This historical experience is said to have lived on in the administrative system. Although Thailand had changed to a democratic system, the people still feel they 'are in the status of a child while the governors are fathers who must give warmth'. Such a legacy is dangerous to democracy because under its influence the people lack responsibility and lack the political consciousness to govern themselves (*pokkhrong tua eng*). A failure to develop the people's ability to govern themselves leads to them falling into the hands of opportunistic politicians.[147] If economic development, education and a traditional political culture are seen as constraints on the development of democracy and influencing the character of the Thais, the manuals also focus more specifically on the Thai disposition.

As in the pre-1960s manuals, the Thai love of freedom is seen in problematic terms: 'The Thais have a specific disposition not to be under the command of others, nor do they like strictness, oppression or want interference in their lives or work'.[148] Equally, the Thais have a sense of honour (*saksri*). Each person's own opinion and needs are self-contained. Reference is made to a saying that sums up the meaning of 'Thainess' (which plays on the double meaning of the word as designating an ethnic group and as meaning freedom): 'Speaking as you wish is the true Thai'.[149]

In summary, it is noted that the love of freedom has allowed the maintenance of independence and ensured that Thailand is free of repressive government, but there is a downside:

> The love of freedom means that Thais do not to like to work under others, such as being an employee... unless there is some compulsion or high reward. This love of freedom makes it difficult to solve conflicts when they arise, as each side believes it is right. They lack the ability to compromise, which is against democratic principles.[150]

Shifting from earlier statements, Buddhism is presented as an obstacle to democracy because it promotes the kind of individualism discussed above. The principles of Buddhism are seen as unduly emphasizing the importance of the individual and their own karma. Buddhism is further described as teaching self-reliance, leading to fierce feelings of privacy and a dislike of forming groups. This is seen as a problem because it allows a government to 'do as it pleases without having to think of the people's interests, such a situation is a danger to democracy'.[151]

Having sketched the meaning of democracy and the social, economic and psychological obstacles to its realization, the text moves on towards defining good citizenship. All citizens, the readers are told, have a duty to defend the nation, to follow the law (which the people themselves, through representatives, have drafted), to pay taxes and to preserve democracy with the king as head of state.[152] In what follows there is an attempt to link good citizenship to safeguarding national ideology.

It is stated that a good citizen is one who assists the community to express its opinions, helps solve local problems, and sacrifices his/her own interests for the common good by offering labour and mental assistance to develop the community. Furthermore, one must 'keep a look out for circumstances which will threaten national security'.[153] Good citizens, then, are ones who carry out moral duties, as derived from religious teachings, including duties towards the family. The father is the head of the family while the mother has the duty of housework and of teaching the children to be good citizens.[154]

A section that did not appear in the earlier versions of PDDC manuals is the section entitled 'National ideology'.[155] This section argues that to develop a democracy appropriate to Thai circumstances and tradition, an instrument is necessary that can bring together the nation. This instrument is national ideology, defined as 'the highest duty of all Thai people to uphold and be patriotic to the nation, the people must remember that the Thai nation is a thing to be treasured above life'.[156]

The meaning of national ideology is further elaborated, noting that the 'nation' is constituted by the people who have a common fate. From this it may be understood that national ideology is the coming together of the people as one to secure the nation's sovereignty.[157] For this to occur the people must uphold the three pillars: the nation, religion and the monarchy. Securing the nation requires external and internal order supported by patriotism. Second, economic prosperity is required, for if people's incomes are good and they live well, communist propaganda will have no effect.[158] Finally, the reader is informed that national ideology is like the end point of a journey; in pointing out the right direction it helps people to behave in the appropriate ways. Thus the basis of democracy is to uphold the national ideology: 'The people who love the nation and uphold national ideology, all can be counted as being in close participation with the government'.[159]

Another liberalism

Although this chapter has focused on LAD, other agents were involved in political education, especially during the 1973–76 period. There were, for example, political development intellectuals who propagated notions of representative and responsible democracy on university campuses to what were effectively adult education classes.[160] One significant non-LAD project was the establishment in 1974 of a 'Back to The Countryside Project' to promote democracy among the rural population, organized by the University Bureau. The project involved sending student teams to not only propagate democracy, but also to make assessments of their assigned areas and provide feedback to the government on communist progress and popular discontent, and provide recommendations for action.[161]

The manual used in this propagation project focused very much on the eradication of certain characteristics which inhibited the formation of a 'democratic personality', such as superstitious beliefs, deference in the face of those with more wealth or power, and lack of conformity to social norms.[162] In terms of practice, the manual avers, a person who follows democratic principles would be one who

- adapts to new situations quickly
- has responsibility for their actions
- is not prejudiced towards other religions or nationalities
- considers others as independent persons, and does not stereotype them as 'militants' or 'leftists'
- does not easily yield to important people, and even though they accept power, that power must be reasonable or have legitimacy[163]

In a seminar to discuss the project, thirty different teams reported back their findings on the level of people's consciousness, the extent of communist activity in the village and the propagation project itself. The reports were uneven, presenting cutting pictures of local influential people bullying the population, and of communist militants or corrupt officials doing likewise. One team reported back that the people were interested more in bread-and-butter issues, and understood by democracy that 'if they are not satisfied [they can] then protest and drive out people'.[164] Another team noted that 'the people understand rights more than duties'.[165] Some reports noted that the villagers have their own form of democracy, such as helping each other without any compulsion.[166] Some groups suggested that previous LAD projects had been successful in the propagation of democracy,[167] while others, more critically, argued that mass organizations were being used for illegitimate ends.[168]

Considering the report-back function of these teams it would not be unfair to suggest that the liberal impulse behind the project found expression in terms not unlike statist democracy: of treating the people as a problem of order and security: democracy and surveillance went hand-in-hand.

Conclusion

The state hegemonic project of identifying democracy with national ideology and good citizenship, described in this chapter, continued to be sustained in Thailand until the mid-1990s, providing state officials with a democratic imaginary that could be deployed for purposes of seeking sacrifice to the wellbeing of the Thai nation. This worked by endeavouring to create an identity between individual practice and the three pillars (nation, religion, monarchy). The attempt to create the mental frameworks of rationality and modernity are evident, if crude.

In this period LAD elaborated a coherent statist notion of democracy that had as its practical activity, or discursive materiality, the project of creating a particular kind of democratic citizen who would act as border police for the fixity of Thainess (the three pillars) and the common good, so defined as to suit the state's authoritarianism and its security imperatives, and the particularistic interests that thrived under their protection. While this modern statist democracy evolved in an accumulative and fragmented way, rather than being related to any particular master text, it exhibited a high level of consistency.

Political development discourse provided state-democratic actors with the framework in which to elaborate programmes for the nurturing of democratic citizens and institutions, and thus supplemented the project of democrasubjection at the hegemonic level – as part of national identity and democracy – with governmental projects at local sites, including community and rural development programmes and democracy propagation campaigns. These projects grew more extensive as time went on, particularly as the emergent liberal challenge from some capitalist forces and political parties grew. Emanating from sites in the state, projects of democrasubjection were disciplinary projections of power attempting to control and limit the emerging power of other groups, and to encase the villages in statist democratic rationale and win allies in the discursive struggle for hegemonic meaning. The propagation of national ideology also provided the ideological means by which the state could politically discipline capitalists, tainting them as selfish and unpatriotic, and unworthy of the tasks of government. This was possible, of course, because of the long history of political marginalization of the Sino-Thai capitalists.

21 Kanok Wongtrangan, *Change and Persistence in Thai Counter-Insurgency Policy,* Bangkok: The Institute of Security and International Studies, Chulalongkorn University, Occasional Paper no. 1, 1983.

22 Phillip Hirsch, 'What is the Thai Village?', in C. Reynolds (ed.) *National Identity and its Defenders: Thailand 1939–1989,* Chiang Mai: Silkworm Books, 1993, pp. 323–40.

23 Phillip Hirsch, 'Bounded Villages and the State on the Thai Periphery', pp. 39–40. By using the term 'bounded villages', Hirsch is pointing out how acts of administrative and ideological control by the state discursively construct the village.

24 Thawin Sunthonsatthun, *'Khaokhrong khrongkan khao thung prachachon'* [Outline of the programme to approach the people], mimeograph, 1960. See also: *Ekkhasan thang wichakan khor phijarana lae miti kieokap panha nai kanborihan rachakan nai suan phumiphak kansammana phathana nakborihan nai radap phuwarachakan jangwat krang thi song, 5 Nov. 2505–1 Dec. 2505, 1962* [Documents for consideration and resolution regarding the problem of regional administration, seminar on developing administrators at the level of governors] mimeograph.

25 *Ibid.,* p. 3.

26 *Ibid.,* pp. 5–6.

27 *Ibid.,* pp. 2, 4, 11.

28 'Prarachadamrat phrarachathan kae khanakammakan jatngan wan nisitjula 13 minakhom 2512' [Royal Edict, graciously conferred to organizing committee for Students Day, Chulalongkorn University, 1969], in *Pramuan prarachadamrat lae prabarom thi prarachathan nai okat tang tang tangtae deuan thanwakhom 2511–2512* [Collected Royal Edicts and royal instructions, graciously conferred on various occasions from December, 1968–1969], pp. 109–10, p. 110.

29 'Phrabaromrachowat phrarachathan kae naksuksa mahawithayalai thammasat nai okat sadet pai song khon tri' [Royal instruction graciously conferred on Thammasat students on the occasion of the king's concert], in *Pramuan phrarachadamrat lae prabaromrchowata* [Collected Royal Edicts 1968–1969], pp. 92–102, p. 95.

30 See Titaya Suvanajata, 'Perceived Leader Role of Community Development Workers in Thailand', M.A. thesis, Cornell University, 1964, p. 3. Perhaps the best overview of Thai community development department in the early period is to be found in Travis King, *The Community Development Programme of Thailand,* Bangkok: USOM, mimeograph, c. 1971.

31 Vichit Sukaviriya, *Facts about Community Development in Thailand,* Bangkok: Community Development Department, 1965, p. 2.

32 *Ibid.*

33 *Ibid.,* p. 6.

34 Winyu Angkhanarak, 'Khambanyai sarup reuang khrongkan phathana phonlameuang rabop prachathipatai' [Concluding lecture on the Project to develop democratic citizens], *Thesaphiban,* 66, 11, 1971, pp. 1359–84, p. 1381.

35 The translation of *Krom kanpokkhrong* as 'Local Administration Department' is a variation of the department's own preferred, but not widely known, translation 'Department of Local Administration'. A more accurate translation would be 'Department of Government', or 'Department of Administration'. Originally LAD was known as the Department of the Interior within the Ministry of the Interior. See Krasuang mahatthai, *100 pi mahatthai krung thep: krasuang mahatthai* [A hundred years of the interior], Bangkok: Krasuang mahatthai, 1992.

36 For the development of administration in the late nineteenth and early twentieth century see Tej Bunnag, *The Provincial Administration of Siam*, Kuala Lumpur: Oxford University Press, 1977.

37 Pasuk Phongpaichit and Sungsidh Piriyarangsan, *Corruption and Democracy in Thailand*, Chiang Mai: Silkworm Books, 1994, pp. 88–90.

38 Chaichana Ingavata, 'Community Development and Local-level Democracy in Thailand: The Role of Tambol Councils', *Sojourn*, 5, 1, 1990, pp. 113–43.

39 With the passing of new legislation in 1994, however, close to 700 subdistricts (clusters of approximately 10–20 villages), out of 7,222, formed Subdistrict Administrative Organizations. The SAO have juristic status and rights to tax and issue ordinances. In July 2005, elections were held for over 3400 SAOs, demonstrating significant progress in formal decentralization.

40 Michael Nelson, *Local Government Reform in Thailand, with Some Comparative Perspectives*, KPI Reports no. 1, Center for the Study of Democracy, King Prajadipok's Institute, 2000.

41 Krom kanpokkhrong, *Phaenkrom kanpokkhrong tam naeo phaen phathanakan setakit lae sangkhom haeng chat chabap thi 4 phor. sor. 2520–2524* [Local administration department plan in accordance with the national economic and social development plan 1977–1981], n.d., p. 11 (underlined in the original).

42 Krom kanpokkhrong, *Raignan prajam pi 2524* [Annual Report, 1981], p. 2; *Krom kanpokkhrong phaen krom kanpokkhrong mae bot chabap thi 3* [Third Master Plan 1], Local Administration Department, 1981, p. 1.

43 *Krom kanpokkhrong, phaen krom kanpokkhrong mae bot chabap thi 4 2525–2529* [The fourth local administration department master plan, 1982–1986], p. 1.

44 *Ibid*.

45 Pinan Anantapong (Director, the Damrong Rachanuphap Institute, Interior Ministry), interview with the author, Bangkok, 28 March 1997.

46 Krom kanpokkhrong, *Raingan prajam pi 2505* [Annual Report 1962], pp. 13, 18. The 1962 report reports the existence of 41,537 village heads and 4,663 subdistrict heads.

47 Krom kanpokkhrong, *Raingan prajam pi 2515* [Annual Report, 1972], p. 10.

48 Krom kanpokkhrong, *Raingan prajam pi 2521* [Annual Report, 1978], p. 76.

49 Krom kanpokkhrong, *Raingan prajam pi 2535* [Annual Report, 1992], p. 12.

50 Krom kanpokkhrong, *Phaen patibatkan prajam pi 2537* [Action Plan 1994], p. 12.

51 Samet Saengnimnuan, 'Or. phor. por. muban prachathipatai khrongkan peua khwamyurot khong chat' [The self defense and development village, democratic village. A project for the survival of the nation], *Thesaphiban*, 74, 1, 1979, pp. 55–66, pp. 56–7.

52 Krom kanpokkhrong, *Raingan prajam pi 2521* [Annual Report, 1978], p. 5.

53 53 See the correspondence of Earl J. Wilson concerning this programme at http://www. library.georgetown.edu/dept/speccoll/fl/f70}1.htm#id28391, retrieved on 3 Feb. 2002.

54 USOM, 'Office Memorandum: United States of American Government from William Berg, USOM Public Administration Adviser, October 12th 1964', mimeograph.

55 William Sommers, 'Prachathipatai baep pakistan' [Pakistan style democracy], *Thesaphiban*, 59, 12, 1964, pp. 1327–44.

56 Phon ek Praphat Charusathian, 'Pathakata reuang ratthathammanun lae kan leuak tang samachik supha phuthaen ratsadon' [Speech on the constitution and the election of the House of Representatives], *Thesaphiban*, 60, 3, 1965, pp. 205–27, pp. 207–8.

57 *Ibid.*

58 *Ibid.*, p. 226.

59 Krom kanpokkhrong, *Raignan prajam pi 2508* [Annual Report, 1965], p. 2.

60 Krom kanpokkhrong, *Lakkan lae hetphon prakop khrongkan phathana phon-lameuang rabop prachathipatai* [Principles and rationale of the project to develop democratic citizens], 1964, p. 1.

61 USOM, 'Report of Community Development Meeting of Training Village Organisers in DPP Areas, Udorn May 26–7 1966', mimeograph, 1966, p. 2. This is a USOM translated document of the meeting.

62 *Ibid.*, p. 4.

63 *Ibid.*, p. 5.

64 Krom kanpokkhrong, *Lakkan lae hetphon* , p. 1.

65 *Ibid.*, p. 2.

66 *Ibid.*, p. 2.

67 *Ibid.*, p. 3.

68 See Chairat Charoensin-O-Larn, *Understanding Post War Reformism in Thailand*, Bangkok: Editions Duangkamol, 1988, pp. 204–6.

69 Toshio Yatsushiro, 'Village Changes and Problems Village: Meeting with 12 Leaders Ban Inplaeng, Subdistrict Kusakam Amphur Wannonirat Sakonnakon Province January 1967', Research Division, USOM Bangkok, May 1967, mimeograph, c. 1967, p. 17.

70 'Security Development in Northern Thailand: Official Villager Contacts and Villager Loyalty', Chulalongkorn University, Department of Local Administration, National Research Council, USOM 1968, mimeograph, p. 12.

71 *Ibid.*, p. 50.

72 See USOM, 'ARD Briefing Information', 1965, mimeograph, in which Thailand is described as 'located within the midst of an all-out struggle between Free World and Communist forces in Southeast Asia' (p. 1). The aim of the ARD was outlined as comprehensive development and teaching Thais 'to help themselves'. Also see 'Memorandum of Joint Agreement Between Local Administration Department and Community Development Department, November 1965', mimeograph.

73 See Office of the Accelerated Rural Development Programme, Prime Minister's Office (1970), The Counterinsurgency of the Government and the Methods of Propagation', mimeograph.

74 Krasuang mahatthai, *Khumu kanpatibatngan rengrat phathana chonabot* [Manual on Aaccelerated rural development), 1974, pp. 79–80.

75 Jerry Wood, 'Thailand Inservice Training Activities of the Department of Local Administration and the Role of USOM, 1963–1970', 1970, p. 5, mimeograph (TIC-23966).

76 See Krom kanpokkhrong, *Withayalai kanpokkhrong krom kanpokkhrong* [College of Administration of the Local Administration Department], 1990, for details of the

college's expansion and course offerings, which included courses in public administration, government, behavioural sciences and social and economic development (p. 14).

77 Sujit Bunbonkan, cited in Phonsak Jinrakraisiri, 'Watthanatham thang kanmeaung khong thai: kho sarup jak wijai chingprajak' [Thai political culture: Conclusions from empirical research], in Ponsak Phongphaew and Phonsak Jinkrairit (eds) *Watthanatham thang kanmeuang thai* [Thai political culture], Bangkok: Samakhom sangkhomsat haeng prathet thai, 1981, pp. 20–44, p. 29.

78 *Ibid.*, pp. 35–6.

79 *Ibid.*, p. 40.

80 *Ibid.*, p. 42.

81 Krom kanpokkhrong, *Raignan prajam pi 2509* [Annual Report, 1966], p. 87.

82 Chaowat Sutlapha, 'Pak kanmeuang nai rabop sangkhom' [Political parties in the social system], *Thesaphiban*, 63, 2, 1968, pp. 157–64.

83 Suthon Srisattana, 'Sathaban kansuksa kap kanphathana thang kanmeuang rabop prachathipatai' [Educational institutions and democratic political development], *Thesaphiban*, 63, 7, 1968, pp. 854–9, p. 857.

84 Hiran Sittkikowit, 'Rao ja fukson prachathipatai hai kae prachacthipatai yangrai' [How will we teach democracy to the people?], *Thesaphiban*, 66, 1, 1971, pp. 61–73, p. 61.

85 *Ibid.*, p. 63.

86 *Ibid.*, p. 69.

87 *Ibid.*, pp. 71–3.

88 Hiran Sittikowit, 'Withikan fukson prachathipatai' [Methods to teach democracy], *Thesaphiban*, 66, 2, 1971, pp. 193–213, p. 194.

89 *Ibid.*, p. 195.

90 *Ibid.*, p. 196.

91 See, for example, Sujin Hangsubut, 'Lakkan pokkhrong rabop prachathipatai' [Principles of democratic government], *The Journal of Social Sciences* (Chulalongkorn) 6, 1, 1969, pp. 52–68. Kramol Thongthammachart, 'Khokhit kieokap panha kanmeuang khong prathet thai' [Ideas relating to the problems of Thai politics], *The Journal of Social Sciences* (Chulalongkorn) 6, 1, 1969, pp. 39–42.

92 Praphat Charusathien, *Khokhit nai kanpathana kanmuang thai* [Ideas on Thai political development], Bangkok: Krom kanpokkhrong, 1973. One informant suggests this book was ghost-written by a key statist intellectual.

93 *Ibid.*, p. 4.

94 *Ibid.*, pp. 11–25.

95 *Ibid.*, pp. 48–9.

96 *Ibid.*, p. 50.

97 *Ibid.*, pp. 54–5.

98 *Ibid.*, pp. 58–61.

99 *Ibid.*, p. 60.

100 *Ibid.*, pp. 62–4.

101 *Bangkok Post*, 11/10/99, p. 2.

102 See Kevin Hewison and Andrew Brown, 'Labour and Unions in an Industrializing Thailand', *Journal of Contemporary Asia*, 24, 4, 1994, pp. 483–514.

103 On the nature of student radicalism as basically liberal and democratic minded, but thwarted by the polarization between right and left, see Chai-Anan Samudavanija, Sombun Suksamran, Kanok Wongtrangan and Sukhumphan Bariphat, *Jak pa su meuang kansuksa kanplianplaeng nai udomkan khong naksuksa thai jak pi 2519* [From the jungle to the city: a case study of the changing ideals of Thai students from 1976], Bangkok: Sathaban suksa khwammankhong lae nanachat khana ratthasat julalongkon mahawhitayalai, 1986. A useful discussion of student politics is provided in Chantana Thanyaset, 'Khabuankan naksuksa kap kanphathana prachathipatai' [The student movement and the development of democracy], unpublished M.A. dissertation, Chulalongkorn University, 1987.

104 A good description of radical publishing in this era may be found in Bunreuang Niamhom, 'Kanwikhro neuaha nangsu thai kiaw kap kanmeuang ti jat phim tantae wan thi 16 tulakhom 2516 thung 26 mokarakhom 2518' [A Content Analysis of Thai Books Regarding Politics Published Between the 14th October, 1973–26 January 1975], M.A. thesis, Chulalongkorn University, 1976.

105 See Pasuk and Baker, *Thailand: Economy and Politics*, pp. 340–3.

106 See Peter Jackson, *Buddhism, Legitimation and Conflict: The Political Functions of Urban Thai Buddhism*, Institute of Southeast Asian Studies, Singapore, 1989, pp. 77–88.

107 See Andrew Turton, 'The Current Situation in the Thai Countryside', *Journal of Contemporary Asia*, 8, 1, 1978, pp. 104–42, pp. 121–9; Kanoksak Kaewthep, 'Mass Movements and Democratization: The Role of the Farmers' Movement in Thailand, 1973–1976', *Warasan wijai sangkhomsat* [Social science research], special 10th issue, 1978–88, pp. 27–47.

108 For a sympathetic account of the CPT from the period, see P. de Beer, 'History and Policy of the Communist Party of Thailand', *Journal of Contemporary Asia*, 8, 1, 1978, pp. 143–57.

109 Katherine Bowie provides an extraordinary study of the use of ritual and indoctrination by one organization of the royal-sponsored right in Katherine Bowie, *Rituals of National Loyalty: An Anthropology of the State and Village Scout Movement in Thailand*, New York: Columbia University Press, 1997.

110 Krom kanpokkhrong, *Khrongkan phathana phonlameuang rabop prachathipatai c.2511/12* [Project to develop democratic citizens c. 1968–9].

111 *Ibid.*, p. 10.

112 *Ibid.*, p. 2.

113 *Ibid.*, pp. 7–8, 10.

114 *Ibid.*, p. 11.

115 Ibid., pp. 26–7.

116 Krasuang mahatthai, *Khumu khanakammakan supha tambon* [Manual for subdistrict council committees], 4th edn, 1973 (henceforth Krasuang mahatthai, *Khumu*, 1973). Although the document is dated 1973, some of the articles are from the late 1960s.

117 Krasuang mahatthai, *Khumu khanakammakan supha tambon dam khrongkan phathana phonlameaung rabop prachathipatai [The manual of the subdistrict committee in accordance with the project to develop democratic citizens]*, 7th edn, 1976 (henceforth Krasuang mahatthai, *Khumu*, 1976).

118 Krasuang mahatthai, *Khumu*, 1973, p. 1.

119 Krasuang mahatthai, *Khumu*, 1976, p. 2.

120 *Ibid.*, p. 1.

121 Krasuang mahatthai, *Khumu*, 1973, p. 2; Krasuang mahatthai, *Khumu*, 1976, pp. 2–3.

122 Krasuang mahatthai, *Khumu*, 1973, p. 10.

123 *Ibid.*

124 *Ibid.*, pp. 4–5; Krasuang mahatthai, *Khumu*, 1976, p. 6.

125 *Ibid.*

126 Krasuang mahatthai, *Khumu*, 1973, p. 5; Krasuang mahatthai, *Khumu*, 1976, p. 6.

127 *Ibid.*, 1976, pp. 7–8; Krasuang mahatthai, *Khumu*, 1973, p. 6.

128 *Ibid.*, pp. 6–7.

129 *Ibid.*, p. 7.

130 *Ibid.*, pp. 26, 34–6.

131 *Ibid.*, p. 7.

132 Krasuang mahatthai, *Khumu*, 1976, p. 9; Krasuang mahatthai, *Khumu*, 1973, p. 7.

133 *Ibid.*, pp. 8–9.

134 *Ibid.*, p. 9.

135 The discussion in Krasuang mahatthai, *Khumu*, 1976, may be followed at pp. 11–14.

136 Krasuang mahatthai, *Khumu*, 1973, p. 10.

137 Krasuang mahatthai, *Khumu*, 1976, p. 12.

138 *Ibid.*, pp. 12–13.

139 Krasuang mahatthai, *Khumu*, 1973, p. 11.

140 *Ibid.*, p. 17.

141 *Ibid.*, p. 20.

142 Krasuang mahatthai, *Khumu*, 1976, p. 23.

143 Krasuang mahatthai, *Khumu*, 1973, pp. 11–12.

144 *Ibid.*, p. 13.

145 *Ibid.*

146 *Ibid.*, p. 14.

147 *Ibid.*, p. 18.

148 *Ibid.*, p. 12

149 *Ibid.*

150 Krasuang mahatthai, *Khumu*, 1976, pp. 14–15.

151 Krasuang mahatthai, *Khumu*, 1973, p. 13.

152 People are said to also have a duty to vote and a duty to be educated and to assist the officials as required by law. See Krasuang mahatthai, *Khumu*, 1973, pp. 25–40.

153 Krasuang mahatthai, *Khumu*, 1973, p. 40.

154 *Ibid.*, p. 41.

155 *Ibid.*, p. 47.

156 *Ibid.*

157 *Ibid.*

158 *Ibid.*, p. 48

159 *Ibid.*, p. 49.

160 One example is the adult education project set up by Chulalongkorn University political scientists that aimed at training middle-class professionals (doctors, lecturers, government officials, businesspersons) on democracy. See Khana ratthasat julalongkon mahawithayalai, *Khrongkan serm khwamru dan kanmeuang lae sangkhom nai rabop prachathipatai [Project to promote political and social knowledge in the democratic system]*, Chulalongkorn University, 1974.

161 The text used in that campaign was reproduced in the early 1980s by a democracy campaign group. See Manun Siriwan lae khana prachathipatai khanathamngan ronarong kaekhai ratthathammanun hai pen prachathipatai, *Prachathipatai [Democracy]*, Working Committee, Campaign for Democratic Constitutional Amendments, 1980. The citations below are from this version.

162 *Ibid.*, pp. 20–1.

163 *Ibid.*, p. 75.

164 Thabuang mahawithayalai, *Sunsongserm prachathipatai sarup raignan kansam-mana ajan naksuksa asa samak khrongkan klapsu chonabot [Summary report of seminar of lecturers, students and volunteers on the back to the Country Project, Centre for the Promotion of Democracy]*, 1974, p. 32.

165 *Ibid.*, p. 96.

166 *Ibid.*, p. 194.

167 *Ibid.*, p. 244.

168 *Ibid.*, pp. 241–2. Names and places which might identify people are blacked out in the copy of the report that I consulted. However, one assumes that relevant names of both local 'influentials' *[phu mi itthiphon]*, communists and corrupt officials were passed on to relevant, and perhaps not so relevant, authorities.

5 Delayed liberalism, the general will

The doctrine entrenched

From late 1976 to the mid-1990s, state actors grappled with reformulating democracy such that it could have some hegemonic sting and carry with it a population accepting of national development. However, coming out of the crisis of the open-democratic period of 1973–76, and with no elite agreement as to the kind of leadership or regime form that were desirable, the next two decades were marked by a tension between liberal and statist democratic tendencies, expressed in constant political rivalry. This chapter charts the uncertain grasping for a 'democratic' solution after the crisis of 1976. It then notes the significant political and economic developments challenging military-bureaucratic rule. Consideration is given to statist responses to these developments by looking at the ideological reformulation of democratic ideology within the military grouping known as 'Democratic Soldiers' (*thahan prachathipatai*) and to the entrenchment of delayed liberalism in LAD.

Interludes: from 'democratic socialism' to liberal democracy

Several months into his term, the palace-favoured Prime Minister Thanin Kriaiwichian,[1] installed after the massacre at Thammasat University in October 1976, gloated about the seeming order his ruthless regime had restored, and told foreign investors, 'Strikes will not bother you anymore … I have a vision. It is of US dollars, Deutschmarks … all flying into Thailand – millions and millions of them for the great reunion.'[2]

Indeed, order and stability were high priorities of this book-banning, union-busting regime. A number of newspapers faced intimidation and closure. One paper was closed for publishing an article suggesting that 'October' was the month of 'jinx' because so many coups had taken place in that month (the month that Thanin would be overthrown in 1977).[3] Additionally, inculcation of national values was to be pursued in the education system with the provision of compulsory courses for tertiary students. Thanin also issued order 42/2519, which abolished all existing laws on student activity and banned political activity. The order required students to gain permission to even hold social activities. However, underground political clubs defied this repressive act.[4] The government also widely distributed *The Democratic System*, authored by Thanin, to educational institutions. As with earlier regimes, democracy was not merely a disguise masking authoritarian rule, for a particular kind of democracy was indeed sought.

In *The Democratic System*, Thanin praised England for having achieved the rule of law, the successful political socialization of its people and the institutionalization of a stable two-party democracy.[5] Seeking a similar system, he proposed the careful evolution of representative democracy in three stages over twelve years.[6] A prime aim was the development of a 'first class' political culture in which 'the majority of the people . . .have knowledge, understanding and interest, and realize the duty of a citizen in a democracy'.[7] Thanin identified the ideal political culture with that espoused in the famous 'Funeral Oration' of Pericles, with its mix of rights and civic duties.[8] Thailand's failure to root democracy was said to lie in a premature giving of rights in a context of great social stratification. Democratic rights coupled with social injustice were seen as fertile ground for communism. His solution, 'democratic socialism', meant a limitation of rights in favour of more economic equality. Such a designation was consciously drawn from elitist and socialist Fabianism, particularly its emphasis on equality of opportunity.[9]

While democracy could serve to secure nation, religion and monarchy,[10] Thanin specified it as a 'democracy with the king as head of state' (*prachathipatai thi mi phramahakasat pen pramuk*).[11] This slogan was given meaning by noting that while, ideally, a king was above politics, specific circumstances required that the Thai king act as a 'second checkpoint' in times of crisis. This 'checkpoint' provided a basis for stability when people had lost faith in government.[12] Describing the king as a key aspect of Thailand's 'identity' (*ekkalak*), Thanin explained:

> The great warrior king is the soul of Thainess, he is the centre of minds and hearts of the whole nation. Therefore, whosoever wants to destroy the monarchical institution must also destroy the people and Thailand.[13]

Thanin's grasping at 'democratic socialism' was not merely the personal Anglophilic odyssey of a crazed man, but reflected an attempt at hegemonic appropriation of popular notions of justice. Thanin spoke the language of economic justice, land reform and equal opportunity, and related these to traditional institutions. Although Thanin's version of 'democratic socialism' would be dropped by subsequent regimes, the attempt to fuse concrete questions of people's livelihoods with the triad of nation, religion and monarchy would become the defining characteristic of post-1976 state ideology.

Thanin's draconianism was, by mid-1977, frustrating the political establishment of palace, bureaucracy, military and capitalists. Repression, it appeared, served only to polarize the situation, making plausible the CPT's claim that only revolution could bring 'real' democracy. Thanin's failure to cohere elites around a new hegemonic project led to a coup against him in October 1977.

The coup signalled a limited liberalization of Thai politics for elite forces. Political dissent could be aired, press censorship was eased and a new constitution was promulgated (1978). There was a great expectation of liberal democracy developing. Even within LAD a new attitude of tolerance was making itself felt, with one official suggesting that Thai society had to accept the existence of 'sharp tongued and critical people' as they helped point out injustices.[14] With Thanin's demise, another opportunity for the propagation of liberal democracy arose. Two manuals, the *Manual on Elections* and the *Manual on Democracy Propagation to the Subdistrict Councils*, highlight the liberal impulse even within the centres of the Thai state in the late 1970s. What is most remarkable about the two manuals is the newly explicit reference to Western thinkers, including Plato, Rousseau, Montesquieu and Mill, reflecting a recovery of pre-Saritian understandings of democratic constitutionalism.

The *Manual on Elections*, aimed at officials conducting democratic education and electoral mobilization, was an educational tool for developing a liberal democratic regime (*prachathipatai baep seriniyom*).[15] While definitions of democracy in Thailand usually refer to Lincoln's 'government for the people, by the people and of the people', the authors of the *Manual* argue that this definition is vague and unhelpful, for it is 'seeing the façade of a building without knowing what is inside'.[16] The *Manual* distinguishes between a formal definition focusing on political form and a broad definition of democracy as a 'philosophy of human society', meaning the use of democratic principles in the economic, social and political spheres of daily life, or, more succinctly, 'a democratic way of life'. Democracy is identified with a set of values supporting freedom of expression, optimism about human rationality, equality, and the sacredness of human life.[17] Arguably following Locke's theory of knowledge, there is a rejection of absolute truth; the empirical nature of knowledge, it is suggested, is just 'probable', and changeable as new things are discovered. The *Manual* explains that

> [t]he special characteristic of democracy is in having great faith in the ability of the human intellect, regardless of class, sex or social status . . .people can use their own reason without others making decisions for them.[18]

The absence of absolute truth requires that there is wide consultation and a diverse expression of opinion so that the (relative) truth of things can be established. This deliberative inflection of democracy is radical when contrasted with the guardian nature of democracy previously propagated by the state. The belief in human reason leads to the next feature of democratic values: a belief in human independence and freedom in determining one's own life without being subject to the arbitrary will of others.[19] The legitimate basis of the state is also presented in liberal terms:

> The political power of the government comes from the acceptance of the governed. This acceptance is equal to the creation of a legitimate force and authority which has the right to rule and be followed.[20]

Such authority, however, may be resisted if governments do not rule in the people's interest. It is further explained that people live under the state because it gives security of life and property and guarantees freedom; thus hinting at a notion of the social contract. True democratic thought, the manual notes, has its roots in liberalism, a philosophy which 'loves freedom'.[21] Earlier versions of 'developmental democracy' suggested that a consensus on the common good would be led and articulated by the guardian state, which would gradually nurture the liberal and democratic temperament of its subject people. Present in this manual is a liberal assumption that processes of deliberation and reflection involving all social forces will define what is good and legitimate. However, as ever, there is still a concern for the production of the good citizen. Thus a reformed family in which tolerance, rationality and a degree of freedom prevail is seen as site for this production. Critically, readers are asked: 'Do we carry out our family lives rationally or emotionally? We all know the proverb "love your cattle, tie them up, love your child, hit it". Concerned that the use of arbitrary punishment without reason instils in the child a preference to use power arbitrarily, rather than reason, the manual warns that if

> the majority of people's lives in a society is characterized by authoritarianism and seeing people as unequal, not respecting each other's rights and freedoms, lacking patience to hear different views, that society will most likely have only the political form of democracy. This is like the citizens in the nation being compared to lotus leaves under water; democracy will not endure, and this will be an opportunity for dictatorship to arise.[22]

In a similar fashion, *The Manual on the Propagation of Democracy to the Subdistrict Councils* takes a strident liberal position, especially regarding the failure to develop local democratic government. The subdistrict council is seen as having failed to develop democracy because of official interference and limited budgets.[23] The liberal tenor of this document is captured by the extensive citation of rights which are, nevertheless, qualified by an extensive list of citizen duties, adding up to civic involvement in society.[24] Interestingly, subdistrict council members are provided with an explanation of why the separation of powers is necessary in a democratic regime, by reference to Montesquieu's point that 'when someone has power they will use it too much'.[25]

Before the consolidation of the ideology of 'democracy with the king as head of state' in the 1980s (see Chapter 6), it was still possible to destabilize royalist readings of democracy. For example, King Ramkhamhaeng's bell is viewed critically in this manual. As the Ramkhamhaeng stone inscription, reputedly from the late thirteenth century, tells it, any one with a grievance needed only to ring the bell and the king would listen to their needs. The authors reinterpret this as a negative thing, for it is seen as producing a culture of citizen dependency, of childlike relations with a father. Thus the old political culture is described as having imparted values of indifference in state matters and a perspective that 'politics is a matter of those above and thus they [the people] have little ambition to go and vote'.[26]

What these two texts signify is the emergent liberalism among factions of Thailand's elites, expressed already in the democratic opening of 1973–76. After

Thanin, such sentiment appeared to have made a rapid recovery. However, circumstances would see this liberalism retreat and become enshrouded once again by the developmental pose of the state. Interestingly, this 'premature' liberalism was not only embracing the growing critique of political culture, but rooting this critique in important symbols of royal mythology. Precisely because, as yet, the newly emergent ideology of 'democracy with the king as head of state' had not yet congealed, commentary along these lines was possible. Increasingly, the space for such introspection would be narrowed, as the monarchy emerged more publicly as a key reference for the myth of a Thai democracy stretching back to time immemorial (see next chapter).

Political openings, ideological closings

Characterized as establishing 'semi-democracy', the constitution of 1978 defined a system of dual power that recognized the emergence of 'extra-bureaucratic' players while seeking to entrench bureaucratic and military power in the upper house. Surviving until 1991, it provided the boundaries of political competition for the next decade.[27] During the 1980s a new dynamic interaction emerged between the ruling bureaucratic and technocratic elites and the capitalist class, with the latter increasingly using parliament to encroach on bureaucratic prerogative.

Under the initial leadership of General Kriangsak Chomanand (1977–80) and then the guardianship of General Prem Tinsulanond (1980–88), the semi-democratic system thrived despite coalition government fall-outs, two attempted coups and economic crisis.[28] Within this structure a party system composed of competing networks of capitalists, military backers, bureaucrats and political entrepreneurs emerged. While formally providing parliament with new input, the party system also gave rise to new informal structures of political patronage and what has been termed 'crony capitalism'. At the same time bureaucratic and military influence was maintained in the appointed Senate.

Throughout the 1980s, liberal forces in various political parties won a series of battles. In 1983 bureaucratic and military forces faced defeat in an attempt to extend a transitional provision in the 1978 constitution by another four years. This would have allowed government officials to hold ministerial office until 1987.[29] The amendment was effectively defeated by the three major political parties, the Democrats, Chart Thai and the Social Action Party. In 1985 the military-bureaucratic position was further eroded when a new electoral bill banning independents (often seen as a significant prop for the Senate and the government party) was passed. Prem quickly dissolved parliament, allowing an election under old rules. Furthermore, against the military's own conception of military-led democracy and after a sustained campaign was waged by parties, academics and students against Prem returning as prime minister, in 1988 an elected MP, General (rtd) Chatichai Choonhaven, a significant provincial capitalist, was chosen as prime minister.[30] In 1989 further constitutional amendments were passed which consolidated the position of the House of Representatives, making the lower house Speaker the Parliamentary President, a move resisted by the bureaucratically dominated Senate.[31] Within less than a decade, the military and bureaucracy were facing a steady decline in political influence and a threat to their corporate position and illegitimate commercial interests.

In February 1991 a military grouping calling itself the National Peace Keeping Council (NPKC) staged a *coup d'état* in a bid to restore the military's deteriorating position. The rationale for the coup was the corruption of the so-called 'parliamentary dictatorship' of the government, a term which hinted at the power-drift away from the military.[32] From the statist point of view, as guardian of the national interest, it was not hard to point to the degenerative body that parliament had become. The inglorious feeding frenzy of capitalist cliques making good on backhanders, licensing irregularities and myriad other income-generating schemes made them easy targets of moral condemnation. One military radio broadcast noted the frequency with which politicians self-interestedly changed parties (following the flow of resources), describing them as 'hopper politicians', 'eating away at the people's faith in democratic rule and destroying … justice in society'.[33]

Considering these developments, Kevin Hewison suggests that deep structural forces were at work in the coup of 1991, forces that recognized the revolutionary implications of the emergent, if corrupt, parliamentary regime for the bureaucratic and military establishment.[34] This was a contest over the desirable state form. The compact of business and state that held throughout the 1980s was clearly breaking up. Yet consensus eluded the elite. Parliamentary democracy had degenerated into a 'buffet Cabinet', the sensible technocracy and collective interests of capital were squandered in the pursuit of interest. Big business groupings were uncertain of their allegiances – could parliament provide the basis for economic growth or did it spread the distribution of rents too thinly and hence undermine the collective project of capital (a stable environment for growth)? The unease of big business explains why, after the coup, so many were eager to embrace the new military-appointed government led by the big-business manager and liberally minded Anand Panyarachun. In the absence of any measures of popular accountability, the Anand government passed numerous laws, including measures to liberalize the economy and the banning of unions in state enterprises.[35] Government without politicking seemed so refreshing. For its part, the military began securing its future political position by intervening in the constitutional drafting process.

Between February 1991 and May 1992, political parties and the military-bureaucratic apparatus engaged in a complex struggle to define the post-coup constitutional order. On the surface, this was similar to the struggles that had marked the 1980s, but in launching the coup with apparent royal assent, the military-bureaucratic apparatus was in an advantageous position. The period in question was marked, then, by a series of debates about the details of political structure, the role of MPs, and the nature of Cabinet. These debates were conducted in the Constitution

Drafting Committee (CDC) appointed by the NPKC in April 1991. Included in the CDC were leading political development theorists such as Suchit Bunbongkarn and Likhit Dhiravegin. Their inclusion was important. As theoreticians of the careful engineering of political change and the requisite compromise necessary for stability and order, they could be counted on to produce a draft not dissimilar to the semi-democracy constitution of 1978. Throughout the drafting period representatives of political parties engaged in a sustained debate on the constitutional structure of Thailand. Interpolating in the debate were liberal academics, public commentators and NGO and labour activists. Two positions distilled. The first, a continuation of the 1980s trend towards greater parliamentary power, resisted the recovery of power by the military and bureaucracy. The political parties so inclined in this direction included the Democrats, Solidarity, the pragmatic New Aspiration Party (NAP) and the Palang Dhamma Party (PDP). While pragmatism and caution marked their strategies of resistance, they nonetheless openly and vehemently opposed the NPKC's attempt to entrench itself. The second position was that of the military-bureaucratic apparatus, which sought to regain lost political prerogative and bring some stability to the executive level of government by imposing a separation of MPs from Cabinet.

The deliberations of the CDC were eagerly reported by the press and followed by activists. While the NPKC leadership had sought a requirement that MPs relinquish their parliamentary seats on becoming Cabinet members, the CDC proposed a compromise solution which was unsatisfactory to both the NPKC and the political parties. The draft constitution presented to the National Legislative Assembly (NLA) (appointed by the NPKC and led by Anand) in August stipulated that two-thirds of Cabinet members be MPs. It also stipulated that they would have no voting rights in the parliament save for constitutional debates. Equally, government officials and military personnel were banned from Cabinet posts. On an issue that would be the catalyst for later mass protests, the draft failed to stipulate the conditions under which a prime minister would assume office, thus paving the way for outsiders (non-MPs). Other features of the compromise draft included provision for the establishment of an ombudsman's office to scrutinize the work of officials, and the ability of the appointed Senate to move motions of no-confidence against the government (but not to participate in them). Importantly, the drafters provided for the establishment of a new constitutional committee. This body would nominate candidates for Senate office and be empowered to investigate electoral irregularities and misconduct by MPs. In his survey of the draft, Vitit Muntarbhorn, a respected law professor, lauded several of the new measures but, noting the powers of the appointed Senate and the possible outsider status of any future prime minister, he concluded that '[t]he new constitution is an instrument which will perpetuate certain absolutist tendencies.'[36] Indeed, despite some liberal elements, the draft was decidedly pro-military, giving the NPKC considerable power to shape the composition of the Senate and which also allowed a non-elected figure to become prime minister. The Senate was to be empowered to initiate no-confidence motions against an elected government. This latter point was considered an important control mechanism by which the bureaucracy could discipline wayward and adventurous governments which might transgress bureaucratic prerogative.[37]

These tendencies were accentuated when the NPKC appointed a Constitution Scrutinizing Committee (CSC) to review the draft after it passed its first reading in the NLA. Its members were closely aligned to the military and bureaucracy. Boonchu Rojanastein, leader of the Solidarity Party, referring to the political affinities of the CSC, mockingly said of them: 'They can read one another's minds only by looking at each others toes.'[38]

Aside from this constitutional entrenchment, forces close to the NPKC had formed a pro-military party, the Samakki Tham Party (STP), that overtly sought an alliance with many of the political figures ousted in the coup. The strategy was clear: set up a military party and invite/compel those politicians subject to an unusual wealth inquiry (set up by the NPKC) into a political alliance. Such blatant manipulation of the constitutional drafting process and political opportunism ignited opposition. Immediately after the coup, the oppositional activities of the Student Federation of Thailand (SFT) and the Campaign for Popular Democracy (CPD) had gained only limited support. Now, in the face of the military's imminent monopolization of power, a broad opposition arose that linked parliamentary parties with NGOs, student organizations and labour groups.[39]

However, in its deliberations the CSC appeared insensitive to public criticism and remained remarkably consistent in its attempt to serve the NPKC. By early November it had dropped the constitutional committee, effectively placing the first Senate nomination in the hands of the NPKC. Furthermore, it included a four-year transitory clause allowing government officials to sit in Cabinet, an issue that had supposedly been settled in the mid-1980s. It increased the number of Senators to 360 and allowed them to take part in nominating a prime minister. While some of these aspects would be watered down as they passed through the second reading in the NLA, by the time the constitution was passed the divisive issue of a non-outsider MP and of an NPKC-appointed Senate remained.[40]

In mid-November pro-democracy groupings held mass demonstrations in Bangkok and other provinces.[41] Under such pressure, Anand finally spoke against elements of the draft constitution. The Finance Minister also argued it would be harmful to the economy.[42] Most significantly, the NLA President announced a compromise that excluded the proposed NPKC-appointed Senate from prime ministerial selection. While the NAP and PDP opposed compromise, the Democrats accepted and succeeded in getting other pro-democracy parties to follow suit.[43] This effectively demobilized the campaign, with the SFT and CPD now turning to monitoring the conduct of the impending election in the newly formed Pollwatch.

The election in March 1992 resulted in a slight victory for the STP and its allies. Following the election, the SFT and CPD again turned to popular mobilization and organized rallies calling for the selection of the prime minister from the body of elected MPs. Having previously promised not to take political office, General Suchinda, the NPKC strongman, became prime minister in early April.[44] Immediately, thousands of protesters demanded Suchinda's resignation. Suchinda embarked on a strategy designed to keep the government together by welding the interests of the parties which had supported him (including those politicians he had ousted in the 1991 coup) while simultaneously placating domestic and international capital through the appointment of professionals to key Cabinet posts. High-level representatives of business were eager to promote an image of business as usual. The Vice-chairperson of the Stock Exchange of Thailand argued that '[f]oreign investors understand that our democracy is a mixture of politicians and military personnel. They must go together in order to have stability.'[45]

Such reassurances became increasingly implausible as the tide of opposition grew. In late April over 50,000 people attended a rally calling for Suchinda's resignation. Days later the four pro-democracy parties formed a bloc to fight for constitutional changes. In early May a demonstration organized by the CPD attracted over 60,000. At that rally Chamlong Srimuang, following others, announced he would fast till death unless Suchinda resigned.[46] Chamlong, an enormously popular politician due to his reputation as the incorruptible Mayor of Bangkok, had raised the stakes.[47] The following week daily rallies of over 100,000 protesters were reported. The scale of opposition was unprecedented, forcing conciliatory gestures on the government. On 9 May the opposing sides agreed to talk on amendments to the constitution. Pressured, even Suchinda hinted at supporting change. Chamlong ended his hunger strike.[48] Despite the apparent possibility of reconciliation, over 200,000 people gathered. The opposition parties, in any case, announced a week-long truce.

The following week the hoped-for compromise faltered as hard-liners reasserted their position.[49] Suchinda clearly had no intention of either amending the constitution or of resigning. Consequently the pro-democracy parties threw their support behind a SFT/CPD rally scheduled for 17 May. The events that followed, now known as Black May, are well documented.[50] On the night of the rally, crowds estimated at between 150,000 and 250,000 began moving towards Government House. Early the next morning troops unleashed a wave of bullets. In the following days the killings continued and over 3,000 protesters were arrested.[51] Approximately forty people were killed although no definitive figure has been established. Defying repression, 80,000 protesters gathered at Ramkhamhaeng University. Across the country, mass rallies broke out protesting the massacre.[52] In the midst of this national crisis universities and businesses closed.[53] Sections of the army sympathetic to the protesters helped them flee the killing fields. Clashes between marines and foot soldiers were reported.[54] On 20 May, ostensibly to end the bloodshed, the king, in a dramatic move, met with Suchinda and Chamlong, calling for a compromise. Hewison suggests that the belated monarchical intervention was an attempt to salvage a compromise before the military turned on itself.[55]

Despite the king's intervention, perhaps because of it, Suchinda remained in power for several days. When, however, government parties conceded amendments, including the requirement that the prime minister be an elected MP, he resigned, but not before securing an amnesty from the king for those involved in the massacre.[56] On Suchinda's resignation the government fell into crisis. The factional nature of the parties and the impossibility of creating a suitable alliance finally led to the dissolution of parliament on 10 June. Calls for dissolution had issued from a broad section of society, including business, pro-democracy groups and the media, but it took the intervention of the king in appointing Anand as interim Prime Minister to end the matter.[57]

Although the subsequent election, held in September 1992, was close, the pro-reform political parties, dubbed the 'angels', won.[58] The most traumatic events in a generation of Thai politics had ended.

Accounting for the change

The May events represented a popular victory for hundreds of thousands of people from both middle-class and working-class backgrounds.[59] Their victory was to force on the establishment a more democratic constitution that banned outsiders from the prime ministership, effectively defeating military and bureaucratic aspirations. Mass struggle succeeded where pious political and constitutional engineers had failed. That Thais, who had 'lacked' democratic culture, according to the development sages, had suddenly trumped their enlightened guardians by engaging in profound politics and social change required some explanation. Modernization theory's argument about the rise of a middle class on the back of economic growth serving as a base for democracy became the standard explanation of the May events. That workers, itinerants, farmers, and students from the less prestigious universities had all figured in the crowd was conveniently overlooked. Nevertheless, where mass intervention provided the impetus for change, it would be the liberal elites who would move to take advantage of the political opening. What is disputed here is not that economic growth and the rise of a more diversified capitalist class and managerial middle class had an impact on political change, rather it is the manner in which these developments are used to further the development narrative of Thai democracy.

From the 1960s onwards, Thailand experienced continuous growth such that a new expanded capitalist class came into being, one that, in the context of the global economy, would outgrow earlier strategies of import substitution and protectionism. Decisive battles against import substitution and protectionism favoured by the military and some business factions were won in the early and mid-1980s as a coalition of technocrats and internationally orientated capitalist groups won economic concessions in their favour.[60] According to Pasuk Phongpaichit, these victories were partly a result of the 'crisis imperative' of the early to mid-1980s and of 'the economic and political demands of a nascent domestic capital working through the emergent democratic system'.[61] The significance of this economic victory lay in the opening up of the economy to new capital forces and investments on an unprecedented scale such that the financial sector boomed, as did real estate and the stock market. It was clear that the new open economy of Thailand was one greatly vulnerable and dependent on world trade.[62] Nevertheless, as spectacular GDP growth was posted, as portfolio investment leaped, the capitalist class seemingly became politically stronger by the quarter. What had seemed a longstanding arrangement of bureaucratic superiority over capitalists was now under pressure because of the emergence of both a vibrant, globally oriented capitalist class and a vibrant, provincial capitalist class claiming entry onto the political stage.

Encouraged by spectacular growth and the riches to be had, status-conscious young graduates flocked to the private sector – leaving the dreary bureaucratic careers for others. It was as if, in a few years, the power of capital and consumption had waved a magic wand to reveal the lumbering and stagnant bureaucracy for what it was. Unmasked or not, bureaucratic power holders remained a force to be reckoned with and, for the most part, rather than take up cudgels, capitalists devised strategies of compromise and mutual interest. In this fulcrum of capitalist riches and bureaucratic power, corruption grew exponentially.

The source of the growing capitalist power lay in economic growth fuelled by the forces of economic globalization: in 1960 exports/imports accounted for only 34 per cent of Thailand's GDP, but by 1991 that figure had jumped to 72 per cent.[63] Massive direct foreign investment, particularly from Japan, and financial inflows from the USA, provided the bourgeoisie with a reason to be confident, but also an imperative to begin to reform. Having failed to claim the mantle of hegemony in 1973–76 period, business now struggled to carve out a realm of autonomy where it could pursue its economic imperatives, while letting the parliamentary regime chip away at other areas of the state in the hands of the bureaucracy and military. This new relationship was politically expressed through representative business associations and their work within the Joint Public Private Sector Consultative Committee (JPPCC) which directly influenced government economic policy, appeasing business interests. This was a significant entry point for business because parliamentary rules on the introduction of laws relating to finance and economic policy effectively limited the legislature's role in formulation and criticism of policy.[64] The new dynamics in this relationship differed from the bureaucratic hegemony of the past. Anek Laothamatas has described the relationship as a system of liberal corporatism.[65] But it was a corporatism of limited partnership, excluding emergent capitalist forces in the provinces. Big business, based in Bangkok, seemed to be able to live with this arrangement throughout the 1980s.

Another player in the opening of the political system to capitalist elites was the provincial bourgeoisie, some known as godfathers (jao poh).[66] Clusters of these entrepreneurs organized politically and succeeded in gaining enough parliamentary seats to win factional control in some of the major parties. To some degree provincial capitalists had been excluded from the post-1976 alliance of business and state, and resented the closed shop that made up the Bangkok elite. Their emergence was a significant pressure on the compromise of the 1978 constitution. Rather than parliament merely rubber-stamping Cabinet decisions and policies devised in the theatre of real power (such as the JPPCC), parliament was used aggressively to pursue particular interests, often in conflict with other elites. The initial power of the provincial capitalists derived from the substantial financial resources with which they were able to bribe local officials. Such resources were built up from local entrepreneurial activities, legitimate and illegitimate. Through patronage of village leaders they also secured leadership in local communities, which would eventually provide them with the leverage to win parliamentary seats, through complex arrangements of vote-buying. As business concerns grew, local power and influence was insufficient to meet their needs and many turned to winning seats in parliament, or having supporters elected.[67] This enabled them to press their demands in a national arena and gain access to the powerful Bangkok bureaucracy. Certainly, provincial businesses had, over the decade, assumed increased economic and political importance. Their networks of influence ran through local bureaucratic offices and into Bangkok, but they also used parliament as an arena for their demands. Nicro's analysis of Khon Kaen province reflects the shift in parliamentary politics.[68] Increasingly, provincial capitalists took an interest in winning seats in parliamentary elections. Nicro notes that the socioeconomic background of candidates shifted from lower middle class before the 1970s to ones entrepreneurially based in the 1980s.

Provincial capitalists, then, began to use their newfound wealth (for some, gained illegally) to enter the national political arena, and began to apply the same kind of illicit tactics they had used in local-level business and politics.[69] With the rise of the provincial capitalists, a new dynamic had emerged in the political process. Major political parties, based on the urban, older established elites, succumbed to the influence of these provincial capitalists, their 'old' money leaderships moved sideways, and the composition of party executives took on a provincial flavour.[70]

The growth of the middle classes in commercial and industrial sectors on the back of foreign investment was also highly significant. The increasing internationalization of the Thai economy in the 1980s is often attributed to increasing the confidence of the new middle classes.[71] For some commentators the capitalist boom had led to a more cosmopolitan outlook among this social grouping.[72] Situated in Bangkok, but working for multinational companies and engaged in export and import, they are said to have recognized the need for political stability as a precondition for economic growth. As Voravidh Charoenlert argues, among the middle class there was a desire for 'peaceful politics' and orderly political succession.[73]

Progressive academics were another force for change was. They saw, in the new capitalist economy, a possibility of building democracy. Following the coup in February 1991, academics petitioned the king, arguing that democratic forms of government were more suitable to Thailand:

In recent years Thailand's economy has ... [become] more complex ... [and] more closely linked to the world economy. Such an economic system can progress further only within a liberal economic and political framework, which permits everyone the freedom to participate and organize to claim their economic rights ... In today's world situation it is vital for Thailand to maintain a good standing as a democratic country in order ... to further Thailand's trading position.[74]

Economic growth and the international environment, then, might be considered the broad canvas on which Thailand's democratization was to be sketched. But this raises the old functionalist question of the relationship between the capitalist class and democracy. Writing of Thailand in 1990, Benedict Anderson argued that parliamentary democracy was the preferred regime of a confident and wealthy bourgeoisie 'because it maximizes their power and minimizes that of their competitors.'[75] Anderson further claimed that

> most of the echelons of the bourgeoisie – from the multimillionaire bankers of Bangkok to the ambitious small entrepreneurs from the provincial towns – have decided that the parliamentary system is the system that suits them best: and that they now believe they can maintain this system against all enemies.[76]

In retrospect, it is clear that Anderson's prognosis glossed over deep political divisions within the bourgeoisie, and indeed its profound ambivalence and, at that time, indifference towards parliamentary forms of government. It may well be true, as Anderson cheekily claimed, that political assassinations, referring to increasing levels of violence during elections, had become a bourgeois class privilege in Thailand. Yet such events should not be seen as a historical portent of the rise of bourgeois democracy, as Anderson ventured.[77] On the contrary, assassinations, rather than merely indicating the importance of parliamentary seats, were an ominous sign of the fragility and uncertainty with which new forms of political regulation were being grasped, to say the least.

More cautiously, Kevin Hewison saw pre-coup developments as compelling the state towards a more bourgeois form in which the bourgeoisie and its intellectual allies would control policy formation.[78] While considering the bureaucratic state as serving capitalist interests, Hewison noted the prime conflict was one in which the bourgeoisie sought effective control.[79] In the 1980s such control began to be exercised in an uneven fashion. For Hewison, events in the late 1980s and early 1990s represented a clear reformulation of the state to better match the capitalist revolution that Thailand had undergone; effectively, a new logic within the state was emergent.[80] However, the new logic that Hewison ventured was gripping the Thai state would only more clearly emerge in the five years following the May events.

Having looked at the politics of the 1980s and early 1990s, the discussion now moves to an examination of the discursive struggle around democracy waged by sections of the bureaucracy and military. Rather than focus on the constitutional debates of 1991–92, the following focuses on the underlying logic of the military-bureaucratic opposition to the emergence of capitalist democracy in Thailand.

Freedom with chains: military responses to communism and parliamentary democracy

By the late 1970s and early 1980s the military began to respond creatively to both communist insurgency and the rise of parliamentary democracy. In response to the increasing liberalization of the 1980s, military leaders asserted the role of the military as guiding Thailand towards a democracy answerable to people's economic, social and political needs. Throughout the 1980s the idea of military leadership in the political affairs of the nation was a potent one, influencing also LAD's democratic practice. Essentially, the military argued that the only effective response to communism was the establishment of a democracy. They envisaged not a capitalist democracy – and indeed they were critical of Thai political parties as being the embodiment of this – but rather what might be called a neo-Thai-style democracy.

Chalermkiat Phiu-nuan, in a scholarly study on the general approach to democracy taken by military democrats, provides an insightful analysis.[81] Chalermkiat concludes, unsurprisingly, that Thai-style democracy discourse is an attempt to create political legitimacy for the military by the harnessing of tradition. What makes his argument compelling is the similarities he notes between Thai-style democracy and the cosmological worldview laid down in the fourteenth-century Thai Buddhist tract *The Three Worlds Cosmology of Phra Ruang*. This theme is also explored by Peter Jackson, who argues for the relevance of this work in contemporary Thai Buddhist discourse.[82] *The Three Worlds*, according to Jackson, presents 'a hierarchical view of the cosmic order which provided a model for the socio-political hierarchy of medieval 'Thai society'.[83] In this model, just as gods and deities were hierarchically ordered in the heavens because of their relative merit, so too, on earth, were humans. Hierarchy was divinely sanctioned. For Chalermkiat, the significant point is that monarchical rule, in *The Three Worlds*, was seen as bringing order to this hierarchicized, but chaotic karmic whole; it is this theme, he argues, that entirely informs Thai-style democracy discourse. For Chalermkiat, the nationalism of Thai democratic discourse, the inculcation of Thainess as a series of moral values conducive to social stability, and the construction of reverence around the monarchy, are all part of the religious belief in the reciprocity of individuals and their circumstances. In Buddhist mythology, a powerful, charismatic leader forebodes well for each individual's karmic wellbeing. The stability and wellbeing of the social order was seen as an outcome of the great merit of the king. It is as if in modern times, Chalermkiat suggests, this sacred function has shifted from the monarch to the nation itself which, in statist discourse, is identified with the state. The state now assumes the function of its people's spiritual and material well-being. In this worldview, Chalermkiat notes, politics is more than just a game of interests—the mundane regulations of the liberal political market; politics, as ownership of the state, is a way of reaching the sacred which, in the contemporary period, is translated as the wellbeing of the nation-state and its security. This sacredness is embodied in concrete rituals of nationalism which give this sacredness tangible meaning.[84] Officially, all military actions, he suggests, are publicly related to the sacred mission of ensuring the wellbeing of the realm: the foundation of a good state for the military must be security. On this, he notes that the conflation of state and nation leads to greater value being given to nation-state security over people and their own rights and freedoms. The state becomes an end in itself: a 'security state'.[85]

In this frame, military intellectuals argue that a democracy appropriate to Thai circumstances will benefit the wellbeing of the nation. Thai-style democracy, then, for Chalermkiat, provides a rationale for the state (its military-bureaucratic aspect); it serves the function of connecting the discourse of security with the necessary political structures of an illiberal democracy seemingly appropriate to the people and their culture. Its unconscious cosmological structure is that which gives it cultural and historical continuity. Sections of the military would mobilize this cosmological structure in order to combat communism, and to counteract the emergence of parliamentary democracy. In what follows below, we look at the manner in which the military sought to emerge as leaders of a national democracy in the 1980s.

Part of the military's response to the civil war with the CPT was to publicly recognize the genuine nature of the insurgency. While previously communists had been characterized as 'un-Thai' and as having only external support, it was now recognized that they gained support because of economic, social and political injustices. Asa Meksawan, a state official, summed up the new thinking somewhat ineloquently: 'I think in the struggle against communists we should not think of killing them, because they are also Thai, rather let them come back and be Thai people.'[86] In their joint study, Chai-Anan Samudavanija, Kusama Snitwongse and Suchit Bunbongkarn argue that the failure to win militarily against the CPT led to the formation of a political strategy to defeat communism, among a grouping known as the 'Democratic Soldiers'.[87] This grouping was centred around the Internal Security Operations Command (ISOC—the anti-communist military intelligence unit) and under the influence of Prasert Sapsunthun, an ex-member of the CPT who had been an influential statist intellectual during the 1960s and had been active within Thai psychological warfare and counter-insurgency circles.[88] Disillusioned with military counter-insurgency, the Democratic Soldiers had been anonymously publishing a series of declarations for some time before the Prem government took up their approach of waging a political struggle against communism.[89]

In one announcement, the Democratic Soldiers attacked the constitutionalism of all previous regimes as pointless: 'If we wish to have a democratic regime we must create democracy and then a democratic constitution can follow.'[90] They argued that cooperation between the military and the people in developing the economic and social systems would provide the basis of democracy.[91] In April 1980, when the Prem government announced its new strategy to fight communism, tensions heightened in the conflicted Thai establishment; the strategy pointed to a long-term expansionary role for the military in economic, social and political development at a time when liberal forces were seeking a containment of the military.

In Order 66/1980 (66/2523) the government stated its determination to protect the three pillars and 'the democratic form of government with the king as head of state'. By using political means to defeat communism, the order stated that it would be possible to preserve Thai national identity, uphold the principle of seeking just and peaceful resolutions to economic and political problems, and to 'inculcate all Thais to uphold the above ideology, especially regarding the sacrifice of private interest for the common interest'.[92] The authors argued that a political offensive was necessary in order to defeat the communists; a political offensive was defined as 'any action that results in the people recognizing that this land is theirs to protect and preserve'.[93]

In a further announcement in March 1981, a 'political offensive' is defined as 'destroying or eliminating military or political conditions which benefit the CPT'.[94] Moreover, a political offensive involved

> destroying dictatorial power and local and national level [dark] influence, to make sovereignty truly the people's, to give people individual freedom, that is true Thai-style democracy, which is democracy with the king as head of state.[95]

In a later announcement on a 'Plan for a Political Offensive', the role of state officials in developing democracy is made clear:

> The personnel who will be the main instrument in creating democracy in the first period will be government officials, and people with democratic ideology, who will join together to create a democracy which will be an example for the further development of democracy in our country.[96]

In effect, this was the idea of developing and extending existing local defence units as mass political organizations led by the military. Efforts were made to mobilize Border Defence Volunteers for such a purpose.[97]

In 1983 the Internal Security Operations Command, under Prasert's influence, issued a blueprint for national reform which was strongly resisted by some military factions for its apparent extremism relating to foreign policy and its neutralist stance on Cambodia and Afghanistan, and for its corporatist suggestion of 'democratization' by appointing people's occupational representatives to the legislature.[98] The blueprint was withdrawn, but not before an accompanying educational text had been widely distributed among soldiers and the bureaucracy. In that text, a chapter dealing with democracy clearly aligned the Democratic Soldiers with Sarit. However, in their presentation of democracy the concept of a social contract (*sanya prachakhom*) is used to define a relationship between people and representatives, thus moving them beyond Sarit's 'despotic paternalism'.[99] Returning to a standard reference of democratic definitions in Thailand, the author (widely believed to be Prasert himself) notes that a government for the people is one in which the will of the people is paramount. However, it is explained that democracy is a system in which the people do not rule directly, but through representatives; the people's will takes the form of a social contract to govern in the interests of the people.[100]

In speaking of government 'by' the people, participation of the people is seen as occurring through either elected or appointed representatives. Indeed, the reader is informed that the king is one of the people's representatives. Another instrument by which the people express themselves is through the military. In a contorted formula, actions by the military were seen as actions by the people:

> When the military is the people's it can do the people's duty because the military, which has power, can use that power in place of the people. This means the people's power is with the military itself.[101]

Finally, government 'for' the people is simply explained as one in the interests of the majority of the people: 'Democracyness must encompass "of" "by" and "for" the people if it is to be "perfect".'[102]

Following a criticism of the existing state of politics as a state of 'parliamentary dictatorship' (*phetjakan ratthasupha*),[103] a Rousseauian argument for non-elective democracy according to the general will (*jetthanarum thua pai*) appears. But first, genuflections are made in the direction of freedom, equality of opportunity and the rule of law.[104] The Rousseauian turn is the key to understanding the whole edifice of the democracy proposed; it provides the logic of 'by the military' described above. Following Rousseau's argument about the state of nature being a free condition, the author argues that once people enter into society they then live under the general will of society.[105] As he explains: 'The general will is not the collection of individual wills, but is, rather, the will of people relating to their collective desires and interests. These collective wishes are sovereign.'[106] Should someone have a will that opposes the general will then that will is wrong:

> society has the compelling power to make humans accept the general will and through this method society will make that person free. Therefore, freedom according to Rousseau is behaving according to the will of society and this is the basic principle of democracy.[107]

In the light of this, an interpretation on the role of elections in democracy is offered: in short, it is stated that elections do not necessarily equal democracy: 'If there is no election but there is the maintenance of the people's interest . . .then this is a democratic government.'[108] While elections are seen as one element of democracy, it is explained that they are the least important, since they may be used democratically or dictatorially.[109] Thai-style democracy, then, as a government in the collective interest, founds itself on the Western philosophy of a mythic social contract instantiated by the moral authority of those in power able to define the will of the people. However, if we follow Chalermkiat's analysis, this was mediated at the deepest level by 'unconscious' efforts to reproduce the stabilizing role of a sacred centre at the heart of a chaotic whole, operationalized by the military, symbolized by the monarchy.

In neo-Thai-style democracy, a mixture of Western philosophy and Thai traditionalism provides a solution to the tension between rights and duties by conflating freedom with actions in accordance with the general will, as expressed in the institutions of monarchy and military.[110] Almost Hegelian, these institutions are seen as containing the most advanced and collective ethos of the people.

In supporting the policies relating to a political struggle against communism, Prem was not necessarily buying into the Prasert position so described. More pragmatically, he was giving shape to an already existing current of thought and practice which provided a united framework in which to focus anti-communist efforts and with which to expand the military's role in developmental terms.[111] Nevertheless, some active military cadres were advocates of Prasert.[112] Prem at times spoke as if he was a supporter of this line of thinking, stressing military leadership over other government bodies.[113] However, his political pragmatism, and his balancing of interests between the bureaucracy and the capitalist parties, belied any principled stand in this regard.

The prime ministerial orders also provided the means by which to coordinate military psychological, security and development operations through the coordination of existing and new mass organizations, and intervention/infiltration in existing organizations. One such mass organization was the Reservists for National Security, which by 1988 was estimated to have had some 600,000 members.[114] Many of these reservists were given training in democracy propagation, and were expected to provide assistance to villagers as well as to participate in other mass organizations and ensure that they were genuinely 'democratic' in terms of carrying out government policy. One project of the reservists was the Democracy Pavilions (*sala prachathipatai*) established in 1983. By 1990 they had spread to 600 subdistricts. Reservists were encouraged to spend time discussing politics with locals at the local community centre or gathering place, and were also encouraged to enter local government and propagate democratic ideology along development lines.[115] The democracy pavilions were partly seen as a response to the crisis of human resource development in Thailand. As Chaiyasit Tanthayakun notes, the government thought reservists to be disciplined and loyal and thus attempted to mobilize them.[116]

Despite the communist threat subsiding by the mid-1980s, Order 66/1980, and related orders, remained key documents in military thinking. Indeed, as Thailand entered its period of 'full' parliamentary democracy in 1988, the military announced on radio, on a number of occasions, the ongoing relevance of the orders:

> The military must uphold Prime Ministers Office's orders 66/2523 and 65/2525 which are correct policy. These policies are not just policies to defeat communists only but can be used as a policy to struggle against all incorrectnesses in the country, for helping the country develop and go towards democracy with the king

> as head of the nation ... the struggle against incorrectness and social injustice, that is a struggle for the success of democracy itself.[117]

Furthermore, as an influential figure behind the adoption of the order, General Chavalit Yongchaiyudh remained associated with the thinking of the Democratic Soldiers during his rise through the military ranks. Most famously in 1987 and 1988 he propagated Prasert's idea of 'democratic revolution'; although similar in effect to the orders we have looked at, this had a more sinister connotation because of the use of the word 'revolution'. The speeches he made at this time were related to criticisms of political parties and their capitalist backers. Chavalit's ideas were a confused mixture of economic and social reforms that would provide for the wellbeing of the people, and a democracy led by the military.[118] Encouraged by Chavalit's rhetorical imitation, in 1988 Prasert and followers held a meeting of their recently formed Revolutionary Council, calling on parliament to delegate all authority to it. Amidst a tense atmosphere of state enterprise industrial disputation, military attacks on capitalist politicians and coup rumours, Prasert explained that as his Revolutionary Council had representatives from all the regions and occupations, it was the only representative body in the nation and should be allowed to rule.[119] Its policies were effectively a repeat of the Democratic Soldiers' ideas.[120] While the Revolutionary Council was attacked by Chavalit's rivals in the military as seeking a presidential form of rule, which implicitly suggested the desire to overthrow the monarchy, others saw the grouping as benign. Prasong Sunsuri, head of the National Security Council, for example, couldn't quite understand the fuss about the call for revolution: 'It's like when a father or mother tells their child to "revolutionize the house" and clean it up. This is not using any force.'[121]

For several years the members of the Revolutionary Council fought charges of treason laid by the Chatichai government – which they finally won. However, as their leaflets and booklets spun off the printing presses, society around them was changing so rapidly that their ideas became almost incomprehensible to most. In the same breath expressing loyalty to the king and Buddhism, they uttered anti-imperialist slogans and attacks on monopoly capitalism. The semi-fascist corporatist element to this grouping, while useful in the days of mass mobilization against the communist insurgency, was an embarrassment to the political establishment, and was mostly politely ignored. The farcical end to neo-Thai-style democracy, with its wizened sage who had curried favour with the worst of dictators, including Thanom and Praphat, and who continued to exert some influence on military thinking into the 1990s, was also symbolic of an end to the military's profound intellectual claims for its right to rule. Perhaps a fitting epithet was the fact that the Revolutionary Council had become known as the 'Joke Council'.[122] A further sign of the decline was Chavalit's entry into the political system and the formation of the New Aspiration Party, showing the increasing acceptance of electoral competition as the basis of power among many military figures.

LAD: security and democracy

While institutionally separate from the military, LAD's work on internal security and its part in counter-insurgency ensured that it was not insulated from developments in military thought. Indeed, one might see LAD, in some respects, as almost an administrative and civil wing of the military, particularly in regard to LAD's involvement with the many paramilitary village organizations.

Asa Meksawan, a conservative Senator in the 1990s and a one-time deputy head of LAD in the late 1970s, was at the forefront of reshaping LAD thinking after the crisis years. LAD published a version of his thesis, which had been written for the National Defence Academy on local government and security.[123] Used by LAD staff as a reference text, the book focuses on the administration of local government as a basis for national security.[124] However, Asa's book concerns more than administration, for it relates governmental structures to issues of political culture and the existing conditions of insurgency. Just as Hiran Sittikowit's articles (see Chapter 4) in the late 1960s embodied the political development concerns of LAD, Asa's work served the same function in the early 1980s.

Asa's writing provides insights into the political rationality of LAD and its attempt to develop a project of citizen reform. In summing up the political culture of Thai people, he argued that Thais were too deferential to superiors and generally indifferent to state affairs. Suggesting fear of officials, Asa observed that people 'dare not defy the civil servants, or express opposition or gather together to oppose the officials of the state'.[125] While this had been good for order it was not, he suggested, a desirable characteristic for developing democracy, which required participation in the political process.[126] In any case, such docility had been upset by economic developments, leading to changing levels of political consciousness in the villages.[127] Considering the implications of the open democratic period, Asa could only see danger looming. As he saw it, the changing political consciousness amongst the people and the rise of opportunistic politicians promising all manner of things had led to a crisis of unfulfilled expectations. The inevitable non-delivery on promises made by politicians had also led to disillusionment with democracy, making the people susceptible to CPT subversion.[128] In this circumstance, local government was now seen as a linchpin in securing the nation.

In 1975 LAD began issuing five year policy and plan documents. The plans were largely a broad statement of objectives and strategies, including issues relating to political development, ideology and democratic education. Significant attention was given to the development of local government as 'schools of democracy', the development of linkages between the state and local people, and the expansion of security mechanisms. However, in one sense the plans are no more than an example of bureaucratic formalism: a litany of objectives, projects, planning statements and budget allocation purportedly aimed at ensuring the people's well being. While they indicate the organisational infrastructure that lies behind the machinations of LAD, the statements on democracy contained in the plans are, on the whole, generally vague and fuse with questions of security.

The first plan (1974–76) was generally seen as a failure, with various offices and directorates in LAD working with little integration, and with few measures of outcomes.[129] The second plan (1977–81) thus aimed at co-ordinating the different bureaucratic offices that made up LAD, and attempted to map out a united strategy with clearly defined goals. With the appointment of Asa, among others to determine the direction of the second plan, the security thrust of democratic development became pronounced.[130] The second plan was to promote and maintain the security of 'the nation, religion and the monarchy'.[131] Of particular importance in this was the establishment and support of 'people's groups' (klum prachachon) that were to be integrated into official projects in order that they acquired 'political understanding, and a capacity for self-organization such that they would be a force for defence and development, and be able to uphold the political ideology of democracy with the king as head of state'.[132] Other objectives involved the provision of basic needs, local democratic development, the eradication of corruption within the bureaucracy, and measures to promote unity, diligence, thrift and self-reliance among the people.[133] In line with developments occurring among the National Security agencies (see next chapter) a new branch was established in LAD to specifically deal with development of political ideology and political processes, with the basic aim being to promote 'people's participation in political activities in appropriate measures both at the local and national level for ensuring such behavior revives national security'.

Noticeably, the third plan (1982–86) was conceived in terms of national security, a recognition of LAD's integral role in nation building and its antisubversive function. Following the National Security Council (see Chapter 6), security was seen in multi-dimensional terms, having military, economic and social-psychological dimensions which, if correctly developed, could bring about internal and external stability.[134] LAD explicitly endorsed order 66/1980 and directly supported 'politics led by the military'.[135] The plan outlined various psychological activities (winning minds and hearts) to be pursued in co-operation with the military – such as the setting up of rice banks, provisions of food and blankets.[136] What is striking about the third plan is its close adherence to the ideas of Asa. Indeed, LAD presented itself primarily as serving a security function, defining its role extensively along these lines, and regurgitating much of Asa's analysis of the contemporary situation.[137]

In the fourth plan (1987–91) emphasis is made yet again on developing the local administrative units and extending their capabilities. The authors of the plan emphasize the importance of officials upholding democracy as an actual practice, and for such officials to extend the political participation of the people.[138] Reflecting the more liberal era, the fifth plan (1992–96) endorses the expansion of democratic education to the people, beyond local officials and village committees, and to make democracy both a form of practice and a way of life, a theme that had been around for almost two decades.[139] The fifth plan, while signalling an expansion of democracy education to all, does not really signal fundamental shifts in orientation towards democracy by the department, merely an expansion of its audience.[140]

Writing LAD democracy

In the aftermath of the crisis of 1976, LAD underwent a period of rethinking regarding its relationship with the people. The themes that are elaborated in its journal, *Thesaphiban*, relate to matters similar to those expressed in the early 1960s on how to approach the people in order to achieve security.[141] The discourse around this question illuminates perfectly the manner in which LAD officials saw their dominant position over the people and their need to lead and supervise them. Reflecting LAD's security orientation, many of the journal articles are extensive discussions of the varied local defence and development organizations in villages. One author saw the aim of these projects as changing villages from 'jungle into towns' so that democracy could become a reality.[142] Not a commonly written observation, the notion of villages as 'jungle' actually underlines much of the civilizing posture held by officials. What is particularly notable is the manner in which officials were to present themselves to the people so as to earn their trust. In one article, trust was seen as the key to government: 'The power of governors is in the trust of the people.'[143] The author suggested that trust could only come from *barami* (prestige): this term, while colloquially used to suggest an underlying power based on goodness, in Buddhist terms implies the possession of virtue related to the positive store of merit a person is said to accumulate. Possession of the virtues is a manifestation of this merit. Furthermore, government officials were told that before governing others one needed to 'to be able to govern oneself'.[144] The governing of the self was then related to the acquisition of the ten royal virtues among other things, which would lead to a projection of the royal *barami* onto officials.[145] Interestingly, then, even if formal democratic objectives were being prescribed, a traditional notion of legitimacy was operative. There are many articles in government journals regarding ethics and administration which draw on royal virtues. These reveal Buddhism as the basis of government apperception. The *Principles for Governors*, issued by the Department of Religion within the Ministry of Education, explains the expectations of a Buddhist ruler as if they were to be practised also by civil servants. Underlying the book is the suggestion that *thammathipatai*, or the sovereignty of Dhamma, is the best form of government. This implies the rule of the righteous, although it is often taken to mean a principle for letting one's life be guided by the sovereignty of Dhamma, or the teachings of the Buddha.[146] The following statement makes things quite clear: 'Since 95 per cent of Thais are Buddhists the most appropriate form of government is according to Buddhism.'[147]

In an insightful comment about the kind of people LAD needed to win to its side, Chalong Kanlayanmit, then head of LAD, noted that

> if we do not have a basis in the masses, then we have a problem. The masses, or the people, I am speaking about are the Village Scouts, the Village Defence Volunteers . . . We must be the ones who are able to maintain their favour and be able to command them to do anything in our support.[148]

With such support, Chalong continued, 'no one will dare touch us'. In conclusion he suggests that 'the smart governor must bring the masses onto our side, and this is the policy of approaching the people'.[149]

It is in the statements above that the militaristic strategy of leading masses of state-mobilized people is most made clear. It is not difficult to see that the democratic education of LAD expressed as principles of self-government and participation is, in context, related to participation in state-sanctioned activities at the local level, and relates to targeted populations, who are subject to formal democratic rule sanctioned by official Buddhist legitimacy. The extent to which LAD could entertain moving away from even its own professed commitment to democracy is evident in the comments of one LAD author, who argued against regular elections of village chiefs and subdistrict heads on the basis that this would introduce 'politics' into the community, by which he meant the divisive activities associated with capitalists and 'dark influences' that had captured the political system at the national level.[150]

During the 1980s and 1990s, LAD was involved in numerous democracy propagation activities. Cumbersome as it would be to discuss them all, a thematic discussion of the texts, documents and articles relating to these projects follows. The texts cover a period spanning almost two decades. Perhaps there are two significant things to note before I look at the projects as a whole. First, in 1988 a new project was launched under the title *Expanding the Basis of Democracy to the People*, a project that coincided with the coming to power of the Chatichai government. The 1988 project reflected the Chatichai government's policy which stressed the role that political parties must play in preserving democracy with the king as head of state.[151] Second, when the military took power in 1991, a leading member of the coup group became interior minister and another democracy project was launched. In terms of the educational material, rationale and objectives, these two democracy projects were identical. LAD continued to call for the development of democracy as a way of life, one that was based on the king as head of state and one that was a representative democracy. It also continued to attack irresponsible political parties, although the attack on 'money-democracy' was more pronounced in the documents relating to the military democracy campaigns of 1991–92. However, one novel aspect of the manuals distributed during the military democracy campaign was the suggestion that a democratic government may be removed from office by *coup d'état*.[152] Otherwise the manual, produced under NPKC direction, was very much in line with the developmental democracy that had evolved in LAD since its inception. Post-1992, another democracy programme was launched which once again presented an argument for development democracy. On the whole, despite the changing nature of the regimes, LAD was in a position to continue to propagate its developmental democracy and its claims for local government as schools of democracy requiring careful supervision.[153] The liberal impulse of the emergent parliamentary regime had not yet penetrated LAD.

The ideal democracy espoused by LAD is a regime in which interest groups and parties, as representatives of the people, participate in a policy and legislative environment, but in which the administrators have the ultimate say.[154] If functioning correctly, the people's representatives will perform as intermediaries between the rulers and the ruled. Sovereignty is owned by the people and is manifest in the monarch's prerogative to rule by law through the three branches of government. However, sovereignty must be alienated from its source because of simple logistics – so many people cannot meet together. In one text people are described as sovereign, but it is noted that not everyone needs to participate and deliberate on problems, rather state officials and other organs of power are delegated to carry out tasks: people's sovereignty is exercised in the sense of choosing the government and in the right to protest through electoral means.[155] The ideal citizenry is rational, civic-minded, tolerant and respectful of others. It abides by majority rule, expressed electorally, but does not tread on the rights of minorities, as defined by rights and freedoms circumscribed by law.[156] The ideal democratic citizenry knows its duty as well as its rights, although effectively duties take precedence, as rights are subject to the constraints of collective interest.

The democracy articulated emphasizes collectivist responsibility to the national interest. Certainly, the citizenship imagined is hardly that of the self-interested bourgeois individual, although regarding rights there is a philosophical inflection in that direction. Yet this aspect, as discussed previously, succumbs to the imperatives of national security. For LAD, democracy is seen in three-dimensional terms: a political system, a way of life and an ideology; and collectively, these dimensions provide the political, moral and social conditions for the establishment of collective happiness and peace.[157] In short, a good citizen is one who sacrifices their own interests for the common good and assists the community.

If this is the idealized picture, then LAD writers see the actual existing situation as a sad façade of democracy. This, indeed, is the underlying premise of all LAD writings on democracy. The fact that Thai democracy is not healthy is universally related to its people lacking 'democracyness'. Thus, despite state attempts at developing democracy, things go astray. It is this contradiction, between the active democratizing state (with its programmes of democracy education) and the 'people problem', that provides both the rationale for a strong state in political development and a plan of action to pursue state democratic development. While the democratic intent and consequence is actualized in the state, Thai society lacks the ability to sustain democratic forms and substance. Rooted in this condition is the state's claim to guide, buttressed by an ideology of delayed liberalism.[158]

As part of its legitimating mission, the state develops democracy by systematically diagnosing the ills of its societal underlings. Thai people are seen as undisciplined.

They tend to take their rights too far. A constant theme is thus the bounded nature of rights and freedoms. Law, convention and morality are invoked as regulating the meaning of rights and freedoms.[159]

It is the virtue of the teaching state that it plots democratic development for its subjects. Each democratic initiative might be taken as one more lesson in the project of democracy. Linked to this educative project is the theme of political participation. From the premise that democracy cannot be simply taught but must be practically inducted, units of state administration and penetration, particularly local-level government, are projected as schools of democracy.[160] Here the possibility of instantiating democratic ideology in local settings is harnessed as a means of inculcating state democratic ideology. The ideological project of state democracy attempts a practical reality. In this setting the themes of self-reliance, cooperation and democratic morality are propounded. Participation becomes a function of acquiring 'democracyness', which, once arrived at, will create clearer communication channels between the people and the state. Liberalism would become a historical possibility were the citizens to act as liberal citizens. That they did not yet act in such a manner seemingly sanctioned delaying the expansion of democracy.

As the parliamentary regime and the system of political parties appeared to be permanent features of the political landscape in the 1980s, the problem of articulating political participation with national democratic institutions became severe. These institutions did not operate in accordance with the stipulations of political development theory. Instead of democratic participation, pathological participation emerged to subvert the state's purported democratic intent. Instead of the much discussed formation of mass parties serving the function of interest articulation, aggregation and political recruitment, a multi-party system built around capitalist short-term group interest emerged.[161]

Lacking a democratic political culture, the people fail to function as democratic citizens, according to LAD. Their electoral choice reflects a debilitating parochialism and rural circumstance. Party choice is based on individual preference rather than allegiance and party preference. The people remain imprisoned in superstition and lack reason. In this mute state they are easy prey to the 'dark influence' of capitalist politicians. The failure to develop democracy in its three dimensions (as ideology, as a way of life, as a system) is attributed to the lack of continuity in the democratic system itself. Each time a broader democratic path was opened it was quickly destroyed by dissent and division, necessitating a restoration of order by state forces, involving the abolition of the constitution and the suspension of parliament and political parties. With no opportunity to practise democracy at this level, the gains made at a local level in democratic consciousness cannot be put into practice, and people slip into their customary ways. In the absence of the democratic mediation of interest, patronage prevails. The prime saboteurs of this blockage to democratic mediation are the political parties. Morally moribund, they pursue private and sectional interest and in the process establish parliamentary dictatorships, that either end in disarray because of interest conflict in a governing coalition or are brought down by military intervention. This parliamentary disorder is seen as symptomatic of sectional interest deviation from the state-defined national interest.[162] The failure of parliamentary democracy and the need to reform its functioning thus becomes another site for state intervention and the continuance of statist democratic ideology.

The basis tenets of classical liberalism seem to provide some of the philosophical basis for the state-centric discourse on democracy. For a democracy to be possible, the various manuals instruct that faith in the positive value of the individual, as a rational being endowed with dignity, is necessary. Democrats must see people in a good light. The democratic way of life is predicated on tolerance and respect of individual rights and freedom. The pursuit of private interest is allowed in the frame of collective interests. But what appears as classical liberalism is really only a shadow; the individual is there only by virtue of prescribed rights afforded by the state: these are not the 'natural' rights of liberalism. Absent too is an existing elaborate theory of the articulation of individual rights. The citation of these rights is a function of according legitimacy to the universal state, as protector and granter of these rights. Furthermore, the ambiguous status of rights is made possible by the nature of developmental democracy, in which the abstract subject of democracy is really the concrete object of reform by state developmental democracy. If democracy is a community of citizens, then those citizens are the subjects of democracy, its wilful agents and constitutive base. But if those subjects are deemed not yet to exist and are awaiting construction, then the people become the raw material upon which the state's citizen design can be operationalized. The non-presence of societal citizens is at the same time the presence of the state project to nurture the ideal citizen. This, if you like, is the project of state democrasubjection. It involved subjecting soon-to-be citizens to the potential good of their own reform as democratic citizens, such that they could sustain a state-prescribed democratic order.

Conclusion

While state ideologues were reeling from the trauma of the communist challenge and reimagining villages as centres of security and schools of democracy, it was the spectre of capitalism that proved most challenging. The new state-compacted relations of business and state at the national level, fragilely expressed in the parliament, threw up new challenges to the security state that surrounded the villages. The challenge was not the threat of a functioning democratic regime such that the statist role would be dramatically diminished, but rather the raw power of wealth and its ability to subvert programmes of development and security towards the needs of newly emerging particularlistic interests outside of the military-bureaucratic complex. The danger was that the venal practices of these new forces which increasingly penetrated the state, lacked any comprehensive legitimacy and had not yet established hegemony over relevant populations. The risk faced by the older and established forces was that the emptiness behind the rallying call of the common good would be exposed. In response, LAD was in a position to claim the mantle of democratic promoter at the rhetorical level against the 'dark influences' of corrupt capitalists, despite the participation of many state officials in corruption.[163]

The paradox of the 1980s is that just as capitalist forces were assembling massive networks of influence which reached down into local villages so as to buy their way into parliament, with scant regard for democratic conventions, it was the security state that was able to wield the language of democracy to discipline capital—which by default was moving towards opening the state up to its influence. This dissonance, between ideological democratization led by the state and political liberalization led by sections of capital, marked a conjuncture in which capital had failed to morally hegemonize the field of democracy as its own, but was able to penetrate the state's rural base so as to buy its way into formally democratic institutions. Statist ideologues aimed to remoralize their democracy projects along the lines of formally constructing a citizen able to withstand the lure of vote-selling, and one buttressed by the moral fibre of civic consciousness.

Presuming to shorthand this period, the ideologies of statist democracy were only partly challenged by liberal sentiments, academics and some reformist politicians. The greater challenge was the capitalization of the political field. The sacred field of the national interest and the people's sovereignty could not withstand the power of money. Soon, though, bourgeois intellectuals would move into this ideological vacuum. For a vibrant capitalist democracy to be legitimate, it required expansive efforts of reform and the removal of the political field from the direct forces of the market. In short, a rethinking of democracy was required that reformed the compact of forces working in the state, enabling the system to claim some authority as a 'democracy'. Such a reform would also entail rethinking the nature of citizenship, away from the strictures of state democrasubjection and its pastoral projects towards liberal and non-state communitarian projects of democrasubjection.

However, before I address these new strategic projects, the following chapter considers the statist turn to constructing national ideology in the 1980s and the attempt to provide a cultural sense of Thai citizenship.

Notes

1 Keyes notes the immediate appointment, by the king, of Thanin to the Privy Council after his overthrow by the military. See Charles Keyes, *Thailand: Buddhist Kingdom as Modern Nation State*, Bangkok: Editions Duang Kamol, 1989, esp. pp. 95–102.

2 See *The Nation*, 26/1/77, p. 1.

3 See *The Nation*, 22/3/77, p. 1; 2/10/77, pp. 1–2.

4 *The Nation*, 19/11/76, p. 1. Also see Chantana Thanyaset, 'Khabuankan naksuksa thai kap kan phathana prachathipatai' [The Thai student movement and the development of democracy], M.A. dissertation, Chulalongkorn University, 1987.

5 Thanin Kriaiwichian, *Rabop prachathipatai* [The democratic system], Bangkok: Krasuang suksathikan, 1977, pp. 4–9, 30, 51.

6 *Ibid.*, p. 83.

7 *Ibid.*, pp. 80–1.

8 *Ibid.*, pp. 112–13.

9 *Ibid.*, pp. 48–9. For Thanin's discussion on Fabianism see pp. 85–7.

10 *Ibid.*, p. 71.

11 *Ibid.*, p. 9.

12 *Ibid.*, pp. 12–13.

13 *Ibid.*, p. 14. On the use of 'identity' by Thanin, it is worthwhile to note that while the term may be traced several generations back, it was gaining a wider currency in the social sciences in the 1970s. Ekkhawit na Thalang suggests its contemporary usage was launched at an academic seminar in 1971, after which it became popular. By 1977 the term was introduced into national education plans. 'Identity' is explored further in Chapter 6. See Ekkhawit na Thalang, 'Ekkalak thai thi mi phon to khwammankhong haeng chat khana anukammakan udomkan khong chat' [Thai identity and its impact on national security], in Khanakammakan ekkalak khong chat samnakngan soemsang ekkalak khong chat samnakngan lekhathikan naiyokratthamontri, *Raignan soemsang ekkalak khong chat kap kanphathana chat thai* [Seminar report on national identity and Thai national development], 1985, pp. 120–32, p. 120.

14 Uthai Hiranto, 'Khon hua runraeng', *Thesaphiban*, 73, 12, 1978, pp. 908–13, pp. 908–9.

15 Krom kan pokkhrong krasuang mahatthai, *Khumu prachasamphan kanleuaktang* [Manual on election public relations], 1978.

16 *Ibid.*, p. 10.

17 *Ibid.*, p. 11.

18 *Ibid.*

19 *Ibid.*, p. 12.

20 *Ibid.*, p. 13.

21 *Ibid.*

22 *Ibid.*, pp. 17–18.

23 Krom kan pokkhrong, *Khumu poei phrae prachathipatai samrap khanakammakan supha tambon* [The manual for the propagation of democracy to the subdistrict council], c. 1978–9, pp. 1–5.

24 *Ibid.*, pp. 17–20.

25 *Ibid.*, p. 28.

26 *Ibid.*, p. 42.

27 Prudhisan Jumbala, *Nation Building and Democratization in Thailand*, Bangkok: Chulalongkorn University Social Research Institute, 1992, pp. 89–117.

28 On political parties, the military, and money-politics, see James Ockey, 'Business Leaders, Gangsters and Civilian Rule in Thailand', Ph.D. dissertation, Cornell University, 1992; James Ockey, 'Political Parties, Factions, and Corruption in Thailand', *Modern Asian Studies*, 28, 2, 1994, pp. 251–77.

29 *The Nation*, 17/3/83, p. 1.

30 *Bangkok Post*, 16/5/88, p. 1.

31 The Charter amendment passed by 496–0, with the military wing of the Senate absent when the vote was taken. *Bangkok Post*, 15/6/88, p. 1.

32 A term mostly associated with Prasert (see below).

33 *Bangkok Post*, 4/10/90, p. 4.

34 Kevin Hewison, 'Of Regimes, State and Pluralities: Thai Politics Enters the 1990s', in K. Hewison, R.Robison and G.Rodan (eds) *Southeast Asia in the 1990s: Authoritarianism, Democracy and Capitalism*, Melbourne: Allen and Unwin, 1993, pp. 161–89.

35 Samnakgnan lekhathikan naiyokratthamontri, *Ngan khong ratthaban anan panyarachun* [Office of the Prime Minister, *The work of the Anand Panyarachun government*], 1992. The first Anand administration passed 248 pieces of legislation, many relating to increasing administrative efficiency, business and financial regulations.

36 Vitit Muntarbhorn, 'A Tied or Thai Constitution', *Bangkok Post*, 22/8/91, p. 4.

37 *Matichon*, 3/7/91, p. 3. The measure was criticized by the liberal intelligentsia, although it was supported by others such as Kramol Thongthammachart. See also *Matichon*, 24/7/91, p. 3.

38 *Bangkok Post*, 30/8/91, p. 5; see *Matichon*, 29/8/91, p. 3.

39 *Matichon*, 22/11/91, p. 1. This article discusses the pact agreed between students and figures in political parties. See also *Siamrat*, 23/11/91, p. 3, on the rising opposition to the NPKC among academics. On political parties' agreement to fight the draft, see *Bangkok Post*, 26/8/91, p. 3; *Bangkok Post*, 7/9/91, p. 4.

40 For a good discussion of the constitutional deliberations see David Murray, *Angels and Devils: Thai Politics from February 1991–September 1992—A Struggle for Democracy?*, Bangkok: White Orchid Press, 1996, pp. 68–88; for a positive account of the first draft see Suchit Bunbongkarn, 'Thailand in 1991: Coping with Military Guardianship', *Asian Survey*, 32, 2, 1992, pp. 131–9.

41 Among the groups were the seven 'pro-democracy' parties and nine pro-democracy activist groups. See *Bangkok Post*, 17/11/91, pp. 1, 4; *The Nation*, 3/12/91, p. A10; *Matichon*, 18/11/91, p. 3.

42 *Bangkok Post*, 24/11/91, p. 1.

43 Chamlong Srimeuang, leader of the PDP, argued that the 'draft gives the military a remote controlled detonator. One push of the button and the government will be gone.' *The Nation*, 1/12/91, p. B1.

44 A scandal surrounded the nomination of STP leader Narong Wongwan: it was revealed that the USA had rejected a visa application because of Narong's alleged drug connections. This provided the pretext for Suchinda to take office. See Economist Intelligence Unit, *Thailand, Burma: Country Report*, no. 2, 1992, p. 11.

45 *Business In Thailand*, April 1992, p. 24.

46 *Bangkok Post,* 8/5/92, p. 1.

47 For the politics of Chamlong Srimeuang see Duncan McCargo, *Chamlong Srimeuang and the New Thai Politics,* New York: St Martin's Press, 1997.

48 *Bangkok Post,* 10/5/92, p. 1.

49 See, for instance, Suchinda's threat to sack the Bangkok Governor for supporting the protests. *Bangkok Post,* 14/5/92, p. 1.

50 See Coordinating Committee of Human Rights Organisations in Thailand, *Crisis in Democracy 17th–20th May 1992, Thailand: The Report of an International Fact-finding Mission,* Hong Kong, 1992.

51 *Bangkok Post,* 19/5/92, p. 10.

52 James P. LoGerfo, 'Beyond Bangkok: The Provincial Middle Class in the 1992 Protests', in Ruth McVey (ed.) *Money and Power in Provincial Thailand,* Copehangen: NIAS, 2000.

53 *Bangkok Post,* 20/5/92, p. 3; 21/5/92, pp. 1, 7.

54 *The Nation,* 20/5/92, p. A5.

55 Kevin Hewison, 'Of Regimes, State and Pluralities: Thai Politics Enters the 1990s', p. 170.

56 Economist Intelligence Unit, *Thailand, Burma: Country Report,* no. 2, 1992, p. 16.

57 *Ibid.,* no. 3, 1992, p. 10. See also *Bangkok Post,* 31/5/92, p. 1; 1/6/92, p. 3; 10/6/92, p. 4.

58 For a breakdown of results see Daniel King, 'The Thai Parliamentary Elections in an Atypical Year', *Asian Survey,* 32, 12, 1992, pp. 1109–23.

59 On the 'myth of the middle-class' revolt see Ji Ungpakorn, *The Struggle for Democracy and Social Justice in Thailand,* Bangkok: Arom Pongpangnan Foundation, 1997, pp. 108–13; Michael Connors, 'When the Dogs Howl: Thailand and the Politics of Democratization', in P. Darby (ed.) *At the Edge of International Relations: Postcolonialism, Gender and Dependency,* London: Pinter, 1997, pp. 125–47, pp. 138–9.

60 Alasdair Bowie and Danny Unger, *The Politics of Open Economies: Indonesia, Malaysia, the Philippines and Thailand,* Cambridge: Cambridge University Press, 1997, pp. 129–56.

61 Pasuk Phongpaichit, 'Technocrats, Businessmen, and Generals: Democracy and Economic Policy-making in Thailand', in A. MacIntyre, A. and K. Jayasuriya (eds) *The Dynamics of Economic Policy Reform in Southeast Asia and the Southwest Pacific,* Singapore: Oxford University Press, 1992, pp. 10–31, p. 27.

62 *Ibid.,* pp. 14–16,18–21.

63 Malcolm Falkus, 'Thai Industrialisation: An Overview', in M. Krongkaew (ed.) *Thailand's Industrialization and Its Consequences,* New York: St Martin's Press, 1995, pp. 13–32, p. 17. The proportion of manufacturing was greatly boosted. In 1960 it was less than 2 per cent of all exports, by 1992 it accounted for 77.8 per cent of all exports (and 24.4 per cent of GDP) compared to agriculture at 16.9 per cent.

64 Rangsan Thanaphon, *Krabuankan amnot naiyobai setakit nai prathet thai* [Economic policy determination in Thailand], Bangkok: Samakhom sangkhomsat haeng prathet thai, 1989, pp. 78–80.

65 See Anek Laothamatas, *Business Associations and the New Political Economy of Thailand: From Bureaucratic Polity to Liberal Corporatism,* Singapore: West View Press, 1992.

66 The term *jao poh* has been translated in the English language press as 'godfather'. The term became increasingly common from the 1970s onwards after the screening in Thailand of the 1970s classic, *The Godfather*. The term is not so inappropriate, as many *jao poh* are renowned for illegal activities and assassinations. Pasuk Phongpaichit and Chris Baker, '*Jao Sua, Jao Poh, Jao Tii*: Lords of Thailand's Transition', paper presented at the Fifth International Conference in Thai Studies, School of Oriental and African Studies, University of London, 1993, p. 17.

67 See McVey (ed.) *Money and Politics in Provincial Thailand*, 2000.

68 Somrudee Nicro, 'Thailand's NIC Democracy: Studying from General Elections', *Pacific Affairs*, 66, 2, 1993, pp. 167–82.

69 Pasuk Phongpaichit and Chris Baker, 'Power in Transition: Thailand in the 1990s', in K. Hewison (ed.) *Political Change in Thailand: Democracy and Participation*, London: Routledge, 1997, pp. 21–41, pp. 29–32.

70 Sungsidh Phiriyarangsan and Pasuk Phongpaichit, *Jitsamnuk lae udomkan khong khabuankan prachathipatai ruam samai* [Consciousness and ideology of the contemporary democracy movement], Bangkok: Sunsuksa sethasatkanmeuang khana settasat kanmeuang julalongkon mahawithiyalai, 1996.

71 Between 1986 and 1988, foreign investment increased from 2.1 thousand million baht to 16.4 thousand million baht, and investment in the form of fixed property rose from 3.1 thousand million baht in 1986 to 49 thousand million baht in 1989 (25 baht approximated 1 US dollar). Figures cited in Anek Laothamatas, 'Thurakit bonsen thang prachathipatai: Tusadi kap khwampenjing' [Business on the Road to Democracy: Theory and Reality], in Sungsidh Piriyarangsan and Pasuk Phongpaichit (eds) *Chonchan klang bonkrasae prachathipatai thai* [The middle class on the road to democracy], Bangkok: Sunsuksa sethasatkanmeuang khana settasat kanmeuang julalongkon mahawithiyalai, 1992, pp. 155–93, p. 181.

72 Pasuk Phongpaichit, 'Botbat chonchan klang nai setakit lae kanmeuang prathet asian NIC lae Thai', in *ibid.*, pp. 91–116, p. 95.

73 Vorawith Chareonlert, 'Chonchanlang kap hetkan phrusaphakhom' [The middle class and the May events], in *ibid.*, pp. 117–53, p. 138.

74 Anonymous, 'Open Statement From Academics Concerning the Recent Coup in Thailand', *Journal of Contemporary Asia*, 21,4, 1991, pp. 563–4.

75 Benedict Anderson, 'Murder and Progress in Modern Siam', *New Left Review*, 181, 1990, pp. 33–48, p. 40.

76 *Ibid.*, p. 46.

77 *Ibid.*, pp. 46, 48.

78 Kevin Hewison, 'Of Regimes, State and Pluralities: Thai Politics Enters the 1990s', p. 170.

79 *Ibid.*, p. 168.

80 *Ibid.*, p. 181.

81 Chalermkiat Phiu-nuan, *Khwamkhit thangkanmeuang khong thahan thai 2519–2535* [The political thought of the Thai military, 1976–1992], Bangkok: Samnakphim phujatkan, 1992.

82 See Peter Jackson, 'Re-interpreting the *Traiphuum Phra Ruang*: Political Functions of Buddhist Symbolism in Contemporary Thailand', in T. Ling (ed.) *Buddhist Trends in Southeast*

Asia, Singapore, Singapore: ISEAS, 1993, pp. 64–100; and Peter Jackson, 'Thai Buddhist Identity: Debates on the *Traiphuum Phra Ruang',* in C. Reynolds (ed.) *National Identity and its Defenders: Thailand 1939–1989,* Chiang Mai: Silkworm Books, 1993, pp. 191–231.

83 Peter Jackson, *Buddhism, Legitimation and Conflict: the Political Functions of Urban Thai Buddhism,* Singapore: Institute of Southeast Asian Studies, 1989, p. 41.

84 Chalermkiat *Khwamkhit thangkanmeuang khong thahan thai,* pp. 20, 177–9.

85 *Ibid.,* pp. 155–6, 189.

86 Asa Meksawan, 'Pramahakasat thai sunruam khong khon thang chat' [The Thai warrior king: The centre of the whole Thai people], *Thesaphiban,* 74, 2, 1979, pp. 77–88, p. 85.

87 Chai-Anan *et al., From Armed Suppression to Political Offensive,* pp. 127–63. For an extended discussion of military politics see Chai-Anan Samudavanija, *The Thai Young Turks,* Singapore: Institute of Southeast Asian Studies, 1982. For a 'revisionist' account of the politics of the military which questions the received wisdom on distinct ideological factions, see Duncan McCargo, *Chamlong Srimeuang,* pp. 19–24.

88 See, for a good biographical account of Prasert, Suriyan Suwannarat, *Lak pokkhrong prachathipatai kap naeokhwamkhit khong nai praset sapsunthon lae phon ek chavalit yongjaiyut 2522–2536* [The principles of the democratic system and the thought of Mr Prasert Sapsunthun and General Chavalit Yongjaiyut: 1979–1993), Bangkok: Suchit Thanrungreuang, 1997, pp. 119–24.

89 Chai-Anan *et al., From Armed Suppression to Political Offensive,* pp. 127–63, pp. 118–21.

90 'Thalaengkan thahan prachathipatai reuang kanrang ratthathammanun thahan prachathipatai' [Declaration of the Democratic Soldiers on Drafting the Constitution], in *Thahan prachathipatai, Kho saneu naeothang kae panha chat khong thahan prachathipatai* [Proposals and approaches to solving national problems of the democratic soldiers], 1987, pp. 14–18, p. 15.

91 'San jak thahan prachathipatai chabap thi 1 chijaeng thalaengkan' [Letter from the Democratic Soldiers, first issue, regarding the Democratic Soldiers' Declaration], in *ibid.,* pp. 19–24, p. 19.

92 'Khwamsang samnakgnan naiyokratthamontri thi 66/2523 reuang naiyobai kantosu peua owchana khommunit' [Order of the Prime Minister's office no. 66/1980 on the policy of struggle to defeat communism], in Phan. ek. Chavalit Yongjaiyut, *Yutthasat kantosu peua owchana khomnunit* [Fighting strategy to defeat communism], n.pl., n.p., 1989, pp. 176–9, p. 176.

93 *Ibid.,* p. 177.

94 'Sarasamkhan khwamsang naiyokratthamontri thi 5/ 2524 reuang chijaeng naiyobai tam khwamsang thi 66/2523' [The substance of Prime Minister's Office order no. 5/1981, Clarifying Prime Minister's Office no. 66/1980], in *Chamlae naiyobai kongthap* [Dissecting military policy], n.d., pp. 20–2. p. 20.

95 *Ibid.,* p. 21. The term 'influence' in Thai *(itthiphon)* is often accompanied with the word dark *(muet)* to indicate non-public forms of illegitimate power.

96 'Khamsang samnakngan naiyokratthamontri thi 65/2525 reuang phaen rukthangkanmeuang' [Prime Minister's Office Order no. 65/1982 on the Political Offensive Plan], in Phan. ek. Chavalit Yongjaiyut, *Yutthasat kantosu peua owchana khomnunit* [Fighting strategy to defeat communism], n.pl., n.p., 1989, pp. 180–7, p. 180.

97 See Krasuang mahatthai, *Kan owchana suk pho. ko. Kho. tam naeo khwamkhit nai kanjattang lae chai prayot muanchon nai ching patipat* [Interior Ministry official on the need to break the relationship between villagers and the CPT by building mass organizations] (p. 12). In this regard the Interior Ministry was following military policy.

98 Chai-Anan *et al.*, *From Armed Suppression to Political Offensive*, p. 121.

99 'Ekkasan prakop kansuksa khrongkan 6601' [Learning Material for Project 6601], in *Chamlae naiyobai kongthap* [Dissecting Military Policy], n.d., pp. 142–56.

100 *Ibid.*, p. 142.

101 *Ibid.*, p. 143.

102 *Ibid.*

103 *Ibid.*, p. 144.

104 *Ibid.*, pp. 150–1.

105 *Ibid.*, p. 152. Note that this Rousseauian term appears in English in brackets as 'general wills'.

106 *Ibid.*

107 *Ibid.*

108 *Ibid.*, p. 154.

109 *Ibid.*, pp. 154–5.

110 *Ibid.*, p. 149. This is seen as non-Western democratic thought.

111 For examples, see the role of the military in the Green Isan Project, also the military role in crime suppression and mass mobilization. Chai-Anan *et al.*, *From Armed Suppression to Political Offensive*, pp. 10, 82.

112 See *The Nation Review*, 31/1/82, which looks at the history of Democratic Soldiers and notes their official disbandment in late 1981. Interestingly, Chai-Anan interprets the orders influenced by Democratic Soldiers and filtered by Chavalit and Harn as 'liberal'. For a counter-interpretation see Sutichai Yoon, 'Pressure Groups Targets of New Political Offensive', *The Nation Review*, 22/7/82, p. 5.

113 See his statement cited in *The Nation*, 7/11/85, p. 4: 'All government agencies must cooperate with the ISOC officers . . .in carrying out the immediate policy for the fiscal year 1986.'

114 Chai-Anan *et al.*, *From Armed Suppression to Political Offensive*, p. 107.

115 Sunsuksa prasanngan thahan kongthun haengchat samnakngan lekhathikan kong amnuaykan raksa khwammankhong phainai [National Reserves Co-ordinating Centre, Office of the Directorate for Maintaining Internal Security], *Sala prachathipatai* [Democracy Pavilions], 1990, pp. 43–50.

116 Chaiyasit Tanthayakun, 'Sala prachathipatai kap kanrianru thang kanmeuang' [The Democracy Pavilions and Political Learning], M.A. Thesis, Chulalongkorn University, 1986, p. 85.

117 See for example the transcripts of radio broadcasts: 'Phai thi yang tongpung ramatrawang' [Dangers of which to be Cautious], in *Pheua phaen din thai dulakhom 2531–mokkharom 2532* [For the land of Thais October 1988–January 1989], pp. 90–3, p. 93.

118 Indeed, even as Minister of Defence in the Chatichai regime, Chavalit remained critical of parliamentary democracy in its Thai form. Earning his royalist credentials, Chavalit emphasized

the important attempts to develop democracy under Rama 7. Supporting parliamentary democracy, Chavalit was, at least publicly, concerned that the representatives were true representatives of the people, a recurring theme of Thai-style democracy. See Phan Ek Chavalit Yongjaiyut, 'Udomkan thangsethakit peua khwammankhong' [Economic ideology for security], *Warasansangkhomsat* [Journal of Social Science], 27, 1, 1990, pp. 3–32, pp. 15–19.

119 *Bangkok Post*, 19/5/88, p. 3. This conference attracted 1,400 delegates, including military and local-level civil servants.

120 See for example Prasert Sapsunthon, *Khadi suphapatiwathaeng chat 2538* [The case of the National Revolutionary Council], n.p., 1995.

121 Cited in *Bangkok Post*, 30/5/88, p. 1.

122 During the constitutional debates of 1995–7 followers of Prasert issued articles and leaflets calling for their version of Thai-style Democracy. See, for example, the article by union leader Wanchai Phonhamapha, 'Naeothang kantosu thangkanmeaung kammakon Thai' [Approaches to the Political Struggle of Thai Workers], *Siam Post*, 17/9/95, p. 22.

123 Asa Meksawan, *Kan pokkhrong radap tambon muban khwammankhong haengchat* [Subdistrict and village level administration and national security], Bangkok: Withayalai pongkan rachaanajak, *c.* 1977.

124 *Ibid.*, p. kho khwai.

125 *Ibid.*, p. 35.

126 *Ibid.*

127 *Ibid.*, p. 38.

128 *Ibid.*, pp. 46–53.

129 The plans were issued in accordance with the NESDB five yearly plans. As LAD's first plan was issued halfway through the 4th National Plan, it only ran three years. See Krom kanpokkhrong, *Phaenkrom kanpokkhrong tamnaeo phathanakan sethakit lae sangkhom haeng chat chabap thi 4* [Local Administration Department Plan in Accordance with the 3rd National Economic and Social Development Plan], pp. 5–6.

130 *Ibid.*, p. 1.

131 Krom kanpokkhrong, *Raignan prajam pi 2521* [Local Administration Department, Annual Report, 1978] p. 4.

132 *Ibid.*

133 *Ibid.*, pp. 4–5.

134 Krom kanpokkhrong, *Phaenkrom kanpokkhrong maebot chabap thi 3 2525–2529* [Third Master Plan, Local Administration Department, 1982–1986], p. 9.

135 *Ibid.*, p. 10.

136 *Ibid.*

137 *Ibid.*, p. 23. It is suggested that an understanding of democracy would lead to a greater faith in the political party system. For this to occur assistance is needed to help parties develop, and indeed to help people set up parties. This, one should note, is a comment that can only be understood in the context of the orientation provided by order 66/2523 publicly allowing for intervention into, or establishment of, mass organizations by the intelligence forces. Additionally, the Subdistrict Council is emphasized as a school of democracy and it is suggested that the PDDC continue (*ibid.*, p. 29).

138 Krom kanpokkhrong, *Raingan prajam pi 2530* [Annual Report, 1987], p. 7.

139 *Ibid.*, 2535 [Annual Report, 1992], p. 13.

140 Limited access to official sources has meant that in some instances other departmental publications were used to gather information on the plans.

141 Sumet Saengnimnuan, 'Or. pho. por. Muban prachathipatai khrongkan peu khwamrot yu khong chat' [Self development and protection villages, village democracy, a project for the survival of the nation], *Thesaphiban*, 74, 1, 1979, pp. 55–66; P. Piyathida, 'Kan kaothung prachachon' [Approaching the people], *Thesaphiban*, 85, 7, 1990, pp. 1–6.

142 Sumet , 'Or.pho. por. Muban prachathipatai', p. 66.

143 Luan Ratthanamongkhon, 'Khunatham kap kanpokkhrong' [Integrity and government], *Thesaphiban*, 74, 3, 1979, pp. 207–15, p. 208.

144 *Ibid.*

145 Chalong Kanyanmit, 'Lak patibat rachakan khong nakpokkhrong' [Principles of conduct for administrators], *Thesaphiban*, 82, 3, 1987, pp. 11–29.

146 Krom Satsana Krasuang Suksathikan, *Lakkan samrap phupokkhrong* [Principles for governors], 1982, pp. 24–32

147 *Ibid.*, p. 32.

148 Chalong Kanyanmit, 'Lak patibat rachakan khong nakpokkhrong' [Principles of Conduct for Administrators], *Thesaphiban*, 82, 3, 1987, p. 23; see also Anek's article which calls for a shift from the language of mass mobilization and military strategy to the language of people's organizations: Anek Sithiprasat, 'Botbat nathi khong fai pokkhrong yuk mai' [The role of new era administrators], *Thesaphiban*, 82, 7, 1987, pp. 4–12.

149 *Ibid*

150 Nakborihan (pseud.), 'Khwammankhong chat kap withikan borihan prachathipatai nai tambon muban' [National security and the mode of democratic administration in the subdistrict and village], *Thesaphiban*, 80, 8, 1985, pp. 17–19. Similar arguments were made about the election of provincial governors, see Pratan Khongrutthisikasakon, 'Kan leuaktang phu wa rachakan jangwat' [The election of provincial governors], *Thesaphiban*, 80, 3, 1985, pp. 21–4. Prathan argues that once the rural areas become urban, when they have formed interest groups and political parties and when they do so with ethics, then and only then might it be time to talk about elected provincial governors (pp. 21–4).

151 See the following material: 'Krasuang mahatthai kap khrongkan khayai thana prachathipatai' [The Ministry of Interior and the Project to Expand the Basis of Democracy], *Thesaphiban*, 84, 10, 1989, pp. 16–21; Krom kanpokkhrong, 'Pak kanmeuang kap kankhayai thana prachachatipatai su puangchon' [Political Parties and Expanding the Basis of Democracy to the People], *Thesaphiban*, 84, 7, 1989, pp. 18–35; Withayalai kan pokkhrong, 'Kankhayai thana prachathipatai su puangchon' [Expanding the basis of democracy], *Warasan kamnan phuyaiban* [Journal of Kamnan and Phuyaiban], 41, 7, 1990, pp. 8–14; Chuwong Chayabut, *Khayai thana prachathipatai su puangchon* [Expanding the basis of democracy to the people], Bangkok: Krom kan pokkhrong, 1992.

152 Krom kanpokkrong krom kanpathathana chumchon krasuang mahatthai, *Khumu patipatkan poei phrae prachathipatai radap muban* [Practical handbook on the dissemination of democracy at the village level], 1991, p. 10.

153 Krom kanpokkhrong krasuang mathathai, *Khumu withayakon phathana prachathipatai radap muban* [Personnel handbook on developing democracy at the village level], 1993.

154 Krom kanpokkhrong, *Prachathipatai radap muban* [Village-level democracy], 1994, pp. 28–9; Pricha Hongkrailert, 'Klum prayot pak kanmeuang mitimahachon' [Interest Groups, Political Parties, and the Will of the People], *Thesaphiban*, 76, 6, 1981, pp. 55–78; Pricha Hongkrailert, 'Kho khithen nai kan sangrabop pakkanmeuang mai prathet thai' [Opinion on building the political party system in Thailand], *Thesaphiban*, 76, 11, 1981, pp. 11–35; *Thesaphiban*, 78, 7, 1983, pp. 3–11.

155 Krom kan pokkhrong, *Khumu kanprachasamphan kanleuaktang* [Election public relations manual], 1978, pp. 12–15.

156 Krom kanpokkhrong krasuang mathathai, *Khumu withayakon phathana prachathipatai radap muban* [Personnel handbook on developing democracy at the village level], 1993, pp. 35–42; Chuwong Chayabut, *Khayai thana prachathipatai su puangchon* [Expanding the basis of democracy to the people], Bangkok: Krom kan pokkhrong, 1992, p. 7.

157 To make this point a familial analogy is used: 'If the father governs by listening to the views of all members of the family, happiness and warmth will arise in the family.' Krom kanpokkhrong, *Prachathipatai radap muban*, 1994, p. 81; P. Piyathida, 'Prachathipatai nan samkhan chanai' [How important is democracy?], *Thesaphiban*, 85, 8, 1990, pp. 17–32, pp. 31–2

158 For a typical statement regarding this see P. Piyathida, 'Kan kaothung prachachon' [Approaching the people], *Thesaphiban*, 85, 7, 1990, pp. 1–6.

159 Such statements will be found in most of the manuals. See also, for example: 'Sarup kansammana phu borihan radap sung krasuang mahatthai reuang prachathipatai nai thang patibat 2527' [Summary of Seminar for High Level Interior Ministry Administrators on Democracy in Practice], 1984, pp. 123–5, mimeograph.

160 Niphon Bunyaphatharo, 'Supah tambon matrakan phathana prachathipatai khanpunthan' [The subdistrict council: the measure of basic democracy], *Thesaphiban*, 75, 4, 1980, pp. 373–9; Jamlong Chukliang, 'Supha tambon rongrian fukson prachathipatai' [The subdistrict council: the training school for democracy], *Thesaphiban*, 75, 5, 1980, pp. 878–83.

161 Lertbut Kongthong, 'Kanpoei phrae prachathipatai radap muban' [Disseminating democracy at the village level], *Thesaphiban*, 87, 2, 1992, pp. 23–5.

162 Krom kanpokkrong krom kanpathathana chumchon krasuang mahatthai, *Khumu patipatkan poei phrae prachathipatai radap muban* [Practical handbook on the dissemination of democracy at the village level], 1991, p. 10.

163 For a cutting sectoral analysis of rampant corruption, see *Ekkasanprakob kan prachum raingan phon wijai sethakit nok kotmai lae naiyobai satharana nai prathet thai* [Materials from meeting on research report illegal economy and public policy in Thailand], 2–3 December 1996, Bangkok, Political Economy Centre, Faculty of Economics, Chulalongkorn University, The Asia Foundation and The Office of Supporting Research Funds. It is argued that the 'informal sector', including drugs, lotteries and sex work, account for between 15 and 18 per cent of total GDP (p. 5).

6

Citizen King

Embodying Thainess

> There are many things I might have become, including a communist, were it not for his majesty the King.
>
> (An alleged remark of Kukrit Pramoj)[1]

FROM THE LOWLIEST OFFICE TO MEGA-MINISTRIES, IMAGES OF the King and royal family appear on bulletins, walls and calendars. The King's aphorisms circulate in memos reminding *kharachakan* (the king's servants) of their duties. His statements lay the basis for thousands of royal projects. This king's apparent omnipresence has intensified since 1976, whereafter all state agencies have complied in propagating the ideology of 'democracy with the king as head of state'. This idea had, in principle, informed previous constitutions; after 1976 it became part of public pronouncements to delineate the specificity of Thai democracy. The deployment of the term pointed to prestigious gains made by the monarchy after its rehabilitation under the Sarit dictatorship and its subsequent mediating and crisis-management roles in the events of 1973 and 1976. For those in the know, the term also resonated with Bhumiphol Adulyadej's newly acquired political power as king. This power has grown as a result of his relatively unscrutinized and shrewd political interventions. If, in the mid-1970s, the fate of the monarchy seemed uncertain, within less than a decade even progressive intellectuals could not conceive of the Thai nation without its wise king. The divine-like status of Bhumiphol is not part of the family treasure, but something that hundreds of officials in the palace and other agencies have contrived to create. Key to this has been the promotion of 'democracy with the king as head of state'.

The ideology of 'democracy with the king as head of state' is a curious mixture of traditionalist conceptions of kingship and democracy. In the traditionalist aspect the king is seen as inviolable and infallible, and remains free of any accusation. His Buddhist-prescribed duties [*rachathami*] to the people include using Buddhism to rule the country in line with the ten virtues. He is also to provide morale to the people, ensure the production of food, recognize the people's achievements and alleviate their suffering. Furthermore, the king must be healthy and have a strong entourage supporting him. He must also be 'born to be king' – this relates to his own karmic merit as well as the high family circle from which he emerges.[2]

Traditional concepts of kingship clearly remain significant in the politics of legitimacy surrounding King Bhumiphol. This traditionalism is bolstered by royal language, which deliberately separates the monarchy from the people. Dictionaries of royal vocabulary list thousands of correct usages for speaking of royals. This royal language elevates royalty above humanity. As Sombat notes, the individuals who address themselves to royal personages begins with the statement, 'May the power of the dust and the dust under the soles of your royal feet protect my head and the top of my head.'[3] For Sombat, court language functions to safeguard and naturalize the sacerdotal/common divide by enforcing and policing a linguistic divide which makes humble and earthly the addressee to royalty. No wonder, then, that the 1932 post-revolutionary regime attacked royal language and attempted to reduce its usage. However, during the Sarit era the court was able to rehabilitate its position and advance its usage.[4]

Given these traditional premises, it would seem paradoxical that Thai kingship, in the contemporary period, is also melded with democratic ideology. Given the threats to stability emerging from social transformation, it was the king who could – as a symbol of order, place and identity – act as a focal point of loyalty. As a central institution from which the state's ideological practices could be referenced and embodied, the monarchy in effect functioned as a central institution in political development. There is a logic to this paradox: the role of the king might be seen as just one form of transitional adaptation by an elite of a traditional institution, and a conscious application of culture and tradition for the purposes of development and order. If democracy is understood as a form of discipline, the role of the monarchy becomes clear: it acts as a strategic site for the production of modern citizens and political order in a modernizing society.

This chapter considers the reconstruction of national ideology after the events of 1976. The focus is on providing a critical exposition of the construction of a national ideology around Thai identity and the king, such that one might speak of an intimate form of democrasubjection. In constructing and deploying a renewed national ideology in the post-1976 period, state actors addressed the people as specifically 'Thai', the attributes of which were exemplified by the king. The task of defining the Thai self was given to the National Identity Board, and it is in that organization that democrasubjection as a hegemonic project (the national imaginary) most clearly met democrasubjection as an embryonic project of directed self government (Foucault's 'conduct of conduct'). The meeting ground was in proposed regimes of self-discipline and self-identification around significant metaphors of Thai selfhood/nationhood. Building a disciplined self/nation was the aim of national ideology. Much of this chapter attempts to map the ideological and organizational planning that went into defining regimes of Thainess. Thainess here is understood as bridging the hegemonic and governmental aspects of democrasubjection, because it gestures both upwards to the nation, and downwards to the Thai self. The material is mundane, but by providing an exposition a clear picture emerges of just how consciously 'Thainess', the nation–religion–monarchy triad and democracy were mobilized for hegemonic and governmental aims.

Renewing the nation/renewing the monarchy

After the tumultuous events of 1973–76, the monarchy became the focus of a new round of ultra-nationalist drum-beating and identity-seeking. The right wing had monopolized the official ideology of nation, religion and monarchy during the polarized political struggles of the 1970s. Many thus associated the triad with the appalling violence of the ultra-right.[5] To counteract this, an aggressive restoration of the monarchy involved integrating the progressive themes of democracy and social development and remoralization of the state around the figure of the monarch. The position of the monarchy was promoted by extensive media manipulation, effectively creating a cult of personality around Bhumiphol.

The restoration of the monarchy, however, should not simply be read as ideological cynicism. Firstly, the Buddhist conception of the monarch required his public exposure as a righteous ruler; his father-like portrayal was functionally required for the maintenance of state-sanctioned Buddhism itself. Secondly, filtered through both conservative and liberal readings of Thai history, there emerged a widespread belief of the king's positive role in democratic evolution. This was bolstered by the citation of critical interventions by the king, including his role in offering political advice to students before 1973, his reputed role in ordering Generals Praphat and Thanom out of the country in 1973, and his rejection of the insertion of certain royal prerogatives in the 1974 draft constitution. Most cited is his intervention in the May 1992 events. On prime time television Bhumiphol lectured protagonists of the May events, Prime Minister Suchinda and Chamlong Srimuang, who lay semi-prostrate before him. However, a critical reading of that event shows Bhumiphol publicly sympathizing with Suchinda. Bhumiphol expressed frustration that his advice to 'promulgate now, amend later' (regarding the military backed 1991 Constitution) had been ignored by those pushing for immediate amendments:

> The draft Constitution had been amended all along; it had been changed even more than originally expected ... let me say that when I met General Suchinda [in late 1991], General Suchinda concurred that the Constitution should first be promulgated and it could be amended later. ... And even lately General Suchinda has affirmed that it can be amended. It can be gradually amended so that it will be eventually improved in a 'democratic way'. Thus, I have already mentioned the way to solve the problem many months ago.[6]

There is, too, the most recent intervention, in which it is rumoured the king sought Anand's involvement in the drafting of the new constitution in 1997, and also instructed the armed forces to support the draft.[7]

It is notable that the word 'rumoured' occurs in the preceding paragraph. This is significant, reflecting the blockage of discussion on a central political institution in Thailand. This has afforded Thai social science little opportunity to offer genuinely critical analyses of the Thai social formation. While negative comments are almost impossible to make in the Thai language, favourable comments abound, both in written and oral form. Genuine attempts at analysing social change, the conditions of hegemony and the position of the monarch, are highly restricted when reference cannot be made to a central economic, political and ideological force. While radical critique suffers, liberal and conservative renderings are sustained by the use of an informal and highly skewed body of knowledge about the king within academic and elite circles. Essentially, a number of royalist liberals are in a position to informally and formally highlight their interpretations of the king through anecdote and official versions of history. This provides the interpretation with some authority. Such interpretations emerge from what may be called the 'insider knowledge complex'. Interviewers are often at the receiving end of this informal production of royal mythology. Many will be asked to turn off tape recorders during interviews so as to hear of the king's positive interventions in politics and the like. Note, here, that even positive insider knowledge cannot be entrusted to the impersonal record of a tape recorder; rather it is dispatched for public consumption in a cautious and controlled way. When the insider puts it on public record, moving it from the level of privileged knowledge to public knowledge, it then becomes part of the staple of democratic justifications about the present monarch. The insider knowledge complex basically valorizes those close to the monarchy as being able to interpret the role of the king, while outsiders, Thai and foreign, are seen as incapable of presenting authentic accounts of the role of the monarch. However, the tenability of insider knowledge is highly dubious. It is produced in relations of domination that allow some things to be said and others not. Insiders are not so much privileged observers of the real, but ideological proponents of skewed interpretations of the informal political role of the royals. It is, one might say, the hearsay of the 'nudge and wink' school. While proffered as individual insight, it is no less vulgar than the exhortatory propaganda of leadership cults.

The king's interventions, his apparent restoration of 'order' and calm, have led to an interpretation of the monarchy as an indispensable para-political institution in Thailand's democracy. Certainly, skilful propaganda and the wilful hopes of royalist liberals aid this image (see Chapter 8). The sum effect of this historical image-making is that the present king is seen as a mediating power between hostile social forces, despite his family's position as leading capitalists and landowners with a personal stake in the wellbeing of Thai capitalism.[8] The palace's unique position as a public exemplar of conservative traditions and its existence as a network of capital have proved an invaluable resource for Thailand's elite democratic development. With the aura of traditional authority, built up since the 1950s, the monarchy is able to strategically intervene in favour of order.

A key ideological resource and active agent of power bloc, the palace has succeeded in partly mobilizing resources for its own ends, but it has also been mobilized by social forces to assume a position at the helm of national ideology. The reciprocity of this relationship remains relatively unexamined.

For many progressive intellectuals, the 1980s brought a reconciliation with the monarchy. As they moved away from projects of radical change and embraced forms of liberal and participatory democracy they came to appreciate the monarchy's role in negotiating a path towards the political institutionalization of democracy. In effect they accepted Thanin's idea that it functioned as a checkpoint in a society where political development faced a number of obstacles including a political culture characterized by patronage, and a political system dominated by military and bureaucratic elements. The elite project of liberalization and institutionalization of democratic institutions could be aided by pragmatic use of royal symbolism. Additionally, some writers see the king's symbolic role of embodying Thainess as a guarantee against the monopolization of power by any one sector. For example, Thirayut Bunmi, the one-time student radical and anti-royalist, claims the term 'democracy with the king as head of state' was popularized *after* the late 1970s precisely as an antidote to military notions of democracy. Thirayut argues that the term 'democracy with the king as head of state' implied that all people had to be part of any democratic settlement. The term is said to encompass all relevant social groups, since the king is the embodiment of all Thais.[9] With this explication of the term, Thirayut can claim that notions of 'democracy led by the military' (a doctrine associated with an influential clique in the military) are effectively an assault on the equality of all parts embodied in the king. This is an ingenious reading, but influential no less, for it informs a progressive strategy that has moved from the mass struggles of the 1970s to the more moderate and symbolic struggles for graduated democratic development under the 'classless' political imaginary of civil society.

The historical processes of the construction of the royal myth cannot be ignored in any attempt to 'progressively' appropriate this institution; it has never been a neutral national symbol. It has, rather, been an active political force working towards what Kevin Hewison, referring to the ideological level, calls a 'conservative capitalist state'. This is a state in which the monarchy ideologically disciplines the rural population through the discourse of thrift, self-reliance, national security and moral selfhood. Pointing to the recurrent themes in the king's speeches that stress discipline and law and order, unity, and the duties of people, Hewison aptly describes the king's thinking as conservative.[10]

The king's thinking on good citizenship certainly conveys a conservative regard for order and discipline. Kanok Wongtrangan's study of Bhumiphol's speeches, spread over thirty years, suggests that the king's thought on good citizens revolves around four central issues.

First, the people must be educated, have quality and ability: this is related to the theme of self-reliance and economic progress.[11] Educated people would help society progress in an orderly fashion and be prosperous.[12] Second, the people must be good and have religion, for religion helps people behave appropriately and 'be a good person, to behave beneficially and not to cause trouble for oneself or others'. Furthermore, knowing one's status and duties 'will lead to happiness and the wellbeing ... for human society'.[13] Third, the people must have unity so that the country can progress and prosper, as well as remain secure. Unity leads to the survival of the nation, pride and dignity.[14] Unity 'is the strongest force in the land

and when it is achieved it will inspire the people in the nation to be unanimous in attempting to . . . create progress and security'.[15] Finally, the people must have strength. On this principle, the king discourses on the importance of self-reliant people who are able to learn and develop both their minds and bodies. Only on this basis will a society prosper. Importantly, here the thematic of the common good is located in the wellbeing of the excellent individual whose path towards self-development has positive consequences for the wellbeing of society as a whole. Thus the moral basis of society, while exemplified in the actions and words of the king and the Buddhist *sangha,* must also be rooted in the self-contained and self-interested activities of strong and capable individuals.[16]

As an exponent of conservative forms of capitalism, the palace has vested interests in the propagation of ideology. As Chairat Charoensin-O-Larn notes, with the fragmentation and competition in and between the state and the bourgeoisie, the monarchy remained a key force for integration.[17] Thus the constancy of the monarchy's political position, its abiding regard for security and productive labour, reflects the concerns of a reflexive capitalist agent empowered by the prestige of royalty, and which has subsequently succeeded in positioning itself at the head of an ensemble of bureaucratic and capitalist forces.

Given the glaring disparity between the rich and the poor, the monarchy's dual position (as an agent of particular political and economic interests and as a symbol of the nation) requires an iron regime of controlled imagery. In the conditions of ideological restoration, post-1976, a new eagerness to police *lèse-majesté* emerged, reflecting the further consolidation of the monarchy and the bureaucratic and capitalist reverence to it.[18] According to Streckfuss, *lèse-majesté* moved from being an offence against the monarchy to being an offence against national security in 1957. Furthermore, in 1976 the Thanin regime increased the length of imprisonment for *lèse-majesté* to fifteen years.[19]

While used as a political instrument by some, overall the policing of *lèse-majesté* has been in the interests of the palace power bloc. Apart from favoured sons, few are spared this ruthless policing. Let me give some examples. A month after Thanin came to power a man was arrested by police on charges of *lèse-majesté* for using a royal village scout scarf to wipe a table.[20] In 1983, more threateningly, a democracy activist was jailed for eight years for the publication of a book, *Nine Kings of the Chakri Dynasty,* which was highly critical of the monarchy and also offered historical argument about the monarchy's less-than-honourable intentions.[21] In 1988 a politician, and one time coup-maker, was sentenced to four years' jail for suggesting that life would have been easier had he been born in the palace.[22] There are many other instances of this kind of arrest, censorship and image-building. Most famously, of course, is the enigmatic case of Sulak Sivalak, the radical conservative who has openly criticized the monarchy for partisanship and failing to fulfil its traditional role.[23] More generally, censorship and self censorship ensures that even historical points are to be policed.[24] Touching on the sensitive point of King Taksin, *King Taksin's Soldiers,* a television drama, was cancelled even though the authorities had already censored it.[25] Furthermore, palace news on every television channel each evening reaffirms appropriate representation of the monarchy.

The existence of *lèse-majesté* should not be seen as a minor blotch on an otherwise clean slate of political opening-up. In the 1980s liberalization was a limited affair, opening a political space for elite conflict and expression, bounded by the triad of nation, religion and monarchy.[26] In villages, newspapers and in relations with the bureaucracy and capitalists, ordinary Thais faced the brute rule of superior power and the strictures of national identity and culture propagated by state ideologues and the palace. The stage-managed role of the monarch, the compulsory respect shown to the institution, and the pressure of social conformity left many people with a taste of bitterness which few felt confident to express.[27] Such was democracy with the king as head of state.

Expectations of reduced policing of *lèse-majesté* in the near future are sanguine to say the least. Thai elites are well aware of how the free press has led to public mockery of the British monarchy, and they are fearful of what would happen were the Thai royal family open to scrutiny. The existence of the law does not suggest that royalty is despised and needs protection, although there are elements of this – but who dares speak with universal sanction and prison waiting? The laws have a more general application in that they point to the monarchy as central to the entire modern ideological complex; around the figure of a righteous king, democracy may be defined in a traditionalistic and disciplinary manner. The king also stands as a model of the citizen; his practices are seen as virtue-in-making. Through him the identity of Thainess can find expression as a moral self/nation beyond the marketplace, providing the people-body with a quasi-religious solidarity.[28]

In 1992 the National Identity Board (NIB) published the king's 1991 birthday speech, which touched on the question of democracy. One component of this speech was to chastise those who continued to protest the draft constitution being debated in parliament at the time (see Chapter 5). The National Identity Board believed the speech to give

> invaluable guidance . . . not only to economic and social progress of Thailand, but also to the development of democracy, especially the concept of 'Know How to Treasure Unity'. The Royal Speech is, without doubt, of great significance to the lives of all Thai people.[29]

In this rambling speech the king touches on the need for theories appropriate to Thai conditions.[30] He argues that the basis of the nation's survival has been that people know how to cherish unity:

> It is very difficult for all the people to be united because it is a near impossibility for a great number of them to really know each other. But 'to know how to treasure unity' is a possibility because it means that everybody knows that he is Thai; if anything happens everyone considers that he is a Thai; if anything happens, everyone knows that there must be unity.[31]

No disciple of Benedict Anderson, Bhumiphol nonetheless concurs on the importance of imagining nationhood. 'Knowing how to treasure Unity', as imagined
nationhood, according to the king, also means compromise even if the outcome for
oneself is not 'a hundred percent'. Furthermore, 'in the affairs of state it is important
that there is a clear directive power, over the people'. Speaking of the need for
representative government, he says:

> Everyone wants to express his opinion on how to do this and that thing . . . . Even
> when only ten persons speak at the same time, nobody can understand anything
> at all. And with 55 million persons, who perhaps don't even know what they are
> talking about, it is worse.[32]

Unity, Thainess, compromise and the gesturing towards a unifying authority, all
these discursive markers make the king an exponent of the general drift of developmental democracy, one whose underlying thematic is the people-problem – of
organizing the people towards productive ends.

Towards national ideology once more

Besides the military and the Local Administration Department, other elements in
the universities, security apparatuses and government ministries were part of an
attempt to re-ideologize Thai society after the trauma of 1973–6. Statists aimed to
formulate elements of past national ideology into a coherent democratic ideology
that could effectively respond to both the challenge of the popular movement and
the rise of money-politics and parliamentary democracy in the centre. As they
cautioned against communism and corruption, state agents deployed the motif of
developing a genuine liberal democracy, appropriate to Thailand, and positioned
themselves as guardians of the process. Unlike LAD, whose democratic ideology
was limited to disciplining its rural constituency while being increasingly truculent
towards the urban political classes, the intellectual forces gathered in committees
located in the Prime Minister's Office moved to elaborate a comprehensive and
historical ideology of 'democracy with the king as head of state', buffered by religious
undertones and moral selfhood. Out of this collaboration between civilian and
military ideologues came the ideology of 'democracy with the king as head of state'
in its fullest sense.[33]

   As with Order 66/1980, this development had its roots in the conflict with communism and the desperate need to re-hegemonize the social field, as well as restore
state influence in the cultural field. As Craig Reynolds notes, attempts to promote
culture and identity were rooted in the loss of prestige the state had suffered in
the preceding years, thus 'the concept of Thai identity, with its disarming ring of
transcendence and permanence, has a specific history and conditions of existence.'[34]

   Indeed, the history of Thainess was continuous and consistent in the sense
that Thai nationalism had begun as a modern enterprise well before the 1932

revolution. After the 1932 revolution, it was a constant theme of militaristic state propaganda, mixed with themes of Thai culture and race. Within these discourses, implicit notions of identity (*ekkalak*) lurked, and sometimes were overtly expressed.[35] Increasingly, since the 1930s, national ideology has been put to work as a beguiling force aiming to moralize the social field, and dehistoricize the social conditions of life. The hope was that a hegemonic effect of moral unity and a perceived community of fate could be created. It was to the production of this effect that state ideologues aspired in the 1970s. Responding to this task, the National Security Council (NSC), an inter-agency body within the Prime Minister's Office, composed of senior military figures, high-ranking public servants and university officials, met to consider options. Their aim was ideological planning and to find an appropriate institutional embodiment of this. A study of documents circulating within the NSC confirms that the National Identity Board (NIB), established in 1980, was the outcome of these deliberations on the need for ideological rearticulation after the experience of rising communist insurgency and political polarization.[36]

In 1976 an initial step was taken by setting up the Project to Promote Identity.[37] As one university text in cultural studies puts it, the Thanin regime knew that defeating communism was not simply a military matter, but involved ideological measures to 'create unity between the people in the nation . . . so that the people are of one heart'.[38] Towards this end a new magazine was published from within the Prime Minister's Office, called *Thai Identity*.[39] The editorial of the first issue, attacked the contaminating foreign influence in Thai culture. A call to arms was issued: '[W]e must help each other to promote the strength of Thai identity to be greater and secure.' The magazine declared its fear that Thai culture was being eroded, and compared its own work to that of a dam: '[D]eveloping the mind or culture is like building a dam, because our culture is being washed away.'[40] The dam metaphor is a fitting one; it provided the magazine with its brief of control and containment of those foreign stormwaters deemed inappropriate.

Concerns such as these were not the property of minor official magazines. In 1976 the NSC was circulating a document on the development of national ideology. That document defines national ideology as 'a system of thought that all people in the nation uphold in order to preserve and build the nation, and which each person aims to act towards together'.[41] The discussion paper notes that ideology is something that can be created, changed and inculcated. Furthermore, it creates morale to fight against obstacles and enemies in pursuit of its realization.[42] National ideology, the argument develops, should be broadened to encompass the dimensions of politics, economics and social psychology. The rationale for this was that existing ideology (nation, religion, king) is too distant from people (*hangklai tua koen pai*) and no longer 'stimulates' (*raojai*) the people.[43] Fearing the consequences of rapid social change and the subsequent instability, the NSC foresaw continuing threats to national security as long as the people were 'confused, anxious, and without a common standpoint'.[44] In this state, the people were seen as vulnerable targets to an 'opposition that has a rigid and stimulating ideology, which will hegemonize [*krongnam lae nam khwamkhithen*] the thinking of the people, before our side'.[45]

In order to develop national ideology, the NSC argues that negative Thai values need to be eradicated and positive Thai values nurtured. These values included: love of freedom; loyalty towards the monarchy; respect of religion; dislike of violence; assimilation; coordination of interests; elevation of money, power and knowledge, seniority, generosity, forgiving, fun and risk-taking; belief in the supernatural; doing whatever one pleases; upholding of tradition and custom; a Buddhist contentedness; and an attitude supportive of non-interference in other people's affairs.[46]

Furthermore, any ideology to be effective should address people's needs. Arguing that 'Thai society does not have clear class divisions'[47] the NSC states that such needs are to based on occupational differentiation. The groups discussed are farmers, merchants, entrepreneurs and bankers, workers, civil servants including the police and the military, and finally students.

What follows is a calculating picture of the conditions and aspirations of major socio-groupings in Thailand, and how these conditions are to be tied to the construction of an ideology enunciated by the watchful security state. Let this be clear: ideology was to be constructed as a response to protests and dissent that had been monitored by the security state. Consider how the NSC sought to make 'ideology' responsive to the needs of various occupational groups. Having studied protests, the NSC groups the grievances and needs of farmers, who are said to make up 80% per cent of the population, into three categories: land and wellbeing, fair prices, and exploitation by capitalists.[48]

Farmers are said to have the following needs and interests:

Economic dimension

- a reasonable income
- a fair price for produce
- to possess their own land
- adjust methods of production to be more efficient
- cheaper basic consumer goods
- do not want exploitative capitalists, merchants or intermediaries

Social dimension

- safety in life and property
- better and equal social welfare from the state such as public health, public infrastructure and education
- uphold religion and the monarchy
- dislike violent and rapid social change

Political dimension

- do not wish to be involved in politics
- they need officials to appropriately give justice and care
- they need a political system which protects their economic and social interests and which preserves religious and monarchical institutions.[49]

Similar mappings are made of the remaining social groups. As with farmers, the demands of workers, gleaned from over 973 protests, are categorized. The NSC notes that workers, 6 per cent of the population, have developed into groups and are conscious of their own interests. Workers' needs and interests are listed as: fair wages and a reduction in wealth disparities between workers and employees; socially, welfare from employers, good working conditions, good relations with management and an ability to express their opinion, equal access to social welfare opportunity and equality, and the need to be accepted as an important class. Politically, workers are seen as wanting to play a role in protecting their own interests, and, more generally, as wanting a political voice.[50]

As for capitalists (merchants/bankers/businesspeople), 9 per cent of the population, it is noted that they pursue their economic interests, and require security and a stable political system to safeguard their interests. The civil service, comprising 5 per cent of the population, is treated as having its own specific interests:

> This interest group ... has power and an important role in leading and building society because the civil service is important in doing the work of the state and it is well educated. Its needs and interests are summarized as follows: an income appropriate to status, it seeks honor and support from society, and prefers gradual change.[51]

Politically, civil servants are said to need a government that follows 'the democratic line'.[52] Finally, students are described as wanting to be the leaders in the struggle for economic and social equality. Furthermore they seek rapid change.

Although unstated, these readings of occupational groupings are informed not just by spying on demonstrations and recording grievances, but also by a typology of political culture. From descriptions of farmers purportedly with little interest in politics who seek comfort under the wings of a benevolent state, to politically conscious students, the research of political scientists on political culture was producing a comprehensive picture of the people-body so that it could be managed. This NSC document served as the basis for discussions on the formation of a national ideology that could creatively respond to social group needs, but which could also unite these groups around a common national interest by expanding the existing contours of national ideology expressed in the triad. The conundrum was how to do this; with remarkable self-consciousness, state ideologists went to work on the problem.

By 1979 the NSC and Cabinet had accepted as a basic statement of national ideology a document submitted by the screening committee of the NSC, written by Professors Kramol Thongthammachart and Sippamon Ketutat. This document follows closely the argument made in 1976 on the need to develop relevant national ideology which could be a reference point for action and common unity. The authors acknowledge that ideology can emerge 'naturally' by letting social institutions and forces influence members of society. However, they argue a case for setting down supervised measures for socio-political institutions to convey effectively, and in unity, ideology.[53] The experience of modern political ideologies such as fascism and communism are cited as demonstrating the need to have unity, comprehensiveness and organizational capacity in order to successfully convey ideology.[54]

The authors note that the NSC, in coordination with government agencies, had elaborated national ideology as follows:

> Preserve the nation, defend independence and democracy, protect religion, treasure and preserve the monarchy, eliminate socio-economic disparities, eliminate suffering and nourish wellbeing, assimilate interests, maintain rights and freedoms, create unity and integrity, uphold the identity of and promote the decent culture of the Thai people.[55]

The authors then note that the above ideology can be divided into two levels: national political ideology, and a practical approach to its realization. Political ideology is described as an approach to the political aspirations of the Thai people, which has the compelling power to defeat ideological currents that 'do not correspond with the identity and disposition of the Thai people.'[56] Such a political ideology is described as:

> Protection and preservation of the nation, symbolized by the monarchy, religion and Thai culture . . . a political, economic and social democracy that affirms the important principle that the interests of the community comes before any other, and the cooperation of all groups.[57]

Addressing how this ideology might be realized meant using the methods of democracy, 'consisting of rights and freedoms under the law which protects the interests of the majority', to address social inequalities on the basis of 'the cooperation of all classes that make up society.'[58]

The authors go on to argue the need to address the concrete grievances of the people and for national ideology to reflect such concerns.[59] In closing, recommendations are presented for the successful propagation of national ideology. These include setting up an organization of language and psychological experts who could simplify ideology into slogans, controlling the media to ensure it does not go against the principles of neutrality and service to the people, nurturing ideologues to convey national ideology in all occupations, and the setting-up of a consultative committee to propose measures on the promotion of national ideology.[60] Many of these recommendations were acted upon. Of particular note were follow-up workshops for radio broadcasters so that they could be effective communicators of ideology. In one such workshop the importance of national ideology was explained:

> Ideology is an instrument of the national leaders, or a doctrine, to use with the masses in order to produce change in the required direction. National ideology should come from the national leaders so that it can be accepted in general.[61]

These vigorous recommendations gestured to the past, when more strenuous effort was given to cultural and ideological propagation. Since the Sarit era, Yukthi Mukdawijit observes, such efforts had become lax and lacked organizational backup.[62] The NSC was effectively recommending a return to more conscious and creative cultural propagation. It was time, some apparently thought, to move beyond the monotonous replaying of nationalist and royalist songs on the radio. Indeed, there was a feeling that the people remained untouched by official ideology, with one NIB notable suggesting that the real ideological triad in Thailand was the 'ideology of three Ss', *saduak, sabai* and *sanuk* (convenience, comfort and fun).[63] The two documents discussed so far are fairly directive, and the intellectual framework behind them, while apparent, is not expounded.

Important in the formation of post-1976 national ideology is the political thought of Kramol Thongthammachart. Reputedly associated with the Praphat and Thanom regime in the late 1960s and early 1970s, Kramol is a leading intellectual of modern statist democracy. His influence was consolidated in the 1980s when he became Minister attached to the Prime Minister's Office under Prem. In this position he was able to influence the ideological work of the regime through the National Identity Board, sitting as an executive member. In an article that sets out the major themes for the 1980s, Kramol reveals his modernist development outlook and reveals the underlying frame to statist democratic thought. Kramol, an ideologue, saw his task in terms of conscious ideological production directed towards people having ideology on the 'tip of the tongue'.

Working with a notion of ideology as the basis for a normative integration of national society,[64] Kramol argues for a governing party to support 'national ideology' and to harness social and political institutions towards ideological ends. Citing as examples Indonesia, Burma and Malaysia, Kramol argues that in conflicted societies it is necessary to meld different ideological strands into a national ideology.[65] However, it is to the experience of China that Kramol looks: 'China was able to use communism as an instrument in leading and mobilizing the people to work for society'.[66] The conditions for this success lay in the fact that the Chinese Communist Party was a mass party with members who persuaded the people to learn and act in accordance with the ideology. More generally, Kramol lays down six conditions for the effective functioning of a national ideology:

1 It must be a system of thought supported by the main social institutions, or which can be moulded into social philosophy.
2 It must be a system of thought that can explain the good things that society should preserve and the bad things that should be eliminated for the purpose of social justice and the common good.
3 It must be based on reason and science that is empirically provable.

4 It must be a system of thought that can point to the methods which people should uphold in order to lead society to an excellent condition.

5 It must be a system of thought which the leader practises continuously and which has good results for society, including being able to resist other ideologies.

6 It must be a system of thought which corresponds with the consciousness and needs of the majority.[67]

Kramol goes on to argue that should a national ideology be successfully established the people would be united. This would help the people perceive their relationship to each other, a necessary process in the creation of common objectives. Such a state of normative integration would inspire action towards a more just society, as well as help members of society to see through the existing societal decadence.[68] An ideologically motivated people could help a sluggish society develop, lead to rationally justified behaviour, and would assist the process of peaceful change.[69] While Kramol follows the general argument that the triad has had a role in uniting the people, he expresses some disquiet because 'the weak point of this ideology is its emphasis on only three institutions of Thai society'. He thus seeks to expand the ideological compass. For him, the problem was not simply that existing ideological propagation was unclear, it also failed to specify how solidarity with the three pillars could be expressed.[70] Also, Kramol argues that the triad provides no incentive in terms of guaranteeing a better life, thus it is necessary

> to expand the three pillars to have wide scope and to encompass approaches and methods to solve various problems of Thai society, even so far that the way of life can be thought of as expressing loyalty to the Nation, Religion and the Monarchy.

This is an important statement, for it provides a link between the three pillars and the ordinariness of everyday life and problems.

Rejecting currents in academia for a form of liberal socialism (seen as being unacceptable to Thai conservatives), Kramol sought to develop an ideology 'that fits with the consciousness of the majority of Thais'.[71] Extrapolating from the findings of an ISOC security-related research project, Kramol reports the people's needs as fivefold:

- Treasure and preserve the nation, religion, the monarchy and the identity of Thainess.
- Develop and build political institutions for a secure democracy.
- Adjust the economic system towards a mixed economy which is just, efficient, and lets the people have a good life, and security of property and life.
- Elevate society and culture of the country so that the people have a simple life, are thrifty, diligent and have a high level of responsibility to society.
- Adjust the administration of the country so that it is a democracy that is clean, pure, just and truly serves the people.[72]

In an attempt to simplify this fivefold schema, Kramol argues for the first point to be known as the 'ideology of the tri-allegiance' (*udomkan trai pak*) and the remaining four points to be named 'the ideology of the four paths' (*udomkan jatumrak*). The four paths were ways of ensuring the maintenance of the three pillars.[73]

What is significant about Kramol's article is the manner in which ideology is seen to be a matter of eloquently composing a formula that connects the lives and wellbeing of the people to the three pillars – such that the conduct of those lives is seen as contributing to the security of the triad, and the security of the triad contributes to the wellbeing of the people. This ideological reformation of people's needs into state ideology would be a constant and aggrandizing practice of the state that took shape in a number of organizations including the NIB.[74]

In 1978 General Kriengsak Chomanand, then Prime Minister, established a secret Committee to Promote National Security to respond to attacks on the 'highest institutions' of the land. This committee later took public shape as the Committee to Promote National Identity before being established as a formal office in 1980 when the many currents of thought among statist intellectuals had coalesced into a practical outcome, the establishment of the National Identity Board. The NIB was charged with considering policy, planning and the promotion of national identity, and the promotion of 'knowledge and correct understanding of national institutions'.[75]

Following its establishment, discussion continued on the question of what constituted national identity and ideology. Following Kramol, others argued the case for social justice, income distribution, economic reform and the need to address the shortfalls of the free market.[76]

Towards national identity: to be a democratic Thai

In 1983, recognizing that the notion of Thai identity had not yet commanded public attention, the NIB hosted a conference, bringing together a broad cross-section of society. The aim was straightforward: to have the NIB definition of national identity accepted and propagated.

In its preparatory documents the NIB defines national identity as 'land, people, independence and sovereignty, government and administration, religion, monarchy, culture and dignity (pride)'.[77] Furthermore, the issue of national identity was to be linked to the development of the country.[78] Clearly these characteristics refer to the people-body within the geo-body, rather than any individual person. Identity, here, is a projection of the nation as a subject. There is a constant slippage between identity of the nation (as a list of characteristics) and identity of the people (as a list of subjective orientations to the nation). This slippage was a mechanism by which interior/exterior identity could be melded together as national identity: a linking of subjective orientations to the objective and moral existence of the nation, an interiorization of the exterior. Nation as self. Here we are speaking of a process of democrasubjection in which governmental technology works on the subjective orientations of citizens such that they sustain the political imaginary of Thainess, hegemonically present as democracy with the king as head of state.

An underlying theme of the conference was an affirmation, but also a recognition, of the need to go beyond the association of Thai identity with Prince Damrong's formula of 'love of national independence, toleration and power of assimilation.'[79]

The outcome of the conference was ultimately the adoption by the Prem government of both a policy statement and plans for ideological and identity development.[80]

In this policy document, the meaning of national identity is finally sealed as the unique characteristics of the nation: 'the people, territory, sovereignty and independence, government and administration, religion, monarchy, culture and pride'. It is also made clear that the most important institutions for national security and development were religion and the monarchy.[81] National identity, and its promotion, was without any doubt, then, about the security of the highest institutions in the land, 'the Nation, Religion, Monarchy and democracy with the king as head of state'.[82] In its policy statement the NIB proposed four operational objectives:

1 Promote the understanding of the people, both in and out of the country, towards the Thai monarchy, especially an understanding of royal graciousness and sacrifice, which are good role models.

2 Promote religion and unity to raise the integrity and virtue of society and develop the minds of the people.

3 Promote the nation by promoting and inculcating virtuous characteristics, promoting graceful characteristics and eliminating ones that obstruct national development.

4 Propagate the value of the democratic system with the king as head of state as well as promote ideology and values that support this system of government.[83]

The various activities that would emerge from the adoption of this policy included propagation of Thainess through the mass media, publications exhorting the beauty of Thainess and exploring the minutiae of Thainess (from the preparation of food to agricultural cultivation, architecture and beliefs). Through these efforts the diversity of people's lives were encompassed in the definition of Thainess.

In 1984 two major publications appeared which set out to strengthen and consolidate the meaning of 'democracy with the king as head of state'. The first was directly attributed to the NIB, *Knowledge about Democracy for the People*.[84] In this book the NIB offers an extended discussion of democracy aimed at the people in general. This publication presents an authoritative view of democracy in the Thai context and may be considered, in some respects, the outcome of the long ideological journey from 1976. It is, in short, an attempt to define democracy in terms integral to Thainess. Significantly, too, it works towards limiting the rhetorical excesses of previous official statements of democracy which stressed the 'people's will'. Instead, it presents an extended definition of representative democracy clearly aimed at justifying the limitation of people's participation and their impact on government. In effect, it seeks to temper the civic idealism (delayed) of LAD with more limited notions of people's participation.

The central component of the Thai character, espoused in the book, is derived from the Damrong formula, including compromise, tolerance and love of freedom. Indeed, 'such things are in the hearts of every Thai'.[85] Nevertheless, it is reported that the subcommittee on national ideology in the NIB notes that there are still aspects of the Thai character that need moulding in a democratic direction, thus the book aims at educating the public about democracy with the king as head of state.[86] A standard liberal definition of democracy is offered in line with those discussed above. Also appearing is the myth that Prachatipok graciously bestowed democracy in 1932. Indeed, an evolution of the rights of the people from the reign of Chulalongkorn is presented. Since 1932 it is stated that all constitutions have been democratic as they have defined people's rights and duties.[87] The book is quite similar to the pre-1960s manuals, and thus hints at the recovery of legalistic liberal democracy with a royal tint. People's duties include extensive loyalties to the state: '[I]f there is a hint of communist activities, people have the duty to inform officials so they [communists] can be caught'.[88] Most of the book is taken up with an explanation of the duties of the people's representatives and officials.[89]

The most interesting section of this book is the discussion relating to the 'will of the people'. The book attempts to present a more realistic and elitist position:

> The people are not the government; taking the opinion of the people as an instrument to define policy is just the same as letting the people be the government, which is likely to lead to a political crisis.[90]

There is, then, a need to separate people from government, and this is done by providing mechanisms for the people's interests to be heard. Although elections are seen as a major mechanism for people's involvement, it is pointed out they are not about defining policy but about electing representatives. Besides, it is noted, that since not all people vote, elections cannot define the true will of the people.[91]

The second text, issued by the Prime Minister's Office, reproduced transcripts from the nationally aired programme *Let's Think Together... Whose Duty is Building Democracy?*[92] In radio broadcasts aired between February and June 1984, a series of discussions on democratic responsibility, discipline and citizen virtues was presented by the secretariat of the Prime Minister's Office. The tone of the discussion left no doubt that the announcers were addressing the rural population, some of whom had migrated to the city. For instance, in one discussion it is noted that Thais lack discipline, and while this was fine in a rural setting, in urban settings it led to the running of red lights and lane-hopping.[93] In effect, the programmes were not so much about defining democracy, although there was plenty of that, but a defining of the projects required for moral improvement of the people. Democracy was therefore related more to self-discipline than political structures. Regarding the need to follow the law, which is issued by the people's representatives, it is noted that 'democracy is an issue of controlling oneself, of governing oneself, for sometimes we can be negligent.'[94] Such self-government extended not simply to following the law but to interiorizing feelings of guilt if one does wrong.[95] That this psychological state had not yet been attained, evidenced by vote-buying and selling, was implicit in the whole discourse of development democracy. It was also, on occasion, explicitly expressed: 'We are probably not yet ready for full democracy ... which means that the people know completely what their interests are and are able to select representatives to be their voice in the government.'[96]

With the rise of money-democracy from the 1980s onwards, the position of the NIB towards democratic thought and development remained the same. Several publications after the crisis of 1991–2, however, intimate a certain disquiet towards democratic development. Rather than present a common stand, the NIB authorized several seminars at which a variety of opinions on democratic development were expressed. Great concern over the state of democracy was expressed, involving detailed critiques of the rise of vote-buying and selling and the failure of state officials to remain neutral. Other issues included the need for a political development plan, the need for a neutral body to watch over elections, and the need for new values. Clearly, a rethinking of democracy was under way, pointing in the direction that would later be taken up by the political reform movement (see next chapter).[97]

The hegemonic work of the NIB

In 1987 the king celebrated his sixtieth birthday. A documentary illustrating the king's practice of the ten virtues was broadcast. The text of this documentary was widely published in 1990 by the NIB, with a preface by the Democracy Subcommittee of the NIB. The book effectively presents a picture of the king as a semi-god, one who has earned enough merit to reach nirvana, but who stays on earth to rule justly over the people. The ten virtues are dealt with chapter by chapter, furnishing concrete examples of the king's conformity to them. Accompanying each chapter is a picture of the actual king as well as an illustration of a semi-god.

Of interest is the telling way in which the king's virtue of non-anger is illustrated. The chapter dealing with this virtue explains that on several occasions when the king went overseas he faced protests. Regarding his Australian trip in 1962, when he faced a number of protests, the book recounts his calm composure 'as if nothing was happening'. A description is given of 'unruly' students at the University of Melbourne opposing his being granted an honorary degree. They are described as impolite in manner and dress, and insistent in their catcalling. The king finally addresses them thus: 'Thank you all very much for giving such a warm and polite welcome to a guest to your city.'[98] The accompanying illustration to this virtue of non-anger is a semi-god calming hostile earthly creatures, animals and humans, with the aura of his sheer goodness. It is made clear that the protests were the work of those who had bad intentions towards Thailand, as if to deflect the idea that the king himself was the target of beastly protest. By using foreign protesters to illustrate the virtue of non-anger, the postulated unity of the king and the Thai nation was not threatened metaphorically. Since Bhumiphol symbolizes the Thais, he may not be transgressed, for that would be a transgression against all Thais. The hegemonic message here was 'we are all one', all tied to the destiny of the 'geo-body' of Thailand. To suggest that a Thai might oppose the king was to suggest someone would slit their own throat.

This intimate relationship between self-identity and the king, as embodiment of the nation, has been central to the attempt to procure forms of behaviour in accordance with order. The constructed moral source of authority resident in the king has been used on countless occasions to restore order. Ideological propagation linked to the construction of Thai identity was the defining characteristic of the NIB throughout the 1980s and 1990s. It sought not only to procure among people an identification of their own interests with the three pillars, but also to define what it was to be Thai. The cultural propagation of this aspect of NIB in its programmes and magazines on Thai culture, art and literature were components of this project. However, as a strategy of democrasubjection it aimed at a total encompassment of Thainess, as self-recognition, within the confines of a legalistic democratic regime, buttressed by what we might call a 'three pillars' civic culture. In this strategy of producing the Thai citizen, democracy was to play a key role, forming a link between identity and ideology: democracy was the political form under which identity would be enhanced, preserved and advanced by the self-governance of rational citizens in the frame of the three pillars. The attempted democrasubjection by NIB consisted in the deployment of the reified technology of tradition (the three pillars) as a means to interpellate 'citizens'. Identity, as construct, was to produce an orientation of loyalty and unity towards what were external manifestations of the Thai self. This deployment also worked conversely, for the identity was to be interiorized and thus it was necessary to make the three pillars hold a lively relevance that could answer to the needs of the citizens it sought to construct.

It was under the 'specific history and conditions of existence' of the post-1976 period that state actors collaborated to revive national ideology by a melding of Thai identity, the triad of nation, religion and monarchy, and adding democracy. While what resulted might appear as a cacophony of identity claims and reckless conflation of ideology/identity, state actors succeeded in constructing an elastic complex of Thai ideology/identity. This complex was attentive to both the strains inherent in developmental needs relating to change, and to the hegemonic needs for stabilizing the social field around Thainess.

National ideology and the part played by democracy were strategic responses to immediate crisis of hegemony as well as the ongoing challenge to elites of the 'people-problem', the human resources contained within the geo-body of Thailand.

In propagating identity as historically, culturally and morally Thai, the strategic aim was to cover over the dangers of non-identification at a subjective level with the symbolic institutions of elite control, the three pillars. Substantiated by extending that identity to encompass ideological objectives of development with social justice and democracy, overcoming the 'people-problem' could be envisioned as a cooperative enterprise of elite subjects and subaltern objects towards a common destiny: the essential objective of Thai ideology being to unite people in a sentiment of common fate, or, in Gramscian terms, a national imaginary. Democrasubjection as a project, in this respect, worked to interiorize the people-problem as a problem of self-morality and development, as Thainess to be something cultivated and aimed towards. This was the meeting ground of hegemony and governance, fully expressed.

In many ways the constructors of national ideology took an ironic stance on the people-problem. The people were the source of sovereignty, but they were not yet able to divest it to legitimate representatives. The people were sovereign and yet this was an imagined state, needing state development and cajolement. The people were sovereign and yet rule should be according to enlightened elites. The people were Thai, but expressions of Thainess was to be cultivated, policed and socialized. The contradiction of requiring ideology to realize identity, when ideology was supposedly an expression of that identity, reflects more generally the contradiction at the heart of the doctrine of political development, a contradiction relating to the baseless claims of popular sovereignty in the absence of a sovereign people (see Chapter 2).

The whole schema of national ideology makes sense not simply as an attempt at normative integration, but as an instance of what might be called meta-ideological insincerity, that is, the giving and propagandizing as essential and ideal that which is to be hegemonically produced. This ironizing stance towards the objects of statist discourse was effectively an addressing of the question of nation building as identity building. If one thinks back to the taxonomy of the people's protests produced by statist apparatuses in the late 1970s, it is possible to see this stance in operation; in attending demonstrations, noting demands, spying and doing the work of security, state actors sought to construct national ideology on the backs of people's protests.

The experience of the NIB and its colleagues in the NSC demonstrates dramatically the self-reflexive manner in which the hegemonic project was mapped by the state. Aggrandizing to itself the capacity of constructing Thai citizenship, it did so through a political development perspective aiming at interpellating the Thai subject by giving it form, objective and ideology, or, in short, Thainess. A key resource for the achievement of this project was the monarchy.

Notes

1 *The Nation*, 5/12/76, p. 9.

2 Somphop Chanthonprapha, 'Phramahakasat thai songtham', in Krom prachasamphan lae samnakngan soemsang ekkalak khong chat [Public relations department and national identity board)], *Naeothang prachathipatai* (The democratic line), 1981, pp. 31–3.

3 Sombat Chantornvong, 'To Address the Dust of the Dust Under the Soles of the Royal Feet: A Reflection on the Political Dimension of Thai Court Language', in *Asian Review*, 6, 1992, pp. 144–63, p. 146.

4 *Ibid.*, pp. 154–5.

5 Several informants have mentioned this perception to me. One only needs to note that after 1976 the CPT attacks on the monarchy grew – confident that there was a popular resentment of the monarchy that could be mobilized.

6 See King Bhumibol Adulyadej, 'Royal Advice Given by His Majesty the King At the Chitralada Villa, Dusit Palace, Wednesday, May 20, 1992, at 21.20', in *Royal Remarks on Various Occasions*, 1992, p. 9.

7 Such 'facts' come from various informants.

8 The royal family is one of Thailand's largest land-owning families, and through the Crown Property Bureau as well as private activities, pursues various capitalist industrial and banking enterprises.

9 Thirayut Bunmi, 'Thangsong phrae khong prachathipatai nai thatsana sangkhom withaya kanmeuang (Thai Democracy at the Crossroads: A Politico-sociological Perspective)', *Warasan sangkhomsat (Journal of Social Science)*, 24, 1, 1987, pp. 6–24, pp. 16–17.

10 See Kevin Hewison, 'The Monarchy and Democratization', in K.Hewison (ed.) *Political Change in Thailand: Democracy and Participation*, London: Routledge, 1997, pp. 63–73, pp. 58–74.

11 Cited in Kanok Wongtrankan, *Naeo phrarachadamri dan kanmeuang khong prabatsomdet phra jao yu hua* (Royal edicts on politics and government of the king), Bangkok: Sathaban thai suksa, julalonkon mahawithayalai, 1988, cited pp. 190–1 (the statement is from 1972).

12 *Ibid.*, p. 191 (1973).

13 *Ibid.*, p. 192(1981).

14 *Ibid.*, p. 194 (1979).

15 *Ibid.*

16 *Ibid.*, pp. 194–5 (1979).

17 Chairat Charoensin-O-Larn, *Understanding Post War Reformism in Thailand*, Bangkok: Editions Duangkamol, 1988, p. 155.

18 David Streckfuss, 'Kings in the Age of Nations: The Paradox of Lese-Majeste as Political Crime in Thailand', in D. Streckfuss (ed.) *The Modern Thai Monarchy and Cultural Politics: The Acquittal of Sulak Sivaraksa on the Charge of Lese Majeste in Siam 1995 and its Consequences*, Bangkok: Santi-Pracha Dhamma Institute, 1996, pp. 54–80.

19 *Ibid.*, p. 76.

20 *The Nation*, 13/11/76, p. 1.

21 *The Nation*, 30/12/83, p. 6.

22 *Bangkok Post*, 23/6/88, p. 1. This was a reduced sentence, on appeal, from the six-year sentence given in October 1987. In any case, several months later he was pardoned by the king. A good discussion of this case may be found in D. Streckfuss (ed.) *The Modern Thai Monarchy and Cultural Politics*, pp. 56–8.

23 D. Streckfuss (ed.) *The Modern Thai Monarchy and Cultural Politics*, 1996.

24 See Annette Hamilton, 'Rumours, Foul Calumnies and the Safety of the State: Mass Media and National Identity in Thailand', in C. Reynolds (ed.) *National Identity and Its Defenders*, pp. 341–78, pp. 355–62.

25 *The Nation*, 4/8/84, pp. 1, 2. Taksin, a hero credited with a restoration of the kingdom after an episode of Burmese sacking, became king, but was overthrown by the first king of the Chakri dynasty.

26 On struggles for liberalization of the religious sphere and the state-managed suppression of this see Jim Taylor, 'Buddhist Revitalization, Modernization and Social Change in Contemporary Thailand', *Sojourn*, 8, 1, 1993, pp. 62–91.

27 It is only through off-the-record information that I can make this statement.

28 As Chai-Anan argues, in the face of rapid industrialization and capitalist consumerism, it is the monarchy and religion which hold out hope, for him, as centres of morality and public good. Chai-Anan Samudavanija, 'State-Identity Creation, State-Building and Civil Society 1939–1989', in C. Reynolds (ed.) *National Identity and Its Defenders*, pp. 59–85, p. 80.

29 King Bhumiphol Adulyadej, 'Royal Speech Given to the Audience of Well-Wishers on the Occasion of the Royal Birthday Anniversary, Wed, 4 December 1991', in *Royal Addresses on Various Occasions*, 1991, Bangkok: n.p., p. 52.

30 *Ibid.*, p. 6.

31 *Ibid.*, p. 12.

32 *Ibid.*, p. 36.

33 For an account of how this ideology is presented at schools one may usefully consult the analysis presented in Niels Mulder, *Inside Thai Society: Interpretations of Everyday Life*, Amsterdam: Pepin Press, 1996, pp. 151–64.

34 Craig Reynolds, 'Introduction: National Identity and Its Defenders', in C. Reynolds (ed.) *National Identity and Its Defenders*, pp. 1–39, p. 14. While the term 'identity' had been coined decades earlier, it gained wider currency after an academic seminar in 1971, even making it into the National Education Plan in 1977. On this see Ekkawit na Thalang, 'Ekkalak thai thi mi phon to khwam mankhong haeng chat' [Thai identity and its impact on national security], in Khana anukammakan udomkan khong chat nai khanakammakan ekkalak khong chat lae samnakngan soemsang ekkalak khong chat samnakngan naiyokratthamontri, *Raignan kansamamana reuang ekkalak khong chat kap kanphathana chat thai* [Seminar report on national identity and Thai national development], 1985, pp. 120–32, p. 120.

35 See B.J. Terwiel, 'Thai Nationalism and Identity: Popular Themes of the 1930s', in C. Reynolds (ed.) *National Identity and Its Defenders: Thailand, 1939–1989*, Chiang Mai: Silkworm Books, 1993, pp. 135–55. Interestingly Praphat Trinarong notes the use of the word 'identity', in an announcement on 3 November 1939 by Phibun regarding patriotism. See Praphat Trinarong, 'Ekkalak thai' [Thai Identity], in Khana anukammakan udomkan khong chat *Raignan kansamamana reuang ekkalak khong chat kap kanphathana chat thai*, 1985, pp. 135–40, p. 136.

36 The National Security Council, established in 1959, is a high-level advisory body to Cabinet comprised of the Prime Minister acting as President, and with various ministers and high-ranking ministry officials sitting as Council members. See *Phrarachabanyat supha khwammankhong* [National security act], 1959, rev. 1964. A speech by the NSC Secretary General in 1968 provides a good overview of its function. Phan Ek Phraya Sriwisanwacha,

'Kham banyai reuang supha khwammankhong haengchat pheu hai khaojai thung amnat nathi lae khwam rapphitchop, 2511' [An address on the national security council: towards an understanding of its power, duties and responsibilities, 1968], in Son Bangyikha, *Pratya waduay khwammankhong* [The philosophy of national security], Bangkok: Mahawithayalai ramkhamhaeng, 1981, pp. 264–71, p. 267.

37 Mahawitthayalai Sukhothaithammathirat University, *Prasopkan Watthanatham suksa* [Cultural studies experience], 1990, p. 365.

38 *Ibid.*, p. 2 .

39 Craig Reynolds, 'Introduction: National Identity and Its Defenders', p. 13.

40 Cited in Praphat Trinarong, 'Ekkalak thai' [Thai identity], p. 136.

41 Supha khwam mankhong haeng chat, 'Patjai kamnot udomkam khong chat' [Determining factors of national ideology], in Khana anukammakan udomkan khong chat nai khanakammakan soemsang ekkalak khong chat, samnakgnan naiyokrathamontri, *Udomkan khong chat* [National ideology], 1983, pp. 17–26, p. 19.

42 *Ibid.*, p. 19.

43 *Ibid.*, p. 20.

44 *Ibid.*, pp. 20–1.

45 *Ibid.*, p. 21.

46 *Ibid.*, pp. 21–2.

47 *Ibid.*, p. 22.

48 *Ibid.*

49 *Ibid.*, p. 23.

50 *Ibid.*, pp. 23–4.

51 *Ibid.*, pp. 25–6.

52 *Ibid.*

53 Kramol Thongthammachart and Sippanon Ketutat, 'Udomkan khong chat naeokhwamkhit lae naeothang kandamnoenngan [National ideology, concepts and operationalization]', in *ibid.*, pp. 11–16, p. 11.

54 *Ibid.*, p. 12.

55 Cited in *ibid.*

56 *Ibid.*

57 *Ibid.*

58 *Ibid.*

59 *Ibid.*, p. 14.

60 *Ibid.*, pp. 15–16.

61 'Udomkan khong thai' [Thai ideology], Khana anukammakan udomkan khong chat samnakngan lekhathikan naiyokratthamontri [Subcommitte on national ideology, national identity board], *Raignan sammana nakjatkanwithayu reuang phoe phrae udomkan khong chat* [Seminar report on radio broadcasters and the propagation of national ideology], 1981, pp. 105–9, p. 105.

62 See Yukthi Mukdawijit, 'Kanmeuang reuang wathanatham nai sangkhom thai' [Cultural politics in Thai society], *Warasan thammasat* [Thammasat journal], 20, 3, 1994, pp. 20–41, p. 29.

63 Yenjai Laohawanit, 'Naeothang sangsan udomkan khong chat' [Ways to construct national ideology], in Khana anukammakan udomkan khong chat *Udomkan khong chat*, pp. 57–65, p. 61.

64 In this respect, Kramol explicitly follows Parsonian functionalism. See Kramol Thongthammachart, 'Udomkan khong chat lae kanpathana chat thai' [National ideology and Thai development], in Khana anukammakan udomkan khong chat *Udomkan khong chat*, pp. 21–42.

65 *Ibid.*, p. 32.

66 *Ibid.*, pp. 32–3.

67 *Ibid.*, p. 33.

68 *Ibid.*

69 *Ibid.*, pp. 33–4.

70 *Ibid.*, p. 4.

71 *Ibid.*, pp. 35–6.

72 *Ibid.*, p. 36.

73 *Ibid.*, pp. 39–40.

74 It was towards this end that Kramol supported the 'Land of Justice and Land of Gold Project', in the 1980s and 1990s. This project attempted to take ideology to the villages in the form of Buddhist virtue, self-reliance, thrift and a commitment to community and nation. On this, see Samnakngan lekhahathikan naiyokratthatmontri khanakammakan songsoem lae prasanngan kanpoei phrae udomkan phaendin tham phaendin thong [The prime minister's office, committee to promote and coordinate the propagation of the ideology of the land of justice and land of gold project], *Khamtop yu thi muban* [The answer is in the villages], 1987.

75 Mahawithiyalai Sukhothathammathirat, *Prasopkan wathanatham suksa* [Cultural Studies Experience], 1990, p. 365 (University, 1990).

76 See for example Nao Wa Akat Prasong Sunsiri, 'Naeo khwamkhit nai kan poeiphrae udomkan khong chat' [translation?], in Khana anukammakan udomkan khong chat *Udomkan khong chat* [National ideology], pp. 43–55, pp. 46–7, 54.

77 'Kantriam kansammana' [Seminar Preparation] in *ibid.*, pp. 1–5, pp. 1–2.

78 'Samphat piset ratthamontri prajam samnakngan naiyokratthamontri, nai kramol thongthamachat, prathan khana anukammakan chaprokit triamkan samamana lae no. to. prasong sunsiri lekhathikan supha khwammankhong haeng chat' [Special interview with Minister of the Prime Minister's Office, Mr Thongthammachart, President of the seminar organizing committee, and Prasong Sunsiri, Secretary General of the national security council], in Khanaanukammakan udomkan khong chat samnakngan lekhathikan naiyokratthamontri [Subcommittee on national ideology, National identity board], *Raignan sammana nakjatkanwithayu reuang phoe phrae udomkan khong chat* [Seminar report on radio broadcasters and the propagation of national ideology], 1981, pp. 16–23, p. 19.

79 'Phradamrat somdet phrajao phi nang theu jao fa kanlayaniwatthana phrarachathan kae ph kao ruam sammamna reuang ekkalak khong chat kap kanphathana chat thai' [Royal edict of Princess Kanlayaniwatthana, graciously conferred to the participants of the seminar on National identity and Thai national development), in *ibid.*, pp. 26–7.

80 'Sarupphon kansammana nayobai khong ratthaban nai soemsang ekkalak khong chat' [Seminar outcomes: government policy to promote national identity], in Khana anukammakan udomkan khong chat *Raignan kansamamana reuang ekkalak khong chat*, pp. 81–4. The policy was adopted on 26 July 1983 (p. 84).

81 *Ibid.*, p. 82.

82 *Ibid.*

83 *Ibid.*

84 Khanaanukammakan udomkan khong chat nai khanakammakan ekkalak khong chat, *Khwamrureuang prachathipatai pheu prachachon* [Knowledge about democracy for the people], 1984.

85 *Ibid.*, p. 4.

86 *Ibid.*, p. 5.

87 *Ibid.*, pp. 9–13.

88 *Ibid.*, pp. 18–19.

89 *Ibid.*, pp. 26–101.

90 *Ibid.*, p. 154.

91 *Ibid.*, p. 156.

92 Samnakngan lekhathikan naiyokratthamontri, *Chuay kan khit kansang prachathipatai pen nathi khong khrai?* [Let's think together . . . Whose duty is building democracy?], 1984.

93 Kosin Wongsurawat and Likhit Thirawekhin, 'Winai khong chaoban' [Discipline of the people], in *ibid.*, pp. 1–8, p. 2.

94 Kosin Wongsurawat and Wisut Phothithaen, 'Seriphap kap prachathipatai' [Freedom and democracy], in *ibid.*, 1984, pp. 58–65, p. 61.

95 *Ibid.*, p. 64.

96 Kosin Wongsurawat and Chaiya Yimwilai, 'Khanton khong prachathipatai [Stages of democracy], in *ibid.*, pp. 66–71, p. 69.

97 See for example Khanakhammakan ekkalak khong chat, *Raingan sammana reuang ja phathana prachathipatai yangrai hai mankhong* (Report on seminar on How can democracy be developed so it is secure?], 1993; Khanaanukhammakan kansongsoem phathana prachathipatai munithi phathana kharachakan lae khana kammakan ekkalak khong chat [Subcommittee to promote the development of democracy, Office to promote national identity, and Foundation for the development of the bureaucracy], *Nana thatsana peu soemsang phathanaprachathipatai* [Many viewpoints for the creative development of democracy], 1990.

98 Samnakngan soemsang ekkalak khong chat, *Thotsaphitrachatham* [The ten royal virtues], 1990, p. 42. Just for the record, the Australian National University, I am informed, declined to offer the degree.

7 New times, new constitution[1]

Between May 1992 and the promulgation of Thailand's sixteenth constitution in October 1997, a remarkable realignment of social forces occurred, enabling a liberal political agenda to emerge as a feasible project. In those years a broad and loose movement for political reform arose to address the impasse marked by perennial politicking within the errant political party system and the crushing corruption and unaccountability of sections of the bureaucracy and many politicians. Motivating this project was the seesawing nature of parliamentary politics. In a report on 'Stability, Efficiency and Accountability of Elected Governments between 1988–1997', Amon Raksasat and Wirat Jianbun note that in the preceding decade there had been twelve changes in the coalition composition of government. Most significantly, and pointing to the lack of continuous leadership, they report that there were over 235 individuals who had served in Cabinet, sharing 445 separate appointments. In important ministries such as Finance, Foreign Affairs and the Interior there had been ten, eleven and nine ministers respectively.[2] Given the imperative of implementing important legislative programmes to maintain the legal basis for a viable capitalism in the era of globalization, such instability worked against improving Thailand's international standing.[3] Reform was necessary. This chapter is an analysis of the movement for political reform. The following chapters take up an analysis of the ideological strands that lay behind the reform and democracy movements of the 1980s and 1990s, seeing these as new attempts to construct pliable subjects.

After May 1992 there was an expectation that a more liberal democratic political order would emerge. Indeed, in 1993 a parliamentary committee on constitutional amendments proposed far-reaching changes that would lead to greater transparency in government and greater avenues for political participation. Among the recommendations were liberal measures such as the establishment of an ombudsman's office, an administrative court, electoral reform, and new counter-corruption and decentralization measures.[4] But the recommendations were lost in the play of government/opposition politics; only minor amendments got through in late 1994. Significantly, the Interior Ministry waged a public campaign against decentralization, rightly seeing it as a threat to its empire.[5] The failure of the 1993–94 constitutional amendments was highly significant. It showed up a politically opportunist Senate safeguarding its own position with the support of the political opposition and, remarkably, the New Aspiration Party (NAP), a key coalition government member, led by Chavalit. Moreover, business groups were not an apparent force in the lengthy constitutional debates of 1993–94, demonstrating how quickly they had lapsed into inactivity after 1992.

Angered by the politicking that had reduced the constitutional package to a punching bag, Chalard Vorachart, a former Democrat MP, began a hunger strike in late May 1994. It was Vorachart's similar actions two years earlier that had inflamed popular interest in ousting Suchinda. Fearing a rerun of 1992, the political establishment panicked, and Parliamentary President Marut Bunnag formed the extra-parliamentary Democracy Development Committee (DDC) in June 1994 to consider proposals for democratic reform. Marut, a lawyer by training, was a long-time exponent of liberal democracy, and was supportive of the reform agenda proposed by the parliamentary committee.

Vorachart's hunger strike merely highlighted a widespread disquiet about the shape of post-May politics in academic circles and the press, but with the semi-democratic option closed and the seeming inability of parliament to introduce constitutional reform, few could grasp a solution. The setting up of the DDC highlighted a third option that had been uttered since 1991. This third option tapped into a longstanding desire for a reform of the parliamentary system among conservative bureaucrats and politically liberal intellectuals, who perceived that state legitimacy was being undermined by money-politics. The 1991 coup had provided an opportunity for reformist views to be aired. In this climate a growing consensus emerged among the elite that the prime minister need not be a politician. This hinted at a broader critique of what was seen as interference by the legislature in the affairs of the executive. The constitutional deliberations of 1991 provoked a wide discussion on the merits of executive and legislative separation among academics and commentators. Against this fertile background for political change, the Institute for Public Policy Studies (IPPS), a small liberal think-tank headed by the influential liberal-royalist Chai-Anan Samudavanija, began to gather around itself a growing band of bureaucrats and intellectuals for reform. In 1991 IPPS held a series of seminars looking at the failure of Thai politics, which were attended by reforming elements in the universities and bureaucracy. In December of that year IPPS launched the Study for the Reform of the Thai Constitution Project, led by Amon Chantharasombun, the former Secretary-General of the Council of State, a high-level legislative review body.[6] In June 1994 IPPS published Amon's work under the title *Constitutionalism: The Way Out for Thailand*.[7] It soon became a bestseller in academic bookshops. IPPS then launched a monthly newsletter, *Political Reform*, as a medium for sharing ideas and for reform advocacy.

Amon's book appeared when many had grown weary of parliament's failure to self-reform. Amon's basic argument epitomized that of a conservative, bureaucratic critique of parliamentary democracy. His main argument was that majority coalition governments could govern with few checks and balances, resulting in both a scramble for parliamentary seats and political parties 'becoming instruments of politicians in controlling the power of parliament and of the state.[8] The state itself had become over-politicized as politicians used democracy as an excuse to claim control over state organs.[9] Amon proposed 'constitutionalism' as a strategy to address Thailand's political instability. 'Constitutionalism', Amon explained, was the principle that had attended the writing of the American constitution, and involved working out an elaborate system of checks and balances against the arbitrary and centralized use of power.[10] It was also, he argued, the principle that informed the post-World War II rationalization of the parliamentary system, particularly in France and Germany.[11] As a major inspiration, Amon cited how De Gaulle had, by diminishing the role of parliament and by placing more power in presidential hands, addressed the weaknesses of government by multi-party coalitions.[12] While endorsing representative democracy as a method for ensuring political legitimacy and limited participation,[13] Amon saw the actual organization of the state as necessarily removed from the representative principle. This ensured the strict division of power, and buffered the state from the pressures of populism and mass emotionalism.[14] For Amon, the principal concern was not democracy as such but how to control the excessive power parliament had accrued. Political reform entailed, therefore, greater accountability, systems of checks and balances, and the separation of executive and legislative power. It was principally about bringing Thailand up to date by rationalizing the parliamentary system.[15]

Amon's recommendations were hardly original – indeed many had been spelt out in both legal and political journals.[16] However, Amon's book lucidly expressed the idea of legislative and executive separation, and combined this with liberal concerns of state accountability and transparency, at a time when significant social forces were grasping for solutions to the inefficient nature of the Thai state and the hidden deals lodged in its many entrails. In one sense procedural democracy, divorced from questions of citizenship and national identity, had arrived as a historical possibility in Amon's work. His emphasis on proceduralism effected a break with classic sovereign notions of an idealized citizens' democracy which had been part of official discourse in Thailand. It also revitalized legal constitutionalism, and thus provided a means by which elites could formulate solutions without the murkiness of 'democratic rhetoric' getting in the way. Political reform, for some, then, was framed as a technicist solution. In this revisionist liberal frame, democratic institutions were no longer about abstract citizenship nor about the metaphor of nation, but rather democracy was institutionally reduced to a rationalized parliament capable of addressing social conflicts. For Amon, there was no such thing as the 'people', this was an abstraction: in effect Amon was driving out of the picture the ubiquitous Lincolnian formula that had been wheeled in by military and civilian regimes alike.[17]

Despite the imaginative limits of Amon's book, it soon became central to political discourse. Media, activists and academics seized on Amon's key idea of excluding politicians from drafting a new constitution and on the need for the separation of powers. That Amon's turgid and legalistic work, and the effort of IPPS in popularizing it, was not in vain is evidenced by the fact that the setting up of the Democracy Development Committee (DDC) was said to have been influenced by Amon's writings.[18]

If the third option was to become a credible solution it required strategic leadership. With military and bureaucratic hegemony declining, and the post-May parliamentary regime lacking legitimacy as an honest articulator of the public interest, one might rightly speak of a crisis in the Thai state. While structural and political forces had effectively conquered the authoritarian state and ripped it asunder, in its place was a shadow play of political democracy underlined by the now exposed and emphatic lines of corruption. In the conditions of this political entropy the capitalist class did not surge forward to fill the leadership vacuum. While it would eventually come on board, the first public stirrings were within academia, the press and the NGOs. Kasian Tejapira, writing of the political reform movement, notes:

> Unexpectedly . . . hope has and could only come from the apolitical quarters outside the official circles of politics. It comes from a bunch of academics and journalists who began the public discourse on political reform, from a lone, quixotic crusader [Vorachart] who launched a hunger strike branded foolhardly and crazy . . . from a senior citizen-doctor [Prawet] whose good faith, moral stature, kindness and generosity is as overwhelmingly astonishing as his political innocence, from an ex-diplomat [Anand] who had twice suffered a great misfortune at the hands of the top executive power during times of crisis and yet still despises power politics in the same manner that a white swan refuses to mingle in the same pond with a flock of black geese.[19]

Senior doctors and white swans

Bringing together a range of politicians, democracy activists, legal and political experts and military figures under the leadership of Dr Prawet Wasi, the DDC proposed a blueprint for political reform influenced by Amon. Amon's dry text and background were hardly the stuff of inspiring political mobilization – *onwards to parliamentary rationalization!* – but under the leadership of Prawet, Amon's realist and formal notions of democracy could be given a different hue. Indeed, Prawet's leadership is important in accounting for the way in which political reform could unite different social forces in Thailand. This unity was achieved by packaging political reform as both a conservative measure to enhance government stability and as an expansion of opportunities for political participation. This successful amalgam allowed support for political reform to be orchestrated from all sides. Public intellectuals like Prawet were able to articulate the need for political reform in terms that encompassed the concerns of both the bureaucrat, the people sector and of big metropolitan capital. A pivotal figure in Thai public discourse in the last decade, Prawet has a respectable background in supporting public health initiatives and the promotion of Thai wisdom. His own personal style and sympathetic media coverage have combined to promote an image of a man with great personal integrity. His activities have brought him into contact with most sectors of society. He is often seen opening civil service, NGO and academic seminars. His opening remarks are always simple and idealistic, expressing simultaneously a great fear for the Thai people, but also a great hope for change. His ubiquity is attributable to the fact that he incarnates a kind of naive idealism that speaks of political, social, economic and spiritual change for the better without too nastily apportioning blame. Furthermore, he speaks, in the same breath, both the language of national ideology (nation, religion, king), and the language of empowerment (community and rights).[20] This syncretism reflects in part the continuing effort by the aristocratic establishment and its supporters (to which Prawet is ideologically wed) to place itself at the moral centre of national development problems: to be, as it is often said, the soul of the nation.[21] This syncretism makes intelligible Prawet's importance, as he is situated halfway between the established aristocratic and bureaucratic critique of unfettered capitalist greed and the recovery of Thai ways, and the emergent NGO critique of capitalist developmentalism.

The DDC's report, *A Proposed Framework for Political Reform in Thailand*, passed to the Parliamentary President in April 1995. It proposed that a Council for Political Development be formed and, more immediately, political reform be enacted to avoid 'parliamentary dictatorship' and continuing political instability.[22] The use of the term 'parliamentary dictatorship' was highly significant, for it situated the DDC within a broader bureaucratic and conservative critique of the emergence of majoritarian parliamentary politics and its subversion by money-politics. Indeed, the military leaders responsible for the 1991 coup had cited parliamentary dictatorship among their reasons for overthrowing the government.[23] The committee proposed an amendment to the existing constitution, enabling an unelected constitutional assembly of ex-prime ministers and experts in law and political science to draft a new constitution. Parliament would be excluded from the process, with the new constitution going to a referendum.[24]

Included in the letter to the Parliamentary President was a 100-page analysis of the problems of Thai politics which, in addition to the critique of money-politics, followed the contemporary arguments about the failure of Thai political culture and the need to establish a system of checks and balances. It is worth considering, briefly, the analysis offered in this document, for it hints at the attempt to redraw the boundaries of Thai democracy. In analysing the failure of democracy the DDC covers many of the typical points raised across the political spectrum: political corruption, parochial political culture, poorly developed democratic mechanisms, and so on. Regarding political culture, Thais are said to be individualistic in their thinking, which results in the absence of political development.[25] One consequence of economic development without political development was social decadence, and, in this case, political reform therefore aimed to refurnish the political house so it might deal with this moral degeneration. Having painted a gloomy picture, the DDC was quick to re-affirm the civic triad of nation, monarchy and religion as continuing to play an important role in generating unity and peace.[26] In another DDC document an emphasis on traditional political values is called for, including making the ten royal virtues the founding virtues of the governors. With these virtues in mind, and rooting rationality in the long Buddhist tradition of self-autonomy, the DDC authors argued that a 'democratic way of life' would be fostered. Furthermore, a balance of powers would frame the government so that abuse would be mitigated.[27] Complementing this analysis, fifteen extensive studies were conducted on areas including rights and freedom, an administrative court, organic laws, and referendums.

The DDC proposed a series of measures to address the problem of parliamentary 'dictatorship' by rationalizing the parliamentary system.[28] These included: potentially allowing an outsider to be appointed prime minister; limiting the right to call votes of no confidence;[29] and the provision of various measures to improve state accountability such as appointment of an ombudsman, establishing an administrative court, and strengthening the house committee system. In addition, the House of Representatives and the Senate would be complemented by a National Consultative Council given power to intervene on matters of national importance.[30]

Amon's parliamentary rationalization, as outlined in the DDC recommendations above, had become, in Prawet's hand, a project of national and moral regeneration. With the stamp of Prawet's wise mediation, 'parliamentary rationalization' was now part of a public debate and would become the focus of a broad movement.

Despite its conservative thrust and its backtracking on the 1992 popular demand for an elected prime minister, the report won support from the press and NGOs.[31] While parliamentary rationalization assured greater executive control over governance, progressive democrats were attracted to the accompanying liberal sentiments concerning a reduction in state power, greater accountability, and the extension of human and community rights proposed by the DDC. However, any reform would be within the parameters of the official ideology of nation–religion–king, and no rights or freedoms could be used antagonistically against these institutions.[32]

It was this mixture of democratic conservatism and the seemingly liberal position on state accountability and rights that secured broad support for political reform. In 1995 the campaign for reform intensified, with the press pushing for the Chuan government to take up the proposals. NGOs also began raising the subject of reform in their newsletters, and organized public seminars. The government, however, preferring gradual constitutional change, shelved the report. Many politicians were against political reform, as it had been presented, because it struck at the new power they had gained, over the past decade, at the expense of the bureaucracy. Also, a central plank of the emerging reform package, and one taken up with gusto by the press, was the exclusion of MPs from Cabinet. If an MP became a Cabinet member they would have to forfeit their parliamentary seat. However, if because of coalition instablity or for any other reason they lost their Cabinet seat, they would then be out in the cold. By such means did the reformers hope to boost executive stability.

Poised for reform

In the course of the DDC deliberations, followed eagerly by the press, the idea of political reform had been popularized and won a wide range of moderately interested supporters. The reform movement had become a discernible phenomenon, forging an unlikely alliance between reforming state technocrats and civil servants, public intellectuals, the press, progressive politicians and developmental NGOs and democracy activists.

This amalgam of social class forces began to forge a loose and largely intellectual alliance to address the failure of the political system. Although inspired by different objectives, each grouping saw a benefit in reforming the political system so that it might be more transparent, accessible and effective. The alliance of liberals, communitarians and supporters of participatory democracy was possible not so much because of shared ideological outlooks, but because of the common experience and disappointment with money-politics. The experience of failed legislative programmes, unresponsive government, poorly planned projects, human rights abuses, unfair monopolies and corruption scandals was the cohesive binding diverse sides to political reform. The social bases of this alliance were widespread, being inter-institutional and cross-class. One defining characteristic of Thai politics in the last generation has been the transitional nature of its economic and political spheres such that no single national hegemonic project has cohered the elite into a unified force.

For generations, civil service and military leaders have attempted to present themselves as representatives of the universal state and as the moral guardians of the people's wellbeing. But with the challenge from political parties and capitalist politicians, this self-image was more hopeful than real. On the whole, bureaucratic elites have tended to pursue regulationist economic policy. Their social values are conservative and their espoused commitment to democracy strictly formal, but rhetorically heavy.[33] Uncertain of the consequences of unregulated capitalism and the headlong rush into a globalizing culture, some from this grouping have, nonetheless, moved towards a modified conservatism and economic liberalism. To be sure, many civil servants had found reprehensible the money-politics of the preceding decade and now, recognizing the impossibility of turning back to the soft authoritarianism of semi-democracy, political reform seemed a fair option. Increasingly, sections of this grouping also had been won over to the liberal project of a globalized economy and a more pluralistic system, and were thus in a position to grudgingly, if not for some enthusiastically, accept the reform project.[34] Around this grouping there are also more enlightened reforming elements in the state. In the various works of the Thai Development Research Institute, a supposedly independent liberal-technocratic economic think-tank, one can sense the unease with which the general distemper of Thai politics is felt by leading governmental advisers and researchers.

As for business groupings, one might simply consider them as self-interested coalitions-of-concessions-and-contracts. Such coalitions had taken the parliamentary system and the political party system by storm. Business, more generally, was fractionalized with, broadly speaking, provincial capitalists seeking to expand the parliamentary arena as a further means of profiteering, and metropolitan business interests opting for a more technocratic form of democracy.[35] Metropolitan business interests, as evidenced by the leadership of Anand Panyarachun, have taken on political reform (see below). While in 1991 big business proved willing to work with the military and bureaucracy, the events of May led to a rethink among some on the nature of the required political regime for stability: they could not countenance a return to military authoritarianism, yet they remained sceptical of the parliamentary system. They feared both the provincial capitalist politicians who had made the parliamentary system their plaything, and that system's intrusion into the economic policy sphere.[36] Interestingly, the Business Club for Democracy arranged a seminar in mid-1995 to win support among business for political reform. At that meeting Anand was invited to speak and a loose monitoring organization was set up.[37]

It was in this context that the political reform movement became increasingly important in providing intellectual leadership for business and reforming technocrats. It should also be noted that as provincial capitalists made it to the national political stage some of them, or at least their party machines, also saw the benefit in a reform of their erstwhile political practices. In other words, the analytical distinction between these two fractions of capital is much more fluid in practice, as is demonstrated by the qualified support finally given by provincial capitalist forces to political reform.

Another significant player consisted of NGOs and more broadly defined civil society organizations. The 1991 *coup d'état* marked a new period of direct democratic activism for the NGOs. While many individuals within the NGO movement had been involved in earlier attempts at constitutional reform in the 1980s, such efforts were overshadowed by the struggle between political parties and the state apparatuses. Nevertheless, the formation of the Campaign for Popular Democracy (CPD) was not without precedent. The formation of that group in 1991 drew on the experience of the early 1980s.[38] Kothom Ariya, who was active in its earlier incarnation, spearheaded the reformation of the CPD.[39] Its focus was on critically watching and protesting the drafting of the NPKC constitution. The CPD was effectively a unifying organization for some 40–50 NGOs and affiliated student and professional interest groups whose delegates sat on the CPD executive.[40] Along with the Student Federation of Thailand, the CPD was a vocal opponent of the NPKC and did much to break down the initial indifference, if not qualified support, surrounding the toppling of the democratically elected government. The pivotal role that this small grouping played in raising critical awareness and mobilizing street action is widely acknowledged. Its strength lay in two areas. First, it had a close relationship with journalists in the print media interested in promoting a broad social justice agenda. Second, the socio-political infrastructure that the NGO movement had built up over half a generation was able to be mobilized, ensuring that democratic support organizations spread to provincial centres.

When elections were announced for March 1992, this network was put to use in Pollwatch, an Anand Panyarachun initiative that aimed at providing independent scrutiny of electoral behaviour and which aimed to stamp out the practice of vote-buying.[41] Pollwatch effectively mobilized a whole national network of activists to monitor the election. By the recruitment of prominent intellectual and activist leaders, Anand set in motion a process whereby progressive currents in the so-called people sector would provide the social pressure and support for political liberalism, packaged as democracy. Anand, through Pollwatch, was to secure an alliance that, despite tensions, would serve sections of the post-May liberal intelligentsia and bourgeoisie well. It provided elites with some societal support for a project of political liberalization, while leaving intact the social-economic framework of capitalism. The loose alliance effected in Pollwatch would repeat itself in different moulds for the next five years, making politically moderate NGOs the footsoldiers for liberal democracy. After the May events, democracy groups and some NGOs turned their attention to ensuring cleaner elections, and later, with the backing of some politicians, to pushing for the election of the centrally appointed provincial governors.[42] Although mass protests were threatened if the Chuan government reneged on an election promise to legislate for elected provincial governors, the NGO activist cadre was not able to mobilize any significant forces in support of their reform agenda. Rather than mass protests, the cadre used public forums and media campaigning to seek the support of progressive sections of the urban middle class.[43] Lacking any powerful social base, the NGO democracy movement became an important, if subordinate, ally to the political reform movement emerging in the elite sector in the first half of the 1990s. Their participation was not naive. There was a hope that once the question of democracy was settled, benefits would accrue for the majority. It was expected that a middle class empowered in the trappings of parliamentary democracy would be in a position to effect positive policy and join with the people sector in alleviating the ills of maldevelopment. This position had crystallized within the NGO peak bodies themselves, as well as among important intellectuals close to the NGOs. Their experience of marginalization in a parliamentary system dominated by money-politics made them reconsider the political forms worthy of support. Many of them embraced political reform as a way of opening new channels for political participation and human rights protection, particularly after their attempts to pressure for political decentralization failed.[44] For this grouping, the democratic agenda was broader than an elected prime minister, with many seeking a restructuring of the political process around participatory democracy, developing human rights and a critique of the development process.

Finally, progressive sections in the labour movement threw their weight behind political reform, with some labour leaders assuming leading roles in democracy organizations. Somsak Kosaisuk, a leader in the State Enterprise Labour Relations Group, is a key member of the Confederation for Democracy (CFD). This is a prominent group of activists who tend to take a harder critical line against the elite than do NGO-sponsored democracy groups. Yet even the CFD ultimately became a central supporter of the reform package, despite its concern that there was an elite bias in its conceptualization.[45]

In 1996 parliament amended the constitution allowing for the formation of a Constitution Drafting Assembly (CDA), from which politicians were barred. The road to this amendment was tortuous and hinted at how divisive the political reform agenda could be. Nonetheless, in passing the amendment power brokers in the political parties were reasonably confident they could determine the composition of the CDA. In December 1996 interested parties struggled to secure seats in the Constitution Drafting Assembly. Bureaucrats, professionals, political parties and sections of NGOs pushed for particular candidates.[46] A requirement that assembly members had at least a bachelor degree ensured that candidates were predominantly from the professions, particularly law and business. In late December 1996, parliament voted on the pool of provincial and specialist candidates. There was great controversy over the selection process. Accusations were constantly made that the governing NAP coalition had circulated a list of preferred candidates, and that its list had generally been followed.[47] For critics, the CDA was expected to be a stooge of the government, which would scuttle hopes of political reform. However, as the CDA deliberated it became clear that connections between the provincial representatives and bureaucratic and political interests had been greatly exaggerated. While some were mediators for political and bureaucratic interests, others were independently minded and open to debate from the core reformist grouping of academic, legal and experienced specialists. The specialists included Bowonsak Uwanno, a new-blood liberal, and previous constitutional framers such as Kramol Thongthammachart and Suchit Bunbongkarn, both skilled in the art of compromise and the balancing of political interests.

The leadership of the assembly, elected by CDA members, demonstrated that the CDA would be an instrument for reform. Uthai Phimchaichon, a liberal democratic politician who had been imprisoned in the 1970s for his stand against the 'unconstitutional' rule of the military, was elected Assembly President, and Anand Panyarachun was elected President of the Drafting Committee itself. Anand and Uthai were important figureheads, legitimizing the reform movement within their respective constituencies – Anand with big business and the middle class more generally, Uthai with liberal-reformist-minded politicians and moderate elements in the NGO movement. Behind them liberal academics and specialists worked on the technicalities of the draft. Of particular note is the key drafter Bowonsak Uwanno, Dean of Law at Chulalongkorn, royalist, former Senator and prominent reform advocate. Bowonsak was elected Secretary-General to the Drafting Committee and later to the Scrutiny Committee of the CDA. He had also played a key role in the DDC and in the House Committee for Constitutional Amendment in 1993–94.

More democratically inclined than Amon, whose tract had informed (inspired would not be the word) the movement, Bowonsak was similarly a French-educated legalist who derived his ideas for political reform from French experience.[48]

After a series of preliminary public hearings and some deliberation, the CDA issued a major document entitled *Preliminary Framework for Drafting the Constitution.*[49] The document clearly positioned the CDA within the reform movement. It begins with the text of a speech made by Anand to a provincial meeting. For Anand,

> political reform means defining the structure and the system of power use so that people have the right to control and scrutinize power, and to prevent the use of power for personal and group interest.[50]

This required providing for greater participation in the political process. However, Anand saw political reform in defensive terms, not as some ideal that would enhance the civic virtues of citizens:

> It [political reform] is not an attempt to make bad people good, but it is a seeking of preventive ways to stop bad people having the opportunity to hold governing power.[51]

Anand had not been known to have great faith in the Thai masses, having made on occasion dismissive and contemptuous comments on their capacity to understand and practise democracy. Now, in an effort at securing popular support for the reform process, he used democratic rhetoric, stressing people's participation as the key to reform. As he put it, the power of the state would be limited by making rights enforceable, through a participatory public scrutinizing the government. Were this the case the new constitution would be a

> rights and freedom constitution: of the people, by the people and for the people and not a power constitution, used as an excuse to disguise the seizure and unlimited use of state power.[52]

The document offered important statements on the three problems the new constitution was to address. It is here that the liberalism of the movement is most evident. First, the extension of rights and freedoms was a priority. Noting that in the past the state had arbitrary power over the people, it is declared that the issue of rights and freedoms is one of also defining the (limited) role of the state. Equally, the failure to clearly define rights and to make them enforceable meant that it was too easy for laws to restrict rights. Furthermore, the right of political participation, it is argued, had been curtailed because of the limited decentralization of power.[53] The document listed measures, therefore, to extend rights and to make them enforceable. These included community rights over resource management, the right to resist an overthrow of democracy with the king as head of state, freedom of information and press, academic freedom and, importantly, any limitation of rights, it was suggested, must find its justification in the constitution. Also proposed was the establishment of a Constitutional Court to deliberate on contentious matters relating to rights violation and unconstitutional behaviour. Such a court would give unprecedented rights to citizens to seek redress if their individual rights were violated, but it would also have the power to determine whether any behaviour was contrary to the nation, religion and monarchy.[54]

Second, regarding state accountability, a series of liberal measures adding up to a comprehensive set of checks and balances for the liberal state were proposed. Such proposals included the establishment of constitutional and administrative courts, an independent counter-corruption agency, a parliamentary ombudsman, the requirement of asset declarations by Cabinet members and senior bureaucrats, and an independent Audit Bureau.[55] Finally, the document proposed a review of the political structure such that 'business politics' would come to an end and legitimacy restored to the political process. Discussed also was political party reform. It was suggested that measures be undertaken to make party structures more democratic and less under the influence of rogue capitalists. Other suggestions included revising the parliamentary system so that the roles of the executive and legislature were clearer. Direct and indirect elections for the Senate were also flagged. Unsurprisingly, the loss of parliamentary status for MPs who become Cabinet members was also discussed.[56]

Subsequent CDA documents, including the circulation of a proposed draft, more or less covered the same ground as this one. There was some disquiet in the CDA itself that the *Frameworks* document had been written with little consultation and that it had pre-empted debate, but nevertheless it became the basis for soliciting comment from public hearing and organized interests including business, NGOs, professional associations and the press.[57] It would not be exaggerating to say that the available evidence suggests a blueprint was well in place before the hearings and was largely followed. Indeed, the National Research Fund had supported various studies aimed at assisting in drafting the constitution, with Bowonsak playing a leading role. Initially it was proposed that proposals from these studies would be put to public hearings of the CDA, but outcries that this was outside interference in the running of the CDA meant the research was utilized discreetly in the drawing up of the CDA frameworks.[58] By setting the agenda for the public meetings and clearly stating the issues to be addressed, the CDA leadership was able to impose strict limits on the issues to be deliberated. In many ways the public meetings served as an excellent means of public relations, a way of legitimating the reform programme.[59]

Input/output and the people's constitution

The CDA was eager to emphasize the popularity of its proposals for reform, and so broad support was demonstrated in a series of reports on particular interest group hearings. Significantly, it publicized support for its suggested measures of state accountability and transparency from business groupings.[60]

Effectively, peak business organizations such as the Thai Chamber of Commerce and Thai Bankers Association more or less repeated the ideas that had been circulating in reform circles for several years. While there was a broad recognition of the need for political change, organized business groups themselves did not consider themselves as leaders in the process. Perhaps the general position of those business reformists, awaiting leadership, is summed up in the words of one provincial business leader: 'The Thai economy has been hundreds of miles ahead of society and politics. We need reforms so that all sectors of the country can move ahead together.'[61] While business had been behind the economic surge, there was no suggestion that it should also lead the political surge. On the influence of organized business, key drafter Bowonsak comments: 'The business sector [was] not interested in the constitution, they know nothing, they just pay politicians . . . they proposed what had already been proposed.'[62] Even towards the end of the drafting process, when efforts had been made to enlist business actively behind the reform process, Bowonsak was still lamenting the lack of business understanding between economics and politics and urged business groups to actively support the draft.[63] Despite Bowonsak's low opinion of organized business, the business sector did seek pro-capitalist statements in the constitution, including measures to support free competition and self-regulation. They sought, also, a greater say in legislative programmes, including laws relating to unfair trading practices and decentralization. They expressed support for decentralization and for the exclusion of MPs from Cabinet.[64] Unlike union demands for the right of trade union association to be written into the constitution, business concerns found their way into the preliminary and final CDA draft, exemplified by an article committing the state to support free trade.

The military's position on political reform was, on the whole, muted. Post-May, the military had been relatively quiet. New leaders, such as General Vimol Wongwanich and his successor General Chettha Thanajaro, have pushed for military professionalism and non-interference in politics.[65] There have been hiccups on this path to professionalism. For instance, top-ranking military officials failed to front up to the parliamentary committee scrutinizing the military budget in 1995–6.[66] Nevertheless, as Chai-Anan observes, a new generation of professional soldiers is emerging who 'are convinced that their best strategy of survival is to keep away from direct political involvement and concentrate on the military's legitimate role and corporate interests'.[67] It was this strategy that marked the military's response to the CDA.

While military figures bemoaned the draft constitution as reflecting a basic mistrust of the armed forces because of a draft article constitutionally sanctioning peaceful resistance to a coup,[68] their greatest concern was Article 40, stipulating that radio, television and telecommunications frequencies were public resources. Furthermore, an independent body was to be set up to allocate frequencies and to supervise their use. In a forewarning of the expected liberalization of control and ownership of frequencies, the independent body was to ensure free and fair competition in the sector. With close to 500 frequencies controlled by various state agencies, and the armed forces, combined, controlling around 200, the military was set to lose control of much of its unaudited corporate income.[69] As expected, the armed forces and other state agencies continue to resist relinquishing their control over this empire.[70] Reporting that the military's radio and television empire was estimated to earn over 2 billion baht a year, Thana Poopat noted

> [m]ost of the money has been spent at the discretion of the commanders in charge of each media unit. Much of the proceeds go towards supplementary welfare benefits for military personnel, but vast amounts are unaccounted for.[71]

The conservatives cave in

In mid-August the CDA passed the draft on to parliament. Its fundamentals were remarkably close to the demands made by the reform movement. Importantly, all the liberal measures were adopted. There were skirmishes within the CDA and with groups outside it over a number of measures described above, but the key plank of ending money-politics through a series of reform measures was adopted. Such measures included: establishing an independent electoral commission and administrative and constitutional courts; an elected Senate; reform of the electoral system; allowing citizens initiatives on legislation and impeachment; and having MPs lose their status once they enter Cabinet. Importantly, an NGO-inspired proposal for the establishment of a human rights commission was accepted.

Even as the CDA presented the draft to parliament in mid-August it remained unclear which way parliament would go.[72] Most political parties remained ambivalent, while a minority in both houses of parliament was stridently against the draft. Equally, a level of criticism, but broad support, was evident among some politicians and bureaucrats. Even the more reputable politicians had reservations about the draft. The greatest bone of contention was the issue of executive and legislative separation of powers. While parties such as the Democrats had pledged support for the draft quite early on, they remained critical of this aspect.[73] For politicians such as Chuan Leekpai, it seemed better to address the problem of political corruption through measures that did not restructure the parliamentary system.[74] This was a standard position for most liberal-reformist politicians who were angered by the CDA's insistence that they be locked out of the drafting process. There were concerns also of too much power being wielded by the prime minister, which worked against the system of checks and balances the CDA was trying to materialize.[75] When presented with the choice of seeing the package of reforms in the CDA constitution either adopted or scuttled, it was expected such politicians would vote for adoption with a wait-and-amend attitude.[76]

Much the same can be said of many Senators, who, on the whole, backed the reform agenda and its elitist assumptions. It is important to note that the Senate remained the basis of the political power of the bureaucracy, with over eighty of its 260 members being serving military or civil servants and another fifty-three coming from their retired ranks. However, Senate appointments made by Banharn in 1996 also introduced more business, professional and progressive elements into the body.[77] They, too, had misgivings about aspects of the constitution (particularly an elected Senate, and the right of 50,000 people to call for an investigation into political corruption and to initiate discussion on legislation), but such issues were seen as peripheral when weighed against the package as a whole. Reformist elements in the state, some sitting as Senators, were keen to see the adoption of the reformist programme, as a decade of political interference into the bureaucracy and growing levels of bureaucratic political corruption had tainted the 'professional royal service' they envisaged themselves providing.

Conservative criticism eased particularly after the onset of the currency crisis in July 1997. It is an open question whether the draft would have passed if the economic crisis had not made it imperative for the elite to present a picture of political stability and consensus. The Senate President, Meechai Ruchapun, a former deputy prime minister under the Anand government, and former minister during the Prem years of the 1980s, used his considerable weight to pull the Senate towards critical support for the draft. Meechai envisaged great chaos if the draft did not pass:

> At the time I changed my position because when the constitution was finished the economic crisis broke out. If we looked around we could see the people had placed their hope in the constitution . . . if we rejected the constitution the people's hope would be exhausted and it would create a severe crisis. We knew that if the constitution passed there would be problems but they would be in the future, but if it didn't pass the problems would break out then and the country would not survive.[78]

The greatest threat to the CDA draft was represented by the governing party itself, which remained opposed to the draft. Key NAP members organized provincial opposition to the draft. Factions within the NAP linked up with conservative elements in the Senate and the bureaucracy to wage an ineffective campaign consisting of attempted mass mobilization as well as constitutional trickery.[79] In the following I present some aspects of the attempt to oppose the constitution. To what extent this was an orchestrated campaign waged from any command centre is unclear, but it is clear that conservative political and bureaucratic elements across the institutional spectrum were involved.[80]

As late as July the NAP remained unclear as to its position on the draft.[81] Pro-draft newspapers considered much of the manoeuvring in the CDA to be the work of the NAP, even suggesting that the decision to push for Senate elections was the work of a key Chavalit adviser, who had engineered this outcome so as to ensure the draft would not pass.[82]

Additionally, Chavalit toyed with the idea of amending Article 211 of the then standing constitution, which would enable parliament to amend the draft when it was presented to parliament.[83] This ploy earned Chavalit protests from democracy groups who reiterated their support for the draft.[84]

There were, of course, sections within the state, the Senate and political organizations, that ideologically and materially saw benefits in retaining the existing system, and were decidedly illiberal. Ideologically, the new draft challenged the statist articulation of 'democracy with the king as head of state' that had emerged after 1976. Enmeshed in this statist mythology and practice, a number of Senators took exception to the CDA draft quite early on. When Article 3 in the working draft of the constitution was amended to read 'sovereignty belongs to the people' instead of 'sovereignty comes from the people', conservative elements saw this as attacking the traditional right of the monarch to exercise sovereignty through the executive, legislature and courts. While this was a symbolic issue, since the king did not exercise any such formal power, opponents hoped that the amendment to Article 3 would lead the CDA draft to being ruled unconstitutional as it altered the position of the monarchy.[85] Meechai also suggested that an article in the draft making it illegal to discriminate on the grounds of different origins in social status was opposed to Thai political culture:

> In a royal palace, the practice of crouching or crawling is normal because there is a specific rule for the palace. What would happen if one day a man talked to the King with arms akimbo (showing disrespect) and he used paragraph 3 of Article 29 to defend himself in court against discrimination? . . . [W]e still recognize differences in origins.[86]

The assumptions here illuminate something of the consensus about the inviolability of the monarchy and that inviolability's link to social order in general. Comments such as these point to a general elite anxiety about the extent of human rights and the evolution of egalitarian culture sought by the NGOs. It also explains why, despite their critical support for the political restructuring sought by the CDA, they were cautious of that other aspect of reform, enforceable human rights.

Aside from opposition articulated in parliament and through the press, there were attempts to mobilize mass organizations and local village leaders against the draft by renowned conservative senators and provincial politicians, such as Poonsak Wannapong and Interior Minister Sanoh Thiengthong. Poonsak attacked Article 3 and the extension of human rights clauses in the constitution, and called on village scouts to protect the king.[87]

Sanoh, as Interior Minister, had also earlier proposed reviving the lagging village scouts, formed in the early 1970s as a bastion of the mass right, by suggesting renewed funding and greater recruitment.[88] Interior Ministry senior bureaucrats, along with Sanoh, also began to stir up opposition to the new constitution among the hundreds of thousands of village leaders and their assistants on the issue of decentralization. The CDA had proposed that all positions in local councils be elected, overturning the ex-officio right of village chiefs to sit there. Village chiefs are elected administrators and law keepers of over 60,000 villages spread across

Thailand, and are identifiable as agents of the state. Many are implicated in the centralized state apparatus, and have been a force for sustaining the power of the mega-sized Interior Ministry against pressure for decentralization. More venally, many see the encroaching democratization at the local level as a threat to the perks and contracts they can secure through their position.[89] Considered a major national force, leading bureaucrats in the Interior Ministry began to mobilize village leaders against the constitution.[90] Interestingly, the Interior Ministry, earlier that year, had proposed extending the term of office for local leaders, turning back reform efforts at the local level. Until 1992 village heads served until death. The Anand regime amended the law requiring retirement at sixty. In 1994 the term of newly elected local leaders was reduced to five years. In proposing a reversal of enforced retirement, the Interior Ministry was attempting to mobilize, through such an incentive, the local leaders in opposition to the articles on decentralization in the draft constitution.[91] While it might be tempting to see such manoeuvring as sheer gross material interest, protecting the existing vertical arrangements of trade-offs, contracts and perks, it is important also to stress the ideological factors at work here, and the unique position of the Interior Ministry, which had not yet been dealt a blow as severe as the military had received in 1992. A whole security state had been built up since the 1960s, with its own particular ideologies of a centralized state and bureaucratic mythology of its service to the king, through service to the people. The Interior Ministry had been central to this ideological reproduction, and had expended great energy in inculcating its values and ideologies to its officials at all levels. This ideological resource was mobilized to stir up provincial opposition to the draft.[92]

The Interior Ministry, which had successfully waged an earlier struggle on decentralization in 1993–94, was, in 1996, beginning to reassess its position. In a revealing strategy discussion document from 1996, there is evidence of bureaucratic anxiety concerning the rise of the market economy, parliament and the inevitable challenges to the ministry's control over the national networks of local governance. As the Interior Ministry saw it, political reform was a threat to national security since 'political reform has a tendency to support political participation of the people and local areas having an increased role in governing themselves.'[93] Interestingly, the strategy document was structured in terms of how the potential changes arising from economic growth and political reform would present the ministry with both opportunities and dangerous obstacles to its work.[94] For example, in terms of decentralization and elections it was expected these would provide the ministry with a greater role in laying down further plans for the development of political parties. The downside, however, was that the ministry's work would come under increasing scrutiny.[95] According to this document, the shift to the power of business was expected to continue, with the bureaucracy and the state increasingly declining in importance.[96] However, as business power grows and further conflicts break out, the bureaucracy, although diminished, would continue to play an important role in managing change from a conservative, gradualist perspective.[97]

The problems of money-politics and vote-buying were not expected to disappear, either, for provincial godfathers were expected to continue to trade money and influence for charisma in local areas; it would only be the slow development of a democratic culture that would stamp out the problem.[98] There is a voiced hope, however, that democracy will emerge, particularly among the middle classes in the urban areas.[99] Typically, fears that decentralization and the subsequent democratization of local government would lead to a scenario of local influential powers unskilled in governance taking the seats of power were aired.[100] Most remarkably, the threat from NGOs in establishing a 'civil society' is discussed.[101] This was ostensibly a threat, since the push for a stronger civil society sector would, it is stated, weaken the state. As the strategy paper put it, private sector organizations 'will push for a sharper and more disciplined struggle between the poor people and capitalists and the state over natural resources, and in developing civil society'. As a balancing force in society it would be increasingly difficult, therefore, for the state to formulate policy independently.[102] It is clear, then, that prior to the 1997 Constitution, Interior Ministry bureaucrats envisaged both further attacks on their administrative integrity and a more fundamental threat in the rise of civil society.

Chavalit, who had used the Interior Ministry several years earlier to defeat constitutional amendments on decentralization, this time abandoned his one-time allies. Feeling the pressure of both the looming economic and political crisis, he capped the mobilization and effectively ordered the Interior Ministry to stop its political interference.[103] Orchestrated mass opposition to the CDA was thus curtailed. Instead, Chavalit desperately lobbied Uthai to amend the draft to no avail. By the time he had succumbed to committing the government to supporting the constitution he had been pressured by the military, business, reformist politicians and the press to do so.[104] All had their own misgivings about the new constitution, but none, in the context of crisis, saw a way out other than for the draft to be accepted. For several days the tamed politicians held a debate to air their grievances.[105] Amidst the parliamentary grumblings, public demonstrations consisting of business supporters and pro-democracy groups rallied in support of the draft.[106] In late September a divided parliament raised its hand in unity to reluctantly pass the constitution.[107] A combination of economic crisis and political manoeuvring had made of Thailand's despised and misunderstood politicians reluctant reformers.

For the next two years parliament would be preoccupied with shaping the new laws required by the constitution. These organic laws would regulate the new electoral system, the administrative court, the constitutional court, the human rights commission and so on. A complex battle emerged between conservatives and liberals and old-style politicians to ensure that the new institutions of the constitution best suited their needs.[108] Several years after the heady hopes of the reform project, results appear somewhat uneven.

In December 2000 the newly empowered National Counter-Corruption Commission found billionaire Thaksin Shinawatra guilty of failing to disclose over 200 million dollars worth of assets while he was Deputy Prime Minister in the dying days of the Chavalit administration. The assets in question had been listed on the stock market under a maid and driver's name, catapulting them into a Thai one-hundred-richest-people list. However, this did not stop Thaksin. Several weeks later his new political party, Thai Rak Thai (TRT) party, came to power in the January 2001 elections, a few seats short of an absolute majority (sorted out by gobbling up a smaller party a few months later). The elections were held under the new constitution. Despite the tainted beginning, and despite the wide acknowledgement that TRT reflected the interests of a range of capitalist groupings, there was a feeling that change was in the air, that TRT would move towards economic and social reform. After all, unusually for Thailand, TRT had campaigned on clear policy issues related to agriculture, health and small and medium enterprises, and a moratorium on farm debt. The policies were seen as a result of consultation with progressive thinkers and consultation with civil society development groups, leading a number of NGO activists to give qualified support to the party in the election.[109] TRT's approach also tapped into general nationalist resentment at the last government's apparent subservience to the IMF. Newly devised and professional electoral campaigns endemic in the West, where electorates are seen as demographic entities requiring communicated political messages, were utilized in parallel with the more certain system of vote-canvassing at local level.[110] It was clear that the dual impact of the economic crisis and the framework established by the new constitution contributed to a new style of campaign. It was as if the high hopes of political reform were, however unevenly, being realized. For example, in the first-ever elections for the Senate, in March 2000, the newly empowered Electoral Commission of Thailand (ECT) had strictly enforced electoral regulations, with the result that over one-third of elected Senators were disqualified and new elections called. In some provinces elections had to be held more than three times. Reform had teeth. In the general elections, the ECT found cause to disqualify sixty-two out of 400 successful candidates, leading to further election rounds. If some political parties were proving reluctant to play a fully clean game, then the new institutions of the reform movement were applied.

As well as a significant re-ordering of politics there were, compelled by the impact of the crisis, significant economic shifts as well. Kevin Hewison identifies a significant nationalist reaction in the face of the enduring economic crisis, which may be said to have impacted on the orientation of the state. As domestic banking capital (historically dominant) has been reorganized and its influence limited – both as a result of the economic boom and the associated rise of other fractions of capital and as a result of the crisis and the concomitant expansion of foreign ownership – new sections of capital have risen and gained political influence. Thaksin is emblematic of this. Thaksin's government, with significant support of other major capitalist groupings, aims to mitigate the expansion of foreign capital into Thailand and to erect protectionist measures.[111] Its 'nationalist' and 'populist' policies are to be seen, then, as aimed at preserving the capacity of domestic capital to dominate in Thailand.[112] In part this explains the small and meduim enterprise craze that hit Thailand in the wake of the crisis, and it was Thaksin's willingness to publicly and aggressively pursue this agenda (while the Democrats were less skilled in publicizing their efforts in this regard) that won much support for his party.[113] It should be noted that the SME agenda, although backed by the World Bank, can with skilful articulation also link up with local and nationalist concerns.[114] Hence a reformist capitalist agenda aimed at building both international export capacity and the development of local markets – nothing particularly offensive to global financial institutions – can, at the domestic level, appear as a progressive programme of nationalism against foreign capital. Nationalist rhetoric, iced with egoism, has been a trademark of Thaksin. Consider comments made in one speech:

> The day before, the IMF came here, probably thinking I was like others, thinking they can say '1, 2, 3, 4, 5 you must do like this'. What did I say? I said 'bankers only know how to collect interest, they don't know how to make money . . . you must listen to me . . . You can say what you like and I will listen, but I don't have to listen . . . I am governing a country that has sovereignty.'[115]

In the early months of office Thaksin spoke-up pro-poor policies, courted NGOs and moved quickly to implement election promises. Then followed a highly controversial and narrow majority decision by the newly established Constitutional Court to nullify the findings of the National Counter-Corruption Commission. Had it not so ruled Thaksin would have been obliged to stand down. The contradictory nature of the court's decision, and accusations of interference, raised questions about the court's integrity and the prospect that the reform programme might be subverted. Lending support to these fears was the manner in which other institutions of the reform project proved less than faithful to the original intention. The Senate's selection of controversial commissioners for the Electoral Commission of Thailand (one was disqualifed from the previous election) has been seen as an attempt at stacking the commission to make it toothless.[116] As press criticism rose of poor implementation of policy, cronyism and Thaksin's highly authoritative style of leadership (he admires Malaysia's Mahathir Mohammed), the government began a none-too-subtle strategy of attrition against the media. These sundry events merely show that the attempt to politically liberalize Thailand remains ongoing, and significant obstacles still need to be tackled. No one expected political reform to be an instant panacea.

The drama that has become the reform project, which is sure to mark the politics of the next decade as different forces battle it out, has been highlighted by the king's dramatic criticism of the Thaksin government. In December 2001, the king used his seventy-fourth birthday to express dissatisfaction with Thaksin's attempt to clamp down on criticism. Noting that Thailand was heading for catastrophe, the king spoke freely:

The prime minister has a long face now after I mentioned catastrophe. But I'm telling the truth, because whatever we do, there seem to be big problems. The prime minister may appear to be happy, but deep down inside he's definitely not . . . Two persons – with different ideas, different experiences and different knowledge – cannot be made to think the same way. When we have an idea and others say it is not right, they have the right to say so. But everybody needs to lower his ego to prevent difference of ideas from being counter-productive.[117]

The king's intervention highlights again the guardianship role the institution has taken over political development. It also highlights a basically liberal view on free expression, although of course this, in the king's own words, is related to the ultimate aim of national unity. While it would be too strong to suggest the intervention was in support of the reform project, it nevertheless makes it difficult for any leader to move towards a more authoritarian control of information.

In summary

In the late 1980s and 1990s the Thai state, in its totality, was experiencing an organic crisis and yet appeared incapable of adaptation and retrieval. The political reform movement offered recovery. If the new constitution signalled reform, it was against the recalcitrant and corrupt elements of capital and the state who had nurtured their own interests through the illegitimate chains of corruption that were (and are?) as organizationally complex as the bureaucracy itself. In effect, the state was serving not just the basic function of securing the conditions for capital accumulation, but was also a site for the pursuit of what Andrew Turton calls 'predatory interests'.[118] Political reform was one response to this crisis. Furthermore, the shift, reflected in the constitution, was part of the emergence of a new invigorated Thai liberalism that was underpinned by the infrastructural logic of Thailand's economic 'miracle', and which compelled a cleaning-up of the stables of government. Indeed, within months of the constitution passing, the Local Administration Department was mapping out a strategy for how it might conform to 'good governance' as exemplified in the principles of participation, efficiency, rule of law and accountability.[119] But, then again, LAD has always been good at appropriation.

Since 1992 there has been a gradual dislocation of statist democracy as represented by the Interior Ministry, the Local Administration Department and the National Identity Board. The statist right and its mass organizations have been marginalized; right-wing populism is seemingly disdained by the palace: to some degree, there has been a tentative embracing of a more liberal technocratic outlook tempered with a new ideology of sustainable development and human rights, filtered through Thai traditionalism (nation, religion, king).[120]

Ideologically in transition, it is not yet clear what will remain of Thai statist ideology into the next decade. It is clear, however, that the reform constitution represents a tentative victory for reformers in the Thai state and opens a space for the emergent liberalism and its supporters to vigorously expand their influence and claim hegemony, within the parameters of a modified ideology of nation, religion and monarchy. Within this ideology, a new rhetoric of state/society relations, participatory democracy and good governance, all more or less packaged in the instrumental notion of political reform and the idealistic ambition of establishing a civil society, will possibly take root. Of course, political struggles will determine the extent to which this becomes entrenched or becomes just a staging post for new developments. Certainly, on the ground there are attempts to root this new logic.

Just as the political opening of 1973–76 brought into being liberal attempts at democracy education, sponsored by the Bureau of Universities, the new constitution spawned a new democracy education project, separate from LAD, in village communities. Sponsored by the Bureau of Universities and the newly formed Electoral Commission of Thailand, some 20,000 non-civil servant 'Constitution Volunteers' began to propagate knowledge about the new constitution in the latter half of 1999. With groups of three-to-four spending up to half a year in a designated subdistrict, it was expected that through public meetings, informal contact, advertising, and with the assistance of local authorities, the critical message of voting on principle and not for cash might transform the landscape of Thai politics.[121] Just like the civil servant predecessors before them, the volunteers were expected to get to know the subdistrict, the local powers, the people's level of wealth and poverty and the local customs. This would presumably enable them better to spread the message of democracy and the importance of casting an honest vote.[122] A booklet used to accompany propagation, *Bunterm Goes to Vote*, signals a shift in the means to compel people to conform to models of the virtuous citizen.[123] The book presents a real-life drama populated by shady politicians, local leaders and corrupt electoral practices, and is animated by the central character's dilemma: to follow old practices or embrace the new. Interspersed with the realistic picture of intimidation by vote canvassers and the lure of monetary incentive, there emerges a picture of an alternative clean electoral system, one in which people make rational decisions based on their own and their community's interest. Gone is the image of the good state watching over people, nurturing their capacity as citizens. Now, the message is that the future really lies in their hands. The good citizen is required to make real the institutional liberalism emergent in sectors of the Thai state.

Notes

1 This chapter is a substantially revised and updated version of an article written in April 1998 and published in 1999. See Michael Connors, 'Political Reform and the State in Thailand', *Journal of Contemporary Asia*, 29, 4, pp. 202–26.

2 Amon Raksasat and Wirat Jianbun, *Raingan kanwijai sathianphap prasithiphap lae khwamrapphitchop khong ratthaban jak kanleuaktang rawang pi 2331–2540* [A research report on stability, efficiency and accountability of elected governments between 1988–1997], Bangkok: Khanakammakan wijai haeng chat, n.p. 1997.

3 See Michael Connors, 'Framing the People's Constitution', in Duncan McCargo (ed.) *Reforming Thai Politics*, Copenhagen: Nordic Institute of Asian Studies, 2002.

4 *Raignan khanakammathikan wisaman phijarana suksa naeothang kae khai ratthammanun ratchaanajak thai 2536* [Report of the Extraordinary House Committee on Constitutional Amendments], 1993.

5 *Siam Post*, 3/4/94. The most significant amendment passed was the lowering of the voting age to eighteen. For a rosy-eyed account that considers the amendments to have been significant, and the role of NGOs to have been somewhat effective, see Kevin Quigly, 'Towards Consolidating Democracy: The Paradoxical Role of Democracy Groups in Thailand', *Democratization*, 3, 3, 1996, pp. 264–86.

6 *Matichon*, 26/8/92, p. 32; 10/12/91, p. 24. A brief history of IPPS involvement in political reform is provided in Chai-Anan Samudavanija, *Kanpatirup thangkanmeuang kheu arai tammai tong patirup peu khrai patirup yangngai* [Political reform: what is it, why is it necessary, who is it for and how can it be done?], Bangkok: Public Policy Institute, 1997.

7 Amon Chantharasombun, *Khonstitichanaelism thang ok khong prathet thai* [Constitutionalism: the solution for Thailand], Bangkok: Public Policy Institute, 1994. This book follows very closely some of the arguments, particularly those related to the relationship between political sociology and constitutionalism, that appear in M.Vile, *Constitutionalism and the Separation of Powers*, Oxford: Clarendon Press, 1967.

8 *Ibid.*, p. 50.

9 *Ibid.*, p. 37.

10 *Ibid.*, pp. 9–11.

11 *Ibid.*, p. 13.

12 *Ibid.*, pp. 27–8.

13 *Ibid*, p. 38.

14 *Ibid.*, pp. 43–4.

15 *Ibid.*, pp. 72–6.

16 See, for example, many articles in the *Warasan kotmai pokkhrong* [Administrative law journal], in particular: Chaiwat Wongwatthanasan, 'Kan baengyaek amnat kantikhwam ratthammanun' [The separation of powers and constitutional interpretation], 1, 2, 1982, pp. 376–411. Chaiwat, a Council of State official, argues that the principle of the separation of powers, in good constitutionalist fashion, is not absolute, but provides an overall orientation for government. His argument is peppered with references to Robert Dahl and Woodrow Wilson. The debate about the separation of powers in the 1990s has principally been about the separation of Cabinet, or the executive, from parliamentary 'interference'. See for example *Siamrat*, 21/3/90, p. 3.

17 *Phujatkan raiwan*, 11/12/96, p. 15.

18 *Patirup kanmeuang* [Political reform], November 1995, p. 5.

19 Kasian Tejapira, 'Post-May Reform is Incomplete', *Bangkok Post*, 20/5/97, p. 8. Anand actually seemed to have no trouble mixing with the black geese when he accepted the office of Prime Minister offered by the NPKC.

20 See, for examples of his moral idealism and societal naivety, Prawet Wasi, *Pheu banmeuang khong rao* [For our home], Bangkok: Samnakngan mo chaoban, 1988; Prawet Wasi,

Kandoen thang haeng khwamkhit patirup kanmeuang [The journey towards political reform thought], Bangkok: Samnakphim mo chaoban, 1997.

21 For an example of the many praises that Prawet Wasi lavishes on the present king see Prawet Wasi, 'Sathaban phramahakasat kap 60 pi prachathipatai' [The institution of the monarchy and 60 years of democracy], in *10 pi ratthasat mo. Sor. Tho.* [10 years of political science], Sukhothaithammathirat University, 1992, pp. 5–11.

22 Khanakammakan phathanakan prachathipatai [Democracy Development Committee], *Kho saneu kropkhwamkhit nai kanpatirup kanmeuang thai* (Proposal for a framework in Thai tolitical reform), 1995, pp. 6–7.

23 *Bangkok Post,* 24/2/91, p. 3.

24 Khanakammakan phathanakan prachathipatai , *Kho saneu kropkhwamkhit,* p. 90.

25 *Ibid.,* p. 6.

26 *Ibid.,* pp. 17–18.

27 See Khanakammakan phathana prachathipatai, *Supha phathana kanmeuang* [Political development council], c. 1994.

28 Khanakammakan phathanakan prachathipatai , *Kho saneu kropkhwamkhit,* pp. 46–8.

29 *Ibid.,* p. 78.

30 *Ibid.,* pp. 53–5. The Committee proposed that this body be composed of ex-prime ministers and parliamentary presidents, permanent secretaries of all ministries, regional military commanders, and the president of both the Federation of Thai Industries and the Thai Chamber of Commerce, and a further seventy members appointed by parliament from the professions and labour. This idea echoed back to some answers to 'excessive' democracy in the mid-1970s. See for example Amon Raksasat, *Anakhot chat thai* [The future of Thailand], Bangkok: Rongphim kromyutsuksa thahanpok, 2519. Amon, one of the 1997 drafters, argues for a political system which combines monarchy-aristocracy-democracy (*rachawutaprachathipatai*).

31 'Sarup praden kanprachum radom khithen pheu phlakdan kanphathana lae patirup rabop prachathipatai thai' [Summarizing the points: brainstorming ideas on pushing for the development and reform of the democratic system], *Jotmai khao kho. ro. Po.* [CPD newsletter], 3, 12, 1995, pp. 26–31.

32 Khanakammakan phathanakan prachathipatai, *Kho saneu kropkhwamkhit,* p. 38.

33 Pasuk Phongpaichit and Chris Baker, 'Power in Transition: Thailand in the 1990s', in K. Hewison (ed.) *Political Change in Thailand: Democracy and Participation,* London: Routledge, 1997, pp. 21–41, pp. 22–5.

34 See Surin on the generational shift in the bureaucracy and technocracy. Surin Maisrikrod, 'Emerging Patterns of Leadership in Thailand', *Contemporary Southeast Asia,* 15, 1, 1993, pp. 80–96, pp. 86–7.

35 *Ibid.*

36 Pasuk and Baker, 'Power in Transition: Thailand in the 1990s', p. 29.

37 *Phujatkan raiwan,* 9/8/95, p. 14.

38 For information on democracy groups in the early 1980s in terms of their modest politics and their attempt to work with mainstream progressive politicians, see Khrongkan ronarong pheu kaekhai ratthathammanun hai pen prachathipatai (Constitution Campaign for Demo-

NEW TIMES, NEW CONSTITUTION   177

cratic Amendments to the Constitution), *Ratthathammanun kho ro po* [The constitution of CPD], Bangkok: Ronarong pheu kae khai ratthathammanun hai pen prachathipatai, 1982.

39 Kothom Ariya, interview with the author, Bangkok, 17/3/97.

40 Parinya Thawanarumitkul, interview with the author, Bangkok, 25/1/94.

41 For a sustained discussion on Pollwatch see William A. Callahan, *Pollwatching, Elections and Civil Society in Southeast Asia,* Aldershot: Ashgate, 2000.

42 See *Bangkok Post,* 3/3/93, p. 1; 31/1/94, p. 1. Also see 'Power Decentralization in Thai Society: Demands From the People', report and analysis from the seminar on 'Local Administration and Creation of People's Organizations' organized by the Local Information Centre for Development, Nakkhon Ratchasima Chamber of Commerce, 12–13 December 1994.

43 See for example 'Phaen ngan lae kitjakam kho ro .po. chuang pi tulakhom 2537-thanwakhom 2538' [CPD plan and activities between October 1994 and December 1995], unpublished paper; 'Sarup raingan prachum samamana kho ro. po. 1994' [Report on CPD seminar, 1994], mimeograph. These internal documents paint a picture of an organization in crisis, with little popular support and having difficulty in attracting people.

44 See *Phujatkan raiwan,* 15/12/95, p. 9. This article argues that the failed attempts at decentralization in 1994/5 led to a broader offensive on the political system, taking shape in the political reform movement.

45 Somsak Kosaisuk, interview with the author, Bangkok, 7/6/97.

46 *Phujatkan raiwan,* 20/11/96, p. 11; 6/12/96, p. 9. An excellent discussion of the extent of NGO and academic mobilization on the CDA election appears in these articles.

47 The provincial CDA 'representatives' were made up of eighteen lawyers, eighteen retired civil servants, fifteen businessmen, five former MPs, four journalists, four farmers, four private sector employees and seven others from varied professions. See *The Nation,* 27/12/96, p. A3, for claims of rigging. Also see *Matichon,* 27/12/96, p. 2. Just under 20,000 candidates ran for the CDA with a third being women. Only six women were selected. See *Bangkok Post,* 14/12/96, p. 1; *The Nation,* 27/12/96, p. A3.

48 See for example Bowonsak Uwanno and Chanchai Sawaengsak, *Kanpatirup kanmeuang farangset khokhithen nai kanpatirup kanmeuang thai* [French political reform: ideas for Thai political reform], Bangkok: Samnakphim nithitham, 1997.

49 Khanakammathikan prachasamphan supha rang ratthammanun [Public relations committee, constitution drafting assembly, *Kropbeuangton rang ratthammanun* [Preliminary framework in drafting the people's constitution], 1997.

50 *Ibid.,* p. 3.

51 *Ibid.,* pp. 3–4.

52 *Ibid.,* p. 4.

53 *Ibid.,* pp. 13–16.

54 *Ibid.,* pp. 14–17.

55 *Ibid.,* pp. 28–39.

56 *Ibid.,* pp. 40–50.

57 See 'Raignan kanprachum supha rang ratthammanun khrang thi 5 4 ko. pho.' [Minutes of the 5th meeting of the constitution drafting assembly, 4th February], 1997; and 'Raingna

prachumsupha rang ratthammanun khrang thi 8 5 mo.kho' [Minutes of the 8th meeting of the constitution drafting assembly, 4th March], 1997.

58 See *Bangkok Post*, 5/12/96, p. 2; 7/12/96, p. 1; *Matichon*, 11/12/96, p. 2.

59 See interview with Kaewsan Ittipoh, *Siam Post*, 27/1/97, p. 2. Kaewsan was a central mover in pushing for participation in the drafting process. However, he saw people as too tied up with their own grievances to understand political reform, and so, he argued, it was necessary to win the support of intellectuals and others to travel and speak in the provinces and drum up participation.

60 Supha rang ratthammanun [Constitution drafting assembly], 'Raingan khong khanatam-ngan rapfang khithen khong onkon thurakit lae onkon ekkachon 3rd April, 2540' [Report of the public hearings committee of business and private organizations], 1997.

61 Kosol Somchida, Deputy President of the Nakhon Ratchasima Chamber of Commerce, cited in *The Nation*, 9/12/96, p. A3.

62 Bowonsak Uwanno, interview with the author, Bangkok, 15/1/98.

63 *Phujatkan raiwan*, 21/8/97, p. 2.

64 See for example 'Khwamhen nai kanyokrang ratthammanun khong nai narong nakhayokhi, phuthaen supha hokankha haeng prathet thai' [Opinion on drafting the constitution of Naron Nakhayokhi representative of the Thai Chamber of Commerce], 1997; Samakhom thanakhan thai (Association of Thai Banks), 'Kanphijarana, rang ratthathammanun' [Con-siderations on the draft constitution], 1997; Supha rang ratthathammanun, 'Raingan khong khanathamngan rapfang khwamkhithen khong ongkon thurakit lae onkon ekkachon 3rd April, 2540' [Report of the public hearings committee of business and private organizations]; *Bangkok Post*, 22/3/97, p. 252.

65 See *The Nation*, 3/7/95, p. A8. Army chief Vimol Wongwanich said of the expected attempts at forming a government after the impending elections, 'We will not get involved. We will leave it to the democracy process.' General Viroj broke precedent in not submitting a list of military names for appointment to the Senate: see *Siamrat sapda*, 24–30 June 1996.

66 Senior military officers objected to a parliamentary committee inquiring into military use of funds. See *Bangkok Post*, 16/7/96, p. 1; 15/9/96, p. 1.

67 See Chai-Anan, 'Old Soldiers Never Die, They are Just Bypassed: The Military, Bureau-cracy and Globalization', in Kevin Hewison (ed.) *Political Change in Thailand: Participation and Democracy*, London: Routledge, 1997, pp. 42–57, p. 55.

68 Deputy Supreme Commander General Preecha Rojanasen is reported as having argued that a clause allowing people to resist any unconstitutional overthrow of a government would lead to arms being hoarded: see *The Nation*, 31/6/97, p. A3. Army Commander in Chief, Chetta Thanajaro, also wanted to ensure that there would be no constitutional ban on amnesty for coup makers; see *The Nation*, 14/6/97, p. A3.

69 See *Matichon*, 28/4/97, p. 4. The remaining 300 are held by: the Public Relations depart-ment (127); Police Department (44); Telecommunications Authority of Thailand (62); with 40 other state agencies sharing the rest. In 1991 alone over one billion baht was earned in advertising revenue from radio stations. By mid-2005 state agencies continued to resist liberalization and to stall the creation of an independent regulator.

70 See Thepchai Yong, 'Broadcasting an anti-reform intent' *The Nation*, 27/4/04. See also *The Nation*, 11/6/05; 21/4/04.

71 *The Nation*, 27/8/99, p. A2.

72 *The Nation* reported a potential vote of 309 in favour of the draft and 343 either against or uncertain. See *The Nation*, 21/8/97, p. A1.

73 *Bangkok Post*, 6/3/97, p. 4; 23/5/97, p. 2. See a broad list of party criticisms of the constitution in *The Nation*, 5/6/97, p. A3.

74 Chuan Leekpai, interview with the author, Bangkok, 26/3/97.

75 *The Nation*, 5/6/97, p. A3.

76 On the governing party's position see *Bangkok Post*, 6/9/97, p. 1.

77 See Sunborikan khomun lae kotmai samnakngan lekhathikan wuthisupha [Secretariat of the Senate, information and legal centre], *Thamniap samachikwuhtisupha 2539* [The Senate Register 1996]. This booklet shows that Banharn's appointments to the Senate marked a decisive shift in reducing the proportion of civil servants (serving and retired) in the Senate from approximately 60 per cent to just over 50 per cent. This shift is all the more dramatic if one considers that Banharn was only in a position to appoint half of the Senate. (The NPKC Senate was appointed for six years, although half of its membership was up for reselection after three years.) See also *Matichon*, 27/7/97, p. 3.

78 Meechai Ruchapun, interview with the author, Bangkok, 8/1/98.

79 *Bangkok Post*, 4/9/97, p. 1.

80 The role of the Interior during 1997 is hard to gauge. Its active and exposed role in defeating amendments on local elections in 1994 meant it pursued its goals more discreetly this time around.

81 See *Bangkok Post*, 25/7/97, p. 1.

82 *Siamrat*, 20/7/97, p. 3.

83 *Bangkok Post*, 2/9/97, p. 1.

84 *Bangkok Post*, 5/9/97, p. 1.

85 *Bangkok Post*, 6/6/97, p. 3.

86 *Bangkok Post*, 10/5/97, p. 1. See also *Watthajak*, 10/5/97, p. 15, on conservative anxiety about the growth of human rights.

87 *Bangkok Post*, 6/6/97, p. 3.

88 *Bangkok Post*, 6/5/97, p. 10.

89 See the statement by Pracha Chatwongwai, head of the Northeast Kamnan and Village Head Association, who was supportive of the draft and critical of the National Association of Kamnan and Village Heads for its opposition: *The Nation*, 3/9/97, p. A3.

90 One of those rumoured to be behind it was the head of LAD, Chuwong Chaiyabut, see *Bangkok Post*, 30/8/97, p. 2.

91 See *Bangkok Post*, 4/5/97, p. 1.

92 *Bangkok Post*, 6/9/97, p. 2.

93 Sathaban Damrongrachanuphap krasuang mahathai (The Damrongrachanuphap Institute, Interior Ministry), *Yuthasat krasuang mahathai 2540–2549* [Strategy of the interior, 1997–2006], 1996, p. 40.

94 *Ibid.*, p. 41.

95 *Ibid.*

96 *Ibid.,* pp. 44–5.

97 *Ibid.,* p. 45.

98 *Ibid.,* pp. 47–8.

99 *Ibid.,* p. 50.

100 *Ibid.,* p. 53.

101 *Ibid.,* pp. 62–5.

102 *Ibid.,* pp. 63–4.

103 *Bangkok Post,* 3/9/97, p. 1.

104 See *Siam Post,* 6/9/97, p. 2. Chavalit had been visited by top military brass and top business leaders. Also people considered close to Prem had expressed a desire for it to pass.

105 Regarding the insider/outsider knowledge complex, I have heard several accounts of the King's intervention. True or not, they clearly fit into the democratic myth. One story has it that the monarchy was instrumental in getting the military to support the draft. General Chetta is said to have then lobbied Chavalit.

106 See *Bangkok Post,* 27/9/97, p. 1.

107 The vote passed by a huge majority, with 578 supporting out of a possible 651. *Bangkok Post,* 28/9/97, p. 1.

108 Duncan McCargo (ed.) *Reforming Thai Politics,* Copenhagen: Nordic Institute of Asian Studies, 2002.

109 *Bangkok Post* (online edition), 7/01/01.

110 See Michael Nelson, 'Thailand's House Elections of 6 Jan. 2001: Thaksin's Landslide Victory and Subsequent Narrow Escape', in Michael H.Nelson (ed.) *Thailand's New Politics: KPI Yearbook 2001,* Bangkok: White Lotus, forthcoming.

111 Kevin Hewison, 'Pathways to Recovery: Bankers, Business and Nationalism in Thailand', Working Paper Series no. 1, April 2001, SEARC, City University of Hong Kong.

112 Pasuk Phongpaichit and Chris Baker, 'Thailand's Thaksin: New Populism or Old Cronyism?', paper presented at the East Asian Institute, Columbia University, 25 October 2001.

113 Philippe Regneir, 'Reform in Post Crisis Thailand (1997–2001): Exploring the Contribution of Small Entrepreneurs to Socio-Economic Change, Democratization and Emerging Populist Governance', paper presented at the 3rd EUROSEAS Conference, 5–8 September 2001, School of Oriental and African Studies, University of London.

114 World Bank, *Beyond the Crisis: A Strategy for Renewing Rural Development in Thailand,* Bangkok: World Bank, 2000.

115 *Siam Rat,* 1/6/01, p. 5.

116 See Michael H. Nelson, 'Thailand's House Elections of 6 Jan. 2001: Thaksin's Landslide Victory and Subsequent Narrow Escape', in Michael H.Nelson (ed.) *Thailand's New Politics: KPI Yearbook 2001,* Bangkok: White Lotus, 2002, pp. 283–441.

117 *The Nation* (online edition), 5/12/01.

118 Andrew Turton, 'Local Powers and Rural Differentiation', in G.Hart, A. Turton and B. White (eds) *Agrarian Transformations: Local Processes and the State in Southeast Asia,* Berkeley: University of California Press, 1989, pp. 70–97, p. 73.

119 Pairot Phromsan, 'Kanborihan thi di mi prasithiphap' [Good governance and efficiency], *Thesaphiban,* 93, 1, 1998, pp. 13–17.

120 The extent to which even state security bodies are changing their outlook can be evidenced in Samnakngan supha khwammankhong, *Nayobai khwammankhong haeng chat 2540–2544* [National Security Policy 1997–2001]. This document speaks of pluralism, the role of NGOs, democracy and human rights.

121 Thabuang mahawithayalai samnakngan khana kammakan kanleuaktang [Bureau of universities and the electoral commission of Thailand], *Khumu asasamak ratthammanun* [Manual for Constitution Volunteers], 1999.

122 *Ibid.*, pp. 7–8.

123 Samnakngan khanakammakan kanleuaktang [Electoral commission of Thailand], *Nangseu songsoem prachathipatai nai chumchon: buntoem pai leuak tang* [Book to promote democracy in the community], *Bunterm Goes to Vote*, 1998.

8   Liberalism, civil society and new projects of subjection

In a satirical book, *A Tyrant's Manual*, Wutiphong Phiapjirawat advises politicians not to succumb to voters seeking favours post-election, instead it was best to shame claimants with the response 'you've already been paid'.[1] The existence of vote-buying and selling has commonly been used to point to the existence of a politically immature electorate incapable of delivering good politicians to government. Others have pointed to the systematic and almost functional nature of the practice in the context of elite competition in Thailand and their commercialization of electoral politics.[2] In turn, this is often seen as a significant failure of Thai political culture and the politics of patronage. Widespread anxiety about the deleterious impact of vote-buying in the early 1990s led to a series of campaigns and educational assaults on local populations.[3] These may be seen largely as extensions state-based approaches to democracy, although a number of civic organizations and NGOs also engaged in this activity. The campaigns have had a rather moral approach. For instance, stickers issued in advance of the 1995 general election advised that 'selling your vote is like selling your nation'. Another moral element has been the gendered nature of some arguments about the need for a pure democracy. For example, at one seminar a facilitator remonstrated the audience on the evils of vote-selling as contaminating the purity of the democratic system. Reaching for imagery that might arouse the interest of male participants he explained, with women in attendance, that no man 'likes to kiss a whore [*phuying mua*], he prefers a virgin [*phuying borisut*], and so it should be with democracy, it should be pure.'[4] Seminars and workshops have been a means by which activists and academics have sought to illuminate the people on the negative social consequences of vote-selling and the importance of good citizenship. In workshops funded by overseas agencies it is not uncommon for participants, ranging from members of village housewives' groups, elderly citizens and students, to line up and receive payment for their involvement. The payment is given at the end, to ensure attendance. Taken by itself, these seminars do not amount to much in particular. They repeat the familiar lessons on good citizenship taught by the state, although with novel pedagogy (group workshops, role plays as opposed to tedious lectures) and with genuine liberal progressive intent. But there is no doubt that there is also continuity in terms of subject/object relations, with 'democracy warriors' defining the legitimate terms of political participation.

If democracy education continues in multiple forms, the context in which it occurs is dramatically changing. For while the invocations to good citizenship and civic duty resonate with statist rhetoric, at a broader level there is an emergent liberal project that is seeking to remake the Thai triad (nation, religion, monarchy) in ways more amenable to its social vision. Civic education projects are occurring in the context of political struggle over state form and ideology, where liberalism may be seen as an emergent position that seeks to embed a new rationality for individual practice related to a newly framed national ideology. In this vision, the state apparatus is displaced, and the good citizen takes centre stage.

Thai liberalism: between society, the state and security

The previous chapter suggested that the domestic seeds of the reform constitution were sowed in the dismay aroused by money-politics and the chagrin of reforming elites towards the electoral habit of vote-buying and selling. More generally, the roots of the new constitution may be located in the historical struggle waged between state-centric visions of regime form and more liberal visions that have been an ongoing feature of Thai political discourse. This places the struggle against authoritarianism and money-democracy into a broader perspective.

Thai liberalism was shaped by the broad historical experience of modernization and development without direct colonialism. Liberal ideals in Thailand were related to ideal notions of civilized polities seen to exist in the West (see Chapter 2). Historically, the success of the Thai state in impeding the progress of territorial imperialism meant that the antagonism often felt by nationalist elites to Western liberalism was less severe in Thailand, notwithstanding the brief Sarit revolution. This made it possible for aspects of the Western liberal tradition to filter into Thai political discourse, and these remain influential today. This is one of the main reasons why Thailand has not been particularly prominent in the 'Asian values' debate. What is significant, though, is the manner in which liberal ideas are mixed with referents in Thai history, so that an 'authentic' Thai liberalism is partly formed around the figure of the monarch. To understand contemporary manifestations of liberalism in Thailand, one needs an appreciation of the links between the monarchy and an assumed historical trajectory. It is not unusual to consider Thai liberalism in a condition of historical inertia, repressed because of state dominance over the Sino-Thai capitalist class (being ethnically differentiated from Thais, this class is understood as not being able to play a role in leading democratization as it could not appeal to the masses).[5] In the absence of this force, the monarchy assumes a significant role in advancing the liberal cause.

The term 'liberalism' in this chapter refers principally to the support of political structures that provide security against the arbitrary use of power and of mechanisms to protect against that old shibboleth, 'the tyranny of the majority', often rendered (implicitly) in Thailand as 'the disease of freedom' (*rok-seriphap*). It is possible to see

Thai liberalism as evolving from this political stance of negative freedom (keeping the state and the masses at bay) towards, more recently, a more philosophical liberalism premised on an ontology of the individual and an embracing of modern liberalism's concerns with positive freedom (providing the conditions for individual potential). Indeed, to the extent that liberalism can reach down to individual subjects and speak to their identity, it must make this move. This has been an uneven and even contradictory movement, since in Thailand supporters of political liberalism may, on social issues, be communitarian, conservative, even socialist in orientation. However, there are adherents of democratic liberalism in Thailand who want to move beyond the state's delayed liberalism and bring about a revolution in state-society relations. This chapter focuses on several relevant organizations and those liberals who have sought to extend Thai liberalism towards a politics of self in relation to the state. Understanding the disciplinary aspect of liberalism allows a more qualified assessment of the democratic nature of Thailand's political transition. Democracy is to be restrained by a liberal ethic.

Historically speaking, Thai political liberalism, in the form of a guaranteed system of checks and balances, and a belief in the rule of law, is traceable to early aristocratic rumblings against the absolute monarchy in the late nineteenth century. Ideas of accountable and consultative government and restraints on absolute power had been aired throughout the early period of the last century, so that notions of the division of power were commonplace parts of political discourse despite the political dominance of the monarchy.[6] However, this is often a forgotten episode, as others prefer to attribute the foundations of Thai liberalism and nationalism to the monarchy.[7]

It may be useful to approach modern elite liberalism by locating elements of its position in the royalist response to 1932. While there is a historically ambiguous relationship between the royalist position and liberalism (see Chapter 6), there is sufficient historical plausibility for modern-day liberals to reach back and create a tradition. With the end of the absolute monarchy and the crushing of the royalist rebellion, royalists sought a settlement based on the British constitutional monarchy, becoming exponents of minimal liberalism. The king's demand to the People's Party before his abdication in 1935 included a British style of democracy with extra powers for the monarchy, including powers of veto, and for the king to have input into procedures relating to petitions to the monarchy.[8] These positions formed the basis for much of Thailand's dominant liberal strand – royal liberalism, understood here as a defensive position against military and bureaucratic government as it emerged in the decades after the overthrow of the absolute monarchy, and a guardianship role for the monarchy until the people were ready for liberal democracy.

The historical irony of modern Thai liberalism, then, is that it may be seen as being forged not in a long historical struggle against the divine rule of kings, nor may it be traced as a gradual evolution of constitutionalism, although there are elements of this; rather, it emerged as a historically significant force in instrumental political discourse against the People's Party and its emergent one-party authoritarianism and militarism. The traumatic experience of the Phibun era (1938–44) – of commoner rule and the abolishment of royal language – may have compelled royalists to support a system of constitutional monarchy as protection against the latent authoritarian republicanism of Phibun. Liberal royalism subsequently became embedded in post-World War II political manoeuvrings for a political 'restoration' of the monarchy, struggles which became encased in a series of constitutions that maintained an exigent tension, *mutatis mutandis*, between liberalism, democracy and authoritarianism.[9] It was the attempt to retain a role for the monarchy in the post-revolutionary period that provided an impetus for a number of writers to seek an emulation of British liberalism with the assured position of a constitutional monarch.[10] Certainly, pragmatic alliances with the military by royalists in the late 1940s aimed at defeating Pridi and the subsequent partnership between the king and Sarit in the late 1950s and early 1960s, stretches the credibility of royal liberalism. However, recognizing this alliance does not mean one should ignore how the king used this interregnum *sans-constitution*, to establish a position from which the monarchy became the entrepôt for graduated liberalism, facilitating order and change management within the conservative cultural bounds of Thainess and security.

Perhaps exemplary of liberal royalism is the work of Seni Pramoj, who in the context of the late 1940s explained:

> The constitutional monarchy offers us an effective tool in defence against dictatorship. So long as the supreme power remains with the monarch, and therefore out of the reach of those ambitious political souls, there will not be a desire among politicians to become a dictator.[11]

Seni, from a minor aristocratic family, helped found the Democrat Party, which has a credible, if compromised history of elite opposition to authoritarian rule and support for private property and inheritance.[12] At the end of World War II he assumed the prime ministership of Thailand very briefly, as he did again for separate stints in 1975 and 1976. His interpretation of Thai democracy has been particularly influential. In an address to schoolteachers in 1968, Seni Pramoj spoke on democracy and freedom.[13] The speech was a summary of much of his writing on this theme, reflecting a broad royalist current in Thai thought.[14] Seni declared that if England was the mother of democracy 'then we are the grandmother, because we achieved democracy sooner.'[15] The basis of the claim is the controversial Ramkhamhaeng Inscription (reputedly late thirteenth century). The inscription is regarded as evidence of the basic liberality of the monarchy, before its corruption by Indianized Brahman practice. The inscription is widely cited in Thai discourse, for it presents a startling picture of freedom, commerce and welfare:

> In the time of Father King Ram Khamhaeng . . . Sukothai is good. In the waters are fish, in the fields is rice. The ruler taxes not his people on travel. They drive oxen to trade; they ride horses to sell. Whoever wants to deal . . . deals.

Over there, at the gateway, a bell is hung. If any folk of the realm seeks court with the King, having anguish in their stomach, grievance in their heart, there is no difficulty. Go ring the bell hung there. Hearing the call, Father King Ram Kham Haeng will sift the case honestly . . . Mango trees abound in this land . . . Whoever plants them, unto him they shall belong.[16]

According to Seni, the Inscription is the first Thai constitution, no less important than Magna Carta, because it describes an implicit social contract between the king and his subjects that guarantees liberties, equality and fraternity.[17] The idea of a social contract here refers back to the idea of a just king who must provide for the welfare of his people. Thus a liberal order (commerce and freedom) is rooted in conservative notions of paternal kingship. However, this early liberal system went into decline owing to the irresponsible use of freedom by the people: 'History's lesson teaches that danger lies not only in abuse of power by the rulers, but also in abuse of liberties by the people.'[18] In a later piece Seni attacked 'the disease of democracy', by which he meant the people's excessive use of liberties and freedoms.[19] An important underlying position of Seni's speech was the stated difference between democracy and liberalism. Acutely aware of these different traditions, anxiety about the tyranny of the majority motivated Seni's attack on excessive freedom. Similar to most liberals, he was inclined to seek the formation of a rational, tolerant and responsible citizen not given to abuse of freedom. These ideas were largely shared by Seni's brother, Kukrit Pramoj, who was also a founder of the Democrat Party and also served as prime minister in the 1975/6 period. Kukrit's historical and fictional writings, as well as ownership of magazines, gave him a platform on which to promote his ideas. Kukrit distinguished liberal and democratic traditions, betraying an obvious concern that democracy not be turned against 'freedom'. As he explained, 'the justice of the liberal system is its respect for the rights of the minority, freedom of speech, freedom of expression and religion'.[20] For Kukrit, were there ever to be a complete democracy (*prachathipatai sombun*), then sovereignty would fully belong to people with grave consequences for the rights of the individual.[21] Democracy is rendered as a system not in which the people rule as such, but a system in which governments have the consent of the people and in which power is divided among the executive, legislature and the courts, all watched over by the king.[22]

What is important here is not the degree to which there was a philosophical congruence between these raw positions and those of Western liberalism, which in any case was a broad and often conflicted body of thought, but rather that modern-day liberals often root their positions in a similar reading of aspects of Thailand's past. Clearly, one could easily read the broad current of thought described above as conservative, given that it relies on traditional notions of legitimacy for the monarchy, and its regard for order. However, there is nothing particularly odd about using a mythic foundational past to enculture a national liberal tradition. If monarchy offends republican liberal sentiment, it has been an enduring feature of several 'liberal' Western societies too. The strategic and ideological use of the institution is the relevant issue. Other components of this enculturing include highlighting the role of Chulalongkorn in freeing slaves and serfs, and the plans of King Prajatipok to introduce a constitution prior to the 1932 revolution.

In terms of modern liberalism, with the political opening of 1973 liberal actors attempted to carve out a space for political freedom and the institutionalization of political democracy. Subsequently, these moves were made in the context of the 'semi-democracy' of the 1980s, the roots of which were laid in the overthrow of the Thanin regime in 1977. Despite the failure of 'semi-democracy' to evolve towards 'full democracy' in this period, actors sought to increase the political leverage of pseudo-representative institutions (parliament) against the monopolized institutions of the national-will-incarnate (the state apparatuses). They primarily exercised their politics in legal and parliamentary circles with an agenda focused on parliamentary reform and cautious democratic development. However, they shared with state actors a concern with security.

Some political development theorists who were to emerge as reformists in the 1990s were writers for journals such as *Psychological Security*, the journal of the National Thai Association of Psychological Security.[23] This association, established in 1970, was composed of intellectuals close to the bureaucratic and military state; its aim was to build political consensus on forms of national security beyond the politics of anti-communism. One long-term member of the association, Pranot Nanthiyakun, explained that one of the aims of building national security was to develop the people to be the 'eyes and ears of the state':

> The communists like to say they can be compared to fish, and the people to water. Whether communists can survive and grow or die depends on the support of the people ... But if our people have true discipline, the people will become poisonous water and the communists, who are fish, will die easily.[24]

Liberal contributions to *Psychological Security* were significant, for they highlighted the shared space between liberals and the national security complexes. This link was mediated in part by a shared discourse of political development. This provided statists and liberals alike with a view that saw development as an engineering process of political, social and economic adjustment to the conditions of modernity. Given that state agencies endorsed and propagated the developmental metaphor, there was a shared discursive space between liberals and the developmental bureaucracy.[25] However, although sharing the same political development language as the articulators of statist democracy, developmental liberal democrats turned that language against the 'universal' state. They saw the overgrown state as a historical condition occasioned by the processes of modernization in the Third World. Largely taking on board Riggs' thesis of the bureaucratic polity, and the larger frame of political development theory, Thai liberals wanted to move beyond bureaucratic dominance and promoted the emergence of a political infrastructure that linked the state to multiple-organized constituencies. Such an image of the state is a classically pluralist one, viewing it as a neutral arbiter of competing societal interests. Furthermore, the state, in turn, is seen as being constrained by social forces. This was to become the liberal project, to develop cautiously a social realm – civil society, as it would become popularly known – that could temper the state.

The relationship to the existing system was not unproblematic for liberals. In the 1980s, modern Thai political liberalism found itself caught between the bureaucratic state apparatus and the money-politics of political parties. Taken as abstract forces, both the state and capital were judged as inhospitable environs for the growth of liberal conduct. However, a good dose of political realism – endemic to the liberal practitioner more likely to work with reform elites in the establishment than be co-opted into the struggles of the 'ignorant' and potentially threatening masses – entailed working with these forces. Thus liberals etched away at smaller areas, building up parliamentary integrity, earnestly attempting to shift the dominant tradition of a military and bureaucratic discourse of democracy away from the ideal of civic virtue to issues of institutionalizing procedural democracy. The issue of citizen virtue would arise as a significant matter only when the conditions for a liberal state had been secured. While the state apparatus had staked its democratic legitimacy on the project of developing the rationality of citizens and perfecting the functioning of democratic institutions, the liberals counter-played, within the same development discourse, on the need to foster a political environment where such virtues and perfection could materialize. This position marked the rise of procedural democracy in Thailand. Many academics and MPs staked the future of democracy on the development of functioning political parties.[26] Duncan McCargo notes that the prevalent desire to develop 'real' parties that has prevailed in Thai political science missed the actual functioning of Thai parties as productive actors in the pursuit of clique-based interest. While this is true, it must be noted that the search for the 'real party' was part of both the bureaucratic ideology of delayed liberalism and part of the liberal ideology of a procedural democracy. It named a project, not a misconception.

Liberals, sharing the same political development frame as the guardian state, were not so much a counter-hegemonic force, but a vanguard element within the integral state as it began its long process of transformation and reformation under the weight of the economic revolution of the 1980s. When, however, the state and capital became mired in the phenomenon of money-democracy, liberalism would move to present itself in counter-hegemonic fashion, as a total reform of the state. This project was not merely a national one, but reflected the growing power of international discourse and elites supporting the establishment of procedural democracy as a means of promoting global liberalization and market access.[27] As indicated in Chapter 7, the events leading to the new constitution were under-written by important structural factors forcing sections of the capitalist and state elite towards reform. Internationally mobile capitalism sought market access and political stability as a condition of long-term entry. These needs were codified in the World Bank's promotion of good governance, encompassing transparent public administration and policy making that is efficient and accountable.[28] In the Thai context, good governance rode on the back of political reform, and became a staple component of political discourse in the mid-to-late 1990s, enabling it to be seen as part of the characteristics of a good democracy. Politically, the significance of the governance discourse was to further increase the legitimacy of liberal conceptions of political order within Thailand. Indeed, the agenda of good governance took institutional shape in the public and political institutions that the reform movement fought for. Key among these elements were: reframing legitimacy in the face of a crisis of the state; promoting freedom of association and participation; an improved judiciary and securing the rule of law; increasing accountability in various spheres of government; freedom of information; and the promotion of state/civil society relations to enhance the efficiency of the governance process.[29] These positions were not merely externally articulated, but found general expression among Thai policy elites and researchers in universities, research institutes and the press.[30]

At the same time, the large international development industry was largely responsible for officializing discourses of participation and civil society throughout the late 1980s and 1990s. 'Participation' and 'civil society', potentially radical oppositional ideas, were to become part of the new regulatory framework involved in restructuring the state in Thailand, as elsewhere (see next chapter). This involved seeking a reduction of state provision of public goods and its replacement by societal and community sectors, and the co-option of significant actors in the name of participation into new development policy frameworks that would ultimately advance market-based capitalism. The World Bank nicely summed up the new thinking in its promotion of an 'effective state' that was to act as a partner rather than providing goods directly. This required a significant ideological shift on the nature of the state:

> Getting societies to accept a redefinition of the state's responsibilities will be one part of the solution. This will include strategic selection of collective actions that states will try to promote, coupled with greater efforts to take the burden off the state, by involving citizens and communities in the delivery of collective goods.[31]

The rallying cry of 'civil society' has largely done this ideological work, with its moral incantation for associational life, self-reliance and anti-statism. Indeed, much of the language of the instruments of global capitalism mirrors that of progressive NGOs. For instance, consider how the World Bank speaks about remaking the state: 'making the state more responsive to people's needs, bringing government closer to the people through broader participation and decentralization.'[32] This could easily be a piece of NGO-speak.

The contested and uneven rise of political liberalism in Thailand, then, should be seen as part of the more general shift that is being effected globally. This shift is principally one in which democratization should be seen as 'an integral aspect of the economic and ideological restructuring accompanying a new stage of globalisation in the capitalist world economy.'[33] Samir Amin writes that the democratic trend is accompanied by

> a kind of generalised offensive for the liberation of 'market forces', aimed at the ideological rehabilitation of the absolute superiority of private property, legitimation of social inequalities and anti-statism of all kinds.[34]

These aspects are all clearly present in the Thai case. The politics of post-reform Thailand have been marked by renewed attempts to reduce the public sector and corresponding programmes of privatization. There is also a general elevation of civil society as a moral force superior to the state in its capacity to produce a caring society. While not the focus of this book, there has been a modest level of foreign involvement in the diffusion of these ideas, with funding agencies from Europe, Australia and North America generally providing aid to governmental and non-governmental organizations in the name of civil society building, anti-corruption, civic education, increasing the capacity of representative institutions, election watches, and so on.

The liberal engagement: developing political institutions

The international nexus promoting Thailand's liberalization is nothing particularly new. Western agencies have in various forms been supportive of liberal democratization in Thailand from the 1970s onwards. In the complex environment of the 1980s, the potential of parliament as a new centre of power became the focus of a significant liberal project that involved a dual strategy of institutionalizing the parliamentary regime and assisting in the political socialization of the elite. At the forefront of this effort was Chai-Anan Samudavanija and the establishment of the Centre for Study of Public Issues in 1984. Eventually becoming the Institute of Public Policy Studies (IPPS), it was initially a unit within the Social Science Association of Thailand (SSAT), and rapidly emerged as an autonomous body, aided by base funding from the Konrad Adenauer Foundation (KAF), a foundation of the German Christian Democrats.[35] While IPPS would always be a small organization with around six full-time staff, its influence was multiplied by the skilful networking of key members.[36]

KAF's support for the IPPS was based on its own foundational charter to promote the development of liberal and constitutional government, federalism and support of the 'ethical foundations' of political life.[37] When IPPS emerged as an autonomous body in 1989, KAF endorsed its fivefold aim to

1 serve as a medium between civil servants, MPs, academics and the public;
2 promote parliamentary democracy;
3 support the dissemination of policy studies;

4 strengthen parliamentary democracy and democratic structures;
5 promote political education.[38]

The story of the IPPS is intimately tied up with the life of Chai-Anan who, through the institute, hoped to revive the liberal agenda that had emerged briefly in the mid-1970s. A prolific writer since the 1970s, Chai-Anan rose to prominence in 1974 when he was appointed to the Constitution Drafting Committee. That Committee's draft was strongly liberal and threatened a delimitation of bureaucratic and military power, although, in a familiar turn of events, conservative elements reasserted their position and watered it down. Undaunted, the youthful, twenty-nine-year-old crusader secured a grant from the Ford Foundation to establish a Legislative Innovation Programme, aiming to provide the new parliamentary government with the necessary information related to legislative programmes. Clearly, the aim was to support the effective operations of parliament and displace the dominance of the bureaucracy in the legislative process.[39] Also appointed as Secretary to the Legislative Reform Committee within the Secretariat of the National Assembly, Chai-Anan found his efforts challenged by a growing conservative backlash as early as 1974. Manoeuvring within the National Assembly led to Chai-Anan and his staff being removed from their positions and, as he notes, 'My 18 month-long effort to create a viable support system for nascent democratic institutions was at an end.'[40]

Chai-Anan, however, found himself rehabilitated in 1980, being appointed as an adviser to Prem, but soon resigned because 'I saw that what was being created under Prem was an entrenched technocratic polity rather than the democracy of my hopes.'[41] His next major initiative was the Centre for Public Policy Issues. The story of Chai-Anan is important. While public exposure may suggest a one-man crusade, in fact there were scores of similarly minded liberal intellectuals and supporters who were involved in various attempts to liberalize the regime. This liberal bridgehead gradually grew stronger throughout the 1980s. Although no doubt the most outstanding of his generation, Chai-Anan's ambitions were shared by many, although a minority. Let his biography be read, then, partly as that of other cautious liberals in Thailand.[42] Chai-Anan summarized his political ambitions thus: 'To explain to my fellow citizens why they should want to make their country a democracy, and to show them how it can be done, have always been my goals.'[43] In very straightforward terms Chai-Anan summarizes the agenda of liberal democrats in Thailand, as well as situating himself clearly within the political developmental frame.

What was central to this agenda was establishing an inter-elite consensus on the rules of the game; this Chai-Anan relates to regime legitimacy:

> Legitimacy in the Thai case involves two levels of consensus. The first is interelite consensus concerning the rules of the game; the second is consensus between the elites and the masses. For the past five years, the Institute [IPPS] has been emphasizing consensus building among elites. The challenge of the future will be to build consensus among the masses.[44]

Chai-Anan also neatly summarizes the modus operandi of many legal and political science intellectuals who, on paper, appear radical but work dangerously close to the circles of power:

> My formal institutional linkages with both the elected House of Representatives and the appointed Senate have been tremendous assets for me. I have been able to work 'within the system' while maintaining very strong links outside it, with academia and non-governmental organizations.[45]

This is the activist Chai-Anan speaking, not always obvious in his academic work, betraying the *élan* of many of the Thai liberals whose academic position and status generates a certain delusional grandeur as to the effectiveness of their practice. Chai-Anan's brand of royal liberalism has been marked by extensive networking among elites and the use of public forums and the media, as well as publishing to propagate representative democracy.[46]

Until the early 1990s IPPS remained in its first phase of attempting to build inter-elite consensus. Although supposedly neutral, IPPS's advocacy for the development of liberal democracy could only be antagonistic to the bureaucratic state.[47] At a time when there were regular tussles between liberalizing political elites and statist bureaucratic actors over contentious issues, IPPS provided a number of academics with an institutional platform from which to address questions beyond those which flared up between the contesting sides. This was important, for while some politicians were – by the logic of their position – fighting for an expansion of parliament's sphere of influence, their efforts were tainted by the dubious backgrounds of many MPs and the constant exposure of corrupt party politics. By virtue of its status as a non-partisan organization, IPPS provided political liberals with a forum in which to address issues of political development and liberalization far from the maddening expletives of actual struggle.

The activities of IPPS were numerous. While primarily a study and policy body in its early years (1984–7), by the late 1980s the institute self-consciously took on an advocacy role. Under the Chatichai government, to which Chai-Anan and Bowonsak acted as advisers, the IPPS was able to move towards closer relations with the legislative and administrative bodies of government. Chai-Anan explains thus:

> This strategy coincided with change in the political arenas in which the semi-democratic regime gave way to an elected government. There was a perceived need to revive and strengthen the parliament.[48]

The shift to advocacy involved working with parliamentary administrative bureaucracies, parliamentary house committees, and raising issues such as appointing an ombudsman.[49] Overarching all this activity was IPPS's advocacy of liberal democracy through a number of media including a newsletter, a radio programme, seminars, books and pamphlets.[50]

Its newsletter, *The People's Representative*, with a print run of 20,000, was widely distributed to members of parliament and supporting organizations, NGOs, schools and civic organizations. While a forum for different views, its combined effect was to advocate the embedding and extension of parliamentary infrastructure in order to increase the efficiency of parliament itself. In general, the newsletter carried articles promoting a greater understanding of democracy, and also presented detailed issues of parliamentary reform and reports of seminars.[51] In terms of mass reach, IPPS also hosted a weekly radio show with an estimated audience of one million people.[52] Furthermore, in league with Sukhothaithamathrat University, IPPS set up a certified political education programme in 1990 to further enlighten relevant political and administrative actors in the parliamentary arena on the mechanisms and principles of liberal democracy. Four targets of education were proposed, from politicians to the general public. Interestingly, the programme was seen as an alternative and, perhaps, a response to the fact that the military had opened some of its National Defence Academy courses to businessmen and politicians in an effort to secure leadership over them.[53]

Perhaps IPPS's most ambitious programme was its effective lobbying, through a parliamentary committee, for the launching of the Parliamentary Development Plan.[54] The plan aimed at increasing the legislative capacity of the lower house and building up networks and links between parliamentary bodies and lower-level representative bodies, as well as foundations and associations.[55] It aimed also at building up relations between political parties and interest groups such that parties could become effective articulators and aggregators of interest.[56] In June 1989 the parliament unanimously endorsed the plan. Clearly the plan was an implicit challenge to the networks of influence that secured bureaucratic dominance throughout the nation. In a discussion of the plan, political scientist Pathan Suwanamongkhon noted that past parliamentary instability, and the negative behaviour of politicians, had resulted in democratic development and education being seen as the prerogative of the Interior Ministry and the Ministry of Education. One of the prime aims of the plan, therefore, was for parliamentary bodies themselves to promote democratic understanding and simultaneously develop the parliamentary regime itself.[57]

In 1993, with a new director and Chai-Anan as President, IPPS moved to its second phase of building mass-elite consensus around the rules of the democratic game. This shift, greatly influenced by the events of 1992, found its lexiconal equivalent when the IPPS explained that it was now moving away from advocating representative democracy towards supporting participatory democracy.[58] As part of this shift, the IPPS began to propagate the institutionalization of public hearings as a way of mediating the growing number of conflicts between government, capitalists and local communities over local resource management. IPPS, along with others, succeeded in getting Cabinet to adopt a resolution on public hearings in 1996.[59] Parallel with this institutional reform was the attempt by IPPS to educate the public on the conduct of public hearings. The new director of IPPS, Parichart Chotiya, explained the role of the organization as being non-partisan and to dis-seminate information: 'I have tried to make it clear to everyone what constitutes a public hearing, and what does not, to create a common understanding of their importance.'[60]

While IPPS had been central in political reform advocacy (see previous chapter), it feared that the immediate institutionalist aims of the reform movement were being subverted by adventurous demands, and so it held seminars to disarm the growing expectations of many:

> political reform cannot be perceived as an instant 'package' which can win support and be implemented in a coup . . . as was misleadingly promoted by some academics. Rather it should be perceived as a process which, when gradually put into place, will lead to changes at a pace that is comprehensible, and acceptable to most parties.[61]

While democratic advocacy and apparent non-partisanship were held in tension in IPPS's work, it was its educational focus that set IPPS apart from activist and 'interested' organizations. Arguing, for instance, that the push for participatory democracy had to some extent succeeded, IPPS defined its role as articulating the limits of the rules of the new participatory game: 'Now that the effort [to promote democracy] starts to bear fruit, it is important that the "empowerment and participation" process be constructive and knowledge based.'[62] This was a theme that would become central to the civil society movement from the mid-1990s onwards. This marks the disciplinary aspect of the liberal movement. The liberal guardian was now engaged in forms of tutelage, defining the legitimate scope of democratization around policy restraint and broad consensus.

If IPPS was symbolic of the liberal strain in Thai politics and was, through its cautious strategy, embedding parliamentary convention and democratic consciousness, it would be wrong to assume it was the only medium. Through the universities, among some members in political parties, and even within the bureaucratic apparatus of the parliament itself, efforts were ongoing. Also, as is widely recognized, the press was increasingly a conduit of liberal opinion and a staging ground for attacks on the state apparatuses. In his critical review of policy advocacy in the Thai media, Duncan McCargo makes a qualified positive assessment of its efforts in the 1990s.[63] From another perspective, however one judges its presentation of policy issues, one thing is clear: the press was a major mouthpiece for the expression of alternative notions of democracy beyond that advocated by the Interior Ministry.[64] Both in its reporting of various seminars and in the pervasive pages of columnists, the press was instrumental in forging a dissensus on the meanings of democracy, problematizing what democracy might be and raising it as an issue of public debate, admittedly among a small audience of readers and columnists.[65]

Liberal politics, expressed in the relatively open press, the struggle to expand the influence of parliament, and the academic and civic support of that objective, should be seen as significantly shifting the terms of legitimacy in Thailand. An alternative base-political infrastructure and discourse, which, while interpolating with official strands of the bureaucracy, had emerged. This broad political infrastructure played a pivotal role in the events following May 1992, translating the broad pro-democracy sentiment of that movement into a coherent reformist strategy aimed at building up the basis of a liberal democratic regime.

Institutions and planning democracy

One manifestation of the collaboration of politicians and liberal academics was the establishment of the King Prachatipok's Institute in 1994. This was initially located within the secretariat of the House of Representatives and later became an independent body by an act of parliament in 1998.[66]

Its aim was to promote an understanding of the 'parliamentary democratic system with the king as head of state'. The addition of 'parliament' in this formulation is significant, for it marked the permanence and connection of parliamentary democracy with the older ideology of democracy with the king as head of state, propagated by the bureaucracy. King Prachatipok's Institute was also required to assist in the legislative process, research democratic development and to make its research public.[67] Marut Bunnag, then Parliamentary President and one-time education minister, claimed to have had a hand in the setting-up of KPI precisely because of his distrust of the Interior Ministry and its dubious capacity to carry through democratic education.[68]

The range of the institute's first curriculum was extensive, covering the principles of democratic government, labour and environmental issues under the conditions of globalization, policy formation and political ethics. The instructors included many familiar faces from the Thai political science scene, including Chai-Anan Samudavanija, Prudhisan Jumbala, Suchit Bunbongkarn, Kramol Thong-thammachart and Anek Laothamatas.[69] Specific curricula were also designed for community leaders, political party members and youth.[70] In effect, with a larger budget, greater recognition and hence greater participation of academics, KPI might be seen as the indirect prodigy of IPPS.

Bowonsak Uwwano, the key framer of the reform constitution, who became Director of KPI in 1999, sees it as playing a crucial role in promoting democratic education for all strata of society from top-level bureaucrats to politicians and right down to villagers. In assuming this new position Bowonsak perhaps sees himself as an intermediary actor between society and the state. Speaking of his role in political reform, Bowonsak observed that

> NGOs, they know only the suffering of the people but they don't know how to cure the suffering, meaning that they know the problems of the people and they suffer with the people but they cannot find anyway out, just to protest, protest and protest. And apart from that, political power and state power in Thailand is very strong. This power more or less ignores the NGO movement. Sometimes they blame the NGOs for threatening the national security by receiving funds

from foreign countries – the gap is very strong. As academics you have one challenging problematic, how you can bridge that gap. You cannot take sides by jumping into NGOs and being activists yourselves, because doing so you are going to share the suffering without finding the way out...you cannot jump into the state power either – doing so you would ignore the suffering of the people. So the role of the academics should be the bridge between the two and that bridge, in order to be strong, has to generate a way out . . . I try to do so.[71]

In the grand tradition of liberal academics exemplified by Chai-Anan, Bowonsak exudes the optimism of one who has the ear of the elite, one who is called on, by the elite, to clean up the stables of government. And yet, in a familiar reversion to the people-problem, of organizing them productively, KPI's strategic focus is largely on building civic capacity for responsible participation. Thus the rationale of the institute is rooted very much in the same manner of Interior Ministry propagation projects; that is, the people do not have democratic consciousness, and this acts as an obstacle to further democratic development:

Government in a democratic regime, even though it began some sixty years ago, has faced the constant problem of people's understanding of that system of government, in realizing their rights and duties as a citizen of the nation that is governed with a parliamentary democratic regime with the king as head of state . . . if this cannot be created it will lead to setbacks in the system of government as in the case of Thailand. This truth may be seen by looking at Western societies which have been able to develop government in all dimensions.[72]

Another manifestation of the new political liberalism was the call for a political development plan among members of the DDC. Among the recommendations of the DDC (see previous chapter) was the establishment of a Political Development Council. This was acted on by the Political Reform Committee, the body established in 1996 by the Banharn government. A number of prominent political development theorists were involved in drafting a political development plan, and while it remains pretty much a white paper, the plan gives an indication of how liberal democratic structures were to relate to the development of a new political culture in Thailand.

The idea for the plan was first aired after the crisis of 1992, when the political science and public administration branches of the National Research Council were called on to develop a plan in order to stabilize political development.[73] Presenting an analysis of the vicious cycle of Thai politics (constitution – parliament – crisis – coup – interim constitution – constitution – parliament – crisis – coup, etc.) rooted in the failure of political parties to develop, in the bureaucracy acting as blocks to political development and the lack of political ethics, the plan sought to map out an orderly progress for political development.[74]

One central objective of the plan was to produce 'democratic personalities', meaning 'individuals realizing their own potential and the potential of others such that they would respect the rights and freedoms of themselves and others'.[75] This would be assisted by the creation of a National Ideology Committee.[76] The vision presented of Thailand in 2555 (AD 2012) was that the bureaucracy and military would have no political role, the bureaucracy itself would be decentralized, political parties would have a mass base and ideology, there would be a guarantee of universal human rights including the right to full participation in the political process, and there would be a high level of democratic culture among the people.[77] As for the role of the monarchy in this new democratic culture, it would 'remain' above political conflicts and would continue to act as a role model for society by ostensibly abiding by the ten virtues of a Buddhist king.[78]

In 1996 the Political Reform Committee selected Likhit Dhiravegin, a political development theorist, to lead the drawing-up of a political development plan.[79] This plan, based on the NRC version, basically sought similar institutional outcomes as those proposed by the political reform lobby. It also took a longer-term view, seeing the need to root democratic culture as the only guarantee of stability. Political development was seen as a long-term and dynamic intervention responding to societal and economic change.[80] It was hoped that in the short term planners could help 'bring into being a political culture that is facilitative of developing and preserving democracy with the king as head of state'.[81] This would be achieved by engineering change through a series of educational measures, intervention into the mass media and creating role models. In the long term a fully developed democratic culture would emerge. In this new culture political participation was expected, but would be guided by the liberal principle of respect for the rights of the minority, and would be within the rule of law. Citizens would live life in a democratic way, which is to say they would be disciplined and responsible. In struggling for their own rights and interests they would be mindful of the common good. In disputes they would act rationally and use 'scientific logic' in order to solve problems peacefully.[82] While much of the rhetoric of democratic education is the same as that preached by LAD, as is the reverence shown to the monarchy, what is significant is that the new agents of political socialization, proposed in this plan, are the family, parliament, political parties and interest groups. The apparatus of the bureaucratic-capitalist state had been dethroned, but its moral projects of citizen construction survived.

Liberal mouthpieces

Prominent individuals have popularized the liberal position. One important latecomer to the cause of political liberalism was Anand Panyarachun. His joining the bandwagon needs to be seen both as a result of the failure of the existing political system as well as his engagement, as a leading representative of globally engaged capital, with the world market. Anand is a member of Transparency International, that agent of 'good governance'.

The economic imperative of the new democrasubjection is best highlighted by a speech made by Anand on the eve of the March election in 1992. In this speech Anand speaks of the end of communism and the success of democracy:

> As for Thailand we do not need to copy anybody's democracy, we only need to uphold the principle of democracy which is that the government must come from the people, it must be of the people, and it must be for the people.[83]

Anand goes on to argue that elections are only one point in the democratic process, and argues that the people, with democratic hearts, need to struggle to take part in policy determination. This struggle and participation is defined by the boundaries of the rules of the game, being the law and the constitution. In linking economy and polity, Anand continues:

> In the last 13 months the policy of the government, whether it be in economic or other dimensions, if it is analyzed well, it will be seen that the policy was open. I had an open economic policy, that was transparent, that was competitive that . . . also had a tax system that was just. These things are important factors in leading towards complete democracy . . . Any country that uses an open economic system . . . history tells us that the political system must follow also, the political system must have competition.[84]

It was imperative, Anand considered, that the open economy in Bangkok be spread to the provinces:

> If and when this takes place, we can see an emergence of a rural middle class that can make better and more effective use of their greater autonomy in managing local affairs and issues.[85]

For Anand, then, a free market economy was the basis of democracy, and, given that this had been established, he urged people not to be demoralized but to be patient with the gradual progress of democracy.[86] Importantly, the growth of democracy would be supported by broadening the participation of 'the young, the learned, and the middle, white-collar and managerial classes in political parties'. For Anand, '[t]hese groups of persons are some of the most important constituent parts of our economic machine.'[87]

The participation of these classes in the provincial politics would support the process of decentralization and help in addressing the economic disparities, which were seen as threat to a stable democracy.[88] Anand adopts the seminal analysis of the problem of Thai democracy developed by Anek Laothamatas regarding transforming peasants into urban citizens (see below). This, presumably, would then provide them with a stake in the system. Anand argued that the cycle whereby rural people elected vote-buying MPs and 'middle-class' Bangkokians brought down governments with cries of corruption and incompetence, would end when the status of the rural population was lifted.[89] Presently, the people were not 'interested in whether the government is good or not', rather they were just interested in a government that 'digs wells and makes roads'.[90] Education and higher social-economic status would lead to a broader social vision, one which would provide rural people with the ability to differentiate between' good and bad governments.

The 'democracy' expressed here is an urban one – dependent on an educated middle class and their assumed rationality. The economic task is how to develop the rural areas so that this form of middle-class citizenship can be made real. To this question, Anek Laothamatas, Anand's apparent inspiration, provides an answer. If the perennial problem of urban/rural split in Thai politics is to be overcome then the rural sector, he argues, needs to be thoroughly commercialized with the consequence of either the embourgeoisment or proleterianization of the Thai peasants.[91] Only on this economic basis can the middle-class rational citizen arise. In this frame, then, economics precedes politics, the subjects of democracy do not yet really exist, and the peasants in the countryside are the ghosts of under-development waiting to be buried. Indeed, it is only by engagement with the liberal regime that the new people will be constructed. Participation becomes a mode of transformation – but this does not rule out the need for democratic instruction.

It would be wrong to imagine that the aims of the liberal project could be confidently achieved in economic processes alone. Many liberals see civic politics and education as a means to ideologize the proposed process from peasant to citizen. Just as state democrasubjection provides concrete steps towards citizen construction, so does the emergent liberal discourse – in its commentary on civic competence – provide steps towards liberal democrasubjection. It should be clear here that the intellectual elites have premeditated the meaning of democracy, its function and its processes. The central task was simply how to make this meaning tangible. This entailed, in part, working on the raw material of the people, making the subjects into citizens in the narcissistic self-image of the virtuous, public-minded and rational intellectual. It is thought that democracy without a 'rational' political culture is unworkable. Anand put it more eloquently:

> Democracy is a reflection of the level of the people who vote . . . if they vote for bad persons, democracy will deteriorate. If people still vote as if they were 2,000 year old turtles, who then should take the blame except the people themselves?[92]

Similarly, Anek argues that one problem for Thailand has been the absence of a long period of democratic development. His basic point is that Western democracy arose gradually as the franchise widened to assimilate lower classes who had been appropri-ately educated to perform their democratic responsibilities.[93] According to Anek, the Westernized revolutionaries who came to power in 1932 'gave' democracy to all people instantaneously. This premature designation of the democratic franchise, he argues, has been the root problem facing Thailand ever since: democracy has been taken like technology, 'before the order of our historical development'.[94] The premature embracing of democracy leads, according to Anek, to the prevalent practice of vote-buying as well as the poor quality of politicians and the strength of the military.[95] For him, then, the project of reconstruction of citizenship becomes a societal revolution of mind and economy. While the economy leads, there is the need for education on citizen virtue in a liberal space (see below).[96]

After the rise of the political reform movement, both Anand and Anek became prominent proponents of liberal democratic development. This has included praising the idea of a 'non-ideological civil society' and the idea of 'good governance'.[97] For Anand, capitalism with a human face is the wave of future. Ideological questions are now seen as obsolete, with new questions being focused on how governments can best serve their citizens.[98] The central question for Anand is no longer any doctrine of government, but a government's capability and legitimacy. On this matter he is full of praise for the practice of governance in Singapore, which is said to have responded well to people's needs.[99] This tension between democracy and good governance, regardless of form, was resolved by linking the instruments of good governance to democracy: transparency, freedom of information, scrutiny, balance of power and rule of law. This is the liberal project writ large, ensuring that any excessive demos and its mutations of freedom are constrained by a properly designed liberal democracy. New channels of communication and institutionalized participation would ensure this.[100]

What of the king in this new liberalism? If the symbol of the monarchy functioned to consubstantiate a nation of difference around embodied Thai identity in the old order, the question now arises of what might the symbol mean in the liberalizing 'democratic' regime. Coming from a prominent spokesperson of the liberal current in Thailand, Anand's speeches on the king reflect the continued importance of this institution in a liberal Thailand.

Anand's writings on the monarchy are far-reaching and not merely ritualistic. He adheres to the royalist version of the king governing not on the basis of divine right but on fulfilling the role of a Buddhist king. He notes the king's 'nearly two thousand projects' have assisted the poor and that the king himself has approached local communities pragmatically by tapping into local wisdom and culture. Such work with the poor has led to the strengthening of the 'social fabric of our society and fortifying our national cohesion and identity'.[101] Anand's speeches on the king are an attempt to constructively integrate the monarchy around the new liberal political project. In one interview he recounts the king's following of the legislative programmes of the parliament and notes that he is 'strict' about using his rights to warn, encourage and to be consulted. Indeed, Anand considers the king as Thailand's 'number one public servant', and furthermore, one who is accountable: '[W]hat he does is seen by the people. Not accountable in the legal sense of the word, but . . . there is transparency in what he does.'[102] Finally, Anand presents a picture of a monarch who has reached the highest stage of wisdom, a position of detachment where the ego is erased.[103] According to Anand, the king has achieved this and is thus able to serve as Thailand's 'guiding light': a king for a liberal society.

Liberal civic education and civil society

If the liberal current recognizes the primacy of economic factors in spawning new historical subjects of democracy – the 'middle class' – this is not left to chance. Hence studies of political culture are part of the liberal project of instilling in would-be citizens liberal dispositions and the capacity for self-rule. This brings forth the necessary project of liberal civic education. As a disciplinary aspect of the new liberal democrasubjection, civic education should be understood by reference to the developmental metaphor and its privileging of subject/object relations between the rulers and the soon-to-be rulers. An examination of the thought of Anek Laothamatas reveals a strong normative bias on the nature of citizenship that requires acquisition of virtue.

Anek is a strong proponent of civic education and a leading liberal intellectual in Thai society. A proponent of political reform, he has also been involved in KPI and civic education programs.[104] For him civic education should be an ongoing process from primary school to university. Speaking of the mass of students in the education system and the purpose of civic education, Anek says: 'Let these people have dignity, even though they have less economic status than others, but they do not have less rights, duties and political respect.'[105] Anek sees such civic education as being bound by the treasured civic culture of Thailand. Anek, however, argues that the official ideology is not 'authentically Thai' but rather has been adapted from other cultures. This is not quite apostasy of the essential 'Thainess' examined in Chapter 6. Certainly, the body of work that deconstructs and challenges the meanings of official ideology, such as Thongchai's, is apostate.[106] However, Anek is disturbing, or nudging, the apperception of the Thai ideology to its constructedness, in order to bolster it. He grasps the developmental metaphor that has haunted 'Thai authenticity' as an unspoken and ideologically productive contradiction, and turns it into the essential virtue of Thainess: Thai identity is marked by its ingenious assimilation of other cultures for its own needs.[107] It is a moving historical body premised on becoming rather than being, or rather on being-in-becoming. This strategic reading by Anek unceremoniously provides liberalism with an entry point into the powerful symbolism of the triad, while not surrendering to the Thai chauvinism of the National Identity Board.

In a book surveying the Western tradition of civil society and citizenship, Anek clearly endorses notions of negative freedom, the minimal state and citizen self-reliance.[108] In an extended discussion on the meaning of civil society, as if it were a living organism, Anek characterizes it as all those associations, groups, forums, foundations and institutes that mediate between the individual and the state and which are characterized by two dispositions:

> 1) [Civil society] dislikes and does not accept state hegemony, even though it will accept assistance from the state and will cooperate with the state, but it is able to appropriately control and resist the state. 2) It does not like the doctrine of

extreme individualism, which promotes selfishness . . . and non-recognition of the common good.[109]

Thus, even though the three elements of society – 'the state, civil society, the individual' – were independent of each other they were also connected in a simultaneous activity of conflict and unity.[110]

The rise of civil society as a counterbalance to the state required a shift from subject consciousness to citizen consciousness. He argues that simply providing the mechanisms of local democracy will not be enough:

> We should not just stress the structure of local government but local civil society as well, by training the people to be citizens; even when they vote they should vote like a citizen, not a client.[111]

He then criticizes the electoral practices of the people as premised on their own private interest rather than the public interest.[112] In his view, elites need to develop 'enlightened self-interest', which is an attitude that disposes one to the pursuit of self-interest without destroying the public interest. This would ultimately foster a more beneficial cooperative environment for the further pursuit of one's interest.[113] Self-described as a 'left-wing liberal', Anek considers one of the duties of civic education as doing away with dependence on the state and developing an ethic of self-reliance, particularly among the poor who, he says, consider democracy as being simply a matter of welfare. The task then was to give new meanings to democracy as 'self-government, or political expressions with dignity'.[114] This would be aided by the fostering of civility, of manners, of a willingness to listen, learn and share.[115] In regard to civic virtue, Anek revisits the Greek *polis*, in search of the characteristics of the 'full human' (a person with civic virtue), and also finds some examples in Thailand of the *polis* where people are directly involved in issues, freely sacrificing themselves, being responsible and using their own resources.[116] While interest groups were part of civil society, for Anek greater emphasis was to be given to groups that stress the public interest. Indeed, Anek is rather negative regarding the contribution interest groups might make to the public good, suggesting here an underlying, already defined 'good' to which groups must conform:

> There might be some groups which raise issues of minorities, or the disadvantaged in society or some whose ideas which are different from mainstream society such as women's groups, disabled groups, homosexual groups . . . such groups are for the minority . . . and are not thoughtful of other interests.[117]

Immediately following this discussion Anek argues:

> If any group that comes together which has interests or principles which contravene the principles of society at large or destroys the integrity of society . . . these are groups that our civil society does not need.[118]

Liberal democrasubjection

The principles of which Anek speaks are to be found in a remade civic triad, liberally integrated with civil society and the market. Anek is among those liberals who would 'wean' people off their state 'dependency' and seek to replace state activities with civil society groups and the market.[119] The project of producing a citizen endowed with self-reliance, one who moves within the spheres of market and civil society, regulated by the state, and encultured by the civic triad, is the project of liberal democrasubjection. It appraises a condition of reliance by the 'people' and 'overbearance' by the state, historically conditioned in the corrupted practices of patron–client relations. Liberalism seeks to revolutionize the mode of interaction such that self-governing agents see the state merely as an instrument of regulation, with some degree of representative function. The substantial matter of life in local environs is to be governed by virtuous citizens, mindful of the social principles presumably established by the broad conventions of a society, but requiring intellectuals such as Anek to define them as changeable when necessary. This privileging of the subject-intellectual over the object-people finds its unspoken rationale in the presupposition that the definition and practice of civic virtue as a universal element of good citizenship is entrusted to enlightened intellectuals. The enlightened were once proponents of the guardian state, supporters of its projects of statist democrasubjection and attempts at instilling particular dispositions and ideologies of the pastoral state. Now, the disciplining space promoted by the enlightened in the neo-liberal era is that of civil society itself, with the 'state' caricatured as the embodiment of subjection and uncivic dependence. This reversal is significant, for while the framing of the citizen in both projects of democrasubjection is sourced from an idealized view of Western citizenship, and while both await development, each is structured by a different logic. Liberal democrasubjection strikes against inhuman servitude to unreason or external compulsion; statist democrasubjection strikes against the savage conditions of pre-modernity as well as against the inhuman and immoral rule of the capitalist market. Yet both projects ultimately seek disciplined subjects as citizens.

Anek's writings on civil society and virtue, characteristic of a generalized and renewed interest in Western theories of citizenship among some Thai intellectuals, fall somewhere within the general continuum of liberal and communitarian perspectives.[120] Certainly, Anek is closer to the liberal frame in general. The appeal to rational and autonomous actors is seen as the basis of the security of the nation-cum-civil society. In this frame the citizen's capacity for the pursuit of rational self-interest provides a filler to the liberal aporia (of what lies between the individual and the public good); it sanctions self-pursuit as the condition of the more general good. Prior to these liberal notions of self and public interest, political development and its metaphors of nation and the common good dominated the field of Thai democratic imagining.

What does the arrival of liberal citizenship signal? While certainly it is contingent on the neo-liberalism of the contemporary age and represents 'Thai borrowings', there is more to it than that. It primarily signals the shift from pastoral or statist democrasubjection to liberal democrasubjection, a project which is only just taking shape. The former was conceived as delayed liberalism, in which a citizen's democracy was a state teleology and to be subject to government was a function of one's own interest as a universal (Thai) citizen. The latter points to a functioning liberalism in which a citizen's democracy is *now* to be actualized in the practices of securely defined citizens. Both are moments of imaginary rule by the citizen body, either delayed or actualized, for both name not actual states but projects of hegemony that require identical rationalities of self-governance, but differ in historical time, one a statist moment and the other liberal. Both are disciplinary projects cajoling actual people into conformity with ethically abstract principles of citizenship that are articulated at the intellectual centre of each state's moment. However, this is not to say the liberal moment has triumphed, for the state is wrought with struggle. One such struggle is the opposition to market liberalism, expressed in the communitarian ethic, to which I move in the next chapter.

Notes

1 Wutiphong Phiapjirawat, *Khumu tonarat thaeknik nai kan khorapchan plon chat yuk prathet lae thamlai khon di* [A tyrant's manual: techniques for corruption, looting the nation and destroying good people], Bangkok: Sathaban nayobai suksa, 2000, p. 63.

2 William A. Callahan and Duncan McCargo, 'Vote-buying in Thailand's Northeast: The July 1995 General Election', *Asian Survey*, 36, 4, 1996, pp. 377–92.

3 See, for particularly insightful accounts of these, Michael H. Nelson, *Central Authority and Local Democratization in Thailand*, Bangkok: White Lotus, 1998.

4 Observed by the author during an anti-vote-buying seminar in Mahasarakham in October 2000.

5 See Chai-Anan, 'Old Soldiers never Die, They Are just Bypassed: The Military, Bureaucracy and Globalization', in Kevin Hewison (ed.) *Political Change in Thailand: Participation and Democracy*, London: Routledge, 1997, pp. 42–57. This position has recently been restated by Chai-Anan Samudavanija and Parichart Chotiya, 'Beyond the Transition', in L. Diamond and M. Plattner (eds) *Democracy in East Asia*, Baltimore: Johns Hopkins University Press, 1998, pp. 147–67, pp. 149–50.

6 See Chai-Anan Samudavanija, *Phaenphathana kanmeuang chabap raek khong thai* [The first political development plan of Thailand], Bangkok: Samnakphim phujatkan, 1995; also see Chanwut Watcharaphuk, 'Prachathipatai baep thai botsuksa phon jak kan naeokhit lae konkai rabop prachathipatai ma chai nai prathet thai' [Thai-style democracy: a study of the results of the application of democratic ideas and instruments in thai politics], M.A. thesis, Chulalongkorn University, 1983, pp. 13–27.

7 See Matthew Phillip Copeland, *Contested Nationalism and the 1932 Overthrow of the Absolute Monarchy in Thailand*, Ph.D. dissertation, Australian National University, 1993, pp. 1–13, 44–6.

8 Eiji Murashima, 'Democracy and the Development of Political Parties in Thailand, 1932–1945', in Eiji Murashima, Nakharin Mektrairat and Somkiat Wanthana, *The Making of Modern Thai Political Parties*, Tokyo: Institute of Developing Economies, Joint Research Programme Series no. 86, 1991, pp. 30–5.

9 That the constitutional struggles might be seen in this light rescues them from the historical obscurity to which they have been dispatched, and might serve as an interesting entry point into a thorough study of Thai liberalism.

10 See, as an example of this sentiment, Kukrit Pramot, 'Prachathipatai lae seriphap' [Democracy and freedom], in *Pathakata khong kukrit* [Addresses of kukrit], Bangkok: Klang witaya, 1960, pp. 6–13, cited in Kriangsak Chetthaphanuanit, 'The Idea of Thai-style Democracy', M.A. thesis, Thammasat University, 1993.

11 Cited in Kobkhua Suwannathat-Pian, 'Thailand's Constitutional Monarchy: A Study of Concepts and Meanings of the Constitutions 1932–1957', paper presented at International Association of Historians of Asia, Chulalongkorn University, Bangkok, 20–4 May 1996, p. 7. The citation is an excerpt from a speech made by Seni Pramoj supporting a new constitution in 1949 which substantially increased royal power, giving the king power to appoint the Senate, to have full control over the Privy Council and hold veto power for 120 days.

12 See Niranitthi Sethabut, *Pak Prachathipat: khwam samret lae khwamloei* [The Democrat Party: success and failure], Bangkok: Samnakphim mahawithiyalai thammasat, 1987, pp. 21–2. As Sangsit Phiriyarangsan notes, despite the Democrat's founding policy statement in 1946 that it would oppose all forms of dictatorship and assist in the development of democracy, it quickly entered a government established subsequent to a *coup d'état* in 1948. However, the party was soon thrown out of office and entered a period of opposition to dictatorship. On the history of the party see Sangsit Phiriyarangsan, 'Pak prachathipat: jak anurakniyom su lathiseriniyom mai' [The Democrat Party: from conservatism to neo-liberalism], in Sungsidh Phiriyarangsan and Pasuk Phongpaichit, *Jitsamnuk lae udomkan khong khabuankan prachathipatai ruam samai* [Consciousness and ideology of the contemporary democracy movement], Bangkok: Sunsuksa sethasatkanmeuang khana settasat kanmeuang julalongkon mahawithiyalai, 1996.

13 Seni Pramoj, 'Stone Inscriptions of King Ram Khamhaeng', in *Presenting Thailand*, Bangkok: n.p., 1968, pp. 10–13.

14 See Kriangsak Chetthaphanuanit, 'The Idea of Thai-style Democracy', M.A. thesis, Thammasat University, 1993, pp. 116.

15 Seni Pramoj, 'Stone Inscriptions of Father King Ram Khamhaeng: First Constitution of Thailand', in Pinit Ratanakul and U. Kyaw Than, *Development, Modernization, and Tradition in Southeast Asia: Lessons from Thailand*, Bangkok: Mahidol University Press, 1990, pp. 21–48, p. 48.

16 'Father King Ram Khamhaeng's Stone Inscriptions', trans. Seni Pramoj, in *ibid.*, pp. 17–20, pp. 18–19.

17 *Ibid.*, pp. 23, 34.

18 *Ibid.*

19 Momratchawong Seni Pramoj, 'Kanmeuang thai' [Thai politics], in *Ratthasat nangsu prajam pi kansuksa 2514 thammasat* [Political science yearbook, 1971, Thammasat], pp. 83–102, p. 83. Seni, in a conservative inflection, goes on to note that the real problem of government is the fact that human beings have vices, so the real issue is not about building a democracy but a good state that can effectively deliver law and order (p. 86).

20 Cited in Kriangsak 'The Idea of Thai-style Democracy', p. 122.

21 *Ibid.*, p. 122.

22 *Ibid.*, p. 124.

23 For example Suchit Bunbongkarn, 'Kanphathana pheu khwammankhong (Development for National Security)', *Jitwithaya khwammankhong* (Psychological Security), 1983, pp. 118–35.

24 See Pranot Nanthiyakun, 'Samakhom Jitwithaya khwammankhong haeng prathet thai' [the National Thai Psychological Security Association], *Jitwithaya khwammankhong* [Psychological security], 1983, pp. 23–46.

25 Indeed, the journal discussed above is one of the prime examples of this, with conservatives and liberals alike contributing, sharing the common critique of the problems associated with building democracy in Thailand.

26 See Duncan McCargo, 'Thailand's Political Parties: Real, Authentic and Actual', in K. Hewison (ed.) *Political Change in Thailand: Democracy and Participation,* London: Routledge, 1997, pp. 114–31.

27 William I. Robinson, *Promoting Polyarchy: Globalization, US Intervention, and Hegemony,* Cambridge: Cambridge University Press, 1996.

28 See for example World Bank, *Governance and Development,* Washington DC: World Bank, 1992; *Governance: the World Bank's Experience,* Washington DC: World Bank, 1994.

29 Martin Minogue, 'Power to the People? Good Governance and the Reshaping of the State', in Uma Kothari and Martin Minogue (eds) *Development Theory and Practice: Critical Perspectives,* Basingstoke: Palgrave, 2002, pp. 117–35, p. 118.

30 See an especially interesting discussion in Barbara Orlandini, 'Consuming "good governance" in Thailand: Re-contextualising development paradigms', Ph.D. dissertation, University of Florence, 2002.

31 World Bank, *World Development Report 1997: The State in a Changing World,* New York: Oxford University Press, 1997, p. 3.

32 *Ibid.* See Paul Cammack, 'Neoliberalism, the World Bank, and the New Politics of Development', in Uma Kothari and Martin Minogue (eds) *Development Theory and Practice: Critical Perspectives,* Basingstoke: Palgrave, 2002, pp. 157–78.

33 Barry Gills, Joel Rocamora and Richard Wilson, 'Low Intensity Democracy', in Barry Gills, Joel Rocamora and Richard Wilson (eds) *Low Intensity Democracy: Political Power in the New World,* London: Pluto Press, 1993, pp. 3–34, p. 4.

34 Samir Amin, 'The Issue of Democracy in the Contemporary Third World', in *ibid.*, pp. 59–79, p. 59.

35 'Introduction to Institute of Public Policy Studies', Bangkok, n.d., mimeograph.

36 Parichart Chotiya (IPPS Director 1993–present), interview with the author, Bangkok, 4/1/98.

37 Konrad Adenauer Foundation, 'Democracy and Development: Information on the activities of the Konrad Adenauer Foundation in the Kingdom of Thailand', 1993, p. 4, mimeograph. The German Christian Democratic Party funds the group.

38 *Ibid.*, p. 9. Also see *Suphaphuthaen ratsadon* [The house of representatives], November 1985. The broadsheet was subsequently renamed *Phuthaen ratsadon*.

39 Chai-Anan Samudavanija, 'Educating Thai Democracy', *Journal of Democracy*, 1, 4, pp. 104–15.

40 *Ibid.*, p. 109.

41 *Ibid.*, p. 110.

42 A cursory glance through journals such as the *Parliamentary Journal* and a number of political and legal journals will identify numerous writers concerned with institutionalizing a liberal regime. For an example see Niyom Ratamrit, 'Klumphon prayot nok rabop rachakan kap kanmeuang nai prathet thai' [Extra-bureaucratic interest groups and politics in Thailand], *Ratthasuphasan* [Parliamentary journal], 35, 1, 1987, pp. 1–34.

43 Chai-Anan Samudavanija, 'Educating Thai Democracy', p. 104.

44 *Ibid.*, p. 115.

45 *Ibid.*, pp. 113–14. Chai-Anan is referring to his appointment as Senator in April 1989 and his taking on the chair of the House Affairs Committee.

46 *Ibid.*, p. 107.

47 In its 1989 Annual Report, IPPS lists its target groups as MPs, academics, Senators, businessmen, local government representatives, provincial chambers of commerce, and the general citizen. As to its aim: 'The Institute defines its role as a mediator in the network of political education. It maintains a strictly non-partisan position, and does not intend to intervene in any decision making process.' Furthermore: 'It aims only to provide the relevant information and policy options among concerned parties at all levels of government and civil society, for the political education of those parties and for the development of democratic institutions.' IPPS, *Annual Report*, 1989, pp. 4, 5.

48 IPPS, 'Introduction to the Institute of Public Policy Studies', n.d.

49 *Ibid.*

50 For standard presentations of liberalism and democracy, see *Phuthaen ratsadon* [The people's representative], January 1986, p. 11, which emphasizes the protection of human rights, government by consent, and the right to change and resist governments.

51 For an example on representations of parliamentary mechanisms, see the article on House Committees in *Phuthaen ratsadon* [The people's representative], November 2528, p. 11.

52 IPPS *Annual Report*, 1989, p. 9.

53 *Phuthaen ratsadon*, January 1990, p. 1. For an explanation of the motives behind this, see *Phuthaen ratsadon*, March 1989, pp. 8–9. An extensive outline of the project is given in *Phuthaen ratsadon*, November 1989, p. 7. See also *Phuthaen ratsadon*, April 1989, p. 1.

54 On the role of the IPPS and Chai-Anan in this see *Phuthaen ratsadon*, December 1988, pp. 1–16 and *Phuthaen ratsadon*, February 1989, p. 4.

55 See *Phuthaen ratsadon*, April 1989, p. 3. This was reported as a historical event, for parliament also provided some 32 million baht to support the project.

56 *Ibid.*

57 Pathan Suwanmongkhon, 'Suphaputhaen ratsadon kap phaen phathana phuthaen ratsadon' [The house of representatives and the parliamentary development plan], *Rathasuphasan* [*Parliamentary Journal*), 37, 12, 1989, pp. 1–3, p. 2. For details on the plan see *Phuthaen ratsadon*, April 1989, pp. 3–4. The challenge to statist projects of democracy is explicit: 'The parliament must be the leaders in the development of democracy' (p. 3).

58 IPPS *Annual Report*, 1993, p. 1.

59 IPPS *Annual Report*, 1996, p. 3.

60 *Bangkok Post*, 17/10/93. One reason for the shift was the formation of the new King Prachatipok's Institute, which was taking on the role of political socialization of the elite: Parichart Chotiya (IPPS Director 1993–present), interview with the author, Bangkok, 4/1/98.

61 IPPS *Annual Report*, 1995, p. 2.

62 IPPS *Annual Report*, 1996, p. 4.

63 Duncan McCargo, 'Policy Advocacy and the Media in Thailand', in D. McCargo and R. Bowra, *Policy Advocacy and the Media in Thailand*, Bangkok: Institute of Public Policy Studies and Konrad Adenauer Stifung, 1997, pp. 24–40, pp. 39–40. See, for an in-depth analysis of the media, Duncan McCargo, *Politics and the Press in Thailand: Media Machinations*, London: Routledge, 2001.

64 Ubonrat Siriyuvasak, 'The Development of a Participatory Democracy: Raison d'être Media Reform in Thailand', unpublished paper, n.d., reports that 30 per cent of participants in the May events were dependent on the print media for their news on the events (p. 2).

65 For an excellent discussion on public intellectuals' use of the press see Kasian Tejapira, 'Globalizers vs. Communitarians: Post May 1992 Debates among Thai Public Intellectuals', paper presented at the Annual Meeting of the US Association of Asian Studies, Honolulu, 11–14 April 1996. For various dissenting views of democracy carried in the press, see for example *Matichon*, 21/1/86, p. 7, where the author 'Seriratthasadon' ['Free subject'] notes: 'I think the time has long past when civil servants can train and instruct local politicians who have been elected from the people.'

66 Prudhisan Jumbala, interview with the author, Bangkok, 17/6/97. Prudhisan notes that in early discussions it was planned to call the body 'The Institute to Develop Democracy', but 'somehow' a consensus emerged to call it the 'King Prachatipok's Institute' to mark the 100th birthday of Rama VII. I would add that such an appellation plays a part in perpetuating the myth that constitutional democracy emerged because the king 'graciously conferred' it.

67 Sathaban phrapokklao (King Prachatipok's Institute], *Laksut kanmeuang kanpokkhrong nai rabop prachathipatai* [Curriculum: government and politics in a democracy], 1996, pp. 25–9.

68 Marut Bunnag, interview with the author, Bangkok, 20/3/97. Marut was a long-term Democrat MP who has persistently presented a liberal democratic line in his various newspaper columns. His past experience as Minister of Education made him feel civil servants and military officers should not sit in the Senate, for there was always a conflict between the Minister and the Permanent Secretary.

69 *Ibid.*

70 Sathaban phrapokklao, 'Khrongkan fukobrom thi damnoen pai lao pi 2538' [Completed training projects 1995], mimeograph; Sathaban phrapokklao, 'Khrongkan fukobrom thi damnoen pai lao pi 2537 (Completed Training Projects 1994], mimeograph; Sathaban phrapokklao, 'Sarup khrongkan thi dai rap ngoppraman pi 2540' [Summary of Budgeted Projects, 1997], mimeograph.

71 Bowonsak Uwanno, interview with author, Bangkok, 15/1/98.

72 Sathaban phrapokklao [King Prachatipok's institute], *Laksut kanmeuang kanpokkhrong nai rabop prachathipatai* [Curriculum: government and politics in a democracy], 1996, p. 1.

73 See *Watthajak*, 10/4/95, p. 3. Interestingly, Kramol Thongthammachart, once Minister to the Prime Minister's Office under Prem, noted that in 1966 an American political scientist had suggested that Thailand should have a political development programme and that the Thanom government had the National Research Council research the issue. In 1968 the plan was proposed to the government but was rejected on the basis that it suggested the prime minister should emerge from elections. See *Matichon*, 17/7/92, p. 2.

74 Khanakammakan supha wijai haeng chat [National research council], 'Phaen phathana kanmeuang' [Political development plan], *c.* 1992/3, pp. 1–8, mimeograph. In the section on developing people's democratic consciousness, typical points are made regarding people lacking principle and worshipping powerful individuals (pp. 18–20). Additionally, the authors of the plan considered the military too involved in politics, political parties as lacking any mass base, and pressure groups as being too attached to their sectional interests to play a role in promoting democratic ideology.

75 *Ibid.*, p. 19.

76 Curiously, this proposal bypasses the National Identity Board and its various sub-committees. Presumably, these were seen as too caught up in the old delayed liberal ideology of the bureaucratic state. It may, equally, have been a simple oversight.

77 *Ibid.*, n.p.

78 *Ibid.*, p. 31.

79 See *Siamrat*, 3/10/95, p. 5.

80 Khana anukammakan jatthamphaen kan phathana kanmeuang [Subcommittee on the Political Development Plan, Political Reform Committee], *Phaen phathana kanmeuang thai* [Thai Political Development Plan], 1996, pp. 2, 5.

81 *Ibid.*, pp. 8–9.

82 *Ibid.*, p. 38.

83 Samnakngan lekhathikan naiyokratthamontri [Office of the prime minister], *Ngan khong ratthaban anan panyarachun* [The Work of the Anand Panyarachun Government], 1992, pp. 249–50.

84 *Ibid.*

85 *Bangkok Post*, 6/7/93, p. 4.

86 See Phairot Yumonthian, *Khamwatha nai anan panyarachun khon di thi sangkhom tongkan* [The words of Anand Panyarachun: the good person that society needs], Bangkok: Saentao, 1993, p. 29.

87 Anand Panyarachun, 'Address of the Prime Minister Mr Anand Panyarachun to the Foreign Correspondents Club of Thailand, 1/7/92 in Thailand', *Foreign Affairs Newsletter*, 1992, pp. 4–7, pp. 4–5.

88 *Ibid.*

89 *Siam Post,* 15/8/95, p. 3.

90 *Ibid.*

91 See Anek Laothamathas, 'Patirupkanmeuang sethakit sang phanthamit prachathipatai' [Politico-Economic Reform: Creating Democratic Allies], in Chalong Sunthonrawanit, *Wiphak sangkhom thai* [Criticizing society], Bangkok: Samakhom sangkhomsat haeng prathet thai lae samnakphim amarin, 1995. Similar arguments appear in Anek Laothamatas, 'A Tale of Two Democracies: Conflicting Perceptions of Elections and Democracy in Thailand', in R. Taylor (ed.) *The Politics of Elections in Southeast Asia,* Cambridge: Woodrow Wilson Center Press and Cambridge University Press, 1996, pp. 201–23.

92 *Bangkok Post,* 16/12/91, p. 4.

93 Anek Laothamathas, *Mop mu thu chonchan klang laek nakthurakit kap phathana kan prachathipatai* [The mobile telephone mob: the middle class, entrepreneurs, and the development of democracy], Bangkok: Samnakphim matichon, 1993, p. 17.

94 *Ibid.,* p. 18.

95 *Ibid.,* pp. 19–31.

96 See for instance Anek Laothamathas, 'Suanruam thi mai chai rat khwammai khong prachasangkhom' [The non-state public sphere: 'the meaning of civil society'], in Anuchart Puangsamli and Kritthaya Achawanitkul (eds) *Khabuankan prachasangkhom thai: khwamkhleuanwai pak phonlameuang* [The Thai civil society movement: citizen sector movements], Bangkok: Khrongkan wijai lae phathana prachasangkom, mahawithayalai mahidol, 1999, pp. 35–61, pp. 51–2.

97 In one meeting Anand praised the activists of 1973 for fighting for rights and liberties. His speech made it clear that civil society, in his eyes, was about individuals knowing their rights and responsibilities, and in terms that were neither left-wing nor right-wing: 'There should be no left and right prejudice. Only when we can establish civil society will we be able to pay back the October 14 heroes and their families.' See *The Nation,* 9/8/98, pp. A1, A2.

98 Cited in Sommai Paritchat, *Mummong khong nai anan* [The perspective of Anand], Bangkok: Samnakphim matichon, 1999, p. 16.

99 *Ibid.,* pp. 17–18.

100 *Ibid.,* p. 19.

101 *The Nation,* 21/5/96, pp. A4–A5.

102 *Bangkok Post,* 12/3/95, p. 17. How so, he cannot say.

103 As Anand puts it, "He is completely detached. When you say people have attachment to persons, or to an object, attachment to love, attachment to jealousy, attachment to individual, attachment to respect, attachment to power, attachment to position, attachment to wealth, to be a really good Buddhist, you must dispossess yourself of all of these attachments". (*ibid.*)

104 Anek was elected as a Party list MP for the Democrats in the 2001 election. In 2004 he defected to nominally lead the Mahachon party for the 2005 election. He failed to get elected. We await to see how Anek's memoirs will square his civic ideas and political pragmatism.

105 Anek Laothamathas, 'Suanruam thi mai chai rat' , p. 51.

106 Here Thongchai's work is perhaps the most challenging, for it remains oppositional and does not attempt to reappropriate the monarchy unlike other former leftists. More than that, the last few chapters of Thongchai's book are an exploration of the symbolic violence perpetrated by the monarchy in its war for Thainess. See Thongchai Winichakul, *Siam Mapped: A History of the Geo-body of a Nation,* Honolulu: University of Hawaii Press, 1994, ch. 8.

107 Anek Laothamathas, *Prachasanghom nai mummong tawantok an lae son thi jon hopkin* [Civil society from the perspective of the west: reading and teaching at Johns Hopkins University], Bangkok: Sathaban kanrainru lae phathana prachasangkhom, 1999, p. 3.

108 *Ibid.,* p. 33.

109 Anek Laothamathas, 'Suanruam thi mai chai rat', p. 35.

110 *Ibid.*

111 Anek Laothamathas, in Chuchai Suphawong and Yuwadi Khatkanklai (eds) *Prachasangkhom thatsana nakkhit nai sangkhom thai* [Civil society: views of Thai thinkers], Bangkok: Samnakphim matichon, 1997, pp. 71–89, p. 79.

112 *Ibid.*

113 *Ibid.,* p. 80.

114 *Ibid.,* pp. 81, 86–7.

115 *Ibid.,* p. 89.

116 Anek Laothamatas, 'Khwampenphonlameuang lae prachathipatai thong thin thammarat thi khuan faiha' [Citizenship and local democracy: the just state we should pursue], in Phitchari Sirirorot (ed.) *Khwamkhatyaeng nai sangkhom thai* [Conflict in Thai society], Bangkok: Khanaratthasat mahawithayalai thammasat, pp. 89–114, p. 100.

117 Ibid., p. 97.

118 *Ibid.*

119 *Ibid.,* pp. 93–5.

120 See the other chapters in Anuchart and Kritthaya (eds) *Khabuankan prachasangkhom thai: khwamkhleuanwai pak phonlameuang* [The Thai civil society movement: citizen sector movements]; *Yutthana Warunpitikul and Suphita Roengchit* (coll.); *Samnuk phonlameuang* [Civic Consciousness]; Bangkok: Munithi kanrianru lae phathana prachasangkom, 1999.

9 Rethinking the nation in times of crisis

Democracy, civic engagement and community

In March 2002 the highly esteemed Dr Prawet Wasi issued a public letter to Thailand's Prime Minister, Thaksin Shinawatra. The letter mirrored the thrust of King Bhumipol's speech in late 2001 to the effect that the government needed to be more tolerant of different opinions. Prawet warned that Thailand was facing the gravest crisis it had ever faced. Having lost economic sovereignty in the 1997 currency meltdown, the country was now faced, he asserted, with the loss of political sovereignty. In response to this threat he called for the government and people to work together as a civil-state (*pracharat*).[1] Such calls for unity have become endemic in Thailand, particularly following the crisis. Perhaps the most famous call came from Thirayut Bunmi, who provided a popular Thai reading of the idea of good governance (*thammarat*) by linking it to a strategy to overcome the economic crisis. Thirayut's intellectual intervention, which kicked off a minor discourse boom on good governance, aimed at taking the reform movement beyond the prevalent liberalism of the new constitution, and towards a new and extensive project of economic revitalization through social and political reform. A good governance 'movement' outside of the state, he argued, was needed. In place of state- or society-centred approaches, Thirayut proposed the creative interaction of state, business and social forces. Economic recovery was possible only through the cooperative effort of all. With his calls for common sacrifice for the nation, alongside the king's call for self-reliance and modesty, Thirayut sought a revisioning of the Thai nation.[2]

These ubiquitous calls for unity have been operationalized through the promotion of civic participation, particularly since the passing of the 'people's constitution'. Civic politics is effectively an attempt to foster informed public opinion that has the capacity to influence the broad policy terrain of governments, and to bring into being a body of citizens capable of free and meaningful association across an array of issues. The contemporary rise of civic politics in Thailand can be traced broadly in the development of a public sphere instantiated by media, publicly engaged NGOs, and intellectuals acting as articulators of the public interest from the 1980s onwards. The density of this sphere has intensified, witnessed by the arrival of many new public formations seeking to broaden the legitimate scope of engagement around anti-corruption, election monitoring, consumer watchdogs and public health – to name a few. Since 1997 one can speak of a qualitative leap in terms of this intensity, with networks of activists, intellectuals and the media using the constitution to push forward social justice agendas and people's participation. Such politics have become influential for several reasons. First, the failure of the party political system to function as an interest aggregator and articulator gives these movements significance despite their relatively small size. Second, their significance is also derived from positive factors: a long accumulation of strategic knowledge and resources, and the formation of dynamic networks. Third, the contested reformation of the state over the last twenty years has provided a space for reformists in the bureaucracy to interact with such currents, leading to a process of appropriation and partnership. What is more, inasmuch as civic education waged by government and non-government bodies is highly abstract, the politics of civic engagement provides, according to its advocates, a greater learning ground for bringing into being informed citizenship. The rise of civic politics marks the shift away from state-based democratic education programmes towards the intervention of new 'civil society' forces into the ideological recomposition of Thailand following the political and economic crisis of 1997.

In focusing on civic politics in this chapter, much of the more radical activity of forces in pro-democracy networks and more radically oriented NGOs is necessarily overshadowed. This focus is warranted because the forces of civic engagement have had a degree of organizational and ideological impact on the state. Moreover, while there is ideological and strategic differentiation among NGOs and social movements, it is clear that in practice there is an orientation to the politics of constituting a functioning public sphere. This project, a reflection of the crisis of development and money-democracy, has been influenced by intellectuals, NGOs and activists who have sought to revisualize Thailand as a place of community, citizenship and nationhood. While the National Identity Board was busy articulating the ideology of the king as head of state, figures elsewhere were eager to break from the fossilization of ideology and seek a reformed nationalism of the people based on local knowledge and wisdom, while still drawing on Buddhism and monarchy. Their communitarian perspective on democracy within a newly imagined nation of Thais has drawn succour from the ideological and real crisis faced by the Thai state, especially after 1997. In the following, a tentative genealogy of the formation of reformed nationalism is offered that highlights the interrelationship of significant actors and circumstances in fuelling new national imaginings. Like liberalism, this is an emergent formation and its origins are fragmentary and circumstantial.

The chapter begins with a discussion of NGOs, not because they are uniformly part of civic politics, but because the context of their operations in the 1980s led NGOs to promote rights-based discourses beyond the more select development aspects of their work. These organizations, working on the ground, through networks, and finding exposure in various media, significantly reworked and challenged the rights and citizenship framework of the state and the liberals. Indeed, through NGO practice and its ideological effects, the state's monolithic ethos of the Thai common good would come to be pluralized into many localized common goods. This undermined the hegemonic effect of conservative national ideology (Thainess), and liberal invocations of the individual. When local peoples and activists raised banners against particular development programmes (dams, for example) that were purportedly 'in the national interest', they put pressure on the delayed liberalism of the state, pushing for a more fertile realization of liberty and responsibility in the locale.

NGOs, rights and development

The emergence of development NGOs, which had their modern origins in the late 1960s among reforming elites, was a matter of great historical consequence. The history of NGOs in Thailand is customarily related to the efforts of the late Puey Ungphakorn, a leading government economic technocrat, who famously began to criticize the government's growth-oriented economic policy and was instrumental in the establishment of the Thailand Rural Reconstruction Movement.[4] The moderately reformist Puey would be later hounded out of the country by right-wing fanatics in the wake of the massacre at Thammasat university. In this atmosphere, NGOs operated under extremely difficult circumstances, with state elements continuing to portray them as communist fronts right into the 1990s.

In considering the influence of NGOs, it will be useful to focus on the small but important and enduring human rights organization, the Union of Civil Liberty (UCL). Formed in November 1973 with figures such as Kothom Ariya and Saneh Chamarik at the forefront, the UCL addressed the issue of democracy from the perspective of institutionalizing human rights.[5] Dedicated to educating and socializing people around constitutional and human rights, the UCL's first constitution expressed its objectives thus:

> At this moment the Thai people have a tacit understanding that any form of government which lacks respect for, and the promotion of, the freedom and rights of the people is but a way for corrupt and decadent state administration . . . which subverts security and the progress of the individual and the nation.[6]

Tirelessly working to propagate rights and dispense advice, the group soon found itself inundated with grievances from farmers and workers.[7] However, in the charged atmosphere of the times, the UCL was hard pressed for credibility. While right-wing paramilitary organizations were gunning down working-class and peasant leaders during 1975–76, the UCL failed to issue condemnations of alleged official involvement. It was also being pressed by left-wing activists to join in the popular movement, while military radio was calling it part of the communist current. Such issues led to great tension as some members sought to join up with the popular movement while others sought to remain formally neutral.[8] In any case, the group was effectively silenced after the 1976 coup.[9] It was revived in July 1979, and thenceforth pursued political neutrality, and explicitly endorsed non-violence.[10]

Throughout the 1980s the UCL bravely functioned as a human rights monitoring group, and as a launching pad for the formation of other groups. A number of Thailand's prominent NGO workers have been associated with the UCL in some way.[11]

In the first half of the 1980s, some communist and student returnees from the jungle, and other left-wingers, debated new strategies for the revolutionary movement, searching for answers to the failure of the CPT and the popular movement. Arguments ranged from seeking a rethinking of radical politics along reformist and socialist humanist lines,[12] to others wanting to rebuild the left along Leninist lines.[13] Others were simply demoralized. Somkiat Wanthana paints a picture of a depressed left:

> The mentality of the age . . . was inert. Among the progressive sector it was melancholy. The glass that cracked, the idol that fell from the shelf, the world that turned upside down . . . were the images that many students and intellectuals surely had in their heads.[14]

The period signalled a shift from broadly Marxist-oriented left politics towards issue-based politics and engagement with the state and political sphere where possible. Considering the failure of the CPT, and given the dual challenge facing the left in the 1980s – the attempt to entrench military and bureaucratic notions of democracy and the rise of parliamentary democracy – Thai Marxists attempted to find a new strategic path.[15] The editors of the radical political economy journal *Warasan Setthasat Kanmeuang* argued that the constitutional struggle of 1983 was essentially an

> argument between the various leaders of the capitalist state, namely: traditional rulers who want an amendment to the constitution so they can receive support . . . of the traditional capitalists who have partly developed from landlords and have influence in the bureaucracy.[16]

The editors gave qualified support to elites struggling to strengthen parliamentary politics, but noted it would be the task of radicals to extend the struggle so that proper principles of democracy were established. These were defined as 'participation of the people in defining their destiny, and opening up opportunities in different types of elections to allow broad social participation in the economy, society and politics'.[17] The idea of civil society (*prachasangkhom*) would come to describe these developments, although the term itself was understood in a broadly Gramscian way in the mid-1980s.[18] With the rise of local struggles and then the emergence of the democratic struggle of 1991–92 the moderate idea of civil society as a normative force against an overbearing state gained wide influence.[19] Based on a critique of older forms of class-based struggle, 'civil society' became a new way of conceptualizing a broad-based struggle for justice around pluralist politics and new norms of civic engagement.

With the political left in organizational and ideological disarray in the 1980s, a modest 'movement' based on local developmental problems gradually took hold.

Indeed, as one NGO activist explains it, between 1979 and 1980 a number of progressive intellectuals involved in the mass movements of the 1970s consciously shifted towards small-scale NGO-type activity, seeing this as localized and less likely to provoke state repression, as it would be perceived as less threatening to those in power than other forms of activity.[20] For many, the politics of the UCL, as neutral and issue-based, seemed more realistic in this situation. Kothom Ariya noted how the 1980s offered the opportunity for a more modest politics to take shape:

> When the left-wing wind is blowing I am lagging behind, at the times when the CPT advocated armed struggle I was speaking about non-violence, so out of tune, but what I claim as a credit is when the opposite wind blew I was in front and many retreated.[21]

Kothom also positively appraises the advances made by the NGO movement in its shift from an oppositionist stance in the early 1980s to winning acceptance among the business and bureaucratic sectors later in the decade.[22] As a one-time president of the Thai Development Support Committee, he was a central player in the Campaign for Popular Democracy, before moving to Pollwatch and becoming a Commissioner of the Electoral Commission of Thailand.[23]

NGOs' local focus provided a breeding ground for new strategies that eventually merged into a loose national network aiming to promote sustainable development and participatory democracy. In this context, groups such as the UCL and its offshoots provided much of the rights discourse, cementing different groups with a common language. UCL's founding president Saneh Chamarik wrote extensively on human rights and also linked the dominant NGO discourse of people-centred development with the recovery of local community culture.[24] Saneh, close to the UN development research community, assumed the chair of the important NGO-Coordinating Committee on Rural Development (NGO-CORD) in 1989–92, and was central in the propagation of community rights over resource management, a position that was fermenting within the multitude of local struggles spread throughout the nation.[25] This provided developmental NGOs with a language that articulated local developmental needs, seen as 'alternative development' with rights-based discourses aimed at constitutional structures and the state, a process that would gain momentum in the 1990s.

The intersection of unbalanced economic growth, its environmental and social consequences for local communities, and the response of critics to this, led to rapid growth of the developmental NGO movement, from some thirty or forty organizations in the early 1980s to over 300 in the late 1990s. Such origins do not offer up an orderly pattern of development. However, it might be useful to follow Suthy Prasartset's discussion of NGO development. Suthy argues that there have been four overlapping strategies within the NGO movement, what he calls the four-corner strategy. In part, each strategy is seen as a phase, but cumulatively the four-corner strategy is held to describe the Thai NGO movement.[26]

To simplify Suthy's schema somewhat, the four-corner strategy is first marked by the 'search for alternative livelihood'. NGOs in the early 1980s promoted self-reliance and people's participation in local development.[27] Such activity was characterized by promoting small cooperatives and various commodity banks for the benefit of small producers.[28] Such a local focus gave rise to popular discourses of community culture, economic delinking from the global economy (present in the form of agribusiness as well as older forms of merchant intermediaries) and integrated farming for self-reliance. Concomitant with this was a promotion of 'local wisdom', which entailed elevating the knowledge of local leaders who were seen as the repository of a community's learning evolution and encyclopaedic in their appreciation of local circumstance.[29] Developing from this first stage was the second corner of NGO strategy, which entailed promoting networking among NGOs and people's organizations. This resulted in the formation of numerous networks across the nation which were based on information exchange and solidarity around common issues.[30] Third, as Thailand entered its accelerated boom in the mid-1980s, placing pressure on natural resources, there emerged a generalized conflict, 'pitting the state and corporate sector against the popular sector'.[31] A consequence of this was the third strategy: the urgent need to articulate policy alternatives and raise public awareness. In this regard NGOs proposed an alternative People's Development Plan, emphasizing, among other things, just development and support for the agriculture sector without linkage to agribusiness.[32] Finally, Suthy notes that NGOs began to consciously devise a strategy of alliance building, the fourth corner, with state officials and others so as to coordinate their projects and win greater legitimacy.[33] Furthermore, they aimed at galvanizing broad support from the urban middle class and academics.[34]

The above may suggest a coherent politics, strategy and historical progression, but it is important to recognize that NGOs did not form a unified movement. Indeed, there were many ideological tendencies in the NGO movement.[35] However, by the mid-1980s many development NGOs presented a generic united front which was critical of mainstream development (macro-economic focused, industrialist, GDP-focused) and authoritarianism. They also rejected strategies of mass mobilization and class struggle. In its *Directory* of 1987, the Thai Volunteer Service[36] provides something of a broad-brush depiction of NGO political orientation:

> The NGDOs [Non-government development organizations] reject the use of power conflicts or violence as a way of solving problems. They associate such methods with dictatorship and feel that their use can only lead to further misery, conflict and violence. NGDOs feel that developing people's consciousness and carrying out small-scale peaceful, practical activities is a more appropriate and secure path to social change in Thai contexts. Thai NGDOs view social development not as an overt struggle but as a long, peaceful process of change in consciousness. A great deal of this theoretical orientation is rooted in prevailing cultural values and an appreciation of current political realities, particularly local government officials' distrust of NGDOs. The unhappy experience of many Thai

intellectuals with constitutional and rapid popular mobilization efforts, right-wing violence and an ideologically backward Communist Party during the 1970s have also played a part in producing a reaction against much radical social theory and the confrontational political activism practiced in other Asian Countries.[37]

If disillusion with older forms of struggle was motivating a more modest practice, as well as a modest expectation of what could be achieved, the overwhelming nature of foreign funding for these organizations further accentuated this tendency. One comprehensive analysis of the staffing and financial structure of 135 NGDO groupings in the late 1980s found them mostly foreign-funded with limited means and staff.[38] International NGOs and foreign governments were funding NGOs according to their own agendas. Some of these funding mechanisms might be seen as promoting the expansion of either international social democracy or liberalism, depending on the funding body.[39] To the extent that NGOs were dependent on funding they were required to plan, justify and develop programmes in line with the international developmental ethos whose endpoint was forms of just capitalism. Equally, this meant developing professionalism, accountability and integration with international agendas of 'just' development.[40] Inevitably, this also entailed a degree of bureaucratization, the existence of career ladders, self-advancement and funding for projects that were not based on popular demands but on NGO prerogative.[41] The pressure to adopt moderate approaches was further felt when, in the early 1990s, it looked as if Thai NGOs would lose a significant proportion of foreign funding (as Thailand was no longer considered a poor nation). The Thai Foundation was set up to develop the fundraising capacities of local NGOs and to promote the philanthropic sensitivity of Thai business and the middle class.[42] Such moves further differentiated NGOs into those promoting a responsible and socially useful image, integral to the public good and Thai society, and those remaining more critical of capitalist development and its greed ethos.[43]

Another significant aspect of the changing nature of development discourses was the active engagement of government with NGO forces and ideas. Reformist elites were by no means outside the development of the NGO 'social-political infra-structure', as Suthy names it. As early as 1984 NGOs proposed the establishment of a joint committee of NGOs and government agencies, a proposal supported and acted on by the National Economic and Social Development Board. Such developments pressed on the NGOs the need for a national coordinating body, which came into being in 1985 as NGO-CORD, to which many NGOs are affiliated while maintaining their own organizational autonomy.[44] As Prudhisan and Maneerat observe, this was not a matter of co-option by the state, but represented a greater negotiating power on behalf of NGOs.[45] To varying degrees, NGOs coordinated their projects with state officials, depending on the campaign and receptiveness of officials.[46] As the boom spread, however, and pressure on resources grew, this relationship became increasingly tense, with some NGOs becoming supportive of people's confrontation with 'maldevelopment' projects. In turn, state and private sector actors resorted to repressive tactics.[47] Nevertheless, attempts were made to seek coordination and dialogue with both the bureaucracy and parliamentary institutions. A series of seminars in the late 1980s and early 1990s, aiming to open a dialogue on mutual work and promote the exchange of information, brought together NGO leaders and MPs. Such moves hinted at the strategic advance of NGOs in staking a legitimate position within the political sphere.[48]

In 1992 important sections of the NGO movement and their intellectual allies issued the *Declaration of the Customary Rights of Local Communities*. In many ways this document provides the clearest exposition of NGO strategic thinking in the 1990s. It presents a critique of development as practised by the state-capital alliance and proposes alternative development measures and outlines a political strategy.[49] Thai industrialization is said to have been achieved by the extraction of the rural surplus from Thai farmers, a process now threatening the rural communities. With the state supporting the private sector, there had been environmental degradation, the impoverishment of rural communities and the emergence of agribusiness. This is said to have occurred against a backdrop of authoritarianism, which had been justified by the need to harmonize and stabilize development. The document notes that state legislation dating from 1964 gave the state ownership of all forest reserves, resulting in the usurpation of traditional ownership by local forest dwellers. As the state moved to enforce its ownership, in order to provide natural resources to the private sector during the boom years, conflicts regularly flared up between officials and locals. Interestingly, the declaration cites one of the king's speeches that pointed to the precedence of the property rights of individuals over retrospective legislation transferring ownership to the state:

> In forests designated as reserved or restricted, there were people there already at the time of delineation. It seems rather odd for us to enforce the reserved forest law on people in the forest which became reserved only subsequently by the mere drawing of lines on pieces of paper. The problem arises in as much as, with the delineation done, these people became violators of the law. From the viewpoint of law, it is a violation, because the law was duly enacted; but according to natural law the violator of the law is he who drew the lines, because the people who has [sic] been in the forest previously possessed the rights of man, meaning that the authorities has [sic] encroached upon individuals and not individuals transgressing on the law of the land.[50]

Having offered a critique of the state of development, the declaration then moves to its political position. It notes that industrial development has spawned a middle class which, it states, is the core of the human rights movement in Thailand:

> The emergence of the human rights movement among the middle class could, to a certain extent, help contain the military dictatorship's role and influence. It also opens up opportunities for business–industrial groups to rise to power in the politico-economic arena. This is the rationale for the formation of the business group for democracy.[51]

The *Declaration* notes some positive developments among business groups relating to democratic development, but strikes a cautionary note on the self-interested attitude of business to democracy. Furthermore, the freedoms and rights of business in the new democracy are said to be at the expense of the 'majority rural-agricultural sector'. Coming to the strategic question of how the NGOs might relate to the capitalist and middle classes, the ball is rhetorically thrown into the potential allies' court:

> A choice is to be made as to whether the newly-emerged capitalist and middle class would continue to follow the authoritarian path . . . Or whether they would take a democratic path which is the common aspiration of all sectors in society, not just for the middle class.[52]

By deed, many NGO activists have answered that question themselves. Suspicious, but hopeful, NGOs pursue a strategy of working with progressive sections in state agencies and business, hopeful that with the institutionalization of democracy they will be in a better position to address the issues of maldevelopment. It is this tension between suspicion and hope that characterizes NGO approaches to the liberal elite, in pursuit of a 'minimum' programme.

This battle to win acceptance of business and the state to alternative development visions and new forms of participatory democracy, which places importance on communities, has shaped public discourse in the last decade. It has served to link local community issues to national political levels and it has spawned a broad current of thought known as 'localism' (*thongthinniyom*), which became something of a generic slogan for a strategy of recapturing a past communitarian ethos to help local communities negotiate their way through the hazards of the global market economy.[53] The guiding theme of localists is the necessity of rooting development (in the sense of people's wellbeing) strategies in people's own practices by a process of consciousness-raising. Localism takes a participatory approach to development as a process of learning, where the reference point is rooted in existing culture and communities. Its focus on community rehabilitation means that localism is also seen as a way of strengthening and remoralizing the nation after the perceived moral collapse into materialism during the economic boom. Against the background of 'maldevelopment' and responding to popular antipathy to unbalanced developmental capitalism, a number of prominent intellectuals theoretically intervened in the NGO movement in an attempt to place a theoretical unity across their diverse practices and constituencies. The intellectual attempt of the so-called community culture school to extract some 'indigenous' core from peasant and rural life practices, as a basis to return cultural dignity to a nation they see being degraded by materialism, was, in the first instance, a radical political critique of existing society. Throughout the 1980s and into the 1990s, intellectuals within and close to state organs such as the National Economic and Social Development Board and the National Culture Commission developed a moderate brand of localism which has come to have a significant impact on reformed notions of national identity and democracy.[54] There is a sense in which it may be said that localism became mainstreamed.[55] What was essentially a counter-hegemonic position in the 1980s was in the 1990s, by a process of appropriation and partnership with state agencies, a key ideological and organizational resource in saving Thai capitalism from itself. It might be useful to see moderate localism as part of a broad ideological current that Somchai Phatharathananunth terms 'elite civil society'. This is characterized by state society cooperation and involves potential domination by the state of civil society forces.[56] At another level, though, it may also be possible to suggest that emergent forms of cooperation are also part of the changing nature of the state; it is not necessarily a strategy of defensive co-option in order for things to stay the same, but a process of adaptation as the integral state undergoes liberal change.

From radicalism to reform

The radical position is articulated in the work of Chatthip Nartsupha, whose Marxist historical work on political economy has, in recent years, been superseded by his shift to a somewhat anarchist position on community culture (*watthanatham chumchon*), and his liberal position on national democratic structures.[57] In a recent preface to an English translation of his *The Thai Village Economy in the Past*, Chatthip tells of how he moved from a study of the economy and culture of the state, to a study of village economy and culture, which meant a shift in research methodology from documents and statistics to 'interviewing ordinary people and listening to the account of their lives, difficulties and struggles for subsistence'.[58] This is a significant observation, for it registers the shift to an epistemology of the local, and a strategy built on local knowledge in the 1980s. The base position of this approach was to turn villagers themselves into crafters of their own development by drawing on local resources of knowledge and community affection. Armed with their own self-knowledge, confident with their local identity, villagers could negotiate development on their own terms.[59] At its most radical, the community culture orientation preached de-linking and a rejection of the market economies. Few villages have actually taken this path, and few NGOs are proponents of this position. Instead a more general theme has emerged on the importance of drawing on local resources for development, rather than development being a project led from the outside.

One implication of the culturalist focus of Chatthip is seen in his argument on the need to Thai-ify development such that the Thai bourgeoisie becomes encultured in village ways of life, rather than slavishly following 'Western' consumerism and the high culture of the royal court. Addressing the failure of the Sino-Thai capitalist class to lead the 'Thai' masses in a bourgeois democratic revolution, Chatthip curiously proposed that the Sino-Thai capitalists mix their tentative embracing of liberal democracy with community culture:

> [I]f the Thai bourgeoisie were to accept this mixed ideology that contains both
> Western liberalism and peasant culture, then the bourgeoisie will be more Thai,
> will more consciously identify with the development of the country. When they
> share the same identity as the majority of Thais, the bourgeoisie will be stronger
> and may become a true vehicle for the advance of ideology in Thailand.[60]

This fusion would be a form of 'progressive' Thai nationalism, which disavows
the high culture of the centre and revalues the ancient Thai traditions of kind-
heartedness, said to be rooted in the spiritual values of village communities.[61] This
suggestion of cultural politics, of changing the identity of the Thai elite, partly
motivates the broad localist current.

One question emerges from all of this: why would the Sino-Thai bourgeoisie
concern itself with peasant culture in a bid to legitimate itself as fully Thai? For
Chatthip, the Thaification of the Sino-bourgeoisie becomes a historical possibility
because, as he argues, community culture discourse and strategy is not one centred
on class polarization but stresses the 'people', a term that encompasses the middle
class. This disavowal of Marxist class struggle seemingly breaks a barrier, for the
progressive bourgeoisie should be willing to form an alliance with the people, since
there is no threat of class revolution. Reflecting his Marxist past, Chatthip lays his
cards on the table:

> [I]n reality, what we face is capitalism. We should therefore have a maximum
> program and a minimum program. The maximum program is anarchism and the
> minimum program is progressive capitalism. In other words, we demand that a
> progressive middle class share administrative power and the management of the
> economy with village communities.[62]

Pasuk and Baker, in a review of Chatthip's recent work, note how he later moved
away from the minimum programme and has instead focused on the building
of rural community networks that retreat from relationships with the state and
capital.[63] Certainly, the anarchism of Chatthip's version of localism places him on
the radical edge of anti-statism.

Others, however, while critical of the state, pursue a politics of collaboration
with state agencies, in the hope of advancing self-capacity as part of a reduction
of the role of the state in an effort to enhance the capacity of 'civil society'. This
current may be termed 'moderate localism'. Moderate localism is a different animal
than earlier manifestations of localism as theorized by Chatthip under the rubric
of the 'community culture school'.

The shifting forms of localism are partly exemplified in the thought of Saneh
Chamarik. Saneh, who is best located between radical and moderate localism,
is an influential thinker and has sought to propagate village culture and local
wisdom within a Buddhist frame, without the Marxist and anarchist colouring of
Chatthip. If Chatthip's work spoke to more radical elements in the development
sector, Saneh has a broader appeal, unclouded as it is by hopes of radical peasant
federations.

Saneh's critique of capitalism is really a critique of capitalism without human values. For Saneh, the neo-classical approach to economic growth places the interests of a minority at the centre while depriving the majority 'of their productive potentials, and, most significantly, right to development'.[64] It is not the market which is the problem but rather the idea that it can rule unregulated. Indeed, the market is described as an outcome of the great evolutionary scheme of history 'when societies and the world at large come to be interdependent'.[65] It is the conditions under which it operates, and whether actors are equally placed to deal with its exigencies, that concerns Saneh:

> The market is a necessity, as is producing for the market, but farmers should not only focus on this dimension because we must accept that the agricultural basis of our farmers is as petty producers.[66]

Thus practical strategies for development have preoccupied Saneh. Among his proposals is the call for state aid in research and development to assist small farmers to be able to respond to the world market.[67] More recently Saneh has connected the issue of local wisdom to the development of small and medium enterprises.[68] Given Saneh's diagnosis, the challenge for NGOs was to enter the policy bodies of the state such that its unbalanced development policies could be addressed.[69]

Saneh's critique of existing conditions is embedded in a critical Buddhism in which good politics can only emerge when linked to wisdom and ethics.[70] For Saneh, Thai Buddhist institutions needed to be more effective in propagating the Buddhist philosophy of a state based on *dharma* and virtue.[71] Such propagation could influence the practice of secular politics. Critical of political reform as simply a technocratic attempt to counter money-politics,[72] Saneh proposes that solutions be found at the local level, where petty producers, working cooperatively, could impact on the national political structures:

> [V]arious community economic networks will combine and become a new social force to change the structure and relations of power towards balance and freedom . . . according to the processes of grassroots democracy.[73]

For Saneh, the economic crisis of 1997 provided an opportunity to commence a debate on development. It could also lead to a highlighting of the need to work towards modest economic growth at local levels, based on self-reliant methods whereby communities raised their own credit and worked through various mechanisms to lift the level of capital within a community. Furthermore, local economic development would ultimately benefit national capital in its dealings with foreigners, for it would provide Thai capitalism with an economy rooted in local strength. This would be aided by a return to Thailand's 'cultural capital' (*thun watthanatham*) held to be embodied in Buddhist wisdom.[74]

Saneh's critique of capitalism, at times rhetorically powerful, becomes, in the circumstances of national crisis, a critique of neo-liberalism and the market's inability to lift the agricultural sector up to a real functioning market level. In essence, Saneh proposes a reformed national capitalism that draws sustenance from local communities so as to be able better to compete in the world economy. Such a position has become influential in directing the work of a number of rural NGOs.

Prawet Wasi similarly argues for the need to develop local capital in Thailand in a manner consonant with local culture and wisdom. The designation of Prawet as an advocate of localism is somewhat limiting, as this is just one aspect of his Buddhist communitarianism. Prawet's localism is conversant with international trends which began to value the local in development from the mid-1980s onwards.[75] Prawet has been a long-term board member of the National Economic and Social Development Board, the body responsible for producing Thailand's broad five-year development plans, and has used that position to push participation and the importance of community in development. At the same time, a central figure in the Local Development Institute, Prawet has been an influential figure among moderate NGOs. Critical of the 'compartmentalized' thinking that produces an emphasis on material development as the measure of progress, Prawet suggests that a more holistic approach to development would see a return to culture – which is simply conceived as situated wisdom and integrated knowledge of local places, within an overarching Buddhist rationality.[76] Following the broad stream of localism, Prawet argues for the need to develop local capital in Thailand in a manner consonant with the local culture and wisdom of the people.[77]

Prawet's basic communitarianism emerges in his conception of communities as places of common locality and identity where citizens come together to solve problems and advance their wellbeing. For Prawet, communities are the basic component of democracy, a place where individuals as members of groups cooperate, share knowledge and work towards creative solutions to common problems.[78] People in communities, not necessarily geographic, share common ideals, beliefs and objectives. They have love, fraternity and collective learning.[79] Supplementing this broad communitarianism is the more developmental concern with growing social capital in communities, and on this Prawet is clearly conversant with the 'Putnam School' and its stress on social capital (norms, networks and trust) as the social underpinnings of growth.[80] In this way of thinking, communities are seen as democratic building blocks because the extent to which they are able to be self-reliant in generating solutions to their problems, is also the extent to which democracy can be consolidated at the national level. It is at local sites that the imperatives of civic responsibility and public mindedness can best be nurtured, and it is therefore there that communities, with adequate social capital, can establish a strong moral base to sustain democracy.

Although broadly embracing a communitarian position, Prawet is first and foremost a thinker who repeatedly integrates his social critique with Buddhist themes; principal among them is the need to possess 'right thinking' (*sammaditthi*) – which is no less than ensuring a full understanding of the Buddha's teachings. For example, regarding development Prawet says:

The Thai path of development is, therefore, not a desperate chase to keep up with *farang* [Westerners]. We have learned that the western model of development is a mistake because it is based on a money chase. Our path must transcend this. We must stay one step ahead of the world by remaining faithful to the right concept, or *sammaditthi*, of development. It is one which focuses on goodness while interlocking the economy with mind, family, community, culture and the environment.[81]

With Prawet's Buddhist position comes an ethic of impermanence and detachment – ideas that are used by Prawet to propagate non-anger and non-violence on the basis of non-attachment to positions, and which seemingly positions him above polarized conflicts based on material interest. Buddhism also provides Prawet with his rationale for human rights and respect of human dignity, which is seen to lie in each individual's capacity for right understanding.[82] As much as Prawet seeks to inculcate right thinking into individuals, he sees it also as immanent in the social whole, by a logic of reciprocity whereby a good society and right understanding are mutually reinforcing. Thus he roots individual potential – or the capacity of right understanding – in the social conditions that prevail.

Underlying these seemingly progressive positions lies a strong current of elitism. The elitism itself comes out in the various pronouncements that Prawet makes about the state of the Thai people. In an open letter to the prime minister, for example, Prawet explained that Thais possess a small conscience and that 'people still cannot think more of the public interest than themselves and their cronies'.[83] Prawet is a disciplinary thinker who makes no bones about the need to educate the masses in the ways of rationality and public-mindedness. Importantly, in discussing the lessons of May 1992 when confrontation between democracy protestors and the Thai military led to scores of people being shot dead, Prawet argued that the hope for Thai democracy was the middle class because they were educated and their lifestyle required rational calculation. Thus he thought more effort needed to be put into making them a new moral force. As for workers and peasants, the vast majority of the Thai population, Prawet implicitly argued that their efforts for social change were prone to violence.[84] For Prawet, then, it is the middle class who best encapsulate the values of the rational citizen. Here the middle class is construed as teachers, shopkeepers, civil servants, business-people, etc. What marks all of these groups is a reasonable degree of economic independence. This underlines one aspect of elite communitarian thought – the need for communities to provide a basis of economic growth such that the people populating them come to have the characteristics of the middle class, namely rationality. 'Self-reliance' and 'self-sufficiency', then, all comes down to providing the material conditions for a deliberative rationality, a prerequisite for democracy. By a long detour one may say that Prawet arrives at a proto-modernist position on the role of the middle classes in democracy.

Prawet's elite communitarianism and democratic outlook converge. Collectively, for him, communities are sites of learning as they endeavour to move towards higher moral states embodied in the principle of self-reliance. In this, intellectuals are seen as having a responsibility to lead by first understanding the conditions and worldview (local wisdom) of the villagers (*chaoban*). This comes about not through abstract discussion or education but through engagement with issues that emerge in communities and which become points of organization, grievance and, hopefully, community deliberation.

In response to the growth of state power, Prawet proposed the strengthening of civil society/community by focusing on increasing people's own power.[85] However, rejecting the idea that the state and business sectors were 'all rotten', he proposed that the state and business sector be utilized in building up the strength of society: 'Don't let us think that they are enemies like communists, we must think in terms of allies.'[86] Influenced by development concepts of participation, and in pursuit of unity between the state and other actors, Prawet proposed new structures for deliberation that bring various groupings under the rubric of what he calls '*penjapakkhi*' or a partnership of five sides, including state officials, NGOs, people's organizations, academics and the private sector. This is, perhaps, Prawet's most important contribution to the 'participatory' aspect of democratization in Thailand, having led to the establishment of *prachakhom*, or provincial-level civic assemblies throughout Thailand. At Prawet's suggestion, the Eighth National Development Plan called for the establishment of *prachakhom*, described as 'assemblies for the purpose of formulating development plans and guidelines for the provinces'.[87] What is significant in this development is the institutionalization of state/society relations through civic assemblies in which each sector discusses development issues. Although the bodies have no binding authority, they are meant to provide popular input into programmes.

In the above we can identify quite clearly the manner in which Prawet is a disciplinary thinker. He aims to mould the nature of citizens by inculcating a form of rationalism which will be educed by taking account of local circumstance and the nature of emergent knowledge in the locale. Any citizen's engagement with this process is to be one that conforms broadly to principles of rational thought (the right way) and which envisages a consensual process of learning which avoids polarity and conflict. Prawet, despite the local, comes to sanction the unity of the Thai, and the *prachakhom* are an organizational embodiment of this.

Socializing political reform, mitigating the economic crisis

While at one level, and corresponding to structural interests, political reform might be conceived as part of the politics of capitalist good governance, at another it may also be seen as a basis on which to build social justice around communitarian ethics encased in a liberal political shell. Taking the latter as their framework, a number of organizations associated with localism have embraced the opportunities for participation afforded by the new constitution and new rhetoric of participatory development embraced by the NESDB and bureaucratic bodies. To illustrate this connection, the following looks at the collaboration between the Local Development Institute (LDI) and Civicnet.

The LDI has, in one form or another, been an influential actor in the domestic NGO scene for close to two decades, its leaders being prominent persons such as Saneh Jamarik and Prawet Wasi. A mediator for international aid, it also relates closely to reformist elements in the bureaucracy. It has long been involved in local development projects and provides support for small-scale development initiatives, assisting in hundreds of these in the last decade. Soon after the crisis the LDI formed the Save the Nation Forum (*prachakhom kopban ku meuang*) to provide an alternative explanation of the economic crisis and to suggest solutions rooted in localism and nationalism. It aimed at forming a pluralistic cross-class movement based on 'collective learning' to overcome materialism, Westernization, patronage culture and corruption.[88] The forum was short-lived (April–May 1998), with limited reach, although it provided a basis for the creation of some new networks countrywide.[89]

Civicnet, formally established in the aftermath of the economic crisis, was an initiative of individuals who had been closely associated with the Bangkok Forum, environmental groups and LDI. One key member, Anuchart Puangsamli, noting how the power of the middle class was traditionally seen to be centred in Bangkok, explains that one motive behind the formation of Civicnet was to tap into the power of emerging middle classes in the provinces. Given the limited engagement of the Bangkok middle class post-1992, it became apparent that new sources of change needed to be identified: 'We tried to look at the people in the provinces, there are a number of educated people there, a number of professionals and business peoples.'[90] While NGOs focused on disaffected groups and organized around particular issues, the provincial urban middle class (itself often the leadership of these NGOs) had few places to congregate and deliberate on public issues. Civicnet would provide an avenue for the formation of a politically engaged middle class that could intersect and inform other movements. Indeed, a key organizing activity of Civicnet is training programmes to equip individuals and groups with the capacity to be 'change agents'. It sees its work as one of providing training to bodies of activists and publicly minded middle-class persons with the skills and wisdom to confront local and national problems through processes of deliberation and learning. As Chaiwat Thirapan, a leading member of Civicnet, explains:

> We don't want to work as a protest or pressure group; we want to create the opportunity of new alternatives, and to develop strength from positive action and thinking ... We work with many groupings and we have observed that through dialogue with other groups and institutions, they start to change their minds.[91]

In line with these politics of dialogue, Civicnet was a supporter, along with LDI and Prawet in the NESDB, of the formation of *prachakhom* (civic assemblies) as new spaces for deliberation:

> We tried to think very hard of how to set up some sort of social space for people at the provincial level to come together and talk, because we think that the citizenship wouldn't happen if people don't have space to exercise their ideas . . . they wouldn't have place to learn. So that is why we try to encourage this idea . . . we didn't mean to set up an organization, rather set up a forum for people to talk.[92]

The *prachakhom* have been subject to significant criticism by several observers who see them as sites where state officials and local notables have come to dominate.[93] These criticisms bring into focus the issue of the nature of deliberative processes when participants come together in cultural settings where power is scripted around status, position, gender, wealth and sexuality.[94] LDI and Civicnet are not oblivious to these problems, indeed they seek a long-term redress to them through participation and the creation of public opinion which will gradually act as a social sanction.[95] Nor are they naive about some state actors' intentions, thus counselling caution in relations with the state.[96] Nonetheless, theirs is a strategy of engagement which follows from a firm belief in the power of dialogue and learning processes, and the possibility of bringing into being moral counterweights to the decadent practices of money-democracy, bureaucratic theft and local thuggery.

In 1997 the LDI shifted its focus from the formation of *prachakhom* to what it termed 'the period of social reform and macro mobilization'. Seeking to expand its influence nationally through various networks, and by propagating the formation of collective learning through deliberative forums and campaigns, the LDI posed for itself a grand quest itemized in a nine-point strategy: the establishment of a social reform fund to 'develop central co-coordinating committees to work with agencies under the principal ministries', help develop consumer networks, assist in the development of media for social reform, assist *prachakhom* to reform education and the value system, assist *prachakhom* to advance reform of law and the macro economy, and open the state to more people's participation in order to strengthen communities.[97]

The work of LDI and Civicnet has largely converged around the project of social reform. In the face of the economic crisis and the resulting national reflection on its causes, localism and its embracing of local wisdom and self-reliance became a key public discourse. Also, calls for fresh and paradigm-breaking thinking were heard. This positioned the two organizations as significant actors in the ideological maelstrom resulting from the crisis. People, and in particular Prawet Wasi, began to speak about utilizing social energy – the power of local communities in interaction and in a process of learning – as a way out of the crisis.

In November 1999 the LDI co-coordinated a number of public intellectuals, including Prawet Wasi, Chai-Anan Samudavanija, Bowonsak Uwanno and Seksan Prasertkul (a mixed bag to say the least) to support a joint statement outlining what was described as the 'Forces of the Land Strategy to Solve the National Crisis'. In the face of foreign domination, the authors counselled that

> Time has proven that the power of the state is not sufficient to solve the national crisis, it is necessary that the social or people sector consolidates its power and

takes part in solving the crisis. There is no power that can solve such complicated problems besides the power of society (SOCIAL ENERGY). Social energy comes from the coming together to think and act – all over the Thai nation, in all places, all organizations, on all issues – as a force of the land (*phalang phaen din*) . . . This social energy should have three methods, act by oneself, work with the state, scrutinise the state . . . In the age of globalization neither the state nor society alone has sufficient power to preserve the country's economic sovereignty. The state and the people need to integrate as a civil-state (*pracharat*).[98]

Although the term *pracharat* is contained in the national anthem, a more recent meaning was elaborated by the liberal royalist Chai-Anan. In a series of articles concerning globalization and change, Chai-Anan tapped into popular writings on the changing nature of the state to produce a broad dichotomy between the older nation-state and the ideal state of the global era. While the nation-state was characterized by such features as uniformity, submission, dependence, compulsion and control, the civil state promotes diversity, freedom, autonomy, pluralism and empowerment and good governance (including institutionalized relations between the state and civil society), as prescribed by the United Nations Development Programme.[99]

If the idealized *prachakhom* might be seen as miniature versions of *pracharat* in local and provincial settings, the next stage was clearly to have the same kind of idealized interaction and integration at the national level. This is what partly lies behind the idea of 'forces of the land'. This is not to say that there is any illusion about a *pracharat* coming into existence; rather, as an ideal it motivates the activities of the organizations concerned, and acts as a regulating goal for their work. The idea of the civil-state articulates liberal and communitarian positions: the civil-state and its inherent liberalism will foster the strength and revitalization of communities. One illustrative example of this kind of politics is the Forces of the Land Forum (*wethi phalang phaendin*), which is discussed below.

The Forces of the Land Forum

In 1998 the newly established Thai-rak-Thai party, in an effort to broaden its appeal and to rebut criticisms of it being just another capitalist party, began to meet with communities, NGOs and public intellectuals in an effort to hammer out a policy platform. In the course of discussions, TRT edged towards a number of seemingly progressive positions including suspension of farmers' debts, cheap health care and increased village funds. Its nominal membership base also rose from tens of thousands to a reputed eleven million by mid-2001. In its policy documents, the party also spoke of harnessing local wisdom for the wellbeing of the nation.[100]

The apparent openness of TRT led to a number of dialogues between the party and public intellectuals, with the Strategy to Save the Nation (see above) clearly being aimed at the electioneering parties. It was Thaksin who most ambitiously drew on localism discourse. Indeed, Phonladej Pinpratip, the Secretary-General of LDI, informs that a number of key reformist members in TRT, including the prime minister himself, began to use the term *phalang phaen din*.[101] There was even talk of the government issuing a general Prime Ministerial Order similar in effect to Order 66/2523 (to defeat communism), but LDI suggested this would just make it too formulaic and defeat its intention.

In the few months after the TRT election victory, dialogue between TRT and LDI continued and in the end TRT gave its formal blessing to LDI, with Civicnet, to launch a forum to gather people's opinions on what could be done to solve local and national problems. According to Phonladej,

> The strategy of *phalang phaen din* is a combined project between the Office of the Prime Minister and my institution, the LDI . . . Both of these work together, with the Office of the Prime Minister needing us, [because] we have connections with many networks all over the country, who can come and help think about the strategy of *phalang phaen din*.[102]

Phonladej was quick to note that although the project had formal government blessing, it was independent of government interference. The basic idea was to gather various networks around the country and to build up a composite picture of local wisdom, mediated by change agents, and to formally present to the government some proposals. Dialogue, learning and communication for social change were to not only influence the government and its policy agenda, but they were also to be seen as part of the process of self-empowerment of communities and individuals alike. Although it would be facile to give too much rigidity to the notion of 'forces of the land', given that it, like so many other Thai phrases, goes through a boom-like use and then becomes redundant, the meaning of the term associated with the LDI comes from Prawet Wasi, in a document distributed at Forces of the Land workshops:

> That Thailand is poor, with no money, doesn't mean that we have nothing. We have something of greater value . . . the Thai people, that is we our very selves, Thai people who love the land are capital (*thun*) that is greater than money, greater than anything.
>
> Thais who come together and think together across the land will be a great force of the land that can defeat any obstacle.

Prawet then goes on to speak about how coming together can solve numerous social ailments:

> A strong community is a force of the land which is a moral force.
> Force of the land is *phumi phala*, *phumi* is land, *phala* is the force of the land. The force of the land is the name of the Rama 9th [Bhumiphol] of Rathanakosin. If you think of the King, think of the force of the land, if you think of force of the land, please think of the power of community.[103]

This sloganistic conflation has purchase in Thailand because the king is constantly invoked as the embodiment of all Thais. However, the reasoning behind this conflation is interesting, for while it would seem to suggest mere homage to the king, Phonladej explains that

> We think in Thailand that the institution of the monarchy is loved by the people, so in thinking of a strategy that can be accepted by the people, we think we need to find something that is symbolic of this, and so the name of king is Bhumiphol, it can be translated as *phalang phaen din* . . . Given that for sometime Thai society has been weakening, we must revive its strength, which corresponds with the name of the king, thus we devise the strategy of *phalang phaen din*.[104]

What we see, then, in the Force of the Land Forum, is the fusion of localism, monarchism, nationalism and the attempt to forge new forms of participatory democracy through civic assemblies. Hardly reactionary nationalism, the movement gives voice to the 'people', who are perceived to be lacking both in the capacity to speak ably as yet, and also lack the space in which to speak. This invocation of 'people' is significant, for it elides significant class differences and purports to see a generalized common interest.

Prawet goes on to speak about needing to interweave the civil-state (*pracharat*) with the force of the land, noting that the people or state alone cannot solve problems. Rather, with the power of society, culture, morality, new organizations and wisdom, national problems could be solved in a sustainable fashion:

> The state is composed of politics and bureaucracy, the people are the villagers, communities, society, localities, business, monks, academics, artists, the media etc. *Pracharat* thus means all sectors of Thai society or Thai people combine together transcending parties . . . [and] cliques, and having a new consciousness which sees the common interest of the nation, ready to create force of the land or force of the nation to defeat the national crisis and move towards wellbeing.[105]

Forces of the Land meetings were held in over ten subregional locations in mid-2001. Approximately 1,000 community leaders, teachers, doctors, villagers, NGO activists and unaffiliated individuals from various *prachakhom* attended the three-day workshops. In a workshop in Khon Kaen held in July 2000, observed by me, participants were treated to introductory speeches in which Prawet's sentiments were recounted by different speakers. Facilitators and speakers addressed the meeting on the nature of social communciation, the power of civic action and the need for the accumulation of knowledge. Equally, there were calls for all sectors of society to work together. Participants broke into teams to consider key problems of Thai society, coming back to share their findings, with facilitators drawing a general picture. Moving from problems, participants were asked to suggest solutions. Most groups were keen to advance 'community strengthening' and local wisdom, with calls even to institutionalize the Forces of the Land movement. In November, delegates from the various subregional meetings met to generalize their findings and prepare a report for the Thaksin government. The findings of the various subregions were divided into four general areas, all seen as falling within the strategy of *phalang phaen din:* creating the power of networks; creating the power of *pracharat;* creating the power of wisdom; and creating the power of the media. Under each topic, prescriptions were given on the necessary organization and structural outcomes for each area to be advanced, as well as a description of the kinds of activity that could be undertaken. The campaign has called for the establishment of a fund for Forces of the Land which would provide umbrella support for various groups: it could support the establishment of an institute for development of regional-level civil society networks; networks of over 100,000 people to work according to the new constitution; support anti-corruption and antidrugs campaigners who confront difficulties in their livelihoods as a result of their work. In practice, these formations are to push forward decentralization and the reform of the bureaucracy, assist in the creation of local economies and self-reliance, scutinize the work of the local authorities and be part of the creation of public space to develop 'healthy public life' and local culture. Second, in creating a people-state an interweaving network of civil society/state groups are to assist in the implementation of the village fund (an initiative of the Thaksin government) and *prachakhom,* assist in moving the bureaucracy away from backward practices, take part in the discussion on amendments to the constitution and push forward anti-corruption measures, strengthen the ECT, push for the Community Forest Law and push for land reform legislation. Third, an 'Institute to Develop Local Wisdom' is to be established, backed also by a local wisdom fund and a 'Local Wisdom Learning Council'. These will assist in research and the drafting of local development plans, drawing up 'corruption maps' and using the media to further local wisdom. Finally, a fund for social and community media is to be established. This will fund radio and television programmes 'of the people, by the people and for the people'.[106]

The proposals, though sidelined as relations between LDI and TRT cooled, are a programme for a revitalized nation organized around rural networks and increased interaction between state and society. In effect the proposals were a crystallization of the politics of civic participation and reformed nationalism. It can be seen that in moderate localism, exemplified in the *phalang phaen din* campaign, localist activists seek a participatory democracy characterized by communitarian institutions, modes of participation and ideologies that, in tying in with the state, try to reform it. In the context of a contested democratic transition, localists and civic activists attempt to bring about institutions and processes that can facilitate the formation of a Thai public consciousness. As has been indicated, it is important to note the disciplinary aspects of this, inasmuch as the ideal citizen becomes one who has regard for the Thai triad and acts through their 'Thainess'. While there is room for local identities in this mode of politics, localist politics are connected to the broader wellbeing of a reformed and reimagined Thai nation. Certainly, it is hard not to see this as a step forward from the atavistic nationalism of the National Identity Board. However, the figures of the 'people', 'citizen' and 'community', so central to localist, communitarian and civic discourses, do not quite exist. The organizational and ideological invocation to be proud of the locality, to be a participant in the locality, is part of the process of bringing them into being as a new ideological reference point for a new Thai nationalism. This process of democrasubjection is steadily gaining ground in Thailand precisely because of the break-up of older modes of association (neo-patrimonialism), and it also works against the formation of a more class-based consciousness. Seen in this light, the politics of civic engagement are not insignificant, despite being pitted against powerful old-style politics. They are part of the process of new forms of order and discipline. With the state in crisis, and the economy in free fall, localism worked to harness the power of the nation in producing order and identity, by relaxing its borders in order that such borders could be strengthened.

Culture and democracy: a campaign

Thus far it has been suggested that there is an emergent reformist discourse that integrates concerns around development, moral personhood, democracy, community and civil society, and that links activists and reformist elites. This intellectual trend is partly manifested in the work of the Office of the National Culture Commission (NCC), established in 1979. The NCC was formed in an attempt to propagate an awareness of the 'oneness of Thais' despite their diverse and regional cultures.[107] Located within the Ministry of Education, the first few years of its activity involved the establishment and integration of provincial- and district-level cultural offices where both local and national culture was displayed.[108] In 1982, The National Culture Commission launched a campaign to address the cultural deficits of Thais in terms of promoting self-reliance, diligence and responsibility, thrift, discipline, law-abiding behaviour, religious ethics and getting the people to follow the slogan of 'nation, religion and monarchy'.[109] According to the commission's secretary-general, this was seen as an important aspect of the struggle against communism.[110] One official of the NCC nicely sums up its reason for existence: 'if we are not the same we will break up'.[111] Certainly, national policy makers were concerned with the destruction of traditional culture and the fading of old ways, as well as what they considered to be bad elements of Thai culture.[112] Premised on anti-communist sentiment and cultural propagation, the NCC would find itself adrift in the late 1980s as the security complex broke up and its rationale of oneness against communism wavered. Furthermore, as the CPT declined and NGO and local struggles emerged, there was a certain ideological crossing of some bureaucrats and NGOs. This is particularly so of Ekkawit Na Thalang, a former high-ranking bureaucrat in the Ministry of Education and Secretary-General of the NCC from 1988 to 1991. Ekkawit was intellectually close to Prawet's reformist Buddhism and the project to promote local wisdom. By the mid-1990s he was arguing for the government to encourage NGOs' involvement in culture propagation.[113] Ekkawit is intellectually important in making respectable the move from notions of unified culture towards an acceptance of diversity as non-threatening and part of a greater uniformity of Thai culture.[114] Within this reformist current of Thai nationalism there is also a more explicit appeal to the religious underpinnings of democracy, such that Buddhist virtue would be the regulating principle of a moral democracy.[115] Cognizant of local wisdom and its varied expressions, there nevertheless remains the attempt by Ekkawit, and Prawet, to project a rational Buddhism onto the communities. The relevance of Buddhist wisdom to political reform, decentralization and self-government in reform Buddhism is expressed best by Peter Jackson:

> In rationalist Buddhism ... rationally guided ethical action is posited as the source of legitimate secular power. This power is immanent in ethical action and is believed capable of transforming the social world for the better. It is universally accessible to all ethical individuals and is thus decentralized, becoming manifest wherever an individual chooses to act ethically and to place reason above unreason.[116]

Important as the reformist elite recognition of community culture and local wisdom was, this was qualified by Buddhist propagation, self-reliance and moral strictures as to the qualities of a self-governing person: this was rationalist Buddhism acting as a disciplinary discourse.

In 1990 the Chatichai government adopted the NCC plan for developing national culture, perhaps reflecting its own apparent cultural anxiety about money and materialism.[117] As a rationale of the plan, the NCC noted the lack of faith in local wisdom and the corresponding elevation of foreign-influenced Bangkok culture. This contamination of culture was said to be spreading to the regions with the result that 'the integrity, honour and pride in old local culture ... is declining everywhere'.[118] In 1994 the NCC launched a major campaign for the preservation of Thai culture. Concerned with the declining interest in things 'Thai' and the rise of materialism, the campaign sought to address the cultural problems that had occurred under a period of accelerated economic development.[119] To distinguish its work from the kind of 'decreed' culture of the Phibun era, an effort was made to emphasize that there was no element of compulsion in its campaign:

> under a democratic system of government there is one thing that is generally accepted and that is democratic culture ... [and thus] the state probably should not be the one to stipulate all cultural standards, since it is a basic freedom of the people to seek their own ways appropriate with their private circumstance.[120]

Yet despite this seeming openness, the eleven issues to be propagated in the campaign were familiar rallying cries of the cultural infrastructure. Starting with the inculcation of nation, religion and monarchy (institutions which are said to 'give pride to being born Thai'), the campaign was to give emphasis to knowing the origins of the Thais, to understanding democracy with the king as head of state, and to have the people realize the king's compassion as expressed in various royal activities.[121] The traits the campaign was to promote were principally not those for 'preservation', but those that the disciplinary agencies of the state had been trying develop. The same contradiction that was noted in the promotion of identity replays itself in this campaign: to be Thai, to have Thai culture, is to develop discipline, orderly family relations, self-reliance, religious virtue, etc. This developmental aspect was of course complemented by the abiding essentialism of Thainess. Thus, as was the case with campaigns of national identity and democracy, the campaign for culture was also one of partly developing what Kasian has called the 'ethno-ideology of Thainess'. In this ideology the Thai nation is 'imagined as a happy and calm village', an immemorial and morally bounded community of intimate ties.[122] Yet there are certain cracks in this ideology, witnessed by the proposed voluntariness of the campaign.

If the cultural warlords have become less belligerent, this owes something to the new democratic openings and the cultural space won by the struggles of local communities. Nevertheless, articulators of the Thai nation, in the age of globalization, are now using those struggles as part of the material to regenerate Thai nationalism within a refurbished traditional frame of the triad, in which the nation is a call to unity; the king is an overarching guardian of the nascent democracy of his subjects, preaching Buddhist virtue and industriousness and generating in the people an affective orientation towards hierarchy and duty; and religion provides the moral codes of the people.[123] What makes this nationalism different from the ultra-right version of the 1970s is that there is a recognition of things not being right, that the nation is more than high culture, that religious institutions are crumbling edifices requiring doctrinal reform, and that the state, as the upholder of Buddhism, has dubious claims on this capacity.[124] There is of course continuity. Reformist nationalists are the inheritors of the seemingly unquestionable position of the monarch, and thus no matter how badly the nation and religion are faring, the prime institution, which in any case embodies the others, is robust and developing an almost god-like status. These are the cultural tensions present in liberal Thailand, a project that requires a new imagining of Thai unity within a democracy.[125]

The new nationalism in Thailand aims to do the work of creating unity, of developing within people affective orientations to the geo-body of Thailand. With no ulterior motive, it is clearly geared towards assisting reformed Thai capital's venture into the global economy.

Liberalism, communitarianism and possible futures

In this and the previous chapter, the focus has been on two major currents of thought: political liberalism and its attachment to the Thai common good, and a communitarianism that subscribes to the institutions of political liberalism. It has been suggested that for the foreseeable future this is the terrain of ideological struggles in Thailand, as both sides will attempt to formulate new democratic imaginaries within the bounds of national ideology. This is, admittedly, a simplistic picture since it misses the monarchy as a nodal point connecting both streams of elite communitarianism and liberalism. This nodal point suggests there is a good deal more unity than division between the two positions. However, this unity is tensely poised, given that liberals are more attached to a national project of economic growth and modernization that would be likely to undermine rural communities.

However, it should be noted that some liberals, taking a developmental perspective on democracy and capitalism, also see 'communities' as a necessary step in the fulfilment of a Thai modernity. Thus while localists speak of communities as if they were impermeable entities, refuges from the perils of globalization and the market, some also think in terms of transition, building up the capital of local communities, of connecting with national and global markets. This tension, which plays itself out in the attempts to rearticulate national ideology around the local, is most apparent in liberal renderings of the 'community'. Bowonsak Uwanno provides some insights into this. Taking the stance that democracy is now a universal phenomenon, Bowonsak attempts to articulate an element of Thainess to it. The new constitution, he believes, reflects Thai philosophy in its support for 'community rights'. Noting that the West had shifted, in the eighteenth century, from collectivism to individualism, he flags the Thai aspect of democracy:

> legally, constitutionally speaking there is in the Western legal tradition the state and the individual but in between there is nothing. We are trying to put something in between, that is to say the community.[126]

Involved with Saneh and Prawet in a three-year research project on community rights, Bowonsak had popularized the idea that such rights existed under the absolute monarchy.[127] Interestingly, he argues it is the section on community rights that provides the new reform constitution with 'the Thai contribution'. This section, he says, 'is more or less eastern'. This is also how he integrates the king to the constitution, for he argues that the king's thought parallels that of many NGOs on community rights.[128] Thus what is seen as among the most radical elements of the constitution – community rights – is presented as having a relationship to 'Eastern' collectivist ways and is linked to the pondering of the philosopher king.[129] Some exploration of this reveals a fairly pragmatic commitment to this 'Thai' aspect. Bowonsak, who would seem to straddle both the liberal and communitarian camps, presents an ideal picture of democracy:

> Democracy is successful in the Western world because the majority of the people in the Western world are middle class. They stand by themselves and are not dependent on others. But the Thai majority are dependent on others, but if we can make them more independent the culture will change.[130]

Bowonsak unexpectedly reveals that the 'Eastern' aspect of the constitution is a stop-gap measure:

> [I]f people depend on community it is better than asking them to be totally independent, the idea of urbanization will take at least fifty years. The middle

path is how to strengthen the communities, it would seem the ideas of Dr Prawet and the King are the way out.[131]

Bowonsak then moves on to speak of the idea of developing civil society to strengthen groups.[132] These supportive comments on civil society clearly situate Bowonsak within a modernizing gesture, for between community and civil society there seems to be an ineluctable transition awaiting Thai peasants. Clearly, some community discourses are part of the transitional ideological underpinnings on the road to a more vital national capitalism. The idea of community need not be seen as a journey into the past, rather it might just as well be seen as a temporary solution to the failures of the market to develop all sectors uniformly.

This posture finds support in an important book analysing participatory rural development in Thailand. Shin'ichi Shigemoti notes that many of the cooperative aspects of contemporary rural communities are truly recent, while traditional communities unpenetrated by the market were likely to have more individualistic and family-orientated activities.[133] What many in the community culture school take to be echoes of an idyllic village past (cooperatives, rice banks, etc.), Shigemoti argues, are really organizations which have emerged to mitigate the direct impact of the larger external money economy; they are essentially about mobilizing local capital in productive ways. Thus the collective pooling of resources is seen to be 'based on a calculation that cooperative organizations are more beneficial than a market economy, even in terms of the individual pursuit of profit.'[134] However, organizational commitments such as these are transitory, a process which provides some individuals with the skills to make the transition to a market economy. Shigemoti argues that when cooperative organizations confront severe competition, the 'know how which the villagers do not yet have (i.e. the ability to manage a private enterprise) will become vital. This opens a new stage of organizing among the villagers.'[135]

The strength of Shigemoti's argument is that it makes explicit the tacit acceptance of the market by many in development circles. It also draws out the logic of this, that many NGOs are assisting in the process of nurturing a capitalist mentality within a transitory cooperative-protective shell. Community, then, is not the fulfilment of Eastern collectivism, but rather the filament that will play its role in the fertilization of local potential for the capitalist transition. Given this, it would appear that the more urban rhetoric of civil society is destined to overwhelm community and, indeed, there has been a growing popularization of this idea among NGOs and related intellectuals.

A communitarianism for a liberal future

Through a broad range of local activities and attempts at policy mobilization, NGOs succeeded in at least flagging their work as a credible alternative or modification of existing state practices of development. NGOs were able to influence political discourse by bringing into the public arena notions such as integrated farming, community rights, self-reliance, local wisdom, and so on, which gradually permeated governmental discourse. The various calls and campaigning for community control over resources, participation in policy determination, public hearings and feasibility studies, were all part of a more generalized political offensive against the hegemonic state that had succeeded in locking out alternative voices through a measure of ideological mobilization and, where necessary, repression and coercion. These movements and the response of the state led to heated conflict and contest over numerous spheres.[136] With state calls for unity increasingly falling on deaf ears, and with new political openings making it difficult to engage in suppression, state and political actors have partly accepted the new institutionalized settings for dispute resolution, but have done much to subvert them towards their own interests. Nevertheless, the myriad forms in which the state/NGO contest was pursued allowed for a constant engagement between the two, with the consequence that in some quarters there was a cross-fertilization of ideas and practices, particularly in the development field. Furthermore, there are actors within and without the state who do seek genuine redress of legitimate grievances, and see a precondition of this the creation of means of communication between conflicting sides, so that – through dialogue – more appropriate action in the pluralized national interest can take place. This broad experience has been significant in reshaping reformist versions of nationalism and democracy.

On a more critical note, it may be noted that a pragmatic communitarianism lies at the heart of some civil society intellectual currents. This does not mean that there is a cynicism about the fate of communities. What it does suggest is that it is a communitarianism that engages with the liberal spaces of the market and the institutions of liberal democracy. It seeks to imprint on these a communitarian concern that morally transcends the enlightened self-interest of elites. Thus communitarianism provides a stronger moral claim on the public good. It is not surprising, therefore, that this current is represented by prominent lay Buddhists, former communists and activists. Nor is it surprising that such claims are taken up and profiled in state centres such as the NCC. There is a logic to this seeming contradiction: in the present circumstances of Thailand, for the rationale of self-governance to be speakable to a moral community, such as intellectuals believe they are addressing, an ethos that binds that community but which articulates it with political liberalism is needed. In all respects the notions of civic virtue, of responsibility, of self-reliance, in communitarian discourse, while located first as principles for the community, are also addressed to individuals. Furthermore, a careful analysis would suggest that ultimately, even if communitarian thinkers believe morally market-based local economies provide the basis of community sovereignty, it would be utopian to imagine the circulation of capital and its attendant commodification of life would not destroy the communitarianism they seek to embed.

What precisely is the democrasubjection sought in this tension between liberal and communitarian? In this space, national ideology emerges as a diverse and encompassing one which interpellates citizens as members of a self-reliant community which, standing on its own, can legitimately speak and address the national arena. It coaxes from such communities uniformity to moral precepts that define the inner life of communities as ultimately self-determining. Citizen Community acts like Citizen Subject: responsible and productive. In this frame the imagined democracy is localized into community and then projected back to the national stage as communities neither in bondage to the state nor degraded by the evils of patronage and subjection to external powers.

Notes

1 Prawet Wasi, *Krungthep thurakit*, 10/3/02, pp. 1, 4.

2 Thirayut Bunmi, *Sangkhom khemkhaeng thammarat haeng chat yuthasat ku hai prathet thai* [Strong society, good governance: a Thailand recovery strategy], Bangkok: Saithan, 1998.

3 Pasuk Phongpaichit, 'Social Movements, NGOs and Environment in Thailand', 8th International Conference on Thai Studies at Nakhon Phanom River View Hotel, Nakhon Phanom Province, 9–12 January 2002.

4 There are also attempts to bind the history of that organization to the benevolence of the monarchy. See, for instance, Rueng Suksawat, 'Behind the Thai NGOs', in Jaturong Boonyayattanasasoonthon and Gawin Chutima (eds) *Thai NGOs: The Continuing Struggle for Democracy*, Bangkok: Thai NGO Support Project, 1995, pp. 51–68, pp. 52–3.

5 Chamophan Suwatthi, 'Botbat sathanaphap khong onkon sitthi manutsayachon' [The Role of Human Rights Organizations in Thai Politics], M.A. thesis, Thammasat University, 1989, pp. 103, 108.

6 Cited in *ibid.*, p. 99.

7 Prudisan Jumbala, interview with the author, Bangkok, 17/6/97.

8 *Ibid.*

9 Nevertheless, some of its members went on to form the Coordinating Group for Religion and Society, which continued to address the issue of political prisoners and information collection and monitoring. See Kothom Ariya, 'Dan sitthi manutsayachon' [The human rights dimension], in Phaisan Sangwoli, *Thotsawat onkon phatthana ekkachon (The Decade of NGOs)*, Bangkok: Munithi asasamak pheua sangkhom, 1991, pp. 136–41, p. 139.

10 Chamophan, 'Botbat sathanaphap khong onkon sitthi manutsayachon [The Role of Human Rights Organizations in Thai Politics], p. 102. In 1983 it was formally registered as an 'association'.

11 Phairot Phongpen (UCL manager), interview with the author, Bangkok, 23/3/97.

12 Thirayut Bunmi, 'Patiwat yuk mai' [New Era Revolution], in Han Linanon, Kriasak Chunhawan, Precha Piemphongsan, Thirayut Bunmi and Weng Tochitrakan, *Patiwat song naeo thang* [Two ways of revolution], Bangkok: Samnakphim athit, 1981, pp. 79–107.

13 Weng Tochirakan, 'Yuthasat yutwithi kanpatiwat prathet thai' [Strategy and Tactics of the Thai Revolution], in *ibid.*, pp. 111–51.

14 Somkiat Wanthana, 'Thai Studies in the 1980s: A Preliminary Remark on the Current State of the Arts', paper presented at 'Thai Studies in ASEAN: State of the Art' conference, September 1987, Bangkok, p. 21.

15 See Lysa Hong, 'Warasan Setthasat Kanmu'ang: Critical Scholarship in Thailand', in Manas Chitakasem and Andrew Turton (eds) *Thai Constructions of Knowledge*, London: School of Oriental and African Studies, University of London, 1991.

16 'Wikrit Prachathipatai baep ratthasupha khong thai nai pi thi 51' [Crisis of Parliamentary Democracy in the Fifty First Year], *Warasan setthasat kanmeuang* [Journal of political economy], 4, 2, 1983, p. 3.

17 *Ibid.*, p. 4.

18 Ahkhom Khanangkun, 'Ratthaniyom rabop rachakan thai: bonsen wa duay rat kap prachasangkhom nai rabop thunniyom thai' [The bureaucratic capitalist state: on the state and civil society in the Thai capitalist system], *Warasan setthasat kanmeuang*, 5, 1–2, 1985, pp. 19–32.

19 See, for instance, the influential book by Thiriyut Bunmi, *Sangkhom Khemkhaeng* [Strong society], Bangkok: Samnakphim mingmit, 1993.

20 Srisuwan Khuankhachon 'Onkon ekkachon kap kanphathana prachatipatai nai prathet thai' [NGOs and the development of democracy in Thailand], in Sungsidh Phiriyarangsan and Pasuk Phongphaichit (eds) *Jitsamnuk lae udomkan khong khabuankan prachathipatai ruam samai* [Consciousness and ideology of the contemporary democracy movement], Bangkok: Sunsuksa sethasatkanmeuang khana settasat kanmeuang julalongkon mahawithiyalai, 1996, pp. 153–71, pp. 156–7.

21 Interview with author, 17/3/97, Bangkok. See also his socialist humanist approach in Kothom Ariya, *Bonsensai prachathipatai* [On the road to democracy], Bangkok: Union of Civil Liberty, 1985.

22 Kothom Ariya, 'Dr Kothom Ariya Prathan kansantiphap lae phathana' [Dr Kothom Ariya, President of the Peace and Development Project], in Phaisan Sanwoli (ed.) *Thotsawat onkon phathana ekkachon*, Bangkok: Munnithi asasamak phu sangkhom, 1991, pp. 35–44, p. 37.

23 Kothom's career might be taken to symbolize the way in which NGO activists have used the new instruments of the liberal state, seeking to advance broadly social democratic politics.

24 Saneh Chamarik, *Phutthasatsana kan sitthi manutsayachon* [Buddhism and human rights], Bangkok: Samnakphim mahawithayalai thammasat, 1988. For a detailed look at Chamarik's engagement with the traditions of Western constitutionalism and human rights, and the position of 'tradition'-bound Asia, see Saneh Chamarik, *Democracy and Development: A Cultural Perspective*, Bangkok: Local Development Institute, 1993.

25 For varied regional experience of NGOs see the regional summaries in Khanakammakan phoei phrae lae songsoem phathana' [Propagation and development promotion committee], *Thamniap onkon phathana ekkachon* [NGO directory], Bangkok, 1997.

26 See Suthy Prasartset, 'The Rise of NGOs as [a] Critical Social Movement in Thailand', in Jaturong and Gawin (eds) *Thai NGOs*, pp. 97–134.

27 An excellent English language source on the early thinking of this movement is Seri Pongphit (ed.) *Back to the Roots: Village Self Reliance in a Thai Setting, Culture and Development*, Bangkok: Series no. 1, Rural Development Documentation Centre.

28 Suthy Prasartset, 'The Rise of NGOs as [a] Critical Social Movement in Thailand', in Jaturong and Gawin (eds) *Thai NGOs*, p. 104.

29 *Ibid.*, p. 106.

30 *Ibid.*, pp. 107–8.

31 *Ibid.*, p. 108.

32 *Ibid.*, pp. 110–11.

33 *Ibid.*, p. 118.

34 *Ibid.*, p. 119.

35 For descriptions of the various activities and perspectives of NGOs see Ernst Gohlert, *Power and Culture: The Struggle Against Poverty in Thailand*, Bangkok: White Lotus, 1991.

36 The Thai Volunteer Service was founded in 1980 and represents an early attempt to stamp some level of coordination on the nascent NGO movement. It also aimed at providing volunteer training to increase the number of NGO cadres as well as serving as a base for information exchange. Its foundation was supported by nineteen NGOs, and it has grown to be an important player in the NGO movement. See Amara Pongsapich, 'Nongovernmental Organizations in Thailand', in Tadashi Yamamoto (ed.) *Emerging Civil Society in the Asia Pacific Community: Non Governmental Underpinnings of the Emerging Asia Pacific Regional Community*, Singapore: Institute of Southeast Asian Studies, pp. 245–70, pp. 255–6.

37 Thai Volunteer Service, *Directory of Non-Government Development Organizations in Thailand.*, unabridged version, Bangkok: Thai Volunteer Service, 1987, p. 10.

38 In this book information is offered on many of the 135 NGDOs and their funding base (*ibid.*). Even the UCL is described as receiving 80 per cent of a 2 million baht budget from non-domestic sources (p. 11).

39 For a more thoroughgoing critique of the role of NGOs see James Petras, 'NGOs: In the Service of Imperialism', *Journal of Contemporary Asia*, 29, 4, 1999, pp. 429–40.

40 See Prawet Wasi, 'So. no. pho. prawet wasi prathan munithi chumchon thong thin phathana' [Prawet Wasi, president of the local community development foundation], in Phaisan Sanwoli, *Thotsawat onkon phathana ekkachon*, Bangkok: Munnithi asasamak phu sangkhom, 1991, pp. 8–14, pp. 9–10.

41 Kothom Ariya, 'Prathan', in *ibid.*, pp. 37–8. On competition and wages for NGO staff, see the comments on p. 31 of the same book.

42 See Stasia A. Obrenskey, 'The Thai Foundation Development Support Consortium: A Plan for Establishing A Coordinated Resource Mobilization Effort', prepared for private agencies collaborating together, Bangkok, 1994, mimeograph. It is reported that by the late 1980s 75 per cent of NGOs had small budgets of less than 1 million baht and 50 per cent had less than five staff (p. 5).

43 Wanlop Tangkhananurak, 'Lekhathikan Munitthi sangsan dek' [Secretary general of the creative children's foundation], in Phaisan Sanwoli, *Thotsawat onkon phathana ekkachon*, Bangkok: Munnithi asasamak phu sangkhom, 1991, pp. 63–7. Wanlop's discussion shows the reliance of some groups on business support.

44 Suthy Prasartset, 'The Rise of NGOs as [a] Critical Social Movement in Thailand', in Jaturong and Gawin (eds) *Thai NGOs*, pp. 102–3.

45 Prudisan Jumbala and Maneerat Mitprasat, 'Non-governmental Organizations: Empowerment and Environment in Thailand', in K. Hewison (ed.) *Political Change in Thailand:*

Democracy and Participation, London: Routledge, 1997, pp. 195–216, p. 201. The authors note that the NESDB had already called for consultation with NGOs in 1981, but they felt unequipped to respond and only did so when they felt in a position of strength.

46 See the case studies presented in *ibid.*, pp. 207–15.

47 A good summary of conflicts from the mid-1990s may be found in Nattaree Prachak, 'Natural Resource Management and the Poor in Thailand', *Thai Development Newsletter*, no. 24, 1994, pp. 8–14. An extensive study of organizational responses of people's organizations and NGOs in the form of the Forum of the Poor, may be found in Praphat Pintoptaeng, *Kanmeuang bonthong thanon 99 wan samacha khon jon* (Politics on the road: 99 days of the Forum of the Poor], Bangkok: Sathaban Naiyonbai lae kanjatkansangkhon mahawithayalai, 1998. Also see Bruce D. Missingham, *The Assembly of the Poor in Thailand: From Local Struggles to National Protest Movement*, Chiang Mai: Silkworm Books, 2004.

48 See *Kansammana rabop ratthasupha kan kankaekhai panha sithi manutsayachon* [Seminar on the parliamentary system and solving the problem of human rights), 1990, mimeograph. *Raingan kansammana botbat so.so. kap panha lae nayobai raeng duan thangsanghom* [Seminar report on the role of MPs and urgent social problems and policies], Bangkok, 14–15 February 1993, mimeograph.

49 See 'Declaration of the Customary Rights of Local Communities: Thai Democracy at the Grass Roots', *Thai Development Newsletter*, no. 24, 1994, pp. 34–6.

50 *Ibid.*, pp. 34–5.

51 *Ibid.*, p. 36.

52 *Ibid.*

53 For discussions on localism after the crisis, see Kevin Hewison, 'Resisting Globalization: A Study of Localism in Thailand', *The Pacific Review*, 13, 2, 2000; Pasuk Pongphaichit and Chris Baker, *Thailand's Crisis*, Chiang Mai: Silkworm Books, 2000; Duncan McCargo, 'Populism and Reformism in Contemporary Thailand', *Southeast Asia Research*, 9, 1, 2001.

54 See Samnakgan khanakammakan watthanatham haeng chat [National Culture Commission], *Sammana thangwichakan phumipanya chao pan kan kandamnoen thang whatthanatham lae phathana chonabot* [Seminar on people's wisdom and carrying out cultural and rural development), 1991.

55 Michael Connors, 'Ideological Aspects of Democratization: Mainstreaming Localism', Working Paper 12, October 2001, Southeast Asia Research Centre, City University, Hong Kong.

56 See Somchai Phatharathananunth, 'Civil Society in Northeast Thailand: The Struggle of the Small Scale Farmers' Assembly of Isan', Ph.D. dissertation, University of Leeds, 2001, Ch. 1.

57 On Chatthip's historical work, see Craig Reynolds and Lysa Hong, 'Marxism in Thai Historical Studies', *Journal of Asian Studies*, 43, 1983, pp. 77–104. For a thorough and probing critique of community culture see Atsushi Kitahara, *The Thai Rural Community Reconsidered: Historical Community Formation and Contemporary Development Movements*, Political Economy Centre, Faculty of Economics, Chulalongkorn University, 1996, especially pp. 65–101.

58 Chatthip Nartsupha, *The Thai Village Economy in the Past*, trans. Chris Baker and Pasuk Phongphaichit, Chiang Mai: Silkworm Books, 1999, p. v.

59 Chatthip Nartsupha, 'The Community Culture School of Thought', in Manas Chitkasem and Andrew Turton (eds) *Thai Constructions of Knowledge*, London: SOAS, 1991, pp. 118–41, p. 120.

60 *Ibid.*, pp. 134–5.

61 *Ibid.*, p. 136.

62 *Ibid.*, p. 138.

63 Pasuk Pongphaichit and Chris Baker, 'Afterword: Chatthip and the Thai Village', in Chatthip Nartsupha, *The Thai Village Economy in the Past*, pp. 114–31, p. 127.

64 Saneh Chamarik, *Democracy and Development: A Cultural Perspective*, Bangkok: Local Development Institute, 1993, p. 61.

65 *Ibid.*, p. 63.

66 'Samphat So. Seneh Chamarik' [Interview with Professor Saneh Chamarik], *Thang Mai* [New way], 4, 1, 1990, pp. 12–22, p. 16.

67 *Ibid.*

68 Saneh Chamarik, 'Naikhwamsamkhan khong po. ro. bo. pa chumchon to sanghom thai' [The importance of the Community Forest Bill to Thai society], paper presented at Thammasat University, 30 May 2001.

69 *Ibid.*, pp. 17–18.

70 Saneh Chamarik, 'Kankaekhai wikrit' [Solving the crisis], in Phitthaya Wongkul (ed.) *Jutjop rathchat su . . . chumchonathipatai* [The end of the nation state: towards community-sovereignty], Bangkok: Samnakngan kongthun sanapsanun kanwijai lae munithi phumipanya, 1997, pp. 9–40, p. 11.

71 *Ibid.*, p. 14.

72 *Ibid.*, pp. 22–3, 30–2.

73 *Ibid.*, p. 36.

74 *Ibid.*, pp. 36–8.

75 See John Brohman, *Popular Development: Rethinking the Theory and Practice of Development*, Oxford: Blackwell, 1996, pp. 337–9.

76 Prawet Wasi, *Watthanatham kap kanphathana* [Culture and development], Bangkok: Samnakngan khanakammakan watthanatham haeng chat, 1995, p. 5.

77 Prawet Wasi, *Setthakit phophiang lae prachasangkhom* [The modest economy and civil society], Bangkok: Samnakphim mo chaoban, 1999.

78 Prawet Wasi, *Kanphatthana prachathipatai lae kanpatirup kanmeaung* [Developing democracy and political reform], Bangkok: Samnakphim mo chaoban, 1994, pp. 14–16.

79. Prawet Wasi, 'Building Learning Global Community: Key for the Future', in Jaturong and Gawin (eds) *Thai NGOS*, pp. 159–64

80 Prawet Wasi and Chuchai Suphawong, 'Botsamphat sattrajan naiphet prawet wasi' [Interview with Professor Prawet Wasi], in Chuchai Supahwong and Yuwadi Khatkanklai, *Prachasangkhom thatsana nakkhit sangkhom thai* [Perspectives of civil society: Thai social thinkers], Bangkok: Samnakphim matichon, 1997, pp. 3–36, p. 6.

81 Prawet Wasi, 'The Thai path of development', *Bangkok Post* (online edition), 14/1/98.

82 See Prawet Wasi, *Saksi haeng khwambenkhon sukkhayaphap haeng khwamsangsan* [The dignity of humanity and creative potential), Bangkok: Mo chaoban, 1995.

83 Prawet Wasi, 'Message to Thaksin from Prawase Wasi', *Bangkok Post* (online edition), 19/5/01.

84 Prawet Wasi, *Potrian jak 18 Proetsaphamahawipyok* [Lessons from the May 18th tragedy], Bangkok: Munithi phumipanya, 1992, pp. 82–3.

85 See Prawet Wasi and Chuchai Suphawong, 'Botsamphat sattrajan naiphet prawet wasi' [Interview with Professor Prawet Wasi], in Chuchai Supahwong and Yuwadi Khatkanklai, *Prachasangkhom thatsana nakkhit sangkhom thai,* Bangkok: Samnakphim matichon, 1997.

86 *Siamrat,* 25/6/96, pp. 33–4.

87 National Economic and Social Development Board, *The Eighth National Economic and Social Development Plan,* (*1997–2001*) at http://www.nesdb.go.th/New_menu/plan8e/content_page.html, retrieved on 31 August 2001.

88 Sathaban chumchon thongthin phatthana (LDI), *Kop ban ku meuang* [Save the nation forum], 1998.

89 Sathaban chumchon thongthin phatthana (LDI) and Sathaban kanrianru lae phatthana prachasangkom (Civicnet), *Bonsen thangkankhonha phalang panya lae jintanakan* [Searching for wisdom and imagination], Bangkok: Sathaban chumchon thongthin phatthana (LDI) and Sathaban kanrianru lae phatthana prachasangkom (Civicnet), 2000, p. 36.

90 Anuchart Puangsamli, interview with the author, Bangkok, 4/8/01.

91 Chaiwat Thirapan, interview with the author, Bangkok, 2/8/01.

92 Anuchart Puangsamli, interview with the author, Bangkok, 4/8/01.

93 Naruemon Thabchumpon, 'State-Civil Society Relations: A New Chapter of Thai Political Reform', paper presented to the International Convention for Asia Scholar (ICAS2) on 10 August 2001, Berlin. Rathana Tosakul Boonmathya, 'Prachakhom: Civil Society in Thailand: The Case of the Khon Kaen Civic Assembly (KCCA)', paper presented to the 7th International Conference on Thai Studies, Amsterdam, 4–8 July 1999.

94 See John Dryzek, *Deliberative Democracy and Beyond: Liberals, Critics, Contestations,* Oxford: Oxford University Press, 2000.

95 Sathaban chumchon thongthin phatthana (LDI) and Sathaban kanrianru lae phatthana prachasangkom (Civicnet), *Bonsen thangkankhonha phalang panya lae jintanakan*], Bangkok: Sathaban chumchon thongthin phatthana (LDI) and Sathaban kanrianru lae phatthana prachasangkom (Civicnet), 2000, pp. 34–5.

96 *Ibid.,* p. 36.

97 Local Development Institute, *7 Years of the Local Development Institute,* Bangkok: Local Development Institute, 1997, p. 14.

98 Sathaban chumchon thongthin phatthana, *Kho saneu yutthasat kae wikrit chat* [A proposed strategy to solve the national crisis], Bangkok: Sathaban chumchon thongthin phatthana, pp. 5–6.

99 Chai-Anan Samudavanija, *Pracharat kap kanplianplaeng* [The civil-state and change), Bangkok: Sathaban nayobai suksa, pp. 60–2.

100 *Siam Post,* 27/3/00, p. 2.

101 Phonladej Pinpratip, interview with the author, Khon Kaen, 28/7/01; see also *Matichon*, 23/4/01, p. 2.

102 Phonladej Pinpratip, interview with the author, Khon Kaen, 28/7/01.

103 Prawet Wasi, 'Phalang chumchom Phalang phaendin' [Force of the community, force of the land], in *Ekkasan prakop radom khwam khit hen weti yutthasat phalang phaendin* (*Documents for Workshop on Forces of the Land Strategy*), 2001, n.p.

104 Phonladej, interview with the author, Khon Kaen, 28/7/01.

105 Prawet Wasi, 'Phalang chumchom Phalang phaendin', n.p.

106 Local Development Institute, *Sarup mattrathan kansang phalang phaendin khong pakprachachon* (Summary of measures to create forces of the land of the people sector], mimeograph, 2001.

107 Phrarachabanyat samnakngan khanakammakan watthanatham haeng chat [Act on the office of national culture], *Ratthasuphasan* (Parliamentary journal], 27, 12, 1979, pp. 124–9. Initially it was quite a small affair with an office of about thirty people. It has grown to over 300 in the late 1990s.

108 Mahawitthayalai Sukhothaithammathirat, *Prasopkan Watthanatham suksa* [Cultural Studies experience], 1990, pp. 358–64. An early Secretary General of the NCC considered that it would be beneficial to stamp out patronizing attitudes towards local culture, for then it could be more productively utilized as part of national culture: see Samnakngan khanakammakan watthanatham haeng chat, *Mong adit pheu anakhot . . . 15 pi samnakngan khanakammakan watthanatham haeng chat* [Looking to the past . . . for the future 15 years of the National Culture Commission], National Culture Commission, 1994, pp. 24–5.

109 Amara Pongsapich, 'Development and Culture: Past, Present and Future Trends in Thailand', in Edwin Thumboo (ed.) *Cultures in ASEAN and the 21st Century*, Singapore: Unipress, 1996, pp. 251–65, p. 256.

110 See Samnakngan khanakammakan watthanatham haeng chat, *Mong adi*, pp. 38–9.

111 *Ibid.*, p. 28.

112 Mahawitthayalai Sukhothaithammathirat , *Prasopkan Watthanatham suksa* [Cultural studies experience), p. 433.

113 Samnakngan khanakammakan watthanatham haeng chat, *Mong adit*), p. 59. Likewise, as Surichai Wun'Gaeo notes, democratization has led to a number of intellectuals making 'discoveries or "rediscoveries" of the various ethnic, regional and religious bases of the national culture', see Surichai Wun'Gaeo, 'The Making of Thai National Culture', in Edwin Thumboo (ed.) *Cultures in ASEAN and the 21st Century*, Singapore: Unipress, 1996, pp. 225–88, p. 237.

114 Samnakngan khanakammakan watthanatham haeng chat, *Mong adit*, pp. 60–1.

115 See Samnakngan khanakammakan watthanatham haeng chat, 'Chiwit lae ngan khong sattrajan phiset dr. ekkawit na thalang phusongkhunnawut watthanatham chat [The life and work of Special Professor Dr Ekkawit Na Thalang, cultural expert], in *Samnakngan khanakammakan watthanatham haeng chat, Chiwit lae ngan phusongkhunnawut thang watthanatham*, 1996, pp. 103–26, p. 122.

116 Peter Jackson, 'Withering Centre, Flourishing Margins: Buddhism's Changing Political Role', in K.Hewison (ed.) *Political Change in Thailand: Democracy and Participation*, London: Routledge, 1997, pp. 75–93, pp. 85–6.

117 See Samnakngan khanakammakan watthanatham haeng chat, *Krop lae thitthang phaen watthanatham haeng chat 2535–2539* [National culture plan 1992–1996, framework and direction], 1990.

118 *Ibid.,* pp. 6–7.

119 Samnakngan khanakammakan watthanatham haeng chat, *Phaen maebot khrongkan-seuapsan watthanatham thai 2537–2540* [Master plan, project for the preservation of Thai culture 1994–1997], 1995, pp. 4–6.

120 *Ibid.,* p. 6. This is why the text explains it is called the 'Campaign for Cultural Preservation'; the term 'campaign' has some measure of choice about it, suggesting the aim was not the enforcement of compulsory cultural measures. For a different interpretation of this campaign as 'atavistic and belligerent' see Kasian Tejapira, 'Cultural Forces and Counterforces in Contemporary Thailand' in Edwin Thumboo (ed.) *Cultures in ASEAN and the 21st Century,* Singapore: Unipress, 1996, pp. 239–50, pp. 240–1.

121 Samnakngan khanakammakan watthanatham haeng chat [National culture commission], *Naoethang nai kansongsoem watthanatham thai 11 prakan* [Methods in promoting 11 points of Thai culture], 1994, p. 3. Other features included promoting good family relations, Thai customs, Thai language, discipline, values, integrity and ethics (five basic values restated as self-reliance, diligence and responsibility, thrift, discipline and abiding by the law, following religious teachings, loving the nation, religion and monarchy).

122 Kasian Tejapira, 'Cultural Forces and Counterforces in Contemporary Thailand', in Thumboo (ed.) *Cultures in ASEAN and the 21st Century,* pp. 239–250, p. 245.

123 For an exploration of the different worldviews that are generated by 'globalization' among Thai intellectuals, and the dialectic between local and global, see Craig Reynolds, 'Globalization and Cultural Nationalism in Modern Thailand', in J. Kahn (ed.) *Southeast Asian Identities: Culture and the Politics of Representation in Indonesia, Malaysia, Singapore and Thailand,* Singapore: Institute of Southeast Asian Studies, 1998, pp. 115–45.

124 See Jim Taylor, 'Buddhist Revitalization, Modernization, and Social Change in Contemporary Thailand', *Sojourn,* 8, 1, 1993, pp. 62–91. This article discusses the breaking up of the state's hegemonic hold over Buddhism.

125 In an NCC seminar held to discuss Thai political culture, the emergent liberal position was endorsed within a Thai frame of the triad, see Samnakngan khanakammakan watthanatham haeng chat, *Nangseua ekkasan thangwichakan reuang kansupsan lae phatthana watthanatham thang kan meuang thai* [National Culture Commission, technical documents on the preservation and development of Thai political culture], 1994.

126 Bowonsak Uwanno, interview with the author, Bangkok, 15/1/98.

127 See Saneh Chamarik and Yot Santasombat (eds) *Pa chumchon nai prathet thai: naoe thang kan phatthana* [Community forests in Thailand: approaches to development], vol. 1, Bangkok: Sathaban chumchon thongthin phatthana, 1996, esp. pp. 67–122, for the section probably written by Bowonsak, although no author is given.

128 Bowonsak Uwanno, interview with the author, Bangkok, 15/1/98.

129 It should be noted that the constitutional provision on community rights is extremely vague, whereas the demands of the NGOs on this had been quite specific about what rights they would have. As of early 2005, NGOs remained locked in a struggle with the government to pass a popularly sponsored Community Forest Bill.

130 Bowonsak Uwanno, interview with the author, Bangkok, 15/1/98.

131 *Ibid.*

132 The above discussion of Bowonsak's ideas comes from the cited interview with him

133 S. Shigemoti, *Cooperation and Community in Rural Thailand: An Organizational Analysis of Participatory Rural Development*, Tokyo: Institute of Developing Economies, Occasional Papers, 1998, no. 35.

134 *Ibid.*, p. 50.

135 *Ibid.*, p. 119.

136 See Praphat Pintoptaeng, *Kanmeuang bonthong thanon* [Politics on the road].

10 From the abstract citizen to concrete struggle

A year into the economic crisis of the late 1990s, an advertisement appeared on Thai television featuring a pale-skinned, upper class Sino-Thai woman joining a rustic dark-skinned peasant family for an evening meal. The voiceover speaks of the beauty of simplicity. Then discreetly the logo of a mobile phone appears. No one could have imagined that this presaged Thai Rak Thai's smart use of the politics of localism to assist Thaksin Shinawatra, the telecommunications giant, to capture the prime minister's seat in 2001. In February 2005, Thaksin's TRT was returned to office in an electoral landslide, gaining close to 19 million votes, delivering it 377 seats in the House of Representatives. The Democrats, the second biggest vote winner garnered 7 million votes, giving it 96 seats in the House of Representatives. TRT's astonishing victory came despite an escalating crisis in the Malay-Muslim southern provinces and an accelerating slide towards authoritarian rule. Armed with a new mandate, Thaksin continued to consolidate his political position, alienating sections of the political establishment, as well as factional elements within TRT.

As political tensions heightened during 2005, a packed forum on royal powers was held at Thammasat University in early September. Pramuan Rujanaseri, a dissident TRT party-list MP and the controversial author of *Phraracha-amnat* (Royal Powers),[1] criticized elements of the parliament for trespassing on royal prerogative. Pramuan centred his attack on the Senate leader (nominally independent but reputedly close to the government) who had attempted to remove the previously royally-endorsed Auditor General. The name of a new nominee had been sent to the palace for endorsement in June, but after three months, the king had yet to return his endorsement or rejection of the new nominee. This royal silence was interpreted by many people as one more sign of disquiet in the palace towards political developments under Thaksin. Civic groups such as the Campaign for Democracy began a campaign to impeach the Senate Speaker for what it alleged was an apparent breach of protocol in regard to royal prerogative.[2] That the struggle for democracy by a number of activists has taken the road to symbolic protection of royal prerogative says something about the narrowing of democratic politics in Thailand, and the strategic use of the monarchy by civic groups.

As a result of these developments, the question of royal power was raised in public discourse in an unprecedented manner. One TRT MP noted: 'Never before since I jumped into the political arena 25 years ago has anyone been talking about His Majesty's powers on such a daily basis.'[3]

Pramuan's book, into its fifth reprint in less than several months, ends with a clear statement of tension between the government and the palace:

> The question today is whether the Thai people still treasure and believe in *phraracha-amnat* (royal powers) of the king . . . or not. Or are they gradually moving towards individuals, and proposals, in the form of a new form of government, to the point that they forget the good things . . . ?[4]

The question, alluding to the emergence of a new power network in Thailand, is rarely posed in public. It would seem to suggest that tensions between the consolidation of Thaksin's power and the older establishment had reached breaking point. This chapter looks at these contemporary developments, as they relate to the key themes raised in this book: the Thaksin episode is one more historical tussle between liberal and authoritarian elites.

The Thaksin interregnum[5]

The 2001 electoral success of Thaksin's party, Thai Rak Thai, was partly due to a mix of savvy campaigning, policy promises and typical practices of money politics. The backdrop to the rise of TRT was the economic crisis. In offering solutions to the crisis, TRT gained traction. Furthermore, the crisis imperative allowed for the unique conditions under which Thaksin could emerge with broad support from erstwhile conflictive capitalist groupings, and from rural and provincial populations.[6] In this unique conjuncture, Thaksin moved to overhaul Thailand's state, political and economic apparatuses in order to achieve a more viable Thai capitalism. The new constitution, which provided several measures for executive stability (see Chapter 7), provided Thaksin with a strong position from which to lead.

During its first term in office the Thaksin government launched substantial bureaucratic reform, so much so that Pasuk and Baker spoke of the 'overthrowing [of] the bureaucratic polity'. Extending executive intervention into the bureaucracy, first seriously attempted under the Chatichai government in the late 1980s, Thaksin has attempted to break senior civil servant tutelage over the political executive, and to turn the bureaucracy into 'implementing agencies'.[7] The advent of the Chief Executive Officer Governor, with direct lines of control and formal accountability, is perhaps most emblematic of this. But this is not some step towards a Weberian type bureaucratic rationality based on impersonalism and merit, rather Thaksin has a decidedly neo-patrimonial angle to his vision, having made personalized appointments across a range of state agencies, perhaps the most notorious being the appointment of Thaksin's cousin, General Chaisit Shinawatra, to Commander-in-Chief, Royal Thai Army, in August 2003.[8] It was not for nothing that Thirayuth Bunmi spoke of 'Thaksinocracy'.[9]

Whether Thaksin is worthy of his own regime nomenclature that defines a distinct organization of power is still uncertain, but it is clear that the idealized liberal constitutional state, aspired to by the political reform movement of the 1990s, has undergone a traumatic assault. Firstly, the government has exerted political influence, often welcomed by politicians on the make, in the nominally independent Senate and in house committees.[10] At the time of writing (September 2005), speculation is rife about which veteran politicians and partisan bureaucrats (especially from the Interior Ministry) will enter the Senate race in 2006. The idea of a non-partisan Senate composed of independent members charged with legislative review and oversight of various independent state agencies is all but gone.[11] Intervention in the Senate is an open secret. A former Senate President, who was critical of the government, was openly replaced by a figure close to TRT in 2003. Similarly, the government has exerted influence on the country's important anti-corruption agency, the National Counter Corruption Commission. Five of the seven new faces selected to the NCCC in December 2003 were in some way associated with TRT.[12] These are simply several examples of the many instances through which the political reform project has been subverted. An increasing number of books and articles on the failure of political reform are now being published, signaling a growing political despair.

Having been supported by many NGO figures for his seemingly pro-poor polices in the lead up to the 2001 elections, Thaksin subsequently moved to undermine the role played by non-governmental organizations (NGOs) in Thailand. Indicative of this was the fact that in May 2003 a rare media scoop in *The Nation* revealed that the government had attempted to get the Ministry of Foreign Affairs to stop foreign funding to NGOs involved in the Assembly of the Poor and specifically around environmental and community protests surrounding the Pak Moon dam. Thaksin, in light of these revelations said, in an almost Mahathirian fashion: 'NGOs are social groups that help bridge the gap between the government and the people. If such a gap no longer exists, the role of NGOs will be automatically diminished and foreign donors will not need to fund them any more.'[13] Furthermore, interference in broadcasting and the print media has diminished Thailand's standing as having one of the freest media in the region.

More bleakly, by the end of the first Thaksin administration extra-judicial murder had become a norm. With due process shelved, and a desultory approach to evidence collection and explanation, the government launched a War on Drugs in 2003, which claimed over 2,000 lives, some of whom are believed to have been vote canvassers for the Democrats.

Violence was also on display in the government's response to a crisis in the Southern provinces of Thailand where, beginning in early 2004 a mix of alleged separatist activity, mafia-like assassinations, the disappearance of Muslim men, and random killings of government officials has turned the Muslim majority provinces of Yala, Narathiwat and Pattani into a playing field of the Thai military and police. The Malay-speaking Muslim majority provinces of the South of Thailand were formally annexed in the early 20th century, and periodically have been the site of resistance against the Thai state, although the origin of the current violence is unclear. The government's implementation of martial law in a number of Southern districts in 2004, and the imposition in mid-2005 of an emergency decree providing excessive powers to the security forces, have in effect led to the area coming under siege by the state.

In 2004 two key events demonstrate the intensification of conflict. On 28 April – reputedly the anniversary of a brutal crackdown on Muslim dissidents in 1948 that left hundreds dead – one hundred Muslim men, including many teenagers, armed mostly with knives, apparently staged attacks on checkpoints, polices stations and army bases. In one case they retreated into the sacred Krue Se Mosque, where over 30 were killed. In total 107 were killed during the crackdown.[14] On 25 October in Tak Bai, Narathiwat province, thousands of protestors called for the release of villagers arrested for allegedly having handed border defence weapons under their supervision to 'militants'. Some protestors were shot during the peaceful demonstration. The military arrested over one thousand people and transported them in overcrowded trucks to an army camp for questioning. En route, 78 people died.[15] Throughout 2005 the killings continued, both of Muslim civilians, religious leaders, and of state officials, bringing the total killed in the region to over one thousand since the beginning of 2004.[16] Indicative of the danger zone the South has become, in mid-September 2005 over one hundred Malay-Muslims sought refuge from state repression by crossing the border to Malaysia.

At this stage, despite the certainties of some terror experts that Thailand is home to 'international terrorism', it is not clear what forces lie behind the renewed violence.[17] The military, police, government, and the local population, all have different accounts of what is happening. Competing accounts focus on as yet unknown elements either in the security forces, mafia networks or revived separatist movements, some with alleged links to 'transnational terrorism'.[18] Some believe that rival complexes composed of military, police, political and business figures are using the alleged insurgency as a cover for gang warfare over illegitimate cross-border trade, drugs and so on. Others believe that Muslim communities have been caught in the crossfire between rival fractions of the state apparatuses, and that this has triggered the renewal of a separatist movement.[19]

Whatever the cause, the most common call issued by the government, the palace and the media is for all Thais to unite. What that means is no longer clear. In December 2004 in an effort to push the theme of national unity, and drawing on the ideological resources that had been built up over a generation, the government sent military planes across the South of Thailand releasing millions of origami peace-birds (*nok-santi*) with messages of peace written by school children and concerned citizens. These showered down upon the people of the South. On the website of the separatist group, Pattani United Liberation Organization, a photo of one of the peace-bird messages is displayed. It reads: '[W]e have sent the bird flu with this Thaksin-bird, not too long, now, you lot will all die.'[20]

The excessive powers granted to the military in 2004 brought into the open the re-politicization of the military that had been ongoing since Thaksin's assumption of power.[21] Concomitantly, there has been the aggressive emergence of reconstituted predatory interests, within the bureaucracy and the police. In a sense, what the war on drugs and the iron-clad militarist reaction to the Southern crisis indicates is the capacity of elements of the national-security complex to act as a kind of shadow state able to determine their own rules with impunity. This is to suggest then that the constitutional state apparatus, genuinely sought by reformist elites, is not a strong and pervasive force with sufficient power to determine the nature of social, political and economic life.

New style, old ways?

Given the above, it looks as if the political reform project and the liberal communitarian aspirations of the localism movement have been dealt, literally, a death blow. Some eight years after the reform constitution, Thailand, in some respects, looks like quite a different country. Yet, a lot remains the same.

It is true that the nature of the capitalist capture of the state in Thailand, represented by the big-business cabinet of TRT, has introduced a forceful new dynamic into the state, as fractions of capital have moved centre-stage, displacing the always-uneasy relationship between state officials and capital during the 1980s and 1990s.[22] But patterns of clientelism and corruption persist, making it too early to say whether Thaksin has fundamentally reshaped the nature of Thai political discourse, politics and the state for the long haul. His regime may well represent the last gasp of a system of money politics, the only difference being that the scale is larger.

Duncan McCargo and Ukrist Pathamanand, see the Thaksin era in historic terms: the replacement on an established elite network with his own. They write:

> Thaksin Shinawatra is not an ideas man. He is a brilliantly successful opportunist, who is gradually taking control of the state and economy of Thailand. His core project is the replacement of the old power group – a network based around the palace, Prem, elements of the Democrat Party, members of prominent establishment families and senior bureaucrats – with his own network of intimates and associates. This enterprise involves defusing political reform and neutralizing the competing players and institutions embodied in the 1997 constitution.[23]

If this is so, Thaksin is just a bigger manifestation of the enduring logic of Thai elite politics: clientelism, cronyism and patrimonial use of the state that the political reform movement sought to eliminate. Given this, it is not at all clear that Thaksin has transformed the fundamental logic of Thai politics, so much as put it into reverse gear. Thaksin has failed to wipe out old style patronage and money politics, although he has shifted the goal posts – absorbing several political parties into TRT's larger structure. Old-style politics where cabinet posts are viewed as personal fiefdoms persist in some quarters. Although much has been made about the possible emergence of a two-party system in Thailand (i.e. the Democrats and TRT), the fact is that both parties, TRT more so, are factionalized along mostly patronage lines rather than ideological lines. TRT then might best be seen as a blanket cover that temporarily lies over a number of fluid clientelist networks, a grand coalition of factionalised interests.[24] This ensures that the government faces the constant threat of implosion as factions seek to advance their own position. Indeed, in the short to medium term, it is possible to envisage that a major defection will bring down the government, leading to the return of the hierarchical pluralism of money-politics.

Another feature of TRT is the heavily personalized funding of the party, which suggests this is not a 'modern' party of interest articulation and aggregation.[25] Apart from undeclared funding from business and individual figures, the official sponsor of the party is Thaksin's wife, to the tune of millions of dollars. Another feature is the persistence of the patron-like role that individual MPs have with their constituents. One report notes that TRT MPs receive an extra 200,000 baht a month from party funding to distribute in their respective electorates. This is not state funding – and its status is legally grey. MPs refer to this as *pasi sangkhom* or a social tax. They use it to help constituents, or at least are instructed to do so.[26] The centrality of local disbursal of funds suggests the importance of locality and a politician's capacity to offer personal patronage. Despite Thaksin's tight control of the media and the popularity of anti-poverty policies, he still requires the mediation of local political intermediaries. In the context of contemporary Thailand, Anek's dream of the autonomous citizen seems just that, a dream (see Chapter 8).

Yet Thaksin and TRT are not Thailand. Elements in the state, within NGOs and social movements continue to press for reform and change. It is notable that even within some state agencies, the liberal language of the 1990s continues to ring out, reflecting the fact that Thaksin is not the sole determinant of Thai politics. The NESDB, the NCC and LAD continue to deploy much of the liberal-communitarian ethos that was emergent in the 1990s.[27] The NESDB in its planning operations for the 10th National Plan continues to use the language of participation, civil society, and even proposes reforms to make agencies such as the NCCC more independent and efficient.[28] The Local Administration Department's (LAD) political language as it appears in its internal journal, *Thesaphiban*, is now a hybrid of managerialism (Thaksin), security (in response to the crisis in the South) and participatory democracy (continuing its reforming stance since the 1990s). In the journal one can encounter articles by officials calling for liberal and democracy-loving officials with an understanding of difference and diversity to try and work out solutions to the crisis in the South.[29] Other officials have returned to the counter-insurgency logic of the 1960s in regard to the politics of the South, calling for the revitalization of mass organizations (such as village tigers and the Self Defence Volunteers) to act as agents to control behaviour and build peace in villages, in line with calls by the palace. These seemingly counterpoised positions are reminiscent of the 'delayed liberalism' of LAD in the 1960s, where liberal intent simultaneously fused and competed with security objectives. This is to say that security and liberal projects, tinged with royalism, continue to compete in domains that are not determined by the instrumental use of the state by capitalist forces.

The National Reconciliation Commission (NRC), established to make recommendations on the crisis in the South, is an example of the continued strength of liberalism. Although, it has no legal power, its establishment in early 2005 came after the government's approach to the South was criticized as counterproductive. Rumour has it that the king played a role in its establishment. On his appointment as Chair of the NRC Anand Panyarachun (the Thai guardian of elite liberalism) announced, 'my boss is the people, not the government'.[30] Given a free hand, he selected Prawet Wasi and other prominent royalist and progressive figures to sit on the NRC. The Commission has cautiously issued advice on peace, diversity and legal process. Prawet Wasi, as a member of the NRC, reprised his former role as a catalyst for political reform by penning an article, which was widely circulated, on how democracy, development, local wisdom, and recognition of historical difference and identity could help bring peace to the region.[31] By the end of 2005 the NRC had become the focus of renewing Thai liberalism in the face of Thaksin's authoritarian slide.

Another reason for the continued ideological relevance of the liberal project is the fact that Thaksin has not forged an ideology (policies and managerial dictate do not an ideology make) which challenges this ethos. Thaksin's mangling of social and political discourse into language fit for an unimaginative MBA class has little power to restructure people's ideological outlook, outside his small band of business minded 'guru-crats' who are eager to consume the latest managerial spin.[32] It is as if Thaksin has left the ideology-producing agencies of the Thai state running on automatic, or at least un-captured, perhaps expecting the market and economy, and the consequences of his economic policy, to do the work of restructuring political subjects. To be sure, Thaksin's nationalist sloganeering and his enthusiasm for management-speak do suggest some ideological concoction, but in some respects he has taken the ideological resources of the 1990s and recast them in a more managerial, economistic and nationalist fashion.[33]

The government has shown an unusual interest in generating support for nationalism (in the past this has been generated by state agencies). It has passed new regulations on flying the national flag and, as part of an effort to maintain Thai identity it established the new Ministry of Culture in 2002.[34] Pasuk and Baker have also identified a group within TRT that actively works to promote nationalism.[35] Nationalism and its various symbols are clearly significant to Thaksin, although the logic driving Thaksin comes from an economic vision of a vibrant Thai economy.[36]

The Thaksin regime earned the label 'populist' for pursuing a number of national-ist and localist innovative economic schemes that have a Keynesian edge. Com-mentators also label it populist because of its various appeals to nationalism, Thainess, and 'the people'.[37] Thirayut suggests that Thaksin pursues a strategy of liberal populism (seriprachaniyom).[38] The government, through its pump priming, aims to create a new layer of local entrepreneurs and small-scale capitalists. This is the market logic of localism, explored in chapter 9, taken to its full logic. Indeed, the economism of the Thaksin regime in its approach to microcredit in rural areas is commensurate with moderate localism, although the fact that it focuses on capitalisation and marketisation in an aggressive fashion opens up the naïve logic of community to contradiction. A multitude of schemes are in place that indicate an activist capitalist government intent on developing a broader middle class in rural areas. Thus, the government targets millions of relatively middle-incomed families in the provinces for its various credit packages, training schemes, and linkage grants, to stimulate small-scale economic growth.[39]

If we accept that under Thaksin the logic of money politics has re-asserted itself, albeit in a different form and under different conditions, then it follows that the agenda of political reform remains pertinent to the contemporary politics of Thailand. This raises the question of whether or not it is possible that a new civic politics of the intensity of the political reform movement of the 1990s will emerge. The development of a substantial extra-parliamentary opposition cannot be predicted. If anything, Thaksin's rise demonstrates how weak and dependent Thailand's progressive social forces are. Bereft of a unified political strategy, they tailed the Thaksin government into the election of 2001, just as they had tailed the liberals in the political reform movement of 1995–97. In the lead up to the 2005 elections Thai Marxist Giles Ji Ungpakorn records a similar political capitulation to pro-capitalist parties. He writes of Thai delegates at the World Social Forum formulating a strategy for the upcoming election:

> Representatives of Thai social movements and N.G.O. networks, including 'Mid-night University', N.G.O., C.O.D. and the People's Assembly announced that their strategy for the February 2005 General Election was to vote for any of the 3 main opposition parties in order to dilute the parliamentary majority of the Thai Rak Thai party. [40]

This voting strategy, known as 'voting to get the dogs to bite each other', demon-strates a significant weakness of the progressive sector in Thai politics, an inability to pose a fully independent alternative to the assorted parties of capitalism that have captured, or bicker over, the Thai state.[41]

Certainly, the conditions for a coalition of progressive and liberal forces exist. The Democrat Party, although savaged by TRT in the 2005 election presented itself as an ostensibly liberal party, while also adapting to some the social policies of the Thaksin government, relating to health, debt and micro-credit funds. One opposition MP claimed that the Democrat's would fight the TRT proclaimed 'air war strategy' of winning 400 seats in the 2005 election with its own 'e-den' strategy (e-den is the colloquial term for a cheap, slow and clunky Thai-made vehicle that moves a bit a like a rhinoceros). Although not a formal description of the party's approach, the 'e-den' imagery suggests a long hard slog against the glittery hi-tech strategy of the government. This repositioning of the party provides Thailand's erstwhile free-floating liberalism with a possible political and institutional base.

In response to the successful use of pro-poor policies by TRT, the Democrats began to articulate concrete policies aimed at winning seats. In the Northeast the party used the slogan 'Adjust, reduce and eliminate debt, revive Thai farmers'.[42] Imitating TRT policy boldness, the Democrats have declared policies aimed at the aspirant 'poor', promising attention to debt eradication on a sustainable basis, as well as offering permanent organizational representation through the formation of a National Farmer's Council.[43] These developments should be seen in the context of the Democrat Party's attempt to build a base in the Northeast, the region that holds most parliamentary seats. Progressive organizations and farmers groups campaigned against the Democrats in the 2001 election, and urged a vote for TRT. In issuing farmer friendly policies the party is undoubtedly trying to remove memories of their wilful suppression of protests and their failure to deal with mass grievances while in office. During 2004, in the run up to the election, the Democrats tried to outdo TRT with promises of free health care, reduced university fees, and debt abolition for those who have acquired debts under the current government's various micro-credit schemes, and so on.[44] The party has also attempted to project an image of itself as a liberal party with concern for the independent functioning of a vibrant civil society.[45] These developments are interesting, for they suggest a party that while committed to the politics of abstract liberalism, in response to Thaksin's pro-poor policies, has begun to experiment with elements of social liberalism. Thus, it is clear that the politics of the 1990s are taking further shape and becoming more concrete.

However, if the party is beginning to speak to real people on the ground, there nevertheless remains a strong element of aristocratic disdain for ordinary people among some policy makers in the party. The urban liberal wing in the party is sceptical about the party's attempt to emulate TRT style policies. For such liberals, the success of TRT in the 2001 election was unrelated to the Democrat's image as a party of the IMF. Instead, they argue, the party lost power because the people were not sufficiently enlightened to elect responsible leaders. Former Democrat deputy leader Drairong summed up this kind of thinking, arguing that Thaksin's only weapon against the Democrats was money, 'Khun Thaksin misunderstands the word naiyokrathamontri, which in English is called Prime Minister, and is abbreviated as PM, Thaksin understands this to mean "POWER and MONEY"'.[46]

The philosopher kings at Democrat party headquarters regularly expressed disgust at the way many provincial people have accepted the many offers of debt relief and new credit by the TRT – seeing this as leading to further problems down the track. Indeed, constant statements were made by the Democrats about the increasing state of indebtedness of ordinary people under the current government.[47] In a sense, despite their stronghold in the South, some Democrat Party liberals despair of ever winning 'upcountry', viewing the people as too unsophisticated to make a good political choice. In this vein, Anek Laothamatas, once a deputy leader of the party, commented that the Democrats are the party of the city because city electorates are more mature and knowledgeable than the provinces.[48] The problem of course is that vast majority of parliamentary seats are in the provinces. Anek has previously given this problem perceptive academic treatment (see Chapter 8). Democrat elitism concerning the rural electorate takes many forms, perhaps the following remark from Anek is the best example:

> At the moment the people (*chao ban*) are only good at transferring debt, they are not skilled at production. Before, they could be compared with a house chicken (*kai ban*) that was able to look after itself, but now they have become like a weak CP chicken, waiting for the government to treat them [CP is an agribusiness company with close links to the government] . . . [49]

From Anand's characterization of the people as 2000 year old turtles to Anek's CP chicken analogy, the elite liberal prescription on good citizenship remains as condescending as ever.

Political reform, again?

Beyond political parties, the 1997 Constitution provided new terrain for the battle between authoritarian and liberal currents in Thailand. Even though Thaksin has sought the neutralization of the independent bodies created by the Constitution, the fact is that progressive forces now exist within these bodies, such as the National Human Rights Commission. The NHRC has been outspoken in relation to the extra-judicial killings that accompanied the government's war on drugs, and it is now acting as an advocate for over 200 hundred families whose relatives have been killed. It has also criticized the government's approach to the crisis in the South.[50] Such developments indicate a changed strategic environment. There are now a number of quasi-state institutions and processes to which recourse can be made. The state is not monolithic and remains open to different social forces.

Outside of the formal political arena progressive formations that move beyond the politics of abstract citizenship remain active. Composed of thousands of individuals involved in unions, NGOs, local community politics, writers and activists, these progressive formations ebb and flow according to issue and circumstance. It is this critical mass that awaits consolidation into a more overtly political force. Such forces are beginning to gain confidence after being demobilized and intimidated in the first few years of the Thaksin government. They have continued to struggle around various issues, but they have not positioned themselves as a national oppositional force to Thaksin.[51]

It is possible to discern a generalized politics among what is known as the 'people sector' (*pak prachachon*) that focuses on a localized economic agenda (a politics of moral markets) and national economic sovereignty, a recognition of the resource management crisis, a desire to create new modes of management, consumption and living, and a democratic reform of the state.[52] These politics are disseminated at multiple sites and through hundreds of small organizations that compose the 'people sector'. There has been some attempt to take these politics into the electoral realm.

During the 2005 election Midnight University and its associates issued a 'Citizen's Manual', that brought to notice the kind of issues people should consider prior to electing politicians.[53] Unlike the state manuals studied in previous chapters in this book, which focus on the abstractly good citizen, the Midnight University manual advises readers to judge politicians on the basis of the politics advocated by progressive NGOs and to consider issues related to local needs and conflicts. Other manuals issued by civil society organizations similarly moved beyond the abstract citizen endorsed by state-educators, and endorse interest based politics.[54] What is significant here is that even if 'the national interest' is invoked in these manuals, and an element of nationalism lies behind the attempt to mobilize voters by the people-sector, the moralism of past anti-vote buying campaigns and the calls for people to act like good citizens is less pronounced. Aggressive concrete political demands are placed up front.

But thus far, despite a number of promising developments – NGO-connected senators, a vibrant on-line dissident community, the continuance of interest based class politics in the Northeast, and the rise of popular protest against Thaksin in the South – organized opposition to Thaksin has not yet cohered into a concrete historical force. It is as if the 'people-sector' is as yet unconnected with a genuine mass base that could lead to a radicalization of its civic-type politics into interest-based politics. Its political strategy remains largely within the liberal-progressive loose alliance that characterised the 1990s.

The extent to which this progressive opposition moves forward depends largely on the lessons learned from the past. In the last decade, progressive social forces have moved to the spotlight when significant segments of the Thai establishment were also seeking political change, such as during the movement for political reform against money politics in 1995–97. Indications of a potential elite opposition to Thaksin are present. Already there has been talk of amending the constitution to ensure that the NCCC and the NHRC remain neutral. In December 2004 liberal elements within the Democrats, Chart Thai and Chart Phattana agreed to push for such an amendment.[55] Even Amon Chantrasombun, who partly defined the politics of the political reform movement, called for a second reform movement against the reemergence of 'parliamentary dictatorship'.[56] Indeed, in some respects the Thaksin period looks a lot like 1995, except that any potential oppositional force faces a new form of grand money politics, and an intensified atmosphere of violence and intimidation.

Should such a movement emerge, it is likely to be characterized, as it was in 1995–97, by liberal elites and progressive activists occupying different spheres of action, but pushing for broad reform. However, the struggle will be so much harder because Thaksin's hold on parliament remains firm (as long as he can juggle competing factional demands), and there is as yet no crisis imperative to reform the system as there was in 1997, when the economy collapsed. The crisis in the South may well prove to be the trigger, with the National Reconciliation Commission becoming the focus of reformists for a second reform movement. What will be crucial for progressive social forces is to define an independent position outside of elite liberalism, and this essentially means pushing for interest style politics and related political programs of social transformation beyond the institutions and procedures of constitutional democracy.[57]

Conclusion

As the Thaksin years show, no amount of democratic decoration and acting as guardians of the abstract public good, informed by currents of nationalism, can protect the interests of ordinary people. In some respects, the great energy expended in the last decade on democracy promotion, civic education and anti-vote buying campaigns (in short – when tens of thousands of people acted as the shock troops for liberal democrasubjection) has done little to abate the influence of money and power in the political system. Indeed, it might be argued that promoting 'good citizenship' in Thailand has led to a moralistic type of politics that permanently displaces questions about power and structure in determining political outcomes.[58] Self-organization is what can transform these democratic institutions into instruments that serve the interests of ordinary people, workers and peasants. Civic politics needs to be complemented with class-based activism in trade unions and farmers federations. Only this can ensure that national politics is not subject to the whims of aggrandizing elites.

In the interests of elite liberalism, and to forestall political instability, action from above may preempt the emergence of a mass progressive movement; and Thaksin may fall in front of a jury of his peers. Indeed, there is considerable concern about the current political situation among elements of the Thai establishment. The king himself has expressed some cogent concerns that indicate fear of mass disaffection with the political system. In late 2003, the king raised some interesting questions about the future implications of Thaksin's mode of rule. Offering sympathetic comments on the 'war on drugs', the king nonetheless suggested that more had to be done to satisfy critics who claimed the government was responsible for thousands of deaths. The king noted that responsibility was continually shifted from the 'superman' prime minister through to ministers, civil servants and through to the people and law, who then might shift responsibility on to the king, 'which is against the constitution, as the constitution says the king has no responsibility at all . . . so we agree that none of us are responsible for the nation.' [59] In the same speech the king notes that those responsible in government should accept criticism when it is warranted:

> [If] they are right then thank them, if they are wrong tell them, quietly . . . The person who is greatly troubled by this is the king, because no one can reproach him . . . We did not tell those who wrote the constitution that no one can reproach or violate the king. Why this was written, I do not know. If one can not be violated how can one know if one is right or wrong?[60]

A system of no accountability is a volatile system, and it is clear that the king's comments relate not just to the war on drugs but extend to the style of governance that Thaksin has embraced. By implication, if the king is open to criticism, although it is not allowed, Thaksin should also be able to tolerate it. By reprising his role as a cautious liberal king, Bhumipol furthers royal mythology.

Whether a popular movement, a push from above, or an implosion from within TRT removes Thaksin is a matter for speculation, as is his longevity. But if Thailand is to break from the familiar tug of war between authoritarian nationalism and royal liberalism, a movement from below that transcends both streams will need to emerge. Otherwise, a return to the royal embrace will be yet one more historical impasse for Thailand's poor.

Notes

1 Pramuan Rujanaseri, *Phraracha-amnat* [Royal powers], Bangkok: Sumet Rujanaseri, 2005. Pramuan is a conservative who rejects Western individualism and the doctrine of separation of powers as inappropriate in the context of Thai political culture, see p. 156.

2 The Constitutional Court had earlier ruled that the appointment of the sitting Auditor General had been irregular because of a technical breach of regulations governing the forwarding of candidate names to the Senate. The Court failed, however, to rule on whether the sitting Auditor General was actually illegitimate. Despite the uncertain status of the sitting Auditor, the Senate speaker forwarded the name of a new nominee. As the king had not yet signed an order removing the sitting Auditor General, the forwarding of the name of a new nominee to the palace was judged to be improper.

3 *Bangkok Post*, 13/09/05, online edition.

4 Pramuan, *Phraracha-amnat*, p. 175. The public discussion about royal powers also occurred when it appeared the palace was stalling on endorsing the annual military promotions list favoured by Thaksin and opposed by Prem.

5 Substantial parts of this section appeared in 'Thaksin's Thailand – to have and to hold', Paper presented to the Thai Update Conference, Macquarie University, 20–21 April, 2004.

6 Hewison, Kevin, *Pathways to Economic Recover: Bankers, Business and Nationalism in Thailand*, Working Paper Number 1, April, 2001. Southeast Asian Research Centre, City University Hong Kong. Available at http://www.cityu.edu.hk/searc/WP1_01_Hewison.pdf.

7 Pasuk Phongpaichit and Chris Baker, *Thaksin: The Business of Politics in Thailand*, Chiang Mai: Silkworm, 2004, pp. 184–188.

8 See Pasuk and Baker, *Thaksin: The Business of Politics in Thailand*, pp.176–=184.

9 Thirayut Bunmi, '*Wikro Sangkom Thai yuj "Thaksinuwat*"' [Analysing Thai society in the era of Thaksinization] *Matichon* 6/1/2003.

10 Suriyasai Katasila, '3 pi wuthisupha bonsenthang patirup kanmuang', [Three Years of the Senate on the road to political reform] *Krungthep Thurakit*, 7/8/03.

11 See *Kanmeaung rewiw*, 14–31 May, 2005, pp. 8–10.

12 *The Nation* 24/10/03; 10/12/03.

13 *The Nation* 10/5/03.

14 The killing of the 'insurgents' remains shrouded in mystery. In late September 2005, as the crisis in the South intensified, the National Human Rights Commission issued a report suggesting that a number of the 'insurgents' had been shot in the head, suggestive of execution after surrender. See *The Nation*, 28/9/05, p. 4A.

15 A government fact finding committee report on Tak Bai— was released in 2005 and reported in *The Nation* on April 26, 2005. On the cause of death it reads:— "Regarding the deaths of the 78 people at the Inkayuth military camp in Pattani, the fact-finding subcommittee on medical aspects inferred their causes of death from physical examinations conducted on injured survivors. Of the injured victims, most suffered crush injuries and four also had compartment syndrome that meant they required urgent operations. Medical specialists said the fact that the protesting Thai Muslims had been fasting without food or liquids for more than 12 hours; that they had been exposed to the scorching sun; and that they had experienced violent treatment during the demonstration, dispersal and transfers on overcrowded vehicles had led to their injuries. The transfers took more than three hours, in some cases on overcrowded vehicles, causing rhabdomyolysis as well as a chemical imbalance in the blood and blood cells. The imbalance was so severe that muscles involved with breathing could hardly function. In the most severe cases the victims died. It was concluded that the above factors caused the deaths of the detainees. Furthermore, the autopsies on the 78 detainees who died on their way from Tak Bai police station in Narathiwat's Tak Bai district to Ingkayuth military camp in Pattani's Nong Chik district showed that most deaths were caused by asphyxiation and pressure on the chest and breathing muscles. There were also some signs of seizures and chemical imbalances in the blood, which could have resulted in death. Therefore, the subcommittee concluded that all 78 detainees died of the same cause – rhabdomyolysis, which causes abnormal breathing. When coupled with the shortage of food and water and long exposure to sweltering heat, the condition can result in death."

16 This figure is unreliable as most shooting deaths in the South are now recorded as in someway related to the 'insurgency'.

17 See Michael Connors 'Thailand: The Facts and F(r)ictions of Ruling' in *Southeast Asian Affairs 2005*, pp. 365–284.

18 For an account that sees much of the violence being perpetrated by the military and police see Koi-lin Anwa and Suphalak Kanjonkhun *Fai tai krai jut* (Who is lighting the Southern Fire?) Bangkok, Indochina Publishing, 2004, 79–122; for an account that views the violence as a consequence of a renewed and united separatist and Islamic movement (PULO, BRN (Coordinate and Congress) Uluma, GMP, GMIP, BIPP under BERSATU) with

extensive roots in Southern villages and a seven point strategy leading to insurrection, see General Kitti *Rattanachaya, Jut fai tai tang rat patani* [Igniting the South, establishing the Patani State] Bangkok, 2004.

19 The English and Thai language press occasionally report on 'insurgents' surrendering and attending re-education camps, seemingly providing evidence of the mass insurgency exposed by Kitti (see note 18). These reports should not be taken literally. Those wishing to indicate non-involvement and innocence *(porisut)* in the events of the South are invited by the military to report to what are effectively re-education camps. In the Southern Border Provinces Peace-Building Command newsletter, *Khao theung khao jai phattana* (Understand, Access, Develop) 1, 1, 15 December, 2004, p. 9, a list of the six-week curriculum provided at an army camp for those who have presented themselves for 're-education' is provided. It is a civics-like education program with some vocational orientation. Some of the subjects, taught mostly by Muslims, include Thai history, Duty of Thai citizen, Ethics and Morality, Thai language and Emotional intelligence. Some believe that many of these alleged 'insurgents' are merely aware that their name may be on a blacklist and hence surrender in order to be processed and not be subject to extra-judicial killing.

20 See website of Pattani United Liberation Organization http://www.pulo.org/ accessed 10/3/05.

21 See Duncan McCargo and Ukrist Pathmanand, *The Thaksinization of Thailand*, Copenhagen: NIAS Press, 2005, pp. 120--=165.

22 Kevin Hewison, 'Neo-liberalism and Domestic Capital: The Political Outcomes of the Economic Crisis in Thailand', *The Journal of Development Studies*, 41, 2, 2005, pp. 310–330; Pasuk Phongpaichit and Chris Baker, ' "Business Populism" in Thailand' , *Journal of Democracy*, 16, 2, 2005, pp. 58–72.

23 Duncan McCargo and Ukrist Pathmanand, *The Thaksinization of Thailand*, Copenhagen: NIAS Press, 2005, p. 252–3.

24 See James Ockey, 'Change and continuity in the Thai political party system', *Asian Survey* 43, 4, 2003, pp. 663–80.

25 See *Corporate Thailand*, 'The Inner Circle' 8, 84, August 2003.

26 *Thai Post* 20/9/03, online edition.

27 See Michael Connors, 'Goodbye to the Security State: Ideological Change in Thailand', *Journal of Contemporary Thailand*, 33, 4, 2003, pp.431–48.

28 See 'Kanprapprung konkai pakrat' *Phaen 10꞊ . . .-* [The Tenth Plan] 3, 5, May, 2005, pp. 2–4.

29 See Parinya Adomsap, 'Kwamkhit kaekhai panha chai din pak tai' [Thoughts on solving the problem of the– Southern Border Provinces] *Thesaphiban*, 100, 6, 2005, pp. 13–17.

30 See *Kanmeaung riwiw* [Politics review], 16--=31 May, 2005, pp. 11--=13. There was talk of Thailand having two Prime Ministers as a result of the re-emergence of Anand.

31 Prawet Wasi, *Samliam dap fai tai* [Triangle to put out the fires in the South], Bangkok: Krongkan pakhi seormsang santisuk nai 3 jangwat chai daen pak tai, 2005.

32 See the discussion on Thaksin's political discourse in McCargo and Ukrist *The Thaksinization of Thailand*, pp. 166–208; For an overview of economic thinking and connection with nationalism see Pasuk and Baker *Thaksin: The Business of Politics in Thailand*, pp. 99–133, 139–144.

33 See McCargo and Ukrist, *The Thaksinization of Thailand*, pp. 180–82.

34 For an analysis of the politics of the Ministry of Culture, see Michael Connors, 'Ministering Culture: The Politics of Hegemony and Identity in Thailand, *Critical Asian Studies*, forthcoming.

35 Pasuk and Baker, *The Business of Politics in Thailand*, p. 79.

36 Jim Glassman, 'Economic "nationalism" in a post-nationalist era', *Critical Asian Studies*, 36, 1, 2004, pp 37–64. The leveraging of Thainess for economic advantage is becoming more pronounced under Thaksin. The NESDB for instance notes, 'Thailand has many competitive advantages . . . these include the identity of Thainess, that no other nation can imitate or compete with.' The article goes on to recommend, in line with the SME strategy, the development of tourism, food, herbal medicines and things that are unique to Thailand. See 'Yuthasat kanprap krongsang sethatkit lae sangkom', *Phaen 10 . . .* 3, 3, 2548, p. 2.

37 Duncan McCargo, 'Populism and Reformism in Contemporary Thailand.' *South East Asia Research* 9, 1.; Hewison, Kevin, 'Responding to Economic Crisis: Thailand's Localism .' in *Reforming Thai Politics*, Duncan McCargo (ed) Copenhagen, Denmark: Nordic Institute of Asian Studies (NIAS), 2002.

38 Thirayut Bunmi, *'Wikro Sangkom Thai'*

39 National Economic and Social Development Board, *'Phonkandamnern Nayobai Kradun Sethakit radab rakya'* [Results of the Grass Root Economic Policy], 2003. http://ie.nesdb.go.th/gd/html/forms/Projects/ProjectIntro/ProjectIntro-1.htm accessed 14/4/04.

40 Giles Ji Ungpakorn, 'Thai Social Movements in an Era of Global Protest" paper presented to the Ninth International Thai Studies Conference, Northern Illinois University, 3–6 April, 2005, p. 2.

41 For a thorough left critique of NGO politics see Ji Giles Ungpakorn, 'Challenges to the Thai N.G.O. movement from the dawn of a new opposition to global capital' in Ji Giles Ungpakorn (ed) *Radicalising Thailand: New Political Perspectives*, Bangkok, Institute of Asian Studies, 2003, pp. 289–318.

42 *Krungthep Thurakit*, 25/8/03. Online edition.

43 Democrat Party, 'Naiyobai' Available at http://www.democrat.or.th/aboutpolicy.asp) accessed 19/4/04.

44 *The Nation* 26/4/04. Online edition.

45 *Prachachart Thurakit* 3/7/03; 7/7/03. Online edition.

46 *Phujatkan*, 26/1/03. Online edition.

47 *Matichon*, 26/8/03. Online edition.

48 See *Thai Post* 4/8/03. Online edition.

49 *Thai Post* 4/8/03. Online edition.

50 National Human Rights Commission '*Kho Saneu to rathaban karani phusiachiwit kiawkhong ya septit*' [Proposals to the Government on the loss of life in relation to drug addition] Available at http://www.nhrc.or.th/news/news1.pdf accessed 18/4/04.

51 By 2004 such an opposition began to take shape against privatization, policy corruption, abuse of human rights and resource livelihood issues and martial law in the South of Thailand. See *The Nation* 22/3/04. It is important to note that between 2001 and 2004 protests of various kinds continued despite the intimidating atmosphere attending the rise of vio-

lence and political authoritarianism of the Thaksin regime. Seksan Prasertkul provides an extensive description of over two hundred actions (including protests, forums, petitions, impeachment proceedings, and meetings) targeted at social, economic and political injustice during the first term of the Thaksin government. See *Kanmeaung pak prachachon nai rabopprachathipatai thai* [People-Sector Politics in the Thai Democratic System], Bangkok: Samnakphim amarin, 2004, pp. 261–360.

52 See Kasian Tejapira, 'Post-Crisis Economic Impasse and Political Recovery in Thailand', *Critical Asian Studies*, 34: 3, 2002, pp. 323–56, pp. 337–38.

53 Mahawhitayalia thieng kheun lae ongkon phantimit *Khumeu phonlameaung chai samrap leauktang lae palaktan nayobai nai anakhot 2548–2551* [Citizens manual: For use in the election and pushing for policy in the future, 2005–2008], 2005. Thanks to Ji Giles Ungpakorn for providing me with a copy of this manual. See his extended discussion of it in Giles Ji Ungpakorn 'Thai Social Movements in an Era of Global Protest'. Midnight University, based in Chiang Mai, is composed of progressive intellectuals and activists interested in holding discussions with villagers and communities. Midnight University took shape in late 1997 in recognition that it was mostly the middle classes who go to university 'during the day'. Its seminars are informal. MU's website is available at http://www.geocities.com/midnightuniv accessed 19/9/05.

54 For example, see Youth Election Project, Political Science, Chulalongkorn, *Voting for Democracy*, 2005.

55 *Phujatkan* 11/12/03. Online edition.

56 *Prachachart Thurakit* 13/3/03. Online edition.

57 For a comprehensive discussion of these type of politics, see Ji Giles Ungphakorn (ed.), *Radicalising Thailand: New Political Perspectives*, Bangkok, Institute of Asian Studies.

58 William Callahan, 'The Discourse of Vote Buying and Political Reform in Thailand', *Pacific Affairs*, 78, 1, pp. 95–=113.

59 Adulyadej Bhumiphol, 'King's Edict graciously conferred on an audience of various persons offering blessings on the occasion of the King's Birthday 4 December, 2003'. Unofficial Thai version available at http://kanchanapisek.or.th/speeches/index.th.html.

60 Ibid. This section of the king's speech is somewhat ambiguous. I checked with a Thai colleague who says that my translation is plausible, but Thais reading the speech in the original might be somewhat confused by the point being made. One possible interpretation of this section is that Bhumipol is making the point that Thaksin is setting himself up to be beyond reproach, but unlike the king, he is responsible for the everyday running of the nation. Thus the king considers the possibility that even a governing king (Thaksin?) must submit to criticism if he is to run the country directly. The speech is littered with light sarcasm directed at Thaksin.

11

Conclusion

The lash of civic virtue, democracy and the politics of democrasubjection

I HAVE INDICATED THROUGHOUT THIS BOOK THE NEED to break from ideologically conceived notions of citizenship, materialized in the politics of civic engagement and the public good, gilded with national ideology. Let me now conclude by retracing my steps and once again argue for 'democrasubjection' as a useful approach to understanding the objectives of elite-defined democracy. The general aim of this book, to explore the aporia of democracy through the obvious contradiction of object–subject relations at the level of discourse and ideology, entailed bracketing questions of subjectivity. This was warranted by the fact that I sought to explore what I consider two relatively new areas, the idea of democrasubjection itself, and the Thai context in which it has been played out. It is this approach that I shall now restate.

I began this book with the suggestion that it would be productive to explore democracy from the dual perspective of hegemony and government, the strategic deployment of which I named democrasubjection. Chapters 3–9 did this, looking for clues to the way that democracy worked at both levels. In doing this I was interested in exploring how, underneath the hegemonic claims of democratic sovereignty, which works at the level of instantiating a political community and projecting notions of common good and national identity, there are specific practices of government that belie the notion of sovereign citizens. Citizens have to be created first in order to be sovereign.

First, this duality was explored through moments of statist democracy, when the state took on a pastoralist pose towards its subjects, working towards a project of guided citizen practice within the folds of a paternalistic and overarching ideological state. This stance, informed by the doctrine of political development, involved an objectification of real subjects as 'the people problem', in order to integrate them into various state projects with the objective of eliciting an identity of nation and self.

Second, I explored how, in Thailand's democratization, new projects of democrasubjection arose which, while rhetorically similar to the statist projects, were framed by a liberal political programme. With the prospect of a diminishing state, there was hope of eliciting citizen practices able to secure a liberal democratic future. The articulators of this project aimed to imprison democratic potential in the storehouse of the liberally constructed citizen. Since the economic crisis, communitarian revisionings of citizenship have strengthened.

In exploring official discourse in Thailand, this work has focused particularly on the internal aspect of the doctrine of political development utilized by the state and emergent state actors. Necessarily, this needs to be complemented with a study of the precise relationship of the new liberalism to the 'global society', represented, for instance, by the transnational foundations seeking to tease out a liberal future for the world. Here one thinks of the Kettering Foundation, the National Endowment for Democracy, and so on. The interaction of this global moment of liberalism with the local attempt to reconstruct liberal pasts, or indeed resurrect fallen and despised outsiders, would present an opportunity for further work on the specific processes of democrasubjection at a transnational level. Such work would need to engage with notions of global citizenship and the accompanying political imaginaries of global governance.

I would not expect that the Thai experience has been replicated elsewhere, so tied to the contingencies of its own history is it. Nevertheless, I suspect that it may be highly relevant to explore the manner in which there is an emergent liberalism within a number of 'developing' countries, not just Thailand. Such work would argue against those who see, on the basis of idealizing features of liberal democracy in the West, developing Asian polities as illiberal democracies. The emergence of Thaksin may well fit the mould of illiberal electoral democracies, but it is a simplistic conclusion to see this as proof of inherent culturally informed political forms. Asian forms of liberalism struggle against powerful enemies, and their intellectual formation is a matter of great interest. The mapping of such non-Western liberalism would not be an invitation to celebrate the end of history, but rather it would entail a study of the new mechanisms of subjection that take root as the discourse of democracy is globalized and is simultaneously meshed with elite-defined national identity. This more often than not leads to 'developmental liberalism'.

As a tool of political analysis, the concept of democrasubjection may allow a critical exploration of democracy at the subjective level of dispositional compliance, and be used to examine the projects geared to this. But these projects must be understood as being articulated to ideological hegemonic projects that seek to bring into being a democratic political imaginary. It is in this dual movement that one can see flashes of contestation, as elites try and construct their ideal subject citizens. More often than not, the success of such projects is permanently suspended, for the people-problem emerges in new and varied ways. I have provided in this book a detailed reading of such projects, partly for the purposes of exposing interesting Thai material, and partly to state a case for democrasubjection. The notion need not be a dogma, but can simply attune us to seeing democracy differently.

The notion of democrasubjection also directs us to the constructed nature of the political community itself. By exploring projects of democrasubjection one can discern, within political development theory, the abiding regard for abstract notions of political community and citizenship as the means towards a modern end. An organizing proposition of development discourse is that national community and national interests exist, even if they must be built and managed. Projects simply bring into being what already lays latent. Development is the metaphor that fields and deals with this constructedness, because it holds out the hope of realization. Only there, through development, is the mundane pragmatic planning that goes into the construction of political community and citizenship transfigured into an idealized state. Yet, if development holds out the promise of national goals, it is also the place where questions on the legitimacy of sovereignty lurk. While some might invoke the artifice of representability, the political development doctrine, when spoken among its practitioners, has a disenchanted regard. It speaks to the technocratic aesthetic of managed social organisms, of imposing onto the social body regulative mechanisms that speak their own worth and need not be identical to the philosophical vocation of democracy and a sovereign people. While political community and citizenship are affirmed as desirable ends, it is the developer, in so many guises, who is the intermediary, fleshing out concrete interpretive and imperative measures towards their realization. In these plans and projects, 'democracy' as both national will and self-virtue is made common and available for technocratic practice and overhaul: How many protests may we count in order to devise national ideology? What part of Thainess will we tease out today? How can culture be deployed so as to bring about a unity of difference?

These questions are now exercising those who seek to embed liberal practice in Thailand. The move towards a liberal rationality implies the articulation of reformed national ideologies. Democracy, as part of this shift, is not merely a rhetorical shift in an authoritarian centralized state, but actually informs a new practice of citizenship geared towards a liberal state, national and international. The people, once more, are the objects of reform: their wayward ways neutered and brought to heel, their grievances channelled into institutions where advocates of the artifice of representability speak to their needs, while all around them the wheels of exploitation turn. In the name of civility and public good it is hoped that rational citizens will submit to the unifying discipline of the nation, symbolized in the benevolent monarchy. When ordinary people struggle, elites always have the lash of civic virtue beckoning them to unity. Such is the work of democracy, hegemonically defined and motivated.

Postscript

A FEARED OUTCOME OF THE EMERGING CRISIS IN Thai politics flagged in Chapter 10 was that the then prime minister Thaksin Shinawatra might lose office by a push from above. I did not expect that push to take the form of a military putsch, believing that Thaksin would be trumped instead by elite machinations. As this book was going to press, the Council for Democratic Reform under Constitutional Monarchy (CDR), a military grouping under the leadership of General Sonthi Boonyaratglin, launched a bloodless *coup d'etat* against Thaksin on 19 September 2006. Inasmuch as other means to dislodge Thaksin had failed, it was a reluctant coup. If under Thaksin the rule of law had been in the intensive care unit, the CDR has taken it to the mortuary table. They annulled the constitution, banned political gatherings, censored the press, and declared their decrees to have the status of law. News soon followed that King Bhumiphol had met with the coup group, bestowing legitimacy on them.

Towards the coup

In the latter half of 2005, in order to build an anti-Thaksin coalition one-time Thaksin supporter Sondhi Limthongkul began to claim that Thaksin was transgressing on the royal prerogative. Sonthi's weekly television show *Muang Thai Rai Sapda* was taken off air in mid-September for its increasingly anti-Thaksin stance. In response, Sondhi began broadcasting the show on the internet and through satellite television. His chosen studio for these broadcasts was public venues including Bangkok's Lumpini Park. Thousands attended at first but numbers began to decline; by January 2006 Sonthi looked liked a spent force. Despite Sonthi's revelations of alleged corruption and lèse-majesté, Thaksin's popularity remained relatively robust because of his image as a pro-poor leader.

Here Thaksin's record needs critical scrutiny. According to the United Nations *Human Development Report*, Thailand's Human Development Index world ranking dropped from 66 in 2002 to 73 in 2005. Income disparities between rich and poor remained largely the same under his government. His pro-poor policies were selectively targeted, smartly packaged and poorly funded. Attempting to consolidate his pro-poor image and rebuild his position, in mid-January 2006 Thaksin appeared in a reality TV show staged in Roi Et. In front of cameras Thaksin lectured community development officials, governors and villagers on self help and small business opportunities. His evening moisturising routine featured in one segment. Several days after, the controversial tax-free sale of his Shin Corp for 73 billion baht to a Singaporean company was announced to a shocked nation. The lagging anti-Thaksin movement was revived, with key democracy and social activists now moving to join with Sonthi.

In early February 2006 I attended a rally at the Royal Plaza Bangkok as an observer. Many people on the left of Thai politics refused to go: although the rally was anti-Thaksin, it was also profoundly royalist. Many different social groups were present, including unionists, farmers and civil servants. While speeches were made against privatization, human rights abuses, and Thaksin's corruption, a key theme at the rally was that Thaksin has consistently and deliberately transgressed the royal prerogative.

Calls were made once again for Thaksin to be removed from office and for 'power to be returned to the king' under Article 7 of the 1997 constitution. That article states that, where there is no constitutional provision to deal with an issue, then a decision may be taken that accords with the 'constitutional practice in the democratic system of government with the King as Head of the State'. That there was indeed constitutional provision for the removal of the prime minister was tendentiously overlooked by those seeking a royal intervention.

Sonthi addressed the assembled crowd of tens of thousands of people. He announced that he would ring an old bell brought to the rally from a royally patronized temple. Explaining that in ancient times aggrieved people could ring a bell and the king would receive them, he struck the bell three times. Its chimes silenced the crowd, transporting them to an idealised era of liberal kingship under King Ramkhamhaeng (see Chapter 8). Sonthi then read a petition, calling for royal intervention to effectively remove the Thaksin government.

Soon after this rally Sonthi joined with the newly formed People's Alliance for Democracy (PAD). The merging of democratic and royalist ideologies explored in Chapters 8 and 9 found expression in PAD. This grouped together leaders of various civic and trade union organizations that had been at the forefront of Thailand's struggle for democracy in the 1990s. Under PAD's leadership more demonstrations followed. Despite the emergence of a broader coalition under PAD, the royalist rhetoric of the anti-Thaksin forces remained undiluted. Calls for royal intervention continued.[1]

Facing fierce and rising opposition over the Shin Corp sale, and after a meeting with the king, Thaksin declared that he would go to the polls in early April. Thai Rak Thai wooed over sixteen million votes; following opposition calls for a boycott over ten million people registered a 'no vote', with millions more ballot papers spoiled. With close to forty seats in the parliament unfilled, a political impasse ensued. Amidst the political confusion, charges of electoral fraud and corruption, King Bhumipol called on the courts to do their job. Speaking to judges in late April, his intention was clear:

Should the election be nullified? You have the right to say what's appropriate or not. If it's not appropriate, it is not to say the government is not good. But as far as I'm concerned, a one party election is not normal. The one candidate situation is undemocratic. (*The Nation*, 27 April 2006)

In early May the Constitutional Court annulled the election. Thaksin had once said that if the king whispered he would leave. The king had more than whispered, but Thaksin continued to fight. Former prime minister Prem Tinsulanond, and president of the Privy Council, now moved to make scarcely disguised comments against Thaksin, and reminded the military that their loyalty was to the king and country, not the government. Open scuffles over military appointments in July 2006 were waged as palace elements sought to diminish Thaksin's influence in the armed forces. Although the coup that followed these events was a surprise to many, its logic is clear for all to see.

The coup group did not move against Thaksin because of corruption, human rights abuses, or erosion of democratic freedoms – a feature of the early years of the Thaksin regime – but because it was clear that Thaksin was fundamentally challenging the power of the palace and the interests that have formed around it. When the coup group say they launched the coup for the sake of democracy, they mean Thailand's 'constitutional monarchy'.[2]

A direct translation of the CDR's name from the Thai language is 'Council for Administrative Reform in a System of Democracy with the King as Head of State'. Drawing on the ideological resources surrounding the enmeshment of Thainess, nation and democracy in the body of the monarchy, the coup group's name takes the ideology of the 'democracy with the king as head of state' (Chapter 6) to a new paradoxical zenith – and by an act of force they have exposed the contradiction in any claim to rule based on fictive sovereignty. Thaksin's fatal weakness was that while in power he did nothing to challenge royal ideology at an ideological level. He did not create a space for new ideological forms to take root. An ex-police officer and businessman, he placed too much faith in sheer force, money and capitalist-inspired manipulation of the poor. Ideology in the form of nationness, Thainess and moral order remain central in strategies of enduring political domination in Thailand. Those elements in the 'people sector' who played the royalist card – by joining the establishment opposition to Thaksin – understood the monarchy's great ideological power, but at the cost of a deeper commitment to self-organization and democratic politics.

It appears as if the coup group, in cooperation with other establishment forces, may move Thailand towards a more conservative law-and-order democracy. Their reported initial approach to former Senate President Meechai Ruchuphan to head a Constitutional Drafting Committee is a sign of the future. Meechai opposed a number of the progressive clauses in the now annulled 1997 Constitution. That constitution was only accepted by conservatives under the duress of a dual economic and political crisis. The recent appointment of retired General Surayud

Chulanont, and formerly a privy councillor, as interim prime minister indicates that Thai royalism will be further embedded in the nation's institutions. A National Legislative Assembly, dominated by business people, bureaucrats and military officers, has been appointed until a new constitution is written and elections are held. The CDR, reconfigured as the Council of National Security, has secured for itself considerable power in the Interim Constitution adopted on 1 October. These powers include the right to remove the prime minister and the right to countersign various appointments.

Yet, the future of Thai democracy may yet be liberal in form, Thai-style. The Preamble of the Interim Constitution reads, in part, that the CDR seized power:

> to correct the deterioration in the government of the realm, and inefficiency in managing the administration of the realm and monitoring the use of state power, which caused widespread corruption and malfeasance ... . This brought about a serious crisis of politics and government, and problems of conflict among the mass of the people...

Article Three of the Interim Constitution reads:

> [T]he human dignity, rights, freedoms and equality of the Thai people which formerly were upheld according to the custom of the government of Thailand as a democracy under Constitutional Monarchy and according to Thailand's international obligations, shall be upheld by this constitution.[3]

Clearly, the historical gains of liberal political order and democratic sentiment are too much part of ideological discourse and the balance of different class and intra-class forces to be simply discarded at this point. It does not appear as if Thailand is on the threshold of a Sarit-style move away from constitutionalism. But it is too soon to say whether a liberal constitution will emerge from the current crisis or whether the Thai elite will now move to adopt a constitution that erodes political freedoms. The composition of the 'second political reform movement', now under the eyes of the military, will greatly determine what direction the constitution takes.

One thing is clear: those who fought in the streets for Thaksin's removal in order to restore democracy – through a royally appointed government – will probably, in turn, now have to contend with a recalibrated form of 'democracy' that, as always, seeks to discipline people just as it seeks to make them into political subjects. The liberalism that could claim a tentative victory in the 1997 'people's constitution' is now deeply compromised. Thaksin's ascendancy underlined its weakness, support for the recent coup its pragmatism. 'Liberalism' has always been profoundly ambivalent about democracy. Currently, Thai politics allows us to see starkly the founding contradiction of developmental democracy in the form of disciplinary royal liberalism: its principal message has always been 'democracy' only when the people are ready for it.

October 2006

Notes

1 For an extended treatment of these events, see Kasian Tejapira, 'Toppling Thaksin', *New Left Review*, 39, May–June 2006.

2 For a prescient discussion of the clash between Thaksin and the palace, see Duncan McCargo, 'Network monarchy and legitimacy crises in Thailand', *The Pacific Review*, 18, 4, December 2005

3 This English translation of the Interim Constitution was provided by Chris Baker and Pasuk Phongpaichit.

Select bibliography

Note: Thai authors have been alphabetized according to first name. All sources, especially official Thai documents and reports, are listed in the relevant chapter endnotes.

Althusser, Louis, *Lenin and Philosophy and other Essays*, 2nd edn, London: NLB, 1977.

Amon Chantharasombun, *Khonstitichanaelism thang ok khong prathet thai* [Constitutionalism: The Solution for Thailand], Bangkok: Public Policy Institute, 1994.

Amon Raksasat, *Anakhot chart thai* [The Future of Thailand], Bangkok: Rongphim kromyuthasuksa thahanpok, 1976.

Anderson, Benedict, *Imagined Communities: Reflections on the Origin and Spread of Nationalism*, London: Verso, 1983.

——— 'Withdrawal Symptoms: Social and Cultural Aspects of the October 6 Coup', *Bulletin Concerned Asian Scholars*, 9, 3, 1977, pp. 13–30.

Anek Laothamatas, *Prachasanghom nai mummong tawantok an lae son thi jon hopkin* [Civil Society from the Perspective of the West: Reading and Teaching at Johns Hopkins University], Bangkok: Sathaban kanrainru lae phathana prachasangkhom, 1999.

——— 'A Tale of Two Democracies: Conflicting Perceptions of Elections and Democracy in Thailand', in R.Taylor [ed.] *The Politics of Elections in Southeast Asia*, Cambridge: Woodrow Wilson Center Press and Cambridge University Press, 1996, pp. 201–23.

——— *Mop mu thu chonchan klang laek nakthurakit kap phathana kan prachathipatai* [The Mobile Telephone Mob: The Middle Class, Entrepreneurs, and the Development of Democracy], Bangkok: Samnakphim matichon, 1993.

——— *Business Associations and the New Political Economy of Thailand: From Bureaucratic Polity to Liberal Corporatism*, Singapore: West View Press, 1992.

Anuchart Puangsamli and Kritthaya Achawanitkul [eds] *Khabuankan prachasangkhom thai: khwamkhleuanwai pak phonlameuang* [The Thai Civil Society Movement: Citizen Sector Movements], Bangkok: Khrongkan wijai lae phathana prachasangkom, mahawithayalai mahidol, 1999.

Asa Meksawan, *Kan pokkhrong radap tambon muban khwammankhong haengchat* [Subdistrict and Village Level Administration and National Security], Bangkok: Withayalai pongkan rachaanajak, *c.* 1977.

Atsushi Kitahara, *The Thai Rural Community Reconsidered: Historical Community Formation and Contemporary Development Movements*, The Political Economy Centre, Faculty of Economics, Chulalongkorn University, 1996.

Barme, Scott, *Luang Wichit Wathakan and the Creation of a Thai Identity*, Singapore: Institute of Southeast Asian Studies, 1993.

Bell, Peter, 'Western Conceptions of Thai Society: The Politics of American Scholarship', *Journal of Contemporary Asia*, 12, 1, 1982, pp. 61–74.

Bowie, Katherine, *Rituals of National Loyalty: An Anthropology of the State and Village Scout Movement in Thailand*, New York: Columbia University Press, 1997.

Bowonsak Uwanno and Chanchai Sawaengsak, *Kanpatirup kanmeuang farangset khokhithen nai kanpatirup kanmeuang thai* [French Political Reform: Ideas for Thai Political Reform], Bangkok: Samnakphim nithitham, 1997.

Burchell, G., Gordon, C. and Miller, P. [eds] *The Foucault Effect: Studies in Governmentality*, Chicago: University of Chicago Press, 1991.

Callahan, William, 'The Discourse of Vote Buying and Political Reform in Thailand', *Pacific Affairs*, 78, 1, 2005. pp. 95–113.

Cammack, Paul, 'Neoliberalism, the World Bank, and the New Politics of Development', in Uma Kothari and Martin Minogue [eds] *Development Theory and Practice: Critical Perspectives*, Basingstoke: Palgrave, 2002, pp. 157–78.

——— *Capitalism and Democracy in the Third World*, London: Leicester University Press, 1997.

Chai-Anan Samudavanija, Kusama Snitwongse and Suchit Bunbongkarn, *From Armed Suppression to Political Offensive: Attitudinal Transformation of Thai Military Officers since 1976*, Bangkok: Institute of Security and International Studies, Chulalongkorn University, 1990.

Chalermkiat Phiu-nuan, *Khwamkhit thangkanmeuang khong thahan thai 2519–2535* [The Political Thought of the Thai Military: 1976–1992], Bangkok: Samnakphim phujatkan, 1992.

Chatthip Nartsupha, *The Thai Village Economy in the Past*, trans. Chris Baker and Pasuk Phongphaichit, Chiang Mai: Silkworm Books, 1999.

Chuchai Supahwong and Yuwadi Khatkanklai, *Prachasangkhom thatsana nakkhit sangkhom thai* [Perspectives of Civil Society: Thai Social Thinkers], Bangkok: Samnakphim matichon, 1997.

Chuwong Chayabut, *Khayai thana prachathipatai su puangchon* [Expanding the Basis of Democracy to the People], Bangkok: Krom kan pokkhrong, 1992.

Connors, Michael, 'Goodbye to the Security State: Ideological Change in Thailand', *Journal of Contemporary Asia*, 33, 4, 2003, pp.431–448

Connors, Michael, 'Ministering Culture: The Politics of Hegemony and Identity in Thailand, *Critical Asian Studies*, forthcoming.

'Declaration of the Customary Rights of Local Communities: Thai Democracy at the Grass Roots', *Thai Development Newsletter*, 1994, no. 24, pp. 34–6.

Escobar, Arturo, *Encountering Development: The Making and Unmaking of the Third World*, Princeton: Princeton University Press, 1995.

Foucault, Michel, 'Governmentality' in G.Burchell, C. Gordon and P.Miller [eds] *The Foucault Effect: Studies in Governmentality*, Chicago: University of Chicago Press, 1991, pp. 87–104.

Gills, Barry, Rocamora, Joel and Wilson, Richard [eds] *Low Intensity Democracy: Political Power in the New World*, London: Pluto Press, 1993.

Girling, John, *Thailand: Society and Politics*, Ithaca NY and London: Cornell University Press, 1981.

Gramsci, Antonio, *Selections from the Prison Notebooks*, London: Lawrence and Wishart, 1971.

Glassman, Jim 'Economic "nationalism" in a post-nationalist era', *Critical Asian Studies*, 36, 1, 2004, pp. 37–64.

Hewison, Kevin, 'Of Regimes, State and Pluralities: Thai Politics Enters the 1990s', in K.Hewison, R.Robison and G.Rodan [eds] *Southeast Asia in the 1990s: Authoritarianism, Democracy and Capitalism*, Melbourne: Allen and Unwin, 1993, pp. 161–89.

——— *Thailand Politics and Power*, Manila: Journal of Contemporary Asia Publishers, 1989.

——— 'Neo-liberalism and Domestic Capital: The Political Outcomes of the Economic Crisis in Thailand', *The Journal of Development Studies*, 41, 2, 2005, pp. 310–330.

Hewison, Kevin [ed.] *Political Change in Thailand: Democracy and Participation*, London: Routledge, 1997.

Hindess, Barry, *Discourses of Power: From Hobbes to Foucault*, Oxford: Blackwell, 1996, pp. 97–113.

Hiran Sitthikowit, 'Withikan fukson prachathipatai' [How Will We Teach Democracy to the People?], *Thesaphiban*, 66, 2, 1971, pp. 193–213.

——— 'Withikan fukson prachathipatai' [How Will We Teach Democracy to the People?], *Thesaphiban*, 66, 1, 1971, pp. 61–73.

Jackson, Peter, *Buddhism, Legitimation and Conflict: The Political Functions of Urban Thai Buddhism*, Singapore: Institute of Southeast Asian Studies, 1989.

Jalong Kanyanmit, 'Lak patibat rachakan khong nakpokkhrong' [Principles of Conduct for Administrators], *Thesaphiban*, 82, 3, 1987, pp. 11–29.

Jaturong Boonyayattanasasoonthon and Gawin Chutima [eds] *Thai NGOs: The Continuing Struggle for Democracy*, Bangkok: Thai NGO Support Project, 1995, pp. 51–68, pp. 52–3.

Jessop, Bob, *State Theory: Putting Capitalist States in Their Place*, London: Polity Press, 1990.

Ji Giles Ungpakorn, *The Struggle for Democracy and Social Justice in Thailand*, Bangkok: Arom Pongpangnan Foundation, 1997.

Ji Giles Ungpakorn [ed], *Radicalising Thailand: New Political Perspectives*, Bangkok, Institute of Asian Studies, 2003.

Kamala Tiyavanich, *Forest Recollections: Wandering Monks in Twentieth-century Thailand*, Chiang Mai: Silkworm Books, 1997.

Kasian Tejapira, 'Globalizers vs Communitarians: Post May 1992 Debates among Thai Public Intellectuals', paper presented to Annual Meeting of the US Association for Asian Studies, Honolulu, 11–14 April 1996.

——— 'Post-Crisis Economic Impasse and Political Recovery in Thailand', *Critical Asian Studies*, 34: 3, 2002, pp. 323–356.

Keyes, Charles, *Thailand: Buddhist Kingdom as Modern Nation-State*, Bangkok: Editions Duang Kamol, 1989.

Khana anukammakan jatthamphaen kan phathana kanmeuang [Subcommittee on the Political Development Plan, Political Reform Committee], *Phaen phathana kanmeuang thai* [Thai Political Development Plan], 1996.

Khanakammakan soemsang ekkalak khong chat samnakgnan naiyokrathamontri, *Raignan soemsang ekkalak khong chat kap kanphathana chat thai* [Seminar Report on National Identity and Thai National Development], 1985.

—— *Khwamrureuang prachathipatai pheu prachachon* [Knowledge about Democracy for the People], 1984.

—— *Udomkan khong chat* [National Ideology], 1983.

Khanakammakan phathanakan prachathipatai [Democracy Development Committee], *Kho saneu kropkhwamkhit nai kanpatirup kanmeuang thai* [Proposal for a Framework in Reforming Thai Politics], 1995.

Khanakammathikan prachasamphan supha rang ratthammanun [Public Relations Committee, Constitution Drafting Assembly], *Kropbeuangton rang ratthammanun* [Preliminary Framework for Drafting the People's Constitution], 1997.

Kobkhua Suwannathat-Pian, 'Thailand's Constitutional Monarchy: A Study of Concepts and Meanings of the Constitutions 1932–1957', paper presented at International Association of Historians of Asia, Chulalongkorn University, Bangkok, 20–4 May 1996.

Kong khosana [Propaganda Office], 'Kanleuaktang phuthean ratsadon' [Election of Members of Parliament], *Thesaphiban*, 1933, pp. 490–9.

Kong khosana krom mahathai samnao [Department of the Interior, Propaganda Office], 'Thalaengkan khong kong khosana kanleuak tang phuthaen tambon' [Announcement of the Propaganda Office: The Election of Tambon Representatives], *Thesaphiban*, 1933, pp. 486–9.

Kramol Thongthammachat, *Kanmeuang lae prachathipatai khong thai* [Thai Politics and Democracy], Bangkok: Ho.jo.kho. bankit trading, 1976.

Krasuang mahathai, *100 pi mahatthai krung thep: krasuang mahatthai* [A Hundred Years of the Interior], Bangkok: Krasuang mahathai, 1992.

—— *Kan owchana suk pho. ko. Kho. tam naeo khwamkhit nai kanjattang lae chai prayot muanchon nai ching patipat* [Winning the War against the Communist Party: Practical Approaches to Establishing and Utilizing the Masses], Bangkok: Krasuang mahathai, 1981.

—— *Khumu khanakammakan supha tambon dam khrongkan phathana phonlameaung rabop prachathipatai* [The Manual of the Subdistrict Committee in Accordance with the Project to Develop Democratic Citizens], Bangkok: Krasuang mahathai, 1976.

—— *Khumu kanpatibatngan rengrat phathana chonabot* [Manual on Accelerated Rural Development], *Bangkok*: Krasuang mahathai, 1974.

Kriangsak Chetphathanuan, 'Naeo khwamkhit prachathipatai paebthai' [The Idea of Thai-style Democracy], M.A. dissertation, Thammasat University, 1993.

Krom kanpokkhrong krasuang mahathai, *Prachathipatai radap muban* [Village-Level Democracy], 1994.

—— *Khumu withayakon phathana prachathipatai radap muban* [Personnel Handbook on Developing Democracy at the Village Level], 1993.

—— *Khumu poei phrae prachathipatai samrap khanakammakan supha tambon* [Manual for the Propagation of Democracy to the Subdistrict Council], c. 1978–9.

—— *Khumu prachasamphan kanleuaktang* [Manual on Election Public Relations], 1978.

—— *Khrongkan phathana phonalameuang rabop prachathipataic.2511/12* [Project to Develop Democratic Citizens], c. 1968–9.

—— *Lakkan lae hetphon prakop khrongkan phathana phonlameuang rabop prachathipatai* [Principles and Rationale of the Project to Develop Democratic Citizens], 1964, mimeograph.

—— *Raingan prajam pi* [various years].

Krom kanpokkrong krom kanpathathana chumchon krasuang mahathai, *Khumu patipatkan poei phrae prachathipatai radap muban* [Practical Handbook on the Dissemination of Democracy at Village Level], 1991.

Krom prachasamphan lae samnakngan soemsang ekkalak khong chat [Public Relations Department and National Identity Board], *Naeothang prachathipatai* [The Democratic Line], 1981.

Krom Satsana Krasuang Suksathikan, *Lakkan samrap phupokkhrong* [Principles For Governors], 1982.

Manas Chitkasem and Andrew Turton [eds] *Thai Constructions of Knowledge*, London: SOAS, 1991, pp. 118–41.

McCargo, Duncan, *Chamlong Srimuang and the New Thai Politics*, New York: St Martin's Press, 1997.

McCargo, Duncan [ed.] *Reforming Thai Politics*, Copenhagen: Nordic Institute of Asian Studies, 2002.

McCargo, Duncan and Ukrist Pathmanand, *The Thaksinization of Thailand*, Copenhagen: NIAS Press, 2005.

McVey, Ruth [ed.] *Money and Power in Provincial Thailand*, Copenhagen: NIAS, 2000.

Morell, David and Chai-Anan Samudavanija, *Political Conflict In Thailand: Reform, Reaction, Revolution*, Cambridge: Oelgeschlager, Gunn and Hain, 1981.

Mulder, Niels, *Thai Images: The Culture of the Public World*, Chiang Mai: Silkworm Books, 1997.

Murashima, Eiji, 'The Origin of Modern Official State Ideology in Thailand', *Journal of Southeast Asian Studies*, XIX, 1, 1989, pp. 80–96.

Murashima, Eiji, Nakharin Mektrairat and Somkiat Wanthana, *The Making of Modern Thai Political Parties*, Tokyo: Institute of Developing Economies, Joint Research Program Series no. 86, 1991.

Nakarin Mektrairat, *Kanpatiwat siam 1932* [The Siamese Revolution of 1932], Bangkok: Samnakphim amarinwichakan, 1997.

—— *Khwamkhit khwamru lae amnatkanmeuang nai kanpatiwat siam 2475* [Thoughts, Knowledge and Political Power in the Siamese Revolution 1932], Bangkok: Sathaban siam suksa samakhom sangkhomsat haeng prathet thai, 1990.

Neher, Clark, *Politics and Culture in Thailand*, Ann Arbor: Center for Political Studies, Institute for Social Research, University of Michigan, 1987.

Nelson, Michael H., *Central Authority and Local Democratization in Thailand*, Bangkok: White Lotus, 1998.

Ockey, James, 'Political Parties, Factions, and Corruption in Thailand', *Modern Asian Studies*, 28, 2, 1994, pp. 251–77.

Ockey, James, 'Change and continuity in the Thai political party system,' *Asian Survey*, 43, 4, 2003, pp. 663–680.

Pasuk Phongpaichit, 'Technocrats, Businessmen, and Generals: Democracy and Economic Policy-making in Thailand', in A.MacIntyre and K.Jayasuriya [eds] *The Dynamics of Economic Policy Reform in Southeast Asia and the Southwest Pacific*, Singapore: Oxford University Press, 1992, pp. 10–31.

Pasuk Phongpaichit and Chris Baker, *Thailand, Economy and Politics*, Oxford: Oxford University Press, 1996.

Pasuk Phongpaichit and Chris Baker, *Thaksin: The Business of Politics in Thailand*, Chiang Mai: Silkworm, 2004.

Pasuk Phongpaichit and Sungsidh Piriyarangsan, *Corruption and Democracy in Thailand*, Chiang Mai: Silkworm Books, 1994, pp. 88–90.

Phaisan Sangwoli [ed.] *Thotsawat onkon phatthana ekkachon* [The Decade of NGOs], Bangkok: Munithi asasamak pheua sangkhom, 1991.

Phonsak Phongpaeo [ed.] *Thitthang khong ratthasat thai* [Directions in Thai Political Science], Bangkok: Samakhom nisit kao julalongkon mahawithayalai, 1985.

Phraya Sunthonphiphit, 'Siam-prachathipatai' [Siam-democracy], *Thesaphiban*, 1937, pp. 407–14.

Piyathida, P, 'Kan kaothung prachachon' [Approaching the People], *Thesaphiban*, 85, 7, 1990, pp. 1–6.

Ponsak Phongphaew and Phonsak Jinkrairit [eds] *Watthanatham thang kanmeuang thai*, Bangkok: Samakhom sangkhomsat haeng prathet thai, 1981.

Poulantzas, Nicos, *Political Power and Social Classes*, London: New Left Books, 1973.

Prachathipatai baep thai lae khokhit kap ratthammanun [Thai-style Democracy and Ideas on the Constitution], Bangkok: Samnakphim chokchaitewet, 1965.

Pramuan prarachadamrat lae prabarom thi prarachathan nai okat tang tang tangtae deuan thanwakhom 2511–2512 [Collected Royal Edicts and Royal Instructions, Graciously Conferred on Various Occasions from December 1968–1969].

Pramuan Rujanaseri, *Phraracha-amnat* [Royal Powers], Bangkok: Sumet Rujanaseri, 2005.

Praphat Charusathien, *Kh khit nai kanpathana kanmuang thai* [Ideas on Thai Political Development], Bangkok: Krom kanpokkhrong, 1973.

Praphat Pintoptaeng, *Kanmeuang bonthong thanon 99 wan samacha khon jon* [Politics on the Road: 99 Days of the Forum of the Poor], Bangkok: Sathaban Naiyonbai lae kanjatkansangkhon mahawithayalai, 1998.

Prawet Wasi, *Setthakit phophiang lae prachasangkhom* [The Modest Economy and Civil Society], Bangkok: Samnakphim mo chaoban, 1999.

——— *Saksi haeng khwambenkhon sukkhayaphap haeng khwamsangsan* [The Dignity of Humanity and Creative Potential], Bangkok: Mo chaoban, 1995.

——— *Watthanatham kap kanphathana* [Culture and Development], Bangkok: Samnakngan khanakammakan watthanatham haeng chat, 1995.

——— *Kanphatthana prachathipatai lae kanpatirup kanmeaung* [Developing Democracy and Political Reform], Bangkok: Samnakphim mo chaoban, 1994.

Prudhisan Jumbala, *Nation Building and Democratization in Thailand*, Bangkok: Chulalongkorn University Social Research Institute, 1992.

Reynolds, Craig, 'Globalization and Cultural Nationalism in Modern Thailand', in J. Kahn, *Southeast Asian Identities: Culture and the Politics of Representation in*

Indonesia, Malaysia, Singapore, and Thailand, Singapore: Institute of Southeast Asian Studies, 1998, pp. 115–45.

Reynolds, Craig [ed.] *National Identity and its Defenders, Thailand: 1939–1989,* Chiang Mai: Silkworm Books, 1993.

Riggs, Fred, *Thailand: The Modernization of a Bureaucratic Polity,* Honolulu: East-West Center Press, 1966.

Saiyud Kerdphon, *The Struggle for Thailand: Counterinsurgency, 1965–1985,* Bangkok: S. Research Centre Co. Ltd, 1986.

Samnakngan khanakammakan kanleuaktang [Electoral Commission of Thailand], *Nangseu songsoem prachathipatai nai chumchon: buntoem pai leuak tang* [Book to Promote Democracy in the Community: Bunterm Goes to Vote], 1998.

Samnakngan khanakammakan watthanatham haeng chat [National Culture Commission], *Phaen maebot khrongkanseuapsan watthanatham thai 2537–2540* [Master Plan, Project For the Preservation of Thai Culture 1994–1997], 1995.

—— *Mong adit pheu anakhot . . . 15 pi samnakngan khanakammakan watthanatham haeng chat* [Looking to the Past . . . for the Future: 15 Years of the National Culture Commission], National Culture Commission, 1994.

—— *Nangseua ekkasan thangwichakan reuang kansupsan lae phatthana watthanatham thang kan meuang thai* [National Culture Commission, Technical Documents on The Preservation and Development of Thai Political Culture], 1994.

—— *Naoethang nai kansongsoem watthanatham thai 11 prakan* [Methods in Promoting 11 Points of Thai Culture], 1994.

—— *Sammana thangwichakan phumipanya chao pan kan kandamnoen thang whatthanatham lae phathana chonabot* [Seminar on People's Wisdom and Carrying out Cultural and Rural Development], 1991.

—— *Krop lae thitthang phaen watthanatham haeng chat 2535–2539* [National Culture Plan 1992–1996, Framework and Direction], 1990.

Samnakngan khosanakan [Propaganda Office], *Khumu phonlameuang* [Citizens Manual], 1948.

—— *Khumu phonlameuang* [Citizens Manual], 1936.

Samnakngan lekhathikan naiyokratthamontri, *Chuay kan khit kansang prachathipatai pen nathi khong khrai?* [Let's Think Together . . . Whose Duty is Building Democracy?], 1984.

Samnakngan soemsang ekkalak khong chat, *Totphitrachatham* [The Ten Royal Virtues], 1990.

Samnakngan supha khwammankhong, *Nayobai khwammankhong haeng chat 2540–2544* [National Security Policy 1997–2001].

Saneh Chamarik, *Democracy and Development: A Cultural Perspective,* Local Development Institute, 1993.

Sathaban chumchon thongthin phatthana, *Kho saneu yutthasat kae wikrit chat* [A Proposed Strategy to Solve the National Crisis], Bangkok: Sathaban chumchon thongthin phatthana, 2000.

Sathaban phrapokklao [King Prachatipok's Institute], *Laksut kanmeuang kanpokkhrong nai rabop prachathipatai* [Curriculum: Government and Politics in a Democracy], 1996.

Seksan Prasertkul, 'The Transformation of the Thai State and Economic Change 1855–1945', Ph.D. dissertation, Cornell University, 1989.

Smart, Barry, *Foucault, Marxism and Critique*, Melbourne: Routledge and Kegan Paul, 1983.

Sombat Chanthonwong, 'To Address the Dust of the Dust Under the Soles of the Royal Feet: A Reflection on the Political Dimension of Thai Court Language', *Asian Review*, 6, 1992, pp. 144–63.

——— *Phasa thangkanmeuang phathana khong naeo athibai kanmeuang lae sap kanmeuang nai kankhian praphet sarakhadi thang kanmeuang khong thai pho. tho. 2475–2525* [Political Language: The Development of Political Explanation and Vocabulary in Thai Political Feature Writings, 1932–1982], Bangkok: Sathabanthai khadisuksa, 1990.

Somboon Suksamran, *Buddhism and Political Legitimacy*, Bangkok: Chulalongkorn University Research Report Series, no. 2, 1993.

Somchai Phatharathananunth, 'Civil Society in Northeast Thailand: The Struggle of the Small Scale Farmers' Assembly of Isan', Ph.D. dissertation, University of Leeds, 2001.

Son Bangyikha, *Pratya waduay khwammankhong* [The Philosophy of National Security], Bangkok: Mahawithayalai ramkhamhaeng, 1981.

Streckfuss, David, 'The Mixed Colonial Legacy in Siam: Origins of Thai Racialist Thought, 1890–1910', in Laurie Sears [ed.] *Autonomous Histories, Particular Truths: Essays in Honour of John Smail*, Madison: Center for Southeast Asian Studies, University of Wisconsin, 1993, pp. 123–53.

Streckfuss, David [ed.] *The Modern Thai Monarchy and Cultural Politics: The Acquittal of Sulak Sivaraksa on the Charge of Lese Majeste in Siam 1995 and its Consequences*, Bangkok: Santi-Pracha Dhamma Institute, 1996.

Sungsidh Phiriyarangsan and Pasuk Phongpaichit, *Jitsamnuk lae udomkan khong khabuankan prachathipatai ruam samai* [Consciousness and Ideology of the Contemporary Democracy Movement], Bangkok: Sunsuksa sethasatkanmeuang khana settasat kanmeuang julalongkon mahawithiyalai, 1996.

Sungsidh Piriyarangsan and Pasuk Phongpaichit [eds] *Chonchan klang bonkrasae prachathipatai thai* [The Middle Class on the Road to Democracy], Bangkok: Sunsuksa sethasatkanmeuang khana settasat kanmeuang julalongkon mahawithiyalai, 1992.

Surin Maisrikrod, 'Emerging Patterns of Leadership in Thailand', *Contemporary Southeast Asia*, 15, 1, 1993, pp. 80–96.

Taylor, Jim, 'Buddhist Revitalization, Modernization and Social Change in Contemporary Thailand', *Sojourn*, 8, 1, 1993, pp. 62–91.

Tej Bunnag, *The Provincial Administration of Siam 1892–1915: The Ministry of the Interior Under Prince Damrong Rajanubhab*, Kuala Lumpur: Oxford University Press, 1977.

Thabuang mahawithayalai samnakngan khana kammakan kanleuaktang [Bureau of Universities and the Electoral Commission of Thailand], *Khumu asasamak ratthammanun* [Manual for Constitution Volunteers], 1999.

——— *Sunsongserm prachathipatai sarup raignan kansammana ajan naksuksa asa samak khrongkan klapsu chonabot* [Summary Report of Seminar of Lecturers, Students and Volunteers on the Back to the Country Project, Centre for the Promotion of Democracy], 1974.

Thahan prachathipatai, *Kho saneu naeothang kae panha chat khong thahan prachathipatai* [Proposals and Approaches to Solving National Problems of The Democratic Soldiers], 1987.

Thak Chaloemtiarana, 'The Sarit Regime 1957–1963: The Formative Years of Thai Polit-
ics', unpublished Ph.D. dissertation, Cornell University, 1974.
Thak Chaloemtiarana [ed.] *Thai Politics: Extracts and Documents 1932–1957*, Bangkok:
The Social Science Association of Thailand, 1978.
Thanin Kriaiwichian, *Rabop prachathipatai* [The Democratic System], Bangkok: Krasuang
suksathikan, 1977.
Thirayut Bunmi, *Sangkhom khemkhaeng thammarat haeng chat yuthasat ku hai prathet
thai* [Strong Society, Good Governance: A Thailand Recovery Strategy], Bangkok:
Saithan, 1998.
Thongchai Winichakul, *Siam Mapped: A History of the Geo-body of a Nation*, Honolulu:
University of Hawaii Press, 1994.
Turton, Andrew, 'Local Powers and Rural Differentiation', in G.Hart, A.Turton and
B.White [eds] *Agrarian Transformations: Local Processes and the State in Southeast
Asia*, Berkeley: University of California Press, 1989, pp. 70–97.
Vandergeest, Peter, 'Constructing Thailand: Regulation, Everyday Resistance and Citi-
0zenship', *Journal for the Comparative Study of Society and History*, 35, 1, 1993, pp.
133–58.
World Bank, *Governance: The World Bank's Experience*, Washington DC: World Bank,
1994.
——— *Governance and Development*, Washington DC: World Bank, 1992.

Newspapers

Bangkok Post
Krungthep thurakit
Matichon
Phujatkan raiwan
Siam Post
Siamrat
Thai Post
The Nation
Wattajak

Index